Microsoft®
Windows®
User Experience

PUBLISHED BY
Microsoft Press
A Division of Microsoft Corporation
One Microsoft Way
Redmond, Washington 98052-6399

Library of Congress Cataloging-in-Publication Data
Microsoft Windows User Experience / Microsoft Corporation.
      p. cm.
    Includes index.
    ISBN 0-7356-0566-1
    1. Microsoft Windows (Computer file)   2. Operating systems
(Computers)   I. Microsoft Corporation.
   QA76.76.063M524395   1999
   005.4'469--dc21   99-36326
                                              CIP

Printed and bound in the United States of America.

1 2 3 4 5 6 7 8 9   WCWC   4 3 2 1 0 9

Distributed in Canada by Penguin Books Canada Limited.

A CIP catalogue record for this book is available from the British Library.

Microsoft Press books are available through booksellers and distributors worldwide. For further information about international editions, contact your local Microsoft Corporation office or contact Microsoft Press International directly at fax (425) 936-7329. Visit our Web site at mspress.microsoft.com.

Acquisitions Editor: Ben Ryan
Project Editor: Sally Stickney

Foreword

Thank you for buying this book. It means that you are concerned about making a great Windows application. That's something we appreciate.

Windows is a platform. This means that we cannot make Windows successful and valuable without your help. Your applications are what make Windows great. The better your applications are, the better the platform is, and ultimately our users are happier. And they are our *shared* users. We need to take care of them together. This book is one example of how Microsoft is trying to help make Windows a better place for our users.

Making a good Windows application used to be about making a good user interface. That's not enough anymore. Making a great Windows application is about making a great user experience. The user experience is about the end-to-end relationship that the user has with your application. To illustrate the difference, sometimes the best user experience is no user interface at all. Every one of our users has experienced unnecessary or unintelligible error messages, gone through terrible installation procedures, or been forced to deal with the lack of our foresight at what might cause them problems or confusion. Every user has been unable to complete their task, been unable to find a command, or gotten frustrated after finding that Help didn't help. This is their pain and our joint responsibility. It's why we called this book *Windows User Experience* instead of Windows User Interface.

Delivering software with a great user experience is not easy. It takes work, it takes testing, and it takes a real desire to connect with our users. At Microsoft, we know just how hard this is. Testament to this fact is that you can find examples of difficult user experiences in applications that have shipped in the past and that currently ship from Microsoft. Please realize that these deficiencies are not intentional violations of the principles in this book, but are the result of decisions made without the benefit of hindsight. This book tries to articulate that hindsight so we can all benefit from the experience.

Your role is clear. You're reading the book. You're looking at your application with a critical eye. You're listening hard to what your customers want to accomplish, and what is keeping them from accomplishing their goals. Microsoft's commitment here needs to be clear as well. This book, our user experience Web site, and other initiatives that will come from Microsoft over the coming months and years are all about Microsoft taking a leadership role in giving our customers the richest, simplest, and most satisfying experience running applications on Windows. We can't do it without your continuing to build great applications or without your feedback. When there are things you need us to do, we need to know. We look forward to hearing how we can help. And we are even more excited to see what fantastic applications you ship.

The Windows User Experience Team
http://msdn.microsoft.com/ui/
winui@microsoft.com

Contents

CHAPTER 3 BASIC CONCEPTS

CHAPTER 4 THE WINDOWS ENVIRONMENT

CHAPTER 5 INPUT BASICS

CHAPTER 6 GENERAL INTERACTION TECHNIQUES

Part 2 Windows Interface Components

CHAPTER 7 WINDOWS

CHAPTER 8 MENUS, CONTROLS, AND TOOLBARS

CHAPTER 9   SECONDARY WINDOWS

Part 3 Design Specifications and Guidelines

CHAPTER 12 WORKING WITH OLE EMBEDDED AND LINKED OBJECTS

CHAPTER 13   USER ASSISTANCE

CHAPTER 14 VISUAL DESIGN

CHAPTER 15   SPECIAL DESIGN CONSIDERATIONS

Part 4 Appendixes and References

Introduction

Welcome to *The Microsoft Windows User Experience: Official Guidelines for User Interface Developers and Designers*, an indispensable guide to designing applications that run with the Microsoft® Windows® operating system. More than anything else, the design of your application's interface affects how a user experiences your product. Here you will find recommendations for well-designed Windows-based applications and hundreds of examples of interfaces — both good and bad — to learn from.

How to Use This Book

This book is intended for people who are designing and developing Windows-based software. It may also be appropriate for people who want a better understanding of the Windows environment and the human-computer interface principles it supports. The contents of this book cover the following areas:

- Summary of new design features and issues — overview of new interface controls as well as the top design issues for applications.

- Basic design principles and process — fundamental design philosophy, assumptions about human behavior, design methodology, and concepts embodied in the interface.

- Interface elements — descriptions of the various components in the interface and instructions on when and how to use them.

- Design details — specific information about the details of effective design and style in an application's interface.

- Additional information — glossary of terms, quick reference information, and a bibliography.

Chapter 1, "Getting Started," includes a summary of the most important information included in this book. If you read only one thing in this book, read this chapter.

This book focuses on the design and elements of an application's user interface. Although an occasional technical reference is included, this guide does not generally cover detailed information about technical implementation or application programming interfaces (APIs), because there are many different types of development tools that you can use to develop software for Windows.

For more information about specific APIs, see the Microsoft Platform SDK on the MSDN Online Web site at http://msdn.microsoft.com/ui/guide/sdk.asp.

How to Apply These Guidelines

This book promotes visual and functional consistency within and across the Windows operating system. Although following all of these guidelines is encouraged, you can adopt only the guidelines that best suit your application. By following these guidelines, you enable users of your application to transfer their skills and experience from one task to the next and to learn new tasks more easily.

However, adhering to these design guidelines does not guarantee usability. The guidelines are valuable tools, but to be part of an effective software design process, they must be combined with other factors such as design principles, task analysis, prototyping, and usability evaluation.

You can extend these guidelines, provided that you do so in the spirit of the principles on which they are based. It is important to maintain a reasonable level of consistency with the visual and behavioral aspects of the Windows interface. In general, avoid adding new elements or behaviors unless the interface does not otherwise support them. More importantly, avoid changing an existing behavior for common elements. A user builds up expectations about how an interface works. Inconsistencies confuse the user and add unnecessary complexity.

These guidelines supersede those issued for Microsoft Windows 95 and all previous releases, and are specific to the development of applications designed for Microsoft Windows 98, Microsoft Windows 2000 Professional, and Microsoft Windows 2000 Server. There is no direct relationship between these guidelines and those provided for other operating systems.

Conventions Used in This Book

The following conventions are used throughout this book:

Book Conventions

This convention	Indicates
	A reference to related topics in this book or to other resources
	Additional or special information about the topic
SMALL CAPITAL LETTERS	Names of keys on the keyboard — for example, SHIFT, CTRL, or ALT
KEY+KEY	Key combinations for which the user must press and hold down one key and then press another — for example, CTRL+P or ALT+F4
Italic text	New terms and variable expressions, such as parameters
Bold text	Win32 API keywords, registry key entries, and user interface elements
Registry text	Examples of registry entries
[ ]	Optional information

Fundamentals of
Designing User Interaction

Getting Started

This chapter includes an overview of the new features and controls provided by Microsoft Windows. It also includes a summary of the key design issues for applications written for the Windows interface.

What's New

This book includes information about designing user interfaces for applications that run on Microsoft Windows 98 and Microsoft Windows 2000. It also describes the new interfaces and conventions used in these operating systems. These features include the following:

- New input conventions
  Automatic (hover) selection, wheel mouse button actions — See Chapter 5, "Input Basics," and Chapter 6, "General Interaction Techniques."

- New controls
  Date picker, HTML control, toolbar frames —
  See Chapter 8, "Menus, Controls, and Toolbars."

- New file common dialog boxes
  File Open, File Save As, File Print, and Browse for File — See Chapter 9, "Secondary Windows."

- New Help support
  HTML Help, balloon tips, InfoTips, simple wizards —
  See Chapter 13, "User Assistance."

- New folder conventions
  My Documents, My Pictures, thumbnails, Web views, Active
  Desktop — See Chapter 11, "Integrating with the System."

- New system integration support and utilities
  Multiple file association support, NoOpen file registration,
  operating system-protected files, Quick Launch toolbar, multiple
  monitor support, Disk Cleanup, Windows Installer — See
  Chapter 11, "Integrating with the System."

If you are designing an application to run on a previous version of
Windows, a Windows Service Pack may be available. The Service
Pack enables you to upgrade the system code to include some of
these new features.

This book also includes information about the evolution of
application design and the impact of the Internet on conventional
application design. While this book does not explicitly include Web
page design guidelines, it does include recommendations about
Web-style applications.

The Importance of a Well-Designed Interface

The usability of your application's design is not just a philosophical
nicety for your consideration; it is essential to the success of your
application. The investment you make in the design of your
application contributes not only to supporting and keeping your
existing customers, but also to expanding your customer base.
Therefore, your investment in the design of your application directly
affects your current and future bottom line.

If you design or develop software for the Windows platform, you are
part of an industry that is creating some of the most exciting and
innovative applications available. More applications and more types
of applications are being written for the Windows platform than for
any other environment. In addition, increased support for
accessibility and localization of applications means that applications
are reaching a larger audience. New hardware initiatives and
innovative technologies are making computers better for end users.

The wide use of features such as common dialog boxes and controls has increased consistency between applications. In short, application developers for Windows are doing a great job of promoting the growth and use of computers everywhere.

The Need for Improved Simplicity

Despite the popular support for Windows, there are still substantial challenges in providing the best experience for users. Computers are still too complicated to use, and support costs are high. Users frequently complain about the number of features they find in applications; they can't find the features they care about, and they can't figure out the features they do find.

Many users expect a computer to be as easy to use, and as predictable and reliable, as an appliance. They want a computer to work in a way that is familiar to them. Therefore, simplicity of design involves issues that must be addressed by everyone building applications for Windows.

Delivering simplicity does not mean just removing functions. It requires work. Even a simple interface can require a significant investment of code. However, the rewards and benefits are substantial, including reduced training and support costs and productive, loyal customers.

Key Areas for Improvement

This book offers many recommendations for designing Windows-based applications. The most common design issues are summarized below. You can find more detail throughout the following chapters.

Confusing or Awkward Setup and Uninstall Design

Often, how users will install an application is not addressed until near the end of the development process. Yet because this is the first interface that users see, it is one of the most crucial elements of your application's design.

Complex, Cluttered Setup

Setup programs often have too many steps, requiring the user to click too many times. You can simplify your setup design by including typical and custom installation options. Use the typical installation option to provide a smooth, easy setup that doesn't overwhelm the user with options, and include default settings that give the user a reasonable configuration. For example, don't require that the user supply the target folder. Instead, you can display the recommended subfolder in the system's Program Files folder as the default. Whenever possible, reduce the number of mouse clicks and pages of options, especially for the typical installation.

Bad setup design is also often characterized by the three "R's": reboots, Readme files, and random windows. Unless it is absolutely necessary, avoid requiring the user to restart the computer. Restarting is not only inconvenient for users, it could cause them to lose data because they didn't save changes to open files. To avoid the need to restart, the installation program should detect whether the currently running dynamic link libraries (.dll) or executable (.exe) files are to be replaced and give the user the opportunity to close any applications that might be affected.

Programs that update system components typically require that the computer be restarted. Generally, this is a bad practice that can make the system unstable and confuse the users. To minimize the need for restarting the computer, avoid modifying core system components or installing files in the Windows System (or System32) folder. For more information, see the Microsoft Platform SDK on the MSDN Online Web site at http://msdn.microsoft.com/ui/guide/sdk.asp and the Windows Logo Program at http://msdn.microsoft.com/winlogo/.

Whenever possible, avoid including unnecessary information in a Readme file. Plan your application's design far enough ahead so that users do not need to be aware of too many special circumstances.

Do not include technical support information on the **Start** menu. This just adds clutter and makes it harder for users to access their applications. Similarly, don't include technical support information as an option in your setup program. Instead, add an entry to your **Help** menu that accesses this information, or just leave the file in your application's folder.

Finally, avoid displaying unnecessary message windows while the user is installing and setting up your application. Consolidate progress messages as much as possible, and use the IShellLink system interface to create your Start menu entries, not the outdated DDE mechanism. For more information about the IShellLink interface, see the MSDN Online Web site at http://msdn.microsoft.com/ui/guide/ishellLink.asp.

Awkward First Experience

Users' overall success with an application can be influenced heavily by their initial experience. A first impression is a critical moment in which to gain a user's trust and confidence. After an application is installed, the user should be able to use it productively within the first five minutes.

Keep in mind that users will often want to use your application immediately after it has been installed. As part of your setup program, include an option to automatically start the application. In addition, let the user know how to start your application in the future by illustrating or referring to your application's **Start** menu entry.

You can help users be productive by promoting your application's key features and functions. A guided feature tour is helpful, but it is often not enough just to highlight your program's capabilities. You might want to include an initial screen that displays key features and functions and shows how to use them.

At the same time, avoid overwhelming users with all the features in your application. Instead, consider exposing features gradually through contextual tips or some form of intelligent help that tracks the user's experience.

Remember that your users' initial experience is not limited to the first five minutes with your product. Your users will have an initial experience every time they use a new feature, so consider the first use of each aspect of your product's design.

Incomplete or Missing Uninstall Option

Your installation design should also include an option to uninstall your application. The uninstall process is frequently neglected in application design, as evidenced by the fact that the most popular tools for Windows are uninstall utilities. But you need to do more than just support the uninstall process. Users often complain about uninstall programs that require them to re-insert the CD, that do not uninstall completely, or that cannot recover from a failed uninstall.

Make sure that you test your uninstall process in a variety of ways. Test it with previous versions of your application and in circumstances where the uninstall process failed before it finished. This could be because of a power failure or because the user tried to end the process without canceling it first. When this happens, the process can leave behind extra files that clutter the user's system, and even more importantly, the user may not be able to re-install the application.

The Windows Installer technology can help you provide well-designed install and uninstall processes. It is available in Windows 2000 and on other platforms through a redistributable operating system component. Use the Windows Installer to make your application resilient and to allow for easy distribution through the Windows 2000 Active Directory. The Windows Installer supports features such as self-repair and Install on Demand, and it is integrated with the Windows Control Panel. For more information about the Windows Installer, see the Microsoft Windows Web site at http://msdn.microsoft.com/ui/guide/install.asp. For more information about designing your uninstall process, see Chapter 11, "Integrating with the System."

Improper Use of the File System

A typical user's hard disk is a mess. Applications often scatter files all over the folder structure, making it hard for users to find their files. This also makes it difficult for users to back up files, *roam* from computer to computer, and replace a computer or move to a new one. Worse, when application files have cryptic names, users don't know what the files are for.

Windows provides several folders that can help you avoid these situations as described below. Do not hard code the names or paths for these folders into your application. Instead, you can use Shfolder.dll to help you identify the appropriate locations for storing files in the file system. For more information about these standard folders, see the following sections and Chapter 11, "Integrating with the System." For information about Shfolder.dll, see the MSDN Online Web site at http://msdn.microsoft.com/ui/guide/shellfolder.asp.

Missing Support for "My Documents"

Use the My Documents folder as the default location for storing documents that the user creates. The My Pictures subfolder provides a location for storing image files. You can create your own subfolders for storing specialized groups of documents, such as the files included in a programming project.

There are several benefits to supporting the My Documents folder. Because this folder is a system default, users can open your documents more quickly from the desktop and by using the File Open command. The system supports storing files on a per-user basis, and therefore also supports user roaming scenarios under Windows 2000. Support for My Documents is especially important for users in large organizations whose IT departments manage user documents.

However, do not hard code the path for the My Documents folder, such as "C:\My Documents," in your application, because the name of this folder may be localized for some language versions of Windows, and its location may vary. Instead, use the system interface (Shfolder.dll) to properly locate this folder.

Improper Placement of Program Files

Avoid installing application files at the root of the user's hard disk. This clutters the hard disk and confuses the user. Instead, create a single folder in the Program Files folder to contain your application files. Store read-only files — such as executable (.exe) files, dynamic-link libraries (.dll files), and Help files — in this folder. The Program Files folder should also include read-only data files, such as clip art, samples, and libraries. Do not place any per-user files in this folder; include only files that your application and uninstall utilities can modify or remove. Store any shared components in the Program Files\Common Files subfolder.

Missing Support for Application Data

For files that don't meet the My Documents or Program Files criteria, create a folder within the Application Data folder and name it using your application's name. For example, use this location to store modifiable application support files such as custom dictionaries, log files, user history, or e-mail stores.

If the files are discardable (such as cached data or temporary files) or do not need to roam with the user from computer to computer, store them in the Application Data\Local Settings subfolder. Files stored in this location are typically data files that the user implicitly generates. There is also an Application Data folder in the All Users folder. Use this folder to store only local dynamic data files — such as log files, hidden databases, or index files — that are not user-specific.

Scattered Temporary Storage

Many applications, including some of those provided by Windows, include their own caches for temporary files. This organization requires the user to purge several different caches to recover this disk space. The Disk Cleanup utility included in Windows provides a simple interface where users can easily manage disk caches. Make sure that any discardable files your application stores can be managed from this utility.

Cryptic File Names

When users encounter files they didn't create that have meaningless or indecipherable names, they have no way of knowing which application they belong to or whether the files are to be backed up or deleted. This is also true for files that have no registered type.

You can improve this situation in a number of ways. Avoid cryptic file names, especially those that include obscure abbreviations. Support for long file names in Windows enables you to define comprehensible names for the files and folders that users see.

Similarly, use appropriate capitalization in file and folder names for a consistent, recognizable appearance. For example, acronyms such as "MS-DOS" should appear in all caps. If you need to localize your file names, you can use registry entries to map file names to your localized folders or file names.

Whenever possible, use existing data types. When you create a new type, the user should be able to identify the type with your application. For every new file type your application installs, do the following, even if files of this type cannot be edited:

- Register the file type.

- Register a user-friendly type description.

- Register an icon.

If the user can open or edit a particular file type, register your application to automatically handle the file type. However, if the file type is not unique to your application, ask the user before you reassociate the file type and provide a way for the user to return the file type to its previous association. For more information about registering your file types, see Chapter 11, "Integrating with the System."

Finally, hiding files that the user does not need to edit better ensures that the files won't accidentally be deleted or moved. If you mark a file as both hidden and system, the file will not be displayed at all in Windows 2000. Hidden system files are accessible only directly from the Address bar or command line and are called "protected." While this is a good way to clean up a potentially cluttered folder, use it with care because users will be unable to see or modify such files.

GUI Overload

Remember that the computer screen is the main work area for user tasks, not a place to advertise or compete for the user's attention. When applications inappropriately use standard Windows graphical user interface (GUI) elements such as the **Start** menu, desktop, or taskbar, it can become confusing to the user, reducing not only user satisfaction, but also productivity.

Start Menu Abuse

The most common design error is how an application is installed on the **Start** menu. Too many entries and too many cascading submenus on the **Start** menu add complexity and reduce user access. Place only entries that a user needs to access frequently on the **Start** menu. As a general rule, limit your application's entry to a single item.

For suites or sets of applications that are used together, include an entry for each significant application on the **Programs** submenu. If you want to provide access to secondary utilities, include a separate group entry. In any case, do not include entries for Help, Readme, and Uninstall.

Finally, avoid installing any entries at the very top (first) level of the **Start** menu. Users expect to find only primary system commands here, as shown in Figure 1.1.

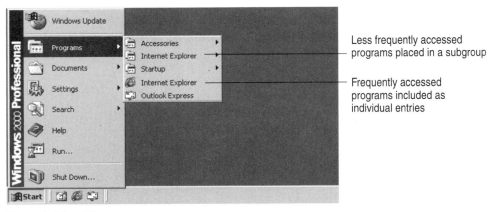

Figure 1.1 Good Start menu usage

Adding to this level of the **Start** menu reduces the user's focus and hampers the user's ability to find key functions, as shown in Figure 1.2.

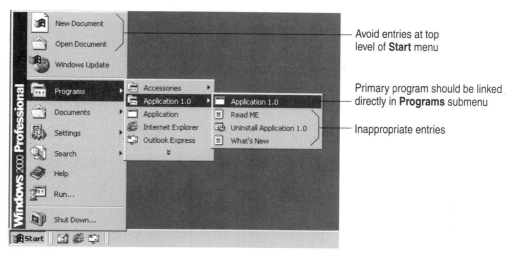

Figure 1.2 Bad Start menu usage

Desktop Icon Abuse

Like the **Start** menu, the desktop is another area where less is more. With the exception of icons that represent access to general information services, such as e-mail, Internet browsers, or online services, avoid creating any icons on the desktop. The Windows desktop provides a general work area and storage location for the user. Usability tests consistently demonstrate that users consider the desktop their space and react negatively to icons appearing there automatically. Furthermore, the **Start** menu is a better location from which to support quick access.

If it's important to give users desktop access to your application's icon, give them the choice by including an option in your application's interface rather than by pre-installing the icon. For example, you could offer to create a shortcut on the desktop in response to a user action, such as creating a dial-up connection. This makes the availability of the icon the user's choice, provides a useful service, and does not leave the desktop cluttered.

Start-up Overload

When a user starts Windows, multiple banners or windows should not compete for attention like a six-car pileup. Even if the information is important, its value may be lost if it is presented in a disorganized way, as shown in Figure 1.3. Whenever possible, follow these guidelines:

- Avoid displaying a dialog box when the system starts.

- Integrate configuration options into your setup design.

- Wait until your application has been started before displaying introductory product information.

If your application needs to open a dialog box when it starts, consider using the support in Windows 2000 that puts your dialog box into a queue, so that dialog boxes are displayed one at a time.

Design your application with these points in mind to improve the user interface and decrease support calls.

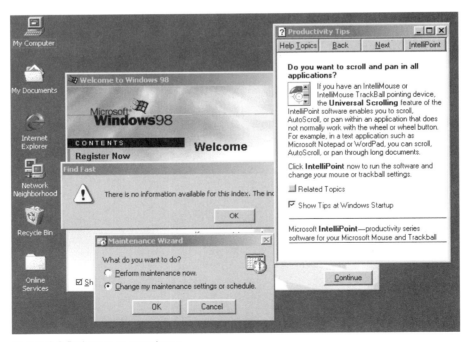

Figure 1.3 Bad start-up experience

Status Notification Area Abuse

Another common mistake is using the taskbar status notification area inappropriately, as shown in Figure 1.4. The Windows taskbar notification area is intended only for quick, short-term notification (for example, a document is printing) or status information for some ongoing process or event (for example, a low battery warning). A taskbar icon should persist only if it is important for a user to have it available, such as for a dial-up connection. This helps ensure that the user will notice changes in the notification area.

Figure 1.4 Bad use of status notification area

Avoid placing automatically included icons in the notification area just to give users quick access to configuration information. If you want to provide this type of support, include an option in your application's interface so that users can display this icon if they choose. Set the default to off.

Windows also includes a special area on the taskbar called the Quick Launch toolbar, shown in Figure 1.5.

Figure 1.5 Quick Launch toolbar

This area provides one-click access to icons that the user chooses to put there and to basic tasks, such as e-mail, and basic locations, such as the Web and the desktop. Therefore, do not install your application here unless it is intended to replace a system-provided function, such as e-mail.

Poor Message Design

Messages are one of the most consistent areas of interface abuse. Users often find messages annoying. They disrupt task flow and are often worded poorly so that at best, they are not very helpful, and at worst, they are incomprehensible and condescending, as shown in Figure 1.6.

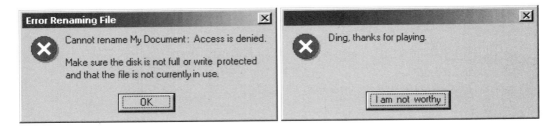

What is displayed on screen   **What the user sees**

Figure 1.6 Poor message design

The best strategy is to avoid messages whenever possible. There are several ways you can do this:

- Disable commands or options when unavailable.

- Handle any input and fail gracefully, when necessary.

- Provide other less intrusive forms of feedback, such as the new balloon-style ToolTips, shown in Figure 1.7.

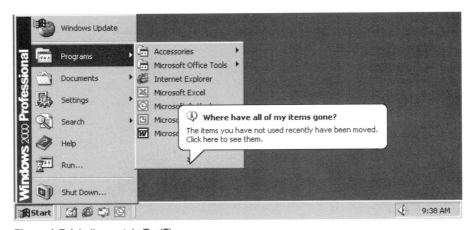

Figure 1.7 A balloon-style ToolTip

When you must write message text, make sure you use non-technical language as much as possible, avoid blaming the user, and provide a clear course of action to resolve a problem.

Missed Opportunities

Many developers of Windows-based applications unintentionally limit their potential audience by overlooking user scenarios that vary from their own. However, it often takes only a little extra effort to support the widest range of users. Time invested here can pay dividends in the form of increasing your application's potential market or meeting governmental requirements. It also provides consistency of operation for all your users.

Overlooking the System Locale

The advent of the Internet makes it possible to quickly and easily distribute software globally. Yet the impact of an application's design on an international audience is often overlooked.

Even if you don't intend to localize your application into other languages, you must carefully consider how your application will operate on configurations set up for other languages. For example, always use the system functions that check for the names and locations of Windows standard folders, such as Program Files and My Documents, because these can differ on other language versions of the operating system. If you assume a specific folder location or name, your application can fail.

If you do plan to localize your application, you will need to consider all elements that are visible and relevant to the user. For example, in double-byte languages such as Japanese, Chinese, and Korean, access-key assignments are formatted differently. Instead of an underlined character in the text label, you include the character in parentheses.

To support multiple languages, create a single worldwide binary with separate language components (.dll files). Your binary should include U.S. English resources that will run on any language system, but it must be designed so that your interface can be changed dynamically.

Remember that localizing the text involves more than translating the words. You should query for and design to accommodate the default interface font. System font metrics such as font name and size can vary widely for different languages and can affect the positioning and spacing of text.

For more information about supporting international users, see Chapter 15, "Special Design Considerations."

Lack of Adequate Keyboard Support

Keyboard support provides efficiency for many users, but for those with sight impairments or repetitive-stress injuries, it is essential. Keyboard support means including keyboard access to all of your application's functions. It takes only a little time to confirm that your application's interface provides a logical tab navigation order.

Complex Secondary Window Design

Your attention to detail most often shows up in the design and layout of controls in property sheets, dialog boxes, and other secondary windows. Because users encounter secondary windows so frequently in the interface, a window that does not follow familiar conventions can disrupt readability and task flow, as users must stop and deal with the inconsistency.

You can improve the usability of your application's secondary windows by observing the following general guidelines:

- Use the appropriate control. Controls are typically optimized for certain types of functions. The wrong control not only affects the user's efficiency, but also confuses the user about the purpose of your design.

For more information about controls and when and how to use them, see Chapter 8, "Menus, Controls, and Toolbars."

- Use recommended layout conventions. For example, buttons such as **OK** and **Cancel** or **Yes** and **No** should be aligned either at the top right or bottom right of the dialog box. (In right-to-left versions of Windows, this alignment can be reversed.) **OK** is always the first button, followed by **Cancel**, and then any other buttons. If you don't have an **OK** button, then **Cancel** follows all the other buttons. Because **OK** and **Cancel** are generally mapped to the ENTER and ESC keys respectively, access key assignments are unnecessary.

- Use appropriate labeling. Always use the appropriate capitalization and access key assignments. Include colons when you use static text to label another control. This not only identifies the text as a label, but also provides a cue for screen-reader utilities.

- Use appropriate alignment. Alignment affects readability and therefore usability and efficiency. It also affects the user's overall impression of the quality of your application. For example, make sure you align the baselines of text labels for text boxes.

- Use appropriate sizing, spacing, and margins. For example, the recommended spacing between controls is seven dialog units (DLUs). The recommended size for buttons is 50 x 14 DLUs, except where a button must be larger to accommodate its text label. Also make good use of your overall space. The guidelines in this book are for the minimum space recommendations. Avoid cramming too many controls together if you have additional space.

> For more information about secondary window design, see Chapter 9, "Secondary Windows" and Chapter 14, "Visual Design."

Lack of Support for User Color and Font Preferences

Windows provides standard font and color settings that users can set to match their preferences. Support for these preferences is important for user satisfaction and also ensures readability and accessibility for users who require high contrast to read the screen.

Wherever possible, use the system settings for fonts, especially for menus, icons, and window title bars. Since your application does not operate in isolation, use the system color settings as well. If you do want to vary colors, consider using colors similar to the user's settings.

In any case, make sure that your application responds appropriately to the High Contrast system flag and to the **WM_SETTINGCHANGE** event.

> For more information about supporting accessibility, see Chapter 15, "Special Design Considerations."

Misuse of Color

Applications often fail to adapt to the color depth settings of the user's display. This can result in palette "flashes" in your application. To avoid this, use the standard halftone color palette when the display is set to 8-bit color. Also be sure to adjust your color usage appropriately to receive the **WM_DISPLAYCHANGE** event.

Icons are an important design element to consider with regard to color and resolution changes. Guidelines for icon design include color and size conventions for your application and all of its file types.

For more information about icon design, see Chapter 14, "Visual Design."

Neglecting Multiple Monitor Support

The latest versions of Windows enable the user to display windows across multiple monitors. If your application overlooks this user scenario, secondary windows can appear on the wrong monitor when the user moves your application's primary window to a secondary monitor, as shown in Figure 1.8.

Primary Monitor   **Secondary Monitor**

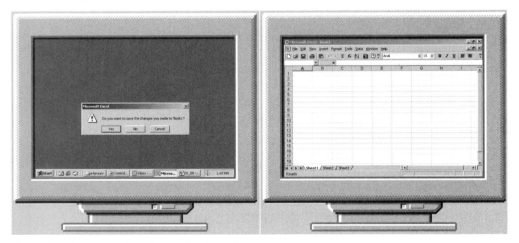

Figure 1.8 The wrong place for a secondary window

To properly support multiple monitors, make sure your application can handle an arbitrarily large coordinate space. Unless a user explicitly moves a secondary window to another monitor, display the secondary window on top of its primary window, as shown in Figure 1.9.

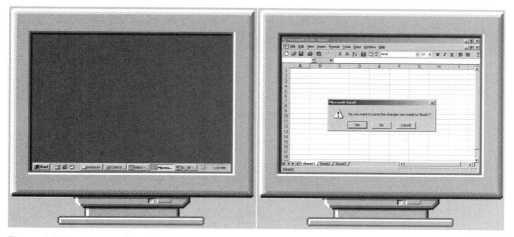

Primary Monitor   **Secondary Monitor**

Figure 1.9 The correct place for a secondary window

The best way to determine whether your application supports multiple monitor configurations appropriately is to test your software with this scenario.

Missing Support for Character Sets

To further address the global market for your application, ensure that your application can deal with input and output for different character sets. This is not hard to do, and it is well worth the effort. Windows provides functions to help you. For example, if you use the rich text box control for input and output of text, it automatically handles and preserves text based on the current character set and code-page settings. Similarly, the Fonts common dialog box ensures that the user has access to the appropriate set of fonts. Finally, make sure that your application can respond appropriately to keyboard language changes using the **WM_INPUTLANGCHANGEREQUEST** event.

For more information about the **WM_INPUTLANG-CHANGEREQUEST** event, see the Microsoft Platform SDK on the MSDN Online Web site at http://msdn.microsoft.com/ui/guide/sdk.asp.

Checklist for a Good Interface

The following checklist summarizes the information in the previous section and in this book. Use it to help you confirm that your application is designed to provide the best user experience:

❏ Your application installs easily in a minimum number of steps.

❏ Your application installation does not require the system to restart.

❏ Users do not have to read a Readme file before using your application.

❏ User-generated data files are stored by default in the My Documents folder.

❏ Your application avoids cryptic file names that are visible to users.

❏ Your application does not create folders outside of the Program Files folder.

❏ Your application does not write files to the root of the hard disk.

❏ If your application uses a disk cache, it also registers with the Disk Cleanup utility.

❏ Your application does not include entries to its Help, Readme, and Uninstall files on the **Start** menu.

❏ Your application does not install icons to the Windows desktop without the user's permission.

❏ If your application is run at startup, it loads without displaying splash screens and dialog boxes.

❏ Your application does not use the taskbar notification area for status, for launching applications or utilities, or for querying properties. It uses the notification area only to alert the user of an important change.

❑ Your application appropriately applies the color choices the user selected in Display properties in Control Panel.

❑ Your application is keyboard accessible.

❑ Your application works correctly if the user increases the size of the default font.

❑ Your application supports the standard set of keyboard shortcuts, where applicable.

❑ Your application's uninstall process leaves no remaining files or registry entries other than files created by the user.

❑ Your application does not use jargon in its user interface text. Use industry-specific or technical terms only if they are clearly understood by the user.

❑ Your application adjusts appropriately when the user changes the display resolution as well as for multiple-monitor configurations.

Design Principles and Methodology

A well-designed user interface is built on principles and a development process that center on users and their tasks. This chapter summarizes the basic principles of the interface design for Microsoft Windows. It also includes techniques and methodologies used in an effective human-computer interface design process.

User-Centered Design Principles

The information in this section describes the design principles on which Windows and the guidelines in this book are based. You will find these principles valuable when designing software for Windows.

User in Control

An important principle of user interface design is that the user should always feel in control of the software rather than feeling controlled by the software. This principle has a number of implications:

- The operational assumption is that the user — not the computer or software — initiates actions. The user plays an active rather than reactive role. You can automate tasks, but implement the automation in a way that allows the user to choose or control it.

- Because of their widely varying skills and preferences, users must be able to personalize aspects of the interface. The system software provides user access to many of these aspects. Your software should reflect user settings for different system properties, such as colors, fonts, or other options.

- Your software should be as interactive and responsive as possible. Avoid modes whenever possible. A *mode* is a state that excludes general interaction or otherwise limits the user to specific interactions. When a mode is the best or only design alternative — for example, for selecting a particular tool in a drawing program — make sure the mode is obvious, visible, the result of an explicit user choice, and easy to cancel.

Here are some other suggested ways of keeping your application's design interactive:

- Use *modeless* secondary windows wherever possible. For more information, see Chapter 9, "Secondary Windows."

- Segment processes, such as printing, so you do not need to load the entire application to perform an operation.

- Run long processes in the background, keeping the foreground interactive. For example, when a document is printing, the user should be able to minimize the window even if the document cannot be altered. The multitasking support in Windows allows you to define separate processes, or *threads*, in the background.

For information about applying the user-in-control design principle, see Chapter 5, "Input Basics," and Chapter 6, "General Interaction Techniques." These chapters cover the basic forms of interaction your software should support.

Directness

Design your software so that users can directly manipulate software representations of information. Whether they are dragging an object to relocate it or navigating to a location in a document, users should see how their actions affect the objects on the screen. Visible information and choices also reduce the user's mental workload. Users can recognize a command more easily than they can recall its syntax.

Familiar metaphors provide a direct and intuitive interface for user tasks. By allowing users to transfer their knowledge and experience, metaphors make it easier to predict and learn the behaviors of software-based representations.

When using metaphors, you need not limit a computer-based implementation to its real-world counterpart. For example, unlike its paper-based counterpart, a folder on the Windows desktop can be used to organize a variety of objects such as printers, calculators, and other folders. Similarly, a Windows folder can be sorted in ways that its real-world counterpart cannot. The purpose of using metaphor in the interface is to provide a cognitive bridge; the metaphor is not an end in itself.

Metaphors support user recognition rather than recollection. Users remember a meaning associated with a familiar object more easily than they remember the name of a particular command.

For information about applying the principle of directness and metaphor, see Chapter 6, "General Interaction Techniques," and Chapter 14, "Visual Design." These chapters cover, respectively, the use of directness in the interface (including drag-and-drop operations) and the use of metaphors in the design of icons or other graphical elements.

Consistency

Consistency allows users to transfer existing knowledge to new tasks, learn new things more quickly, and focus more attention on tasks. This is because they do not have to spend time trying to remember the differences in interaction. By providing a sense of stability, consistency makes the interface familiar and predictable.

Consistency is important through all aspects of the interface, including names of commands, visual presentation of information, operational behavior, and placement of elements on the screen and within windows. To design consistency into software, you must consider the following:

- Consistency within an application. Present common functions using a consistent set of commands and interfaces. For example, avoid implementing a **Copy** command that immediately carries out an operation in one situation but in another displays a dialog box that requires a user to type in a destination. As a corollary to this example, use the same command to carry out functions that seem similar to the user.

- Consistency within the operating environment. By maintaining a high level of consistency between the interaction and interface conventions provided by Windows, your software benefits from the users' ability to apply interactive skills they have already learned.

- Consistency with metaphors. If a particular behavior is more characteristic of a different object than its metaphor implies, the user may have difficulty learning to associate that behavior with an object. For example, an incinerator communicates a different model than a wastebasket as far as recovering the objects placed in it.

Although applying the principle of consistency is the primary goal of this book, the following chapters focus on the elements common to all Windows-based software: Chapter 7, "Windows"; Chapter 8, "Menus, Controls, and Toolbars"; and Chapter 9, "Secondary Windows." For information about closely integrating your software with the Windows environment, see Chapter 11, "Integrating with the System," and Chapter 12, "Working with OLE Embedded and Linked Objects."

Forgiveness

Users like to explore an interface and often learn by trial and error. An effective interface allows for interactive discovery. It provides only appropriate sets of choices and warns users about potential situations where they could damage the system or data, or better, makes actions reversible or recoverable.

Even in the best-designed interface, users can make mistakes. These mistakes can be both physical (accidentally pointing to the wrong command or data) and mental (making a wrong decision about which command or data to select). An effective design avoids situations that are likely to result in errors. It also accommodates potential user errors and makes it easy for the user to recover.

For information about applying the principle of forgiveness, see Chapter 13, "User Assistance," which provides information about supporting discoverability in the interface through the use of contextual, task-oriented, and reference forms of user assistance. For information about designing for the widest range of users, see Chapter 15, "Special Design Considerations."

Feedback

Always provide feedback for a user's actions. Good feedback helps confirm that the software is responding to input and communicates details that distinguish the nature of the action. Effective feedback is timely and is presented as close to the point of the user's interaction as possible. Even when the computer is processing a particular task, provide the user with information about the state of the process and how to cancel the process if that is an option. Nothing is more disconcerting to users than a "dead" screen that is unresponsive to input. A typical user will tolerate only a few seconds of an unresponsive interface.

It is equally important that the type of feedback you use be appropriate to the task. You can communicate simple information through pointer changes or a status bar message; for more complex feedback, you may need to display a progress control or message box.

For information about applying the principle of visual and audio feedback, see Chapter 14, "Visual Design" and Chapter 15, "Special Design Considerations."

Aesthetics

Visual design is an important part of an application's interface. Visual attributes provide valuable impressions and communicate important cues to the interactive behavior of particular objects. At the same time, it is important to remember that every visual element that appears on the screen potentially competes for the user's attention. Provide a coherent environment that clearly contributes to the user's understanding of the information presented. The skills of a graphics or visual designer can be invaluable for this aspect of the design.

For information and guidelines related to the aesthetics of your interface, see Chapter 14, "Visual Design." This chapter covers everything from individual element design to font use and window layout.

Simplicity

An interface should be simple (not simplistic), easy to learn, and easy to use. It must also provide access to all functionality of an application. Maximizing functionality and maintaining simplicity work against each other in the interface. An effective design balances these objectives.

One way to support simplicity is to reduce the presentation of information to the minimum required to communicate adequately. For example, avoid wordy descriptions for command names or messages. Irrelevant or verbose phrases clutter your design, making it difficult for users to extract essential information easily. Another way to design a simple but useful interface is to use natural mappings and semantics. The arrangement and presentation of elements affects their meaning and association.

Simplicity also correlates with familiarity; things that are familiar often seem simpler. Whenever possible, try to build connections that draw on your users' existing knowledge and experiences.

You can also help users manage complexity by using progressive disclosure. *Progressive disclosure* involves careful organization of information so that it is shown only at the appropriate time. By hiding information presented to the user, you reduce the amount of information the user must process. For example, you can use menus to display lists of actions or choices, and you can use dialog boxes to display sets of options.

Progressive disclosure does not imply using unconventional techniques for revealing information, such as requiring a modifier key as the only way to access basic functions or forcing the user through a longer sequence of hierarchical interaction. This can make an interface more complex and cumbersome.

For information about applying the principle of simplicity, see Chapter 8, "Menus, Controls, and Toolbars." This chapter discusses progressive disclosure in detail and describes how and when to use the standard (system-supplied) elements in your interface.

Design Methodology

Effective interface design is more than just following a set of rules. It requires a user-centered attitude and design methodology. It also requires early planning of the interface and continued work throughout the development process.

A Balanced Design Team

An important consideration in the design of an application is the composition of the team that develops and builds it. Always try to balance disciplines and skills, including development, visual design, writing, human factors, and usability assessment. Rarely are all these characteristics found in a single individual, so create a team of individuals who specialize in each area and who can contribute uniquely to the final design.

Ensure that the design team can effectively work and communicate together. Locating them in close proximity or providing them with a common area to work out design details often fosters better communication and interaction.

The Design Cycle

An effective user-centered design process involves a number of important phases: designing, prototyping, testing, and iterating. The following sections describe these phases.

Design

The initial work on a software's design can be the most critical. During this phase, you decide the general shape of your application. If the foundation work is flawed, it is difficult to correct later.

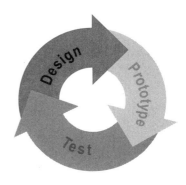

This part of the process involves not only defining your application's objectives and features, but understanding who your users are and their tasks, intentions, and goals. For example, an order-entry system may have very different users and requirements than an information kiosk. Designing for your users involves understanding the following factors:

- Background — age, gender, expertise, experience level, physical limitations, and special needs.

- Work environment — equipment, social and cultural influences, and physical surroundings.

- Current task organization — steps required, dependencies, redundant activities, and output objective.

At this point, begin defining the conceptual framework to represent your application with the knowledge and experience of your target audience. Ideally, you should create a design model that fits the user's conceptual view of the tasks to be performed. Consider the basic organization and different types of metaphors that can be used. Observing users at their current tasks can provide ideas about effective metaphors.

Document your design. Writing down your design plan not only provides a valuable reference and form of communication, but often helps make the design more concrete and reveals issues and gaps.

Prototype

After you have defined a design model, prototype some of the basic aspects of the design. This can be done in a variety of ways:

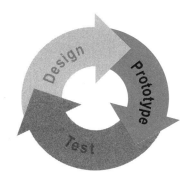

- Pencil-and-paper models — where you create illustrations of your interface to which other elements can be attached.

- Storyboards — comic book-like sequences of sketches that illustrate specific processes.

- Animation — movie-like simulations.

- Operational software using a prototyping tool or standard development tools.

A prototype is valuable in many ways. It provides an effective tool for communicating the design. It can help you define task flow and better visualize the design. And it provides a low-cost vehicle for getting user input on a design. This is particularly useful early in the design process.

The type of prototype you build depends on your goal. Functionality, task flow, interface, operation, and documentation are just some of the different aspects of an application that you may need to assess. For example, pen-and-paper models or storyboards may work when you are defining task organization or conceptual ideas. Operational prototypes are usually best for the mechanics of user interaction.

Consider whether to focus your prototype on breadth or depth. The broader the prototype, the more features you should try to include to gain an understanding about how users react to concepts and organization. When your objective is focused more on detailed usage of a particular feature or area of the design, use depth-oriented prototypes that include more detail for a given feature or task.

Test

Usability testing a design, or a particular aspect of a design, provides valuable information and is a key part of an application's success. Usability testing is different from quality assurance testing in that, rather than finding programming defects, you assess how well the interface fits user needs and expectations. Of course, defects can sometimes affect how well the interface will fit.

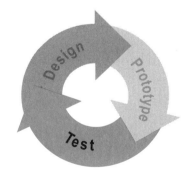

There can be different reasons for testing. You can use testing to look for potential problems in a proposed design. You can also focus on comparative studies of two or more designs to determine which is better given a specific task or set of tasks.

Usability testing provides you not only with task efficiency and success-or-failure data, it can also provide you with information about the user's perceptions, satisfaction, questions, and problems, which may be just as significant as the ability to complete a particular task.

When you test your design, it is important to use participants who fit the profile of your target audience. Using fellow workers from down the hall might be a quick way to find participants, but software developers rarely have the same experience as their customers. For details about conducting a usability test, see "Usability Assessment in the Design Process" later in this chapter.

Iterate

Because testing often uncovers design weaknesses, or at least provides additional information you will want to use, repeat the entire process, taking what you have learned and reworking your design or moving on to reprototyping and retesting. Continue this refining cycle throughout the development process until you are satisfied with the results. At a minimum, plan for at least one full iteration of your design and include it up front in your schedule.

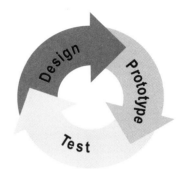

During this iterative process, you can begin substituting the actual application for prototypes as the application code becomes available. However, avoid delaying your design cycle waiting for the application code to be complete enough; you can lose valuable time and input that you could have captured with a prototype. Moreover, by the time most applications are complete enough for testing, it is difficult to consider significant changes, because it becomes easier to live with usability defects due to the time resources already invested. In addition, the time resources required to make significant changes at this point may affect the application's delivery schedule.

Usability Assessment in the Design Process

As described in the previous section, usability testing is a key part of the design process, but testing design prototypes is only one part of the picture. Usability assessment should begin in the early stages of development, when you can use it to gather data about how users do their work. You then incorporate your findings into the design process. As the design progresses, usability assessment continues to provide valuable input for analyzing initial design concepts and, in the later stages of application development, can be used to test specific tasks. Assess the usability of your application early and often.

Make sure you allocate adequate time in your development schedule to address the issues that may arise from your usability testing. Don't assume that the results will always confirm your design. How you respond to what the assessment reveals determines its real value.

When you are working through the details of individual features, don't neglect to evaluate how these integrate into the design. The usability assessment should include all of an application's components. Consider the user's entire experience as part of the usability assessment for your product. To help ensure overall usability, define a list of the top twenty most important and frequent tasks users should be able to do with the product, then test all of these tasks regularly. At a minimum, do this on the previous version as a baseline, then at each preliminary and final release for the product being developed.

Usability Testing Techniques

Usability testing involves a wide range of techniques and can involve an investment in resources, including trained specialists working in soundproof labs with one-way mirrors and sophisticated recording equipment. However, even the simplest investment in an office or conference room, tape recorder, stopwatch, and notepad can produce benefits. Similarly, all tests need not involve great numbers of subjects. More typically, quick iterative tests with a small, well-targeted sample and six to ten participants can identify most design problems.

Like the design process itself, usability testing begins with defining the target audience and the test goals. When you design a test, focus on tasks, not features. Even if your goal is to test specific features, remember that your customers will use those features within the context of particular tasks. It is also a good idea to do a dry run of the testing environment itself. You need to make sure that the task scenarios, prototype, and equipment run smoothly.

It is best to do usability testing in a quiet location, free from distractions. Make participants feel comfortable. Unless you have had the experience of participating in a usability test yourself, the pressure many test participants feel may surprise you. You can alleviate some tension by explaining the testing process and equipment to the participants, and by stating that your objective is to test the software, not them. Let the test participants know that if they become confused or frustrated, it is more of a reflection on the test itself than it is on them.

Give the user reasonable time to try to work through any difficult situations. Although it is generally best not to interrupt participants during a test, they may get stuck or end up in situations that require intervention. This need not necessarily disqualify the test data, as long as the test coordinator carefully guides or hints around a problem. Give general hints first before providing specific advice. For more difficult situations, you may need to stop the test and make adjustments. Keep in mind that less intervention usually yields better results. Be sure to record the techniques and search patterns that users employ while attempting to work through a difficulty, as well as the number and type of hints you use to help them.

Ask participants to think aloud as they work, so you can hear the assumptions and inferences that they are making. As they work, record the time taken to perform a task and any problems they encounter. You may also want to follow up the session with a questionnaire that asks the participants to evaluate the application or tasks they performed.

Record the test results using a portable tape recorder, or better, a video camera. Since even the best observer can miss details, reviewing the data later will prove invaluable. Recorded data also allows more direct comparisons between multiple participants. It is usually risky to base conclusions on observing a single participant. Recorded data also allows the entire design team to review and evaluate the results.

Whenever possible, involve all members of the design team in observing the test and reviewing the results. This ensures a common reference point and better design solutions as team members apply their own insights to what they observe. If direct observation is not possible, make the recorded results available to the entire team.

Other Assessment Techniques

You can use many techniques to gather usability information. In addition to those already mentioned, focus groups are helpful for generating ideas or trying out ideas. A focus group requires a moderator who directs the discussion about aspects of a task or design but allows participants to express their opinions freely. You can also conduct demonstrations, or walk-throughs, in which you take the user through a set of sample scenarios and ask their impressions along the way. In a "Wizard of Oz" technique, a testing specialist simulates the way the interface interacts with the user. Although these latter techniques can be valuable, they often require a trained and experienced test coordinator.

Understanding Users

The design and usability techniques described in the previous sections have been used in the development of Microsoft Windows and in many of the guidelines included in this book. This process has yielded the following general characteristics about users. Consider these characteristics in the design of your software:

- Beginning Windows users often have difficulty using the mouse. For example, dragging and double-clicking are skills that may take time for beginning mouse users to master. Dragging can be difficult because it requires continued pressure on the mouse button and involves properly targeting the correct destination. Double-clicking is not the same as two separate clicks, so many beginning users have difficulty handling the timing necessary to distinguish these two actions, or they overdo it, assuming that everything needs to be double-clicked. Design your interface so that double-clicking and dragging are not the only ways to perform basic tasks; allow the user to conduct the basic tasks using single-click operations, as well as through the keyboard.

- Beginning users often have difficulty with window management. They do not always realize that overlapping windows represent a three-dimensional space. As a result, when a window hides another, a user may assume it no longer exists.

- Beginning users often have difficulty with file management. The organization of files and folders nested more than two levels is more difficult to understand because it is not as apparent as it would be with physical files and folders.

- Intermediate users may understand file hierarchies but have difficulty with other aspects of file management, such as moving and copying files. This may be because most of their experience working with files is from within an application.

- Advanced, or power, users want efficiency. The challenge in designing for advanced users is providing efficiency without introducing complexity for less-experienced users. Developing shortcuts is often a useful way to support these users. In addition, advanced users may be dependent upon particular interfaces, making it difficult for them to adapt to significant rearrangement of or changes in an interface.

- To develop for the widest audience, include international users and users with disabilities. Address the needs of these users as part of your planning and design cycles to ensure that you can accommodate them.

Design Tradeoffs

A number of additional factors may affect the design of your application. For example, marketing considerations for a product may require you to deliver your application with a minimal design process, or comparative evaluations may force you to consider additional features. Remember that shortcuts and additional features can affect the application. There is no simple equation for determining when a design tradeoff is appropriate. So in evaluating the impact, consider the following factors:

- Every additional feature potentially affects performance, complexity, stability, maintenance, and the support costs of an application.

- It is harder to fix a design problem after an application is released because users may adapt to, or even become dependent on, a peculiarity in the design.

- Simplicity is not the same as being simplistic. Making something simple to use often requires a good deal of code and work.

- Features easily implemented by a small extension in the application code do not necessarily improve a user interface. For example, if the primary task is selecting a single object, extending it to support selection of multiple objects could make the frequent, simple task more difficult to carry out.

3

Basic Concepts

Microsoft Windows supports the evolution and design of software from a basic graphical user interface to a data-centered interface that is better focused on users and their tasks. This chapter outlines the fundamental concepts of data-centered design. It covers some of the basic definitions used throughout this book and provides the fundamental model for defining your interface to fit well within the Windows environment.

Data-Centered Design

Data-centered design means that the design of the interface supports a model where a user can browse for data and edit it directly instead of having to first locate an appropriate editor or application. As a user interacts with data, the corresponding commands and tools to manipulate the data or the view of the data become available to the user automatically. This frees a user to focus on the information and tasks rather than on applications and how applications interact.

In this data-centered context, a *document* is a common unit of data used in tasks and exchanged between users. The use of the term is not limited to the output of a word-processing or spreadsheet application, but it emphasizes that the focus of design is on data rather than on the underlying application.

Objects as Metaphor

A well-designed user interface provides an understandable, consistent framework in which users can work without being confounded by the details of the underlying technology. To help accomplish this, the design model of the Windows user interface uses an object metaphor, a representation of the natural way we interpret and interact with the world around us. In the interface, *objects* not only describe files or icons, but any unit of information, including cells, paragraphs, characters, and circles, and the documents in which they reside.

Object Characteristics

Objects, whether real-world or computer representations, have certain characteristics that help us understand what they are and how they behave. The following concepts describe the aspects and characteristics of computer representations:

- Properties — Objects have certain characteristics or attributes, called *properties*, that define their appearance or state — for example, color, size, and modification date. Properties are not limited to the external or visible traits of an object. They may reflect the internal or operational capability of an object, such as an option in a spelling check utility that automatically suggests alternative spellings.

- Operations — Things that can be done with or to an object are considered its *operations*. Moving or copying an object are examples of operations. You can expose operations in the interface through a variety of mechanisms, including commands and direct manipulation.

- Relationships — Objects always exist within the context of other objects. The context, or *relationships*, that an object may have often affects the way the object appears or functions. Common kinds of relationships include collections, constraints, and composites.

Relationships

The simplest relationship is a *collection*, in which objects in a set share a common aspect. The results of a query or a multiple selection of objects are examples of a collection. The significance of a collection is that it enables operations to be applied to a set of objects.

A *constraint* is a stronger relationship between a set of objects, in that changing an object in the set affects some other object in the set. The way a text box displays text, a drawing application layers its objects, and a word-processing application organizes a document into pages are all examples of constraints.

A relationship between objects can become so significant that the aggregation itself can be identified as an object with its own set of properties and operations. This type of relationship is called a *composite*. A range of cells, a paragraph, and a grouped set of drawing objects are examples of composites.

Another common relationship found in the interface is containment. A *container* is an object that holds other objects, such as text in a document or documents in a folder. A container often influences the behavior of its content. It may add or suppress certain properties or operations of an object placed in it. In addition, a container controls access to its content as well as the type of object it will accept as its content. This may affect the results of transferring objects from one container to another.

All of these aspects contribute to an object's *type*, a descriptive way of distinguishing or classifying an object. Objects of a common type have similar traits and behaviors.

Composition

As in the natural world, the metaphor of an object implies a constructed environment. Objects are composed of other objects. You can define most tasks supported by an application as a specialized combination or set of relationships between objects. A text document is a composition of text, paragraphs, footnotes, or other items. A table is a combination of cells. A chart is a particular organization of graphics. If you consistently define user interaction with objects at all levels of the interface, you can create complex constructions while maintaining a small, basic set of conventions.

These conventions, applied throughout the interface, increase ease of use. In addition, using composition to model tasks encourages modular, component-oriented design. Objects can then be adapted or recombined for other uses.

Persistence

In the natural world, objects persist in one state unless changed or destroyed. When you use a pen to write a note, you need not invoke a command to ensure that the ink is preserved on the paper. The act of writing implicitly preserves the information. This is the long-term direction for objects in the interface as well. Although it is still appropriate to design software that requires explicit user actions to preserve data, you should identify when to preserve data automatically. In addition, view-state information — such as cursor position, scroll position, and window size and location — should be preserved so that it can be restored when an object's view is reopened.

Putting Theory into Practice

The use of objects in an interface design does not guarantee usability. But the application of object-based concepts does offer greater potential for a well-designed user interface. A user-centered design process is the best way to ensure a successful, high-quality interface.

The first step to object-based design should begin as any good design begins—with a thorough understanding of the users' objectives and tasks. In the task analysis, you will want to identify the following information:

- The basic components or objects used in the tasks.

- The behavior and characteristics that differentiate each kind of object.

- The relationships of the objects to each other and to the user.

- The actions to be performed, the objects to which they apply, and the state information or attributes that each object in the task must preserve, display, and allow to be edited.

After the analysis is complete, you can start designing the user interfaces for the objects you identified. Define how the objects are to be presented, either as icons or as data elements in a form. Use icons primarily to represent composite or container objects that need to be opened in separate windows. Present attribute or state information as properties of the associated object, usually with property sheets. Map behaviors and operations, such as menu commands and direct manipulation, to specific kinds of user interaction. Make these available when the user selects an object.

The information in this book will help you define how to apply the interfaces provided by the operating system.

The Windows Environment

This chapter provides a brief overview of some of the basic elements included in the Microsoft Windows operating system that allow the user to control the computing environment (sometimes known as the *shell*). These elements are the basis of the user's environment and also the sources of the user's interaction with your application.

The Desktop

The Windows desktop is shown in Figure 4.1.

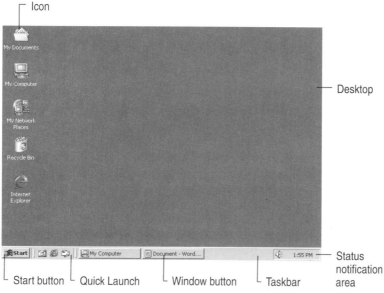

Figure 4.1 The desktop

The *desktop* represents a user's primary work area; it fills the screen and forms the visual background for all operations. However, the desktop is more than just a background. It is a convenient location for the user to place and easily reach objects that are stored in the file system. The desktop also serves as a private workspace for a networked computer, through which a user can browse for and access objects on the network.

The Taskbar

The taskbar is a special component of the desktop that is used to switch between open windows and to access global commands and other frequently used objects. As a result, it provides a home base — an operational anchor for the interface.

As with most toolbars, the user can configure the taskbar. For example, a user can move the taskbar from its default location and relocate it along another edge of the screen, as shown in Figure 4.2.

Figure 4.2 The taskbar in another location

The user can configure display options for the taskbar. The taskbar gives the user access to your application and provides notifications even when your application is not active. The taskbar is an interface shared across applications, and the conventions and guidelines for its use are covered in this book. For more information about integrating your application with the taskbar, see Chapter 11, "Integrating with the System."

The Start Button

The **Start** button at the left side of the taskbar displays a special menu that includes commands for opening or finding files. You can include a **Start** menu entry during your application's installation by placing a shortcut icon in the system's Programs folder. For more information about including entries on the **Start** menu, see Chapter 11, "Integrating with the System."

The Quick Launch Bar

Next to the **Start** button is the Quick Launch bar. This special toolbar area has been designed to provide users with easy access to the Web, e-mail, the desktop, and other basic system services, and to programs or other icons they use most frequently. This toolbar is generally reserved for the user to customize. Before adding your program to the Quick Launch bar, read the guidelines in Chapter 11, "Integrating with the System." Chapter 1, "Getting Started," also includes information about common design mistakes involving the Quick Launch bar.

Window Buttons

Whenever the user opens an application, a primary window opens and a corresponding button is placed on the taskbar. This button provides access to the open application window and is a convenient way for users to switch between open applications. The taskbar automatically adjusts the size of the buttons to accommodate as many as possible. When the button size requires an abbreviated window title, the taskbar automatically supplies a small pop-up window, called a *ToolTip* (as shown in Figure 4.3), that displays the full title.

Full title of the window

Figure 4.3 A pop-up window with a full title

When a window is minimized, the window's button remains on the taskbar. When the window is closed, the button is removed from the taskbar.

A user can also drag and drop objects onto a taskbar button. When the user drags an object onto a taskbar button and holds the pointer there, the system opens the associated window, allowing the user to drop the object within that window.

For more information about drag-and-drop operations, see Chapter 6, "General Interaction Techniques."

The Status Notification Area

On the opposite end of the taskbar from the **Start** menu is a special notification area. By default, this area includes the clock and the volume indicator. For guidelines on when it is appropriate to add your own entries to the status notification area, see Chapter 11, "Integrating with the System." Chapter 1, "Getting Started," also includes information about common design mistakes involving the status notification area.

Icons

Icons can appear on the desktop and in windows. *Icons* are pictorial representations of objects. Your software should supply and register icons for its application file and for any of its associated document or data files. For more information about the use of icons, see Chapter 11, "Integrating with the System." For information about icon design, see Chapter 14, "Visual Design."

Windows includes a number of icons that represent basic objects, such as the following.

Icons that Represent Basic Objects

Icon	Type	Function
My Computer	System folder	Provides access to a user's private storage.
My Network Places	System folder	Provides access to the network.
Folder	Folder	Provides organization of files and folders.
Shortcut to My Favorite Folder	Shortcut	Provides quick access to another object. A shortcut icon uses the icon of the type of file it is linked to, overlaid with the link symbol.
Windows Explorer	Application	Displays the content on a user's computer or on the network.
Recycle Bin	System folder	Stores deleted files and folders.

Icons that Represent Basic Objects *(continued)*

Icon	Type	Function
Control Panel	System folder	Provides access to the properties of installed devices and resources (for example, fonts, monitors, and keyboards).
My Documents	System folder	Provides a standard location for storing user-generated document and data files.
My Pictures	System folder	Provides a standard location for storing user-generated picture files.

Windows

You can open windows from icons. The Windows interface provides a means of viewing and editing information and viewing the content and properties of objects. You can also use windows to display information such as the following:

- The parameters and user input necessary to complete commands.

- Palettes of options, settings, or tools.

- Messages to inform the user of a particular situation.

Figure 4.4 shows some of the different uses for windows.

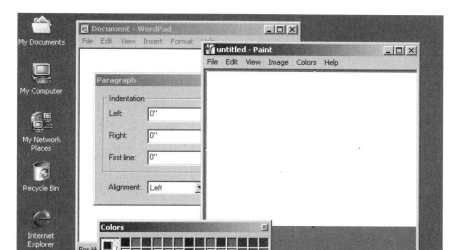

Figure 4.4 Different uses of windows

For more information about windows, see Chapter 7, "Windows,"
and Chapter 9, "Secondary Windows."

Input Basics

A user interacts with objects in the interface by using different types of input devices. The most common input devices are the mouse and the keyboard. While this chapter discusses the basic behavior for these devices, it does not exclude other forms of input.

Mouse Input

The mouse is the primary input device that users employ to interact with objects in the Microsoft Windows interface. The term "mouse" also applies to other types of pointing devices that emulate a mouse, such as trackballs.

> For more information about interaction techniques such as navigating, selecting, viewing, editing, transferring, and creating new objects, see Chapter 6, "General Interaction Techniques."

Mouse Pointers

The mouse is operationally linked with a graphic on the screen called the *pointer* (also referred to as the *cursor*). By positioning the pointer and clicking the primary and secondary buttons on the mouse, a user can select objects and their operations.

As a user moves the pointer across the screen, its appearance can change to indicate a particular location, operation, or state. The following table lists some common pointer shapes and their uses.

Common Pointer Shapes

Shape	Screen location	Available or current action
⬦	Over most objects	Pointing, selecting, or moving
I	Over text	Selecting text
⧖	Over any object or location	Processing an operation
⬦⧖	Over any screen location	Processing in the background (application loading), but the pointer is still interactive
⬦?	Over most objects	Context-sensitive Help mode
⌕	Inside a window	Zoom-in view
↕	Over a sizable edge	Resizing an edge vertically
↔	Over a sizable edge	Resizing an edge horizontally
⬉	Over a sizable edge	Resizing an edge diagonally
⬈	Over a sizable edge	Resizing an edge diagonally
←|→	Along column gridlines	Resizing a column
↕	Along row gridlines	Resizing a row
←||→	Over split box in vertical scroll bar	Splitting a window (or adjusting a split) horizontally
↕	Over split box in horizontal scroll bar	Splitting a window (or adjusting a split) vertically
⦸	Over any object	Not available as a drop target
☝	Over any object	Navigate to linked reference

Each pointer has a particular *hot spot* that defines the exact screen location of the mouse. The hot spot determines which object is affected by mouse actions. Screen objects can additionally define a *hot zone*, the area where the hot spot is considered to be over the object. Typically, the hot zone coincides with the borders of an object, but it may be larger or smaller to make user interaction easier.

Mouse Actions

Basic mouse actions in the interface use the primary or secondary mouse buttons. By default, the primary button is the left button and the secondary button is the right button. The operating system allows the user to swap the mapping of the buttons. Secondary button actions typically duplicate functions already accessible by using the primary button, but typically they provide a shortcut that's easier for the user.

For a mouse with three buttons, the secondary button is the right button, not the center button.

The following table describes the common actions performed with the mouse.

Common Mouse Actions

Action	Description
Pointing	Positioning the pointer so it "points to" a particular object on the screen without using the mouse button. Pointing is usually part of preparing for some other interaction. Pointing is often an opportunity to provide visual cues or other feedback to a user.
Clicking	Positioning the pointer over an object and then pressing and releasing the mouse button. Generally, the mouse is not moved during the click, and the mouse button is quickly released after it is pressed. Clicking identifies (selects) or activates objects or hyperlinks.
Double-clicking	Positioning the pointer over an object and pressing and releasing the mouse button twice in rapid succession. Double-clicking an object typically invokes its default operation, such as selecting text or opening an icon.

Common Mouse Actions *(continued)*

Action	Description
Pressing	Positioning the pointer over an object, then holding down the mouse button. Pressing is often the beginning of a drag-and-drop operation.
Dragging	Positioning the pointer over an object, then pressing down and holding the mouse button while moving the mouse. Use dragging for actions such as selecting and directly manipulating an object.

For most mouse interactions, pressing the mouse button only identifies an operation. User feedback is usually provided at this point. Releasing the mouse button activates (carries out) the operation. An auto-repeat function — for example, pressing a scroll arrow to continuously scroll — is an exception.

This guide does not cover other mouse behaviors such as *chording* (pressing multiple mouse buttons simultaneously) and multiple-clicking (triple- or quadruple-clicking). Because these behaviors require more user skill, they are not generally recommended for basic operations. However, you can consider them for special shortcut operations.

Because not every mouse has a third button, no basic action is defined for a third (middle) mouse button. It is best to assign operations to this button only in environments where the availability of a third mouse button can be assumed or to provide shortcut access to operations supported elsewhere in the interface. When you assign actions to the third mouse button, you need to define the behaviors for the actions already described (pointing, clicking, dragging, and double-clicking).

Some types of mouse also include a wheel button that supports click-and-drag actions as well as a rolling action. Assign viewing operations — such as scrolling, panning, and zooming — to the wheel button.

For more information about using the wheel button, see Chapter 6, "General Interaction Techniques."

Keyboard Input

The keyboard is used primarily for entering and editing textual information. However, the Windows interface also supports the use of the keyboard to navigate, toggle modes, modify input, and, as a shortcut, invoke certain operations. The fact that users can navigate through the interface by using the keyboard as well as by using the mouse is a fundamental principle and one of the key advantages of the Windows user interface.

Below are the common interactive behaviors performed by using the keyboard.

> For more information about using the keyboard for navigation, selection, and editing, see Chapter 6, "General Interaction Techniques." Additional information is also available on the Microsoft Accessibility Web site at http://microsoft.com/enable/training/keyboard.htm.

Common Keyboard Actions

Action	Description
Pressing	Pressing and releasing a key. Unlike mouse interaction, keyboard interaction occurs on the downstroke of the key. *Pressing* typically describes the keyboard interaction for invoking particular commands or for navigation.
Holding	Pressing and holding down a key. *Holding* typically describes interaction with keys such as ALT, SHIFT, and CTRL that modify the standard behavior of other input such as another key press or mouse action.
Typing	Typing in text with the keyboard.

Text Keys

Text keys include the following:

- Alphanumeric keys (a–z, A–Z, 0–9)

- Punctuation and symbol keys

- TAB and ENTER keys

- The SPACEBAR

> Most keyboards include two keys labeled ENTER, one on the main keyboard and one on the numeric keypad. Because these keys have the same label, assign both keys the same functionality. (Note that on some keyboards, the latter may not be available.)

In text entry, pressing a text key enters the corresponding character and typically displays that character on the screen. Except in special views, the characters produced by the TAB and ENTER keys are not usually visible. In some contexts, text keys can also be used for navigation or for invoking specific operations.

Access Keys

An *access key* is an alphanumeric key — sometimes referred to as a *mnemonic* — that, when used in combination with the ALT key, navigates to and activates a control. The access key matches one of the characters in the text label of the control. For example, pressing ALT+O activates a control whose label is "Open" and whose assigned access key is "O". Typically, access keys are not case sensitive. The effect of activating a control depends on the type of control.

In Windows 2000, access keys are hidden by default to simplify the user interface. However, the operating system displays the access keys whenever the user initiates a keyboard command — for example, by pressing the ALT key.

Use the following guidelines to assign access key characters to controls in your application (in order of preference):

- The first letter of the label for the control, unless another letter provides a better mnemonic association

- A distinctive consonant in the label

- A vowel in the label

Avoid assigning a character where the visual indication of the access key cannot be distinguished from the character. For example, access keys may not be visible if you format a menu item using underlined text. Also, avoid using a character usually assigned to a common function. For example, when you include an **Apply** button, reserve the "A" — or its localized equivalent — as the access key for that button. In addition, do not assign access keys to the **OK** and **Cancel** commands when they map to the ENTER and ESC keys, respectively.

Define an access key to be unique within the scope of its interaction — that is, the area where the control exists and where keyboard input is currently being directed. If duplicate access keys are assigned within the same scope, the first control is activated when the access key is pressed. Depending on the control, pressing the access key a second time may or may not activate another control with the same assignment.

Controls without explicit labels can use static text controls to create labels with assigned access keys. Software that supports a writing system other than roman, such as Kanji, and that runs on a standard keyboard, can prefix each control label with a roman alphabetic character as its access key.

For more information about static text controls, see Chapter 8, "Menus, Controls, and Toolbars."

Mode Keys

Mode keys change the actions of other keys (or other input devices). There are two kinds of mode keys:

- Toggle keys — A toggle key turns a particular mode on or off each time it is pressed. For example, pressing the CAPS LOCK key toggles between uppercase and lowercase alphabetic keys; pressing the NUM LOCK key toggles between numeric and directional input using the keypad keys.

- Modifier keys — Like toggle keys, modifier keys change the actions of normal input. Unlike toggle keys, however, modifier keys establish modes that remain in effect only while the modifier key is held down. Modifier keys include the SHIFT, CTRL, and ALT keys. Such a "spring-loaded" mode is often preferable to a "locked" mode because the key must be activated continuously by the user. This makes using the modifier key a conscious choice and allows the user to cancel the mode easily by releasing the key.

Users who cannot hold down two keys at one time can use the StickyKeys accessibility feature that enables them to simulate key combinations by pressing keys sequentially. This function is supported only for the SHIFT, CONTROL, and ALT keys, so your application should not require multiple-key combinations that do not include one of these three keys.

Because it can be difficult for a user to remember multiple modifier assignments, avoid using multiple modifier keys as the primary way to access basic operations.

In some contexts, the keyboard may not be available. Therefore, use modifier-based actions only to provide quick access to operations that are supported adequately elsewhere in the interface.

Shortcut Keys

Shortcut keys (also referred to as *accelerator keys*) are keys or key combinations that users can press for quick access to actions they perform frequently. CTRL+*letter* combinations and function keys (F1 through F12) are usually the best choices for shortcut keys. By definition, a shortcut key is the keyboard equivalent of functionality that is supported adequately elsewhere in the interface. Therefore, avoid using a shortcut key as the only way to access a particular operation.

When you define shortcut keys, keep the following guidelines in mind:

- Assign single keys whenever possible. These are the easiest actions for the user to perform.

- Do not make modified letter+key combinations case sensitive.

- Use SHIFT+*key* combinations for actions that extend or complement the actions of the key or key combination used without the SHIFT key. For example, pressing ALT+TAB switches windows in a top-to-bottom order. Pressing SHIFT+ALT+TAB switches windows in reverse order. However, avoid using SHIFT+*text* key combinations, because the effect of the SHIFT key may differ for some international keyboards.

- Use CTRL+*key* combinations for actions that represent a larger scale effect. For example, in text editing contexts, pressing HOME moves the cursor to the beginning of a line, and pressing CTRL+HOME moves the cursor to the beginning of the text. Use CTRL+*key* combinations for access to commands where a letter key is used — for example, use CTRL+B for bold. Remember that such assignments may be meaningful only for English-speaking users.

In international versions of your software, there may be no mnemonic relationship between a command and its shortcut key. In this case, it may be more useful to use function keys instead, even though they are harder for most users to remember. For a list of the most common shortcut key assignments, see Appendix B, "Keyboard Interface Summary."

- Avoid ALT+*key* combinations because they may conflict with the standard keyboard access for menus and controls. The ALT+*key* combinations — ALT+TAB, ALT+ESC, and ALT+SPACEBAR — are reserved for system use. ALT+*number* combinations enter special characters.

- Avoid assigning the shortcut keys defined in this guide to other operations in your software. That is, if CTRL+C is the shortcut for the **Copy** command and your application supports the standard copy operation, don't assign CTRL+C to another operation.

- Whenever possible, enable the user to change the shortcut key assignments in your application.

- Use the ESC key to stop a function in process or to cancel a direct manipulation operation. It is also usually interpreted as the shortcut key for a **Cancel** button.

Some keyboards also support three new keys: the Application key and the two Windows keys. The primary use for the Application key is to display the shortcut menu for the current selection (the same as pressing SHIFT+ F10). You may also use it with modifier keys for application-specific functions. Pressing either of the Windows keys — left or right — displays the **Start** menu. These keys are also used by the system as modifiers for system-specific functions. Do not use these keys as modifiers for non-system-level functions.

General Interaction Techniques

This chapter covers basic interaction techniques, such as navigating, selecting, viewing, editing, and creating. Many of these techniques are based on an object-action paradigm in which a user identifies an object and an action to apply to that object. By using these techniques consistently, you enable users to transfer their skills to new tasks.

Where applicable, support the basic interaction techniques for the mouse and keyboard. When you add to or extend these basic techniques, consider how the feature or function can be supported across input devices. Techniques used for one device need not be used for all other devices. Instead, tailor techniques to optimize the strengths of a particular device. For example, Windows supports direct keyboard access to menus and controls using access keys rather than requiring the user to use arrow keys to mimic how the mouse moves the pointer. In addition, make it easy for the user to switch between devices so that an interaction started with one device can be completed with another.

Navigation

One of the most common ways of identifying or accessing an object is by navigating to it. The following sections include information about mouse and keyboard techniques.

Mouse Navigation

Navigation with the mouse is simple; when a user moves the mouse left or right, the pointer moves in the corresponding direction on the screen. As the mouse moves away from or toward the user, the pointer moves up or down. By moving the mouse, the user can move the pointer to any location on the screen.

Keyboard Navigation

Keyboard navigation requires a user to press specific keys and key combinations to move the *input focus* — the indication of where the input is being directed — to a particular location. The appearance of the input focus varies by context; in text, it appears as a text cursor or insertion point. In most other contexts, it is represented by a dotted rectangle. You should display the input focus location in any active window.

For more information about displaying the input focus, see Chapter 14, "Visual Design."

Basic Navigation Keys

The navigation keys are the four arrow keys and the HOME, END, PAGE UP, PAGE DOWN, and TAB keys. Pressed in combination with the CTRL key, a navigation key increases the movement increment. For example, where pressing RIGHT ARROW moves right one character in a text field, pressing CTRL+RIGHT ARROW moves right one word in the text field. The following table lists the common navigation keys and their functions. You can define additional keys for navigation.

Basic Navigation Keys

Press this key	To move the cursor	Press CTRL+this key to move the cursor
LEFT ARROW	Left one unit	Left one (larger) unit
RIGHT ARROW	Right one unit	Right one (larger) unit
UP ARROW	Up one unit or line	Up one (larger) unit
DOWN ARROW	Down one unit or line	Down one (larger) unit
HOME	Beginning of line	Beginning of data or file (top-most position)
END	End of line	End of data or file (bottom-most position)

Basic Navigation Keys *(continued)*

Press this key	To move the cursor	Press CTRL+this key to move the cursor
PAGE UP	Up one screen (previous screen, same position)	Left one screen (or previous unit, if left is not meaningful)
PAGE DOWN	Down one screen (next screen, same position)	Right one screen (or next unit, if right is not meaningful)
TAB	Next field (SHIFT+TAB moves in reverse order)	Next larger field

Unlike mouse navigation, keyboard navigation typically affects existing selections. Optionally, you can support the SCROLL LOCK key to enable scrolling navigation without affecting existing selections. If you do so, the keys scroll the appropriate increment.

For more information about keyboard navigation in secondary windows, such as dialog boxes, see Chapter 9, "Secondary Windows."

Other Forms of Navigation

Navigation can also be supported with specific commands or interface elements. For example, viewing operations can sometimes be considered a form of navigation. Opening a document, clicking a link, or switching windows are forms of moving from one context to another.

Selection

Selection is the primary means by which the user identifies objects in the interface. Consequently, the basic model for selection is one of the most important aspects of the interface.

Selection typically involves an action that the user takes to identify an object. This is known as an *explicit selection*. Once the object is selected, the user can specify an action for the object.

In some situations, the identification of an object can be derived by inference or implied by context. An *implicit selection* works most effectively where the association of object and action is simple and visible. For example, when the user drags a scroll box, the user selects and moves the scroll box at the same time. Implicit selection may result from the relationships of a particular object. For example, selecting a character in a text document may implicitly select the paragraph of which the character is a part.

A selection can consist of a single object or multiple objects. Multiple selections can be contiguous or disjoint. A *contiguous selection* set is made up of objects that are logically adjacent to each other, also known as a *range selection*. A *disjoint selection* set is made up of objects that are spatially or logically separated.

Multiple selections can also be classified as *homogeneous*, where all objects in the selection reflect the same type or same property settings, or *heterogeneous*, where they differ. Even a homogeneous selection might include certain aspects that are heterogeneous. For example, a text selection that includes bold and italic text can be considered homogeneous with respect to the basic object type (characters), but heterogeneous with respect to the values of its font properties. The homogeneity or heterogeneity of a selection can affect what operations or properties you expose for the objects in the selection.

Selection Feedback

Always provide visual feedback for explicit selections when the user makes the selection, so that the user can see the effect of the selection operation. Display the appropriate selection appearance for each object included in the selection set. The form of selection appearance depends on the object and its context.

You may not need to provide immediate selection feedback for implicit selection; you can often indicate the effects of implicit selection in other ways. For example, when the user drags a scroll box, the scroll box moves with the pointer. Similarly, if the effect of selecting a word in a paragraph implicitly selects the paragraph, you would not use selection appearance on the entire paragraph, but rather reflect the implicit selection by including the paragraph's properties when the user chooses the **Properties** command.

For more information about how to visually render the selection appearance of an object, see Chapter 14, "Visual Design." For more information about how the context of an object can affect its selection appearance, see Chapter 12, "Working with OLE Embedded and Linked Objects."

Scope of Selection

The *scope* of a selection is the area, extent, or region within which any other selections are considered to be part of the same selection set. For example, you can select two document icons in the same folder window. However, the selection of these icons is independent of the selection of the window's scroll bar, a menu, the window itself, or selections made in other windows. So, the selection scope of the icons is the area viewed through that window. Selections in different scopes are independent of each other. For example, selections in one window are typically independent of selections in other windows. Their windows define the scope of each selection independently. The scope of a selection is important because you use it to define the available operations for the selected items and how the operations are applied.

Hierarchical Selection

Range selections typically include objects at the same level. However, you can also support a user to elevate a range selection to the next higher level if that level extends beyond the immediate containment of the object (but is within the same window). When the user adjusts the range back within the containment of the start of the range, return the selection to the original level. For example, extending a selection from within a cell in a table to the next cell, as shown in Figure 6.1, should elevate the selection from the character level to the cell level. Adjusting the selection back within the cell should reset the selection to the character level.

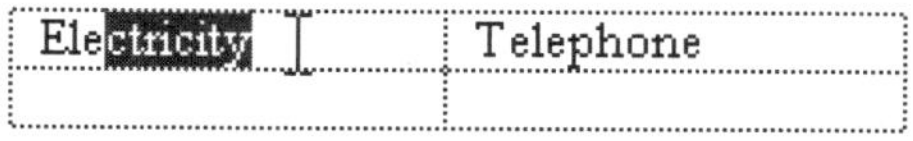

1. User selects within a table cell.

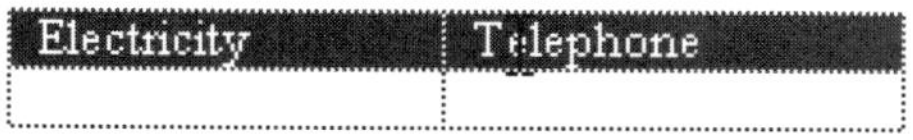

2. User extends selection into next cell, resulting in selection of both cells.

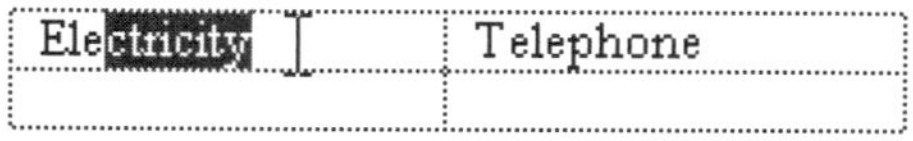

3. User returns to original cell, returning to character selection.

Figure 6.1 Hierarchical selection

Mouse Selection

Selection with the mouse relies on the basic actions of clicking and dragging. In general, clicking selects a single item or location. Dragging selects a single range consisting of all objects logically included from the button-down to the button-up point. If you also support dragging for object movement, use keyboard-modified mouse selection or region selection to support multiple selection.

Basic Selection

Support user selection using either mouse button. When the user presses the mouse button, establish the starting point, or *anchor point*, of a selection. If, while pressing the mouse button, the user drags the mouse, extend the selection to the object nearest the hot spot of the pointer. If, while continuing to hold the mouse button down, the user drags the mouse within the selection, reduce the selection to the object nearest to the pointer. Tracking the selection with the pointer while the user continues to hold the mouse button down allows the user to adjust a range selection dynamically. Use appropriate selection feedback to indicate the objects included in the selection.

For more information about the appearance of selection feedback, see Chapter 14, "Visual Design."

The release of the primary mouse button ends the selection operation and establishes the *active end* of the selection. If the user presses the secondary mouse button to make a selection, display the shortcut menu for the selection when the user releases the mouse button.

For more information about shortcut menus, see Chapter 8, "Menus, Controls, and Toolbars."

The most common form of selection optimizes for the selection of a single object or a single range of objects. In such a case, creating a new selection within the scope of an existing selection (for example, within the same area of the window) cancels the selection of the previously selected objects. This allows simple selections to be created quickly and easily.

When using this technique, reset the selection when the user presses the mouse button and the pointer (hot spot) is outside, not on, any existing selection. If the pointer is over a selected item, however, don't cancel the selection. Instead, determine the appropriate result according to whether the user pressed the primary or secondary mouse button.

If the user presses the primary mouse button and the pointer does not move from the button-down point, the effect of releasing the mouse button is determined by the context of the selection. You can support whichever of the following best fits the nature of the user's task:

- The result may have no effect on the existing selection. This is the most common and safest effect.

- The object under the pointer may receive a special designation or distinction — for example, it can become the next anchor point, or the release of the mouse button can create a subselection.

- The selection can be reset to be only the object under the pointer.

If the user presses the secondary mouse button, the selection is not affected, but the shortcut menu for the selection is displayed.

Although selection is typically done by positioning the pointer over an object, it may be inferred based on the logical proximity of an object to a pointer. For example, when selecting text, the user can place the pointer on the blank area beyond the end of the line; the resulting selection is inferred as being the end of the line.

Selection Adjustment

Selections are adjusted (elements added to or removed from the selection) using keyboard modifiers with the mouse. The CTRL key is the disjoint, or toggle, modifier. If the user presses the CTRL key while making a new selection, preserve any existing selection within that scope and reset the anchor point to the new mouse button-down point. Toggle the selection state of the object under the pointer — that is, if it is not selected, select it; if it is already selected, cancel it. Disjoint selection techniques may not apply to all situations where you support selection.

If a selection modified by the CTRL key is made by dragging, the selection state is applied for all objects included by the drag operation (from the anchor point to the current pointer location). This means that if the first item included during the drag operation is not selected, select all objects included in the range. If the first item included was already selected, cancel it and all the objects included in the range regardless of their original state.

For example, the user can make an initial selection by dragging.

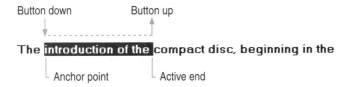

The user can then press the CTRL key and drag to create a disjoint selection, resetting the anchor point.

The user must press the CTRL key before using the mouse button for a disjoint (toggle) selection. After a disjoint selection is initiated, it continues until the user releases the mouse button (even if the user releases the CTRL key before releasing the mouse button).

The SHIFT key adjusts (or extends) a single selection or range selection. When the user presses the mouse button while holding down the SHIFT key, reset the active end of a selection from the anchor point to the location of the pointer. Continue tracking the pointer, resetting the active end as the user drags, similar to a simple range drag selection. When the user releases the mouse button, the selection operation ends. You should then set the active end to the object nearest to the mouse button release point. Do not reset the anchor point. It should remain at its current location.

Only the selection made from the current anchor point is adjusted. Any other disjoint selections are not affected unless the extent of the selection overlaps an existing disjoint selection.

The effect on the selection state of a particular object is based on the first item included in the selection range. If the first item is already selected, select (do not toggle the selection state of) all objects included in the range; otherwise, cancel (do not toggle the selection state of) the selection of the objects included.

The user must press and hold down the SHIFT key before pressing the mouse button for the action to be interpreted as adjusting the selection. When the user begins adjusting a selection by pressing the SHIFT key, continue to track the pointer and adjust the selection (even if the user releases the modifier key) until the user releases the mouse button.

Pressing the SHIFT modifier key always adjusts the selection from the current anchor point. This means the user can always adjust the selection range of a single selection or a CTRL key–modified disjoint selection. For example, the user can make a range selection by dragging.

The same result can be accomplished by making an initial selection.

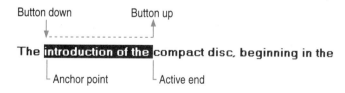

The user can adjust the selection with the SHIFT key and dragging.

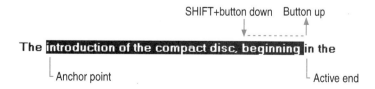

The following sequence illustrates how the user can use the SHIFT key and dragging to adjust a disjoint selection. The user makes the initial selection by dragging.

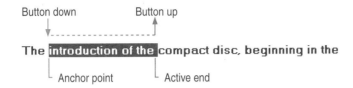

The user presses the CTRL key and drags to create a disjoint selection.

The user can then extend the disjoint selection using the SHIFT key and dragging. This adjusts the selection from the anchor point to the button-down point and tracks the pointer to the button-up point.

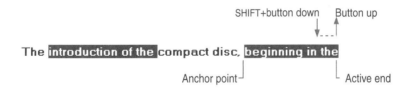

Figure 6.2 shows how these same techniques can be applied within a spreadsheet.

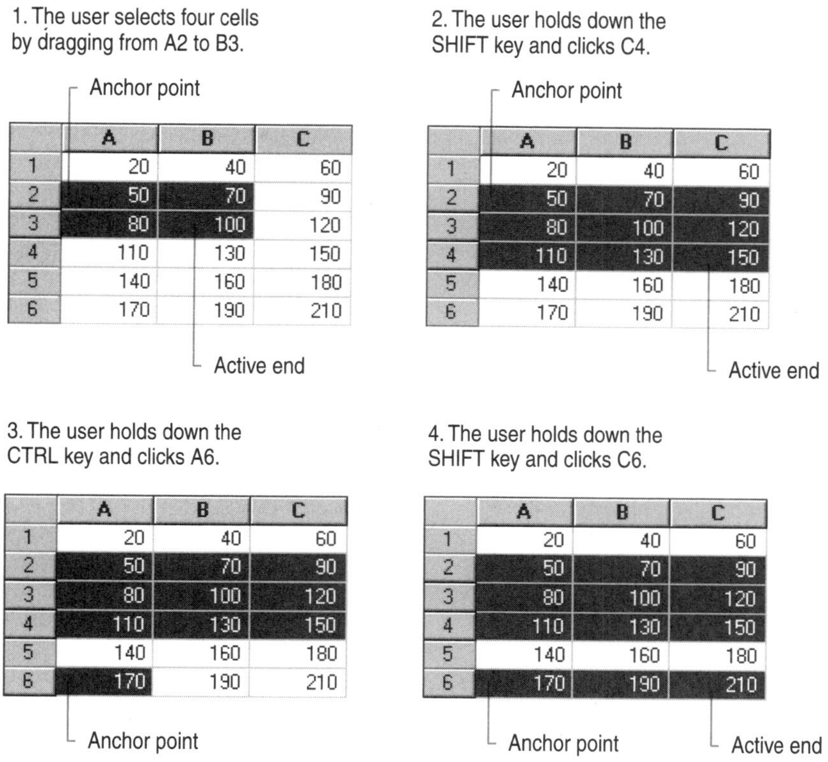

1. The user selects four cells by dragging from A2 to B3.

Anchor point

	A	B	C
1	20	40	60
2	50	70	90
3	80	100	120
4	110	130	150
5	140	160	180
6	170	190	210

Active end

2. The user holds down the SHIFT key and clicks C4.

Anchor point

	A	B	C
1	20	40	60
2	50	70	90
3	80	100	120
4	110	130	150
5	140	160	180
6	170	190	210

Active end

3. The user holds down the CTRL key and clicks A6.

	A	B	C
1	20	40	60
2	50	70	90
3	80	100	120
4	110	130	150
5	140	160	180
6	170	190	210

Anchor point

4. The user holds down the SHIFT key and clicks C6.

	A	B	C
1	20	40	60
2	50	70	90
3	80	100	120
4	110	130	150
5	140	160	180
6	170	190	210

Anchor point   Active end

Figure 6.2 Selection within a spreadsheet

Figure 6.3 shows how these same techniques can be applied to object selection.

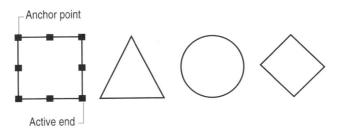

1. The user makes an initial selection by clicking the first item.

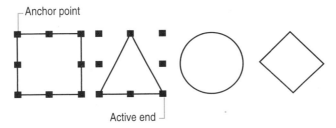

2. The user extends the selection by holding down the SHIFT key and clicking the next item.

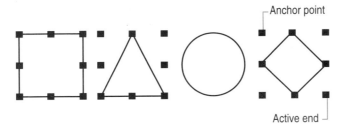

3. The user makes a disjoint selection by holding down the CTRL key and clicking another item.

Figure 6.3 Selection of objects

The following summarizes the mouse selection operations.

Mouse Selection Operations

Operation	Mouse action
Select object (range of objects)	Click (drag)
Make disjoint selection of noncontiguous objects (range of objects)	CTRL+click (drag)
Adjust current selection to object (or range of objects) (drag)	SHIFT+click

For more information about the mouse interface, including selection behavior, see Appendix A, "Mouse Interface Summary."

Region Selection

In Z-ordered, or layered, contexts, in which objects may overlap, user selection can begin on the background (sometimes referred to as *white space*). To determine the range of the selection in such cases, a bounding outline (sometimes referred to as a *marquee*) is drawn. The outline is typically a rectangle, but other shapes (including free-form outline) are possible.

When the user presses the mouse button and moves the pointer (a form of selection by dragging), display the bounding outline, as follows.

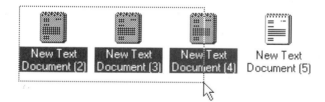

You set the selection state of objects included in the outline by using the selection guidelines described in the previous sections, including operations that use the SHIFT and CTRL modifier keys.

You can use the context of your application and the user's task to determine whether an object must be totally enclosed or only intersected by the bounding region to be affected by the selection operation. Always provide good selection feedback during the operation to communicate to the user which method you support. When the user releases the mouse button, remove the bounding region, but retain the selection feedback.

Auto-Selection

Windows also supports a form of automatic selection known as Web-style or *hover selection*. When the user positions the pointer over an object and pauses briefly for a system-defined time-out, the object is selected, enabling the user to click once to carry out an action on the object.

You can use hover selection to simplify selecting and activating items or to emulate Web-style interfaces. If you use this form of selection, always provide feedback to cue the user about the difference in functionality, such as the visual feedback recommended for displaying links. Also provide audio feedback by playing the system selection sound. When using hover selection to support the selection of non–text-based objects, such as icons, check to see whether the current system setting supports conventional selection or hover selection. Hover selection is automatically supported for the system-supplied List View controls when the user sets this option in Control Panel.

For more information about the mouse interface, including selection behavior, see Appendix A, "Mouse Interface Summary."

Keyboard Selection

When keyboard selection is used, selected objects are defined by the input focus. The input focus can be an insertion point, a dotted outline box, or some other visual indication of where the user is directing keyboard input.

For more information about input focus, see Chapter 14, "Visual Design."

In some contexts, selection may be implicit with navigation. When the user presses a navigation key, move the input focus to the location (as defined by the key) and automatically select the object at that location.

In other contexts, it may be more appropriate to move the input focus and require the user to make an explicit selection with the Select key. The recommended keyboard Select key is the SPACEBAR, unless this assignment directly conflicts with the specific context — in which case, you can use CTRL+SPACEBAR. (If this conflicts with your software, define another key that best fits the context.) In some contexts, pressing the Select key may also cancel the selection of objects; in other words, it will toggle the selection state of an object.

Contiguous Selection

In text contexts, the user moves the insertion point to the desired location by using the navigation keys. Set the anchor point at this location. When the user presses the SHIFT key with any navigation key (or navigation key combination, such as CTRL+END), set that location as the active end of the selection, and select all characters between the anchor point and the active end. (Do not move the anchor point.) If the user presses a subsequent navigation key, cancel the selection and move the insertion point to the appropriate location defined by the key. If the user presses the LEFT ARROW or RIGHT ARROW keys, move the insertion point to the end of the former selection range. If UP ARROW or DOWN ARROW are used, move the insertion point to the previous or following line at the same relative location.

You can use this technique in other contexts, such as lists, where objects are logically contiguous. However, in such situations, the selection state of the objects logically included from the anchor point to the active end depend on the selection state of the object at, or first traversed from, the anchor point. For example, if the object at the anchor point is selected, then select all the objects in the range regardless of their current state. If the object at the anchor point is not selected, cancel the selection of all the items in the range.

Disjoint Selection

You use the Select key for supporting disjoint selections. The user uses navigation keys or navigation keys modified by the SHIFT key to establish the initial selection. The user can then use navigation keys to move to a new location and subsequently use the Select key to create an additional selection.

In some situations, you may prefer to optimize for selection of a single object or single range. In such cases, when the user presses a navigation key, reset the selection to the location defined by the navigation key. Creating a disjoint selection requires supporting the Add mode key (SHIFT+F8). In this mode, when the user presses navigation keys, you move the insertion point without affecting the existing selections or the anchor point. When the user presses the Select key, toggle the selection state at the new location and reset the anchor point to that object. At any point, the user can use the SHIFT+navigation key combination to adjust the selection from the current anchor point.

When the user presses the Add mode key a second time, toggle out of the mode, preserving the selections the user created in Add mode. But now, if the user makes any new selections within that selection scope, return to the single selection optimization — canceling any existing selections — and reset the selection to be only the new selection.

Selection Shortcuts

Double-clicking with the primary mouse button is a shortcut for the default operation of an object. In text contexts, it is commonly assigned as a shortcut to select a word. When supporting this shortcut, select the word and the space following the word, but not the punctuation marks.

> Double-clicking as a shortcut for selection applies only to text. In other contexts, double-clicking may perform other operations.

You can define additional selection shortcuts or techniques for specialized contexts. For example, selecting a column label may select the entire column. Because shortcuts cannot be generalized across the user interface, however, do not use them as the only way to perform a selection.

Common Conventions for Supporting Operations

There are many ways to support operations for an object, including direct manipulation of the object or its control point (*handle*), menu commands, buttons, dialog boxes, tools, or programming. Support for a particular technique does not necessarily exclude other techniques. For example, the user can size a window by using the **Size** menu command and by dragging its border.

Design operations or commands to be *contextual*, or related to, the selected object to which they apply. That is, determine which commands or properties, or other aspects of an object, are made accessible by the characteristics of the object and its context (relationships). Often the context of an object may add to or suppress the traits of the object.

Operations for a Multiple Selection

When determining which operations to display for a multiple selection, use an intersection of the operations that apply to the members of that selection. The selection's context may add to or filter out the available operations or commands displayed to the user.

It is also possible to determine the effect of an operation for a multiple selection based on a particular member of that selection. For example, when the user selects a set of graphical objects and chooses an alignment command, you can make the operation relative to a particular item identified in the selection.

Limit operations on a multiple selection to the scope of the selected objects. For example, deleting a selected word in one window should not delete selections in other windows (unless the windows are displaying the same selected objects).

Default Operations and Shortcut Techniques

An object can have a default operation. A *default operation* is an operation that is assumed when the user employs a shortcut technique, such as double-clicking or drag-and-drop. For example, double-clicking a folder displays a window with the content of the folder. In text editing situations, double-clicking selects the word. The behavior differs because the default commands in each case differ: for a folder, the default command is **Open**; for text, it is **Select Word**.

Similarly, when the user drags and drops an object at a new location by using the primary mouse button, there must be a default operation defined to determine the result of the operation. Dragging and dropping to some locations can be interpreted as moving, copying, linking, or some other operation. In this case, the drop destination determines the default operation.

For more information about supporting default drag-and-drop operations, see "Transfer Operations" later in this chapter. Also see Chapter 12, "Working with OLE Embedded and Linked Objects."

Shortcut techniques for default operations provide greater efficiency in the interface, an important factor for more experienced users. However, because they typically require more skill or experience and because not all objects may have a default operation defined, avoid using shortcut techniques as the exclusive way to perform basic operations. For example, even though double-clicking opens a folder icon, the **Open** command appears on a menu.

Viewing Operations

Following are some of the common operations associated with viewing objects. Although these operations may not always be used with all objects, when supported they should follow similar conventions.

Common Viewing Operations

Operation	Action
Open	Opens an object in its primary viewer. For container objects, such as folders and documents, this window displays the content of the object. Whether the view enables the user to modify the contents of the object shown in the window depends on that object's properties.
Close	Closes a window.
Edit	Opens a container object for modification. Where possible, the object should be editable in the existing view. If that view does not support editing the object in place, open the object in another window.
Go	Displays another location, typically in the same window.
Refresh	Updates the view of the information in a window.
Browse	Browses folders, tree structures, or Internet sites.
Find	Locates a specific file, object, computer, Web site, server, term, or phrase.
New Window	Opens another primary window for the object or data being viewed in the current window.
Properties	Displays the properties of an object, typically in a property sheet window.

When the user opens a new window, you should display it at the top of the Z order of its peer windows and activate it. Primary windows are typically peers with each other. Display supplemental or secondary windows belonging to a particular application at the top of their local Z order — that is, the Z order of the windows of that application, not the Z order of other primary windows.

For more information about opening windows, property sheets, and Help windows, see Chapter 7, "Windows," Chapter 9, "Secondary Windows," and Chapter 13, "User Assistance," respectively.

If the user interacts with another window before the new window opens, the new window does not appear on top; instead, it appears where it would usually be displayed if the user activated another window. For example, if the user opens window A, and then opens window B, window B appears on top of window A.

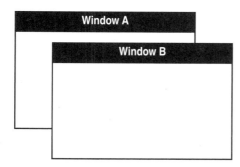

If the user clicks back in window A before window B is displayed, however, window A remains active and at the top of the Z order; window B appears behind window A.

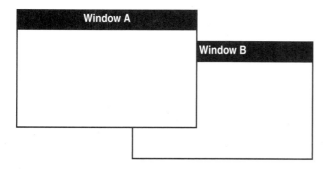

Whether to allow a user to edit information in an open window's view depends on a number of factors. These factors may include user permissions, the type of view being used, and the content being viewed.

After the user opens a window, re-executing the command that opened the window should activate the existing window instead of opening another instance of the window. For example, if the user chooses the **Properties** command for a selected object whose property sheet is already open, the existing property sheet is activated instead of a second window being opened.

This guideline applies per user desktop. Two users opening a window for the same object on a network can each see separate windows for the object from their individual desktops.

Closing a window does not necessarily mean quitting the processes associated with the object being viewed. For example, closing a printer's window does not cancel the printing of documents in its queue. Quitting an application closes its windows, but closing a window does not necessarily quit an application. Similarly, you can use other commands in secondary windows that result in closing the window — for example, **OK** and **Cancel**. However, the effect of closing the window with a **Close** command depends on the context of the window. Avoid assuming that the **Close** command is the equivalent of the **Cancel** command.

If the user has made changes in a window and then clicks the **Close** command, and those changes will be lost if not applied, display a message asking whether the user wants to apply or discard the changes or cancel the close operation. If there are no outstanding changes or if pending changes are retained for the next time the window is opened, remove the window.

Shortcuts for Viewing Commands

Following are the recommended shortcut techniques for the common viewing commands.

Recommended Shortcuts for Viewing Commands

Shortcut	Operation
CTRL+O	Opens a primary window for an object. For container objects, such as folders and documents, this window displays the contents of the object.
ALT+F4	Closes a window.
F1	Displays a window that contains contextual Help information.
SHIFT+F1	Starts context-sensitive Help mode.
Double-click (primary mouse button) or ENTER	Performs the default command.
ALT+double-click or ALT+ENTER	Displays the properties of an object in a window, typically in a property sheet window.

For more information about reserved and recommended shortcut keys, see Appendix B, "Keyboard Interface Summary."

Use double-clicking and the ENTER key to open a view of an object when that view command is the default command for the object. For example, double-clicking a folder opens the folder's primary window. But double-clicking a sound object plays the sound; this is because the **Open** command is the default command for folders, and the **Play** command is the default command for sound objects.

Scrolling

When a view, such as a List view, contains more information than can be displayed in it current size, you can provide access to the hidden information by supporting scrolling or panning or both.

Scrolling most often refers to moving up and down in a document. However, more generally, scrolling refers to moving back and forth in any data stream. Scrolling is more general than traversing text, as it can apply to any data stream. For example:

- Slide shows — Next Slide/Previous Slide

- Forms — Next Record/Previous Record

- Calendars — Next Day/Previous Day (or Week, Month, Year)

Keep in mind that data always moves relative to the frame in which it appears:

- Scrolling up means to move toward the beginning of the data, which moves the data in the view downward.

- Scrolling down means to move toward the end of the data, which moves the data in the view upward.

- Scrolling left means to move toward the left side of the data, which moves the data in the view to the right.

- Scrolling right means to move toward the right side of the data, which moves the data in the view to the left.

With the mouse, you provide scrolling through a scroll bar or other control that includes components that support clicking or dragging actions to move the view. Scrolling typically does not change the selection state (unless the SHIFT or CTRL key is also pressed) or move the input focus.

If you support scrolling, include support for mice that have a wheel button, using the following functionality:

- When the user rotates the wheel forward (toward the monitor), scroll up.

- When the user rotates the wheel backward (toward the user), scroll down.

- For documents that scroll only horizontally, when the user rotates the wheel forward, scroll to the left. This is equivalent to clicking the left scroll arrow on a horizontal scroll bar. The current selection should not be affected.

- For documents that scroll only horizontally, when the user rotates the wheel backward, scroll to the right. This is equivalent to clicking the right scroll arrow on a horizontal scroll bar. The current selection should not be affected.

In applications that support long documents, consider scrolling three lines of text by default for each scroll operation (moving the wheel one notch). Controls used for very short documents or lists might scroll one line at a time. In all cases, scrolling should never be more than the number of lines showing in the window.

With the keyboard, you can support scrolling by using the arrow keys and optional navigation keys such as HOME, END, PAGE UP, and PAGE DOWN. Typically, these keys also move the input focus and change the selection state (unless the SHIFT or CTRL key is also pressed).

For related information about scroll bars and scrolling a window, see Chapter 7, "Windows." For more information about scroll controls, see Chapter 8, "Menus, Controls, and Toolbars."

For more information about using the keyboard for scrolling, see the Microsoft Accessibility Web site at http://microsoft.com/enable/training/keyboard.htm.

Panning

Panning is similar to scrolling, except that it is a continuous operation. When the user is panning, the data scrolls continuously until the desired location is reached and the user terminates the operation. The user controls the speed and direction. The object that is selected does not change.

Panning begins when the user presses the mouse button down to establish the origin point; the data is moved relevant to that point as the user drags the mouse. You can support panning with the mouse by providing a special panning tool or command that changes the standard use of the mouse to enable the view to move with the pointer.

The origin is important in panning, because you should use the distance the pointer moves from to determine the panning speed. You can provide a reference bitmap, called the origin mark, which is continuously displayed at the origin. Remove it when the user completes the operation.

The following table lists the common images to support an origin mark.

Panning Origin Marks

Shape	Use
	Two-dimensional panning
	Vertical-only one-dimensional panning
	Horizontal-only one-dimensional panning

If you support panning, include support for mice that have a wheel button. When the user presses the wheel button to establish the origin point and then drags the wheel button, move the view as follows. When the user drags up, move toward the data above the origin point; when the user drags left, move toward the data to the left of the origin point.

During the panning operation, change the pointer to provide feedback. The pointer you use varies based on the direction the user is panning.

The following table lists the common pointer shapes to support panning feedback.

For more information about programming the Microsoft IntelliMouse, see the IntelliMouse SDK on the MSDN Online Web site at http://msdn.microsoft.com/ui/guide/mouse.asp.

Panning Pointers

Shape	Screen location	Use
	Over the origin mark	Two-dimensional panning
	Over the origin mark	Vertical-only one-dimensional panning
	Over the origin mark	Horizontal-only one-dimensional panning
	Over the drag location	Pan up
	Over the drag location	Pan down
	Over the drag location	Pan left
	Over the drag location	Pan right
	Over the drag location	Pan up-left
	Over the drag location	Pan up-right
	Over the drag location	Pan down-left
	Over the drag location	Pan down-right

When you implement support for panning, make sure you consider the relationship between the speed of panning and the distance the mouse moves from the origin. This relationship has a significant impact on how easy panning is to use.

There are three panning zones or phases that you should consider as a part of your design:

- Neutral zone – This is an area four pixels wide around the origin where no panning occurs.

- Delayed panning zone – In this area, the panning speed is slow and typically scrolls by the smallest logical unit of your data.

- Accelerated panning zone – In this area, you accelerate the speed exponentially, increasing the size of the scrolled area to its maximum as the user moves the mouse further from the origin point. Generally, the maximum scroll unit is equivalent to the amount of data that can be viewed at one time within the frame of the data. If you support faster panning, keep in mind that the user may not be able to follow the data being scrolled.

For more information about how to implement an acceleration scheme, see the Microsoft Platform SDK on the MSDN Online Web site at http://msdn.microsoft.com/ui/guide/sdk.asp.

Automatic Scrolling

If you are supporting a mouse that has a wheel button, you may also want to support an automatic scrolling mode where the document scrolls by itself. This form of scrolling is ideal for reading long documents and for skimming data. As with panning, the user controls the mouse to control the direction and speed (although you should use a flatter acceleration curve to provide finer control speeds for reading).

Start automatic scrolling when the user clicks the wheel button. Cancel the scrolling operation when the user clicks the wheel button again or clicks any other mouse button. Also cancel the operation if the user presses any key. You should ignore any function assigned to that key and return the application to the state it was in before automatic scrolling was started. You can use the same origin mark images and pointers as defined for panning unless you provide your own automatic scrolling controls.

Zooming

Zooming refers to changing the magnification level of a document or set of data. You can provide support for zooming by using a special control or command.

You can also support zooming with mice that include a wheel button. In this situation, use the CTRL key and rotation of the wheel button to enable the user to zoom the view. Rotating the wheel forward, toward the monitor, increases the zoom percentage (zooms in). Rotating the wheel backward, toward the user, decreases the zoom percentage (zooms out). Note that settings in the Mouse properties in Control Panel may enable the user to reverse the direction.

Define the zooming increment based on the range and logical granularity of your levels of zoom support. Typical changes are 10 to 20 percent for each notch on the wheel. If the typical working level is 100 percent, set this as the upper or lower bound of the range so that users can easily return to this level without having to keep track of the number of notches traversed. Of course, some applications, such as mapping software, may not have an inherent typical magnification level. In this situation, you may want to make sure it is easy for users to move between the maximum and minimum levels. Target your range to be no more than seven levels.

Zooming can also be used to move between other representations of data, such as changing outline levels, navigating hierarchies, or performing other operations to show a greater or lesser amount of detail. To support this form of data zooming with a wheel-button mouse, use the SHIFT key with the rotation of the wheel button. When the user rotates the wheel forward (toward the monitor), show more detail — for example, expand an outline or hierarchy. When the user rotates the wheel backward (toward the user), show less detail — for example, collapse an outline or hierarchy. Set the zoom relative to the item being pointed to, not to the current selection. This enables the user to easily traverse a hierarchy without having to select at each level.

Editing Operations

Editing involves changing (adding, removing, replacing) some fundamental aspect about the composition of an object. Not all changes constitute editing of an object, though. For example, changing the view of a document to an outline or magnified view (which has no effect on the content of the document) is not editing. The following sections cover some of the common interface techniques for editing objects.

Editing Text

Editing text requires that you target the input focus at the text to be edited. For mouse input, the input focus always coincides with the pointer click or drag location. For the keyboard, the input focus is determined by using the navigation keys. In all cases, the visual indication that a text field has the input focus is the presence of the text cursor, or insertion point.

Inserting Text

Inserting text involves the user placing the insertion point at the appropriate location and then typing. For each character typed, your application should move the insertion point one character to the right (or left, depending on the language).

If the text field supports multiple lines, the text should *wordwrap*; that is, the text should move to the next line automatically as the textual input exceeds the width of the text-entry area.

Overtype Mode

Overtype is an optional text-entry mode that operates similarly to the insertion style of text entry, except that you replace existing characters as new text is entered — with one character being replaced for each new character entered.

Use a block cursor that appears at the current character position to support overtype mode, as shown in Figure 6.4. This looks the same as the selection of that character and provides the user with a visual cue about the difference between the text-entry modes.

The 1893 statistics are complete

Figure 6.4 An overtype cursor

Use the INSERT key to toggle between the normal insert text-entry convention and overtype mode.

Deleting Text

The DELETE and BACKSPACE keys support deleting text. The DELETE key deletes the character to the right of the text insertion point. The BACKSPACE key removes the character to the left. In either case, move text in the direction of the deletion to fill the gap — this is sometimes referred to as *auto-joining*. Do not place deleted text on the Clipboard; instead, include at least a single-level undo operation in these contexts.

For a text selection, when the user presses DELETE or BACKSPACE, remove the entire block of selected text. Delete text selections when new text is entered directly or by a transfer command. In this case, replace the selected text with the new input.

Handles

Objects may include special control points, called *handles*. You can use handles to facilitate certain types of operations, such as moving, sizing, scaling, cropping, shaping, or auto-filling. The type of handle you use depends on the type of object. For example, the title bar acts as a move handle for windows. The borders of the window act as sizing handles. For icons, the selected icon acts as its own move handle.

For more information about the design of handles, see Chapter 14, "Visual Design."

A common form of handle is a square box placed at the edge of an object, as shown in Figure 6.5.

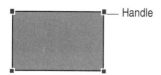 — Handle

Figure 6.5 A graphic object with handles

When the handle's interior is solid, the handle implies that it can perform a certain operation, such as sizing, cropping, or scaling. If the handle is hollow, the handle does not currently support an operation. You can use such an appearance to indicate selection even when an operation is not available.

To be visible and easily targeted with a mouse, handles should never be smaller than the size of a resizable window border. Because handles are typically dragged only with the mouse, provide a separate mechanism for moving or resizing objects using the keyboard. For example, you can provide a property sheet where the user can view and enter values for location and size, and you can also allow the user to "nudge" an object using the arrow keys.

Transactions

A *transaction* is a unit of change to an object. The granularity of a transaction may span from the result of a single operation to that of a set of multiple operations. In an ideal model, transactions are applied immediately, and there is support for rolling back, or undoing, transactions. Because there are times when this is not practical, specific interface conventions have been established for committing transactions. If there are pending transactions in a window when it is closed, always prompt the user to ask whether to apply or discard the transactions.

Transactions can be committed at different levels, and a commitment made at one level may not imply a permanent change. For example, the user may change the font properties of a text selection, but these text changes may require saving the document file before the changes are permanent.

Use the following commands for committing transactions at the file level.

File Level Transactions

Command	Function
Save	Saves all interim edits, or checkpoints, and begins a new editing session. If the document has not been named, this command prompts the user for a name, the same as the **Save As** command.
Save As	Saves the file (with all interim edits) to a new file name and begins a new editing session.
Close	Prompts the user to save any uncommitted edits. If confirmed, the interim edits are saved and the window is removed.

Use the **Save** command in contexts where committing file transactions apply to transactions for an entire file, such as a document, and are committed at one time. It may not necessarily apply to transactions committed on an individual basis, such as record-oriented processing.

On a more granular level, you can use the following commands for handling common transactions within a file.

Commands for Common Transactions

Command	Function
Repeat	Duplicates the last/latest user transaction.
Undo	Reverses the last, or specified, transaction.
Redo	Restores the most recent, or specified, "undone" transaction.
OK	Commits any pending transactions and removes the window.
Apply	Commits any pending transactions, but does not remove the window.
Cancel	Discards any pending transactions and removes the window.

Following are the recommended commands for handling process transactions.

Commands for Process Transactions

Command	Function
Pause	Suspends a process.
Resume	Resumes a suspended process.
Stop	Halts a process.

Although you can use the **Cancel** command to halt a process, **Cancel** implies that the state will be restored to what it was before the process was initiated.

Properties

Defining and organizing the properties of an application's components are a key part of evolving toward a more data-centered design. Commands such as **Options**, **Info**, **Summary Info**, and **Format** often describe features that can be redefined as properties of a particular object (or objects). The **Properties** command is the common command for accessing the properties of an object; when the user chooses this command, display a secondary window with the properties of the object.

For more information about property sheets, see Chapter 9, "Secondary Windows."

Defining how to provide access to properties for visible or easily identifiable objects — such as a selection of text, cells, or drawing objects — is straightforward. It may be more difficult to define how to access properties of less tangible objects, such as paragraphs. In some cases, you can include these properties by implication. For example, requesting the properties of a text selection can also provide access to the properties of the paragraph in which the text selection is included. Another way to provide access to an object's properties is to create a representation of the object. For example, the properties of a page could be accessed through a graphic or other representation of the page in a special area (for example, the status bar) of the window.

Yet another technique to consider is to include specific property entries on the menu of a related object. For example, the shortcut menu of a text selection could include a menu entry for a paragraph. Or consider using the cascading submenu of the **Properties** command for individual menu entries, but only if the properties are not easily made accessible otherwise. Adding entries for individual properties can easily clutter a menu.

For more information about shortcut menus, see Chapter 8, "Menus, Controls, and Toolbars."

The **Properties** command is not the only way to provide access to the properties of an object. For example, folder views display certain properties of objects stored in the file system. In addition, you can use toolbar controls to display properties of selected objects.

Transfer Operations

Transfer operations are operations that involve (or can be derived from) moving, copying, and linking objects from one location to another. For example, printing an object is a kind of transfer operation because it can be defined as copying an object to a printer.

Three components make up a transfer operation: the object to be transferred, the destination of the transfer, and the operation to be performed. You can define these components either explicitly or implicitly, depending on which interaction technique you use.

The operation defined by a transfer is determined by the destination. Because a transfer may have several possible interpretations, you can define a default operation and other appropriate operations based on information provided by the source of the transfer and the compatibility and capabilities of the destination. For example, attempting to transfer an object to a container can result in one of the following alternatives:

- Rejecting the object

- Accepting the object

- Accepting a subset or transformed form of the object (for example, extracting its content or properties but discarding its present container, or converting the object into a new type)

Most transfers are based on one of the following three fundamental operations.

Transfer Operations

Operation	Description
Move	Relocates or repositions the selected object. Because a move operation does not change the basic identity of an object, it is not the same as copying an object and deleting the original.
Copy	Makes a duplicate of an object. The resulting object is independent of its original. Duplication does not always produce an identical clone. Some of the properties of a duplicated object may be different from the original. For example, copying an object may result in a different name or creation date. Similarly, if some component of the object restricts copying, then only the unrestricted elements may be copied.
Link	Creates a connection between two objects. The result is usually an object in the destination that provides access to the original.

There are two different methods for supporting the basic transfer interface: the command method and the direct manipulation method.

Command Method

The command method for transferring objects uses the **Cut**, **Copy**, and **Paste** commands. Place these commands on the **Edit** drop-down menu and on the shortcut menu for a selected object, and support the standard shortcut keys for these operations. You can also include toolbar buttons to support these commands.

For more information about the standard shortcut keys, see Appendix B, "Keyboard Interface Summary."

To transfer an object, the user must do the following:

1. Make a selection.

2. Choose either **Cut** or **Copy**.

   The **Cut** command removes the selection and transfers it (or a reference to it) to the Clipboard. The **Copy** command duplicates the selection (or a reference to it) and transfers it to the Clipboard.

3. Navigate to the destination (and set the insertion location, if appropriate).

4. Choose a **Paste** command.

   The **Paste** command completes the transfer operation.

For example, when the user chooses **Cut** and **Paste**, remove the selection from the source and relocate it to the destination. When the user chooses **Copy** and **Paste**, insert an independent duplicate of the selection and leave the original unaffected. When the user chooses **Copy** and **Paste Link** or **Paste Shortcut**, insert an object at the destination that is linked to the source.

Choose a form of the **Paste** command that indicates how the object will be transferred into the destination. Use the **Paste** command by itself to indicate that the object will be transferred as native content. You can also use alternative forms of the **Paste** command for other possible transfers, using the following general form.

Paste [*type name*] [**as** *type name* | **to** *object name*]

For more information about object names, including their type name, see Chapter 11, "Integrating with the System."

For example, **Paste Cells as Word Table**, where [*type name*] is Cells and Word Table is the converted type name.

The following table summarizes common forms of the **Paste** command.

Common Paste Commands

Command	Function
Paste	Inserts the object on the Clipboard as native content (data).
Paste [*type name*]	Inserts the object on the Clipboard as an embedded object. The embedded object can be activated directly within the destination.
Paste [*type name*] as Icon	Inserts the object on the Clipboard as an embedded object. The embedded object is displayed as an icon.
Paste Link	Inserts a data link into the object that was copied to the Clipboard. The object's value is integrated or transformed as native content within the destination, but remains linked to the original object so that changes to it are reflected in the destination.
Paste Link to [*object name*]	Inserts a linked object, displayed as a picture of the object copied to the Clipboard. The representation is linked to the object copied to the Clipboard so that any changes to the original source object will be reflected in the destination.
Paste as Hyperlink	Inserts a hyperlink into the object that was copied to the Clipboard to support navigation to that object.
Paste Shortcut	Inserts a linked object, displayed as a shortcut icon, into the object that was copied to the Clipboard. The representation is linked to the object copied to the Clipboard so that any changes to the original source object will be reflected in the destination.
Paste Special	Displays a dialog box that gives the user explicit control over how to insert the object on the Clipboard.

For more information about these **Paste** command forms and the Paste Special dialog box, see Chapter 12, "Working with OLE Embedded and Linked Objects."

Use the destination's context to determine what form(s) of the paste operation to include based on what options it can offer to the user, which in turn may depend on the available forms of the object that its source location object provides. It can also be dependent on the nature or purpose of the destination. For example, a printer defines the context of transfers to it.

Typically, you will need only **Paste** and **Paste Special** commands. The **Paste** command can be modified dynamically to reflect the destination's default or preferred form by inserting the transferred object — for example, as native data or as an embedded object. The **Paste Special** command can be used to handle any special forms of transfer. However, if the destination's context makes it reasonable to provide fast access to another specialized form of transfer, such as **Paste Link**, you can also include that command.

Use the destination's context also to determine the appropriate side effects of the paste operation. You may also need to consider the type of object being inserted by the paste operation and the relationship of that type to the destination. The following are some common scenarios:

- When the user pastes into a destination that supports a specific insertion location, replace the selection in the destination with the transferred data. For example, in text or list contexts, where the selection represents a specific insertion location, replace the destination's active selection. In text contexts where there is an insertion location but there is no existing selection, place the insertion point after the inserted object.

- For destinations with non-ordered or Z-ordered contexts where there is no explicit insertion point, add the pasted object and make it the active selection. Also use the destination's context to determine where to place the pasted object. Consider any appropriate user contextual information. For example, if the user chooses the **Paste** command from a shortcut menu, you can use the pointer's location when the mouse button is clicked to place the incoming object. If the user supplies no contextual clues, place the object at the location that best fits the context of the destination — for example, at the next grid position.

- If the new object is automatically connected (linked) to the active selection (for example, table data and a graph), you may insert the new object in addition to the selection and make the inserted object the new selection.

You also use context to determine whether to display an embedded or linked object as content (a view or picture of the object's internal data) or as an icon. For example, you can decide what to display based on which paste operation the user selects. The **Paste Shortcut** command implies pasting a link as an icon. Similarly, the **Paste Special** command includes options that allow the user to specify how the transferred object should be displayed. If there is no user-supplied preference, the destination application defines the default. For documents, you typically display the inserted object as an item of content in the destination container. If icons better fit the context of your application, make the default paste operation display the transferred object as an icon.

The execution of a **Paste** command should not affect the content of the Clipboard. This allows data on the Clipboard to be pasted multiple times, although subsequent paste operations should always result in copies of the original. However, a subsequent **Cut** or **Copy** command replaces the last entry on the Clipboard.

You can also optionally support **Move To** and **Copy To** commands. In this situation, you must also supply a dialog box that lists the possible destinations and enables the user to select a list entry.

Direct Manipulation Method

The command method is useful when a transfer operation requires the user to navigate between source and destination. However, for many transfers, direct manipulation is a natural and quick method. In a direct manipulation transfer, the user selects and drags an object to the desired location. Because this method requires motor skills that may be difficult for some users to master, avoid using it as the exclusive transfer method. The best interfaces support transfer by the command method for basic operations and transfer by direct manipulation as a shortcut.

You can support direct manipulation transfers to any visible object. The object (for example, a window or icon) need not currently be active. For example, the user can drop an object in an inactive window. The drop action activates the window. If an inactive object cannot accept a direct manipulation transfer, it (or its container) should provide feedback to the user.

The destination's context determines how the transferred object is integrated and displayed in the drop destination. A dropped object can be incorporated either as native data, an object, a partial form of the object — such as its properties — or a transformed object. You determine whether to add to or replace an existing selection based on the context of the operation, using such factors as the formats available for the object, the destination's purpose, and any user-supplied information such as the specific location that the user drops to or commands (or modes) that the user has selected. For example, an application can supply a particular type of tool for copying the properties of objects.

Default Drag-and-Drop Transfers

A user transfers an object in a *default drag-and-drop operation* with the primary mouse button. The operation is interpreted by what the destination defines as the appropriate default operation. As with the command method, the destination determines this based on information about the object (and the formats available for the object) and the context of the destination itself. Avoid defining a destructive operation as the default. When that is unavoidable, display a message box to confirm the user's intentions.

Using this transfer technique, the user can directly transfer objects between documents defined by your application, as well as to system resources, such as folders and printers. Support drag-and-drop operations by following the same conventions that the system supports: the user presses the primary mouse button while pointing to an object, moves the mouse while holding the button down, and then releases the button at the destination.

The most common default transfer operation is **Move**, but the destination can reinterpret the operation to be whatever is most appropriate. Therefore, you can define a default drag-and-drop operation to be another general transfer operation such as **Copy** or **Link**, a destination-specific command such as **Print** or **Send To**, or even a specialized form of transfer such as **Copy Properties**.

Nondefault Drag-and-Drop Transfers

A user transfers an object in a *nondefault drag-and-drop* operation with the secondary mouse button. In this case, rather than executing a default operation, the destination displays a shortcut menu when the user releases the mouse button, as shown in Figure 6.6. The shortcut menu contains the appropriate transfer completion commands.

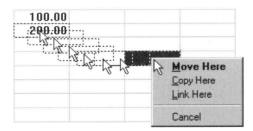

Figure 6.6 A nondefault drag-and-drop operation

The destination always determines which transfer completion commands to include on the resulting shortcut menu, usually factoring in information about the object supplied by the source location.

The form for nondefault drag-and-drop transfer completion verbs follows similar conventions as the **Paste** command. Use the common transfer completion verbs — **Move Here**, **Copy Here**, and **Link Here** — when the object being transferred is native data of the destination. When it is not, specify the type of transfer being completed. You can also display alternative completion verbs that communicate the context of the destination; for example, a printer displays a **Print Here** command. For commands that support only a partial aspect or a transformation of an object, use more descriptive indicators — for example, **Copy Properties Here** or **Transpose Here**.

Use the following general form for nondefault drag-and-drop transfer commands.

[*Command Name*] [*type name* | *object name*] **Here** [**as** *type name*]

The following summarizes common forms for nondefault transfer completion commands.

Nondefault Transfer Completion Commands

Command	Function
Move Here	Moves the selected object to the destination as native content (data).
Copy Here	Creates a copy of the selected object in the destination as native content.
Link Here	Creates a data link between the selected object and the destination. The original object's value is integrated or transformed as native data within the destination, but remains linked to the original object so that changes to it are reflected in the destination.
Move [*type name*] Here **Copy [*type name*] Here**	Moves or copies the selected object as an embedded object. The embedded object is displayed in its content presentation and can be activated directly within the destination.
Link [*type name*] Here	Creates a linked object displayed as a picture of the selected object. The representation is linked to the selected object so that any changes to the original object will be reflected in the destination.
Move [*type name*] Here as Icon **Copy [*type name*] Here as Icon**	Moves or copies the selected object as an embedded object and displays it as an icon.
Create Shortcut Here	Creates an object that is linked to the selected object; displayed as a shortcut icon. The representation is linked to the selected object so that any changes to the original object will be reflected in the destination.

For more information about how to display default menu commands, see Chapter 14, "Visual Design."

Define and appropriately display one of the commands in the shortcut menu to be the default drag-and-drop command. This is the command that corresponds to dragging and dropping with the primary mouse button.

Canceling a Drag-and-Drop Transfer

When a user drags and drops an object back onto itself, interpret the action as cancellation of a direct manipulation transfer. Similarly, cancel the transfer if the user presses the ESC key during a drag transfer. In addition, include a **Cancel** command in the shortcut menu of a nondefault drag-and-drop action. When the user chooses this command, cancel the operation.

Differentiating Transfer and Selection When Dragging

Because dragging performs both selection and transfer operations, provide a convention that allows the user to differentiate between these operations. The convention you use depends on what is most appropriate in the current context of the object, or you can provide specialized handles for selection or transfer. The most common technique uses the location of the pointer at the beginning of the drag operation. If the pointer is within an existing selection, interpret the drag to be a transfer operation. If the drag begins outside of an existing selection, on the background's white space, interpret the drag as a selection operation.

Scrolling When Transferring by Dragging

When the user drags and drops an object from one scrollable area (such as a window, pane, or list box) to another, some tasks may require transferring the object outside the boundary of the area. Other tasks may involve dragging the object to a location not currently in view. In this latter case, it is convenient to scroll the area automatically (also known as *automatic scrolling* or auto-scroll) when the user drags the object to the edge of that scrollable area. You can accommodate both these behaviors by using the velocity of the dragging action. For example, if the user is dragging the object slowly at the edge of the scrollable area, you scroll the area; if the object is being dragged quickly, do not scroll.

To support this technique during a drag operation, you sample the pointer's position at the beginning of the drag each time the mouse moves, and on an application-set timer (every 100 milliseconds recommended). If you use drag-and-drop support, you do not need to set a timer. Store each value in an array large enough to hold at least three samples, replacing existing samples with later ones. Then calculate the pointer's velocity based on at least the last two locations of the pointer.

To calculate the velocity, sum the distance between the points in each adjacent sample and divide the total by the sum of the time elapsed between samples. Distance is the absolute value of the difference between the x and y locations, or (abs(x1 - x2) + abs(y1 - y2)). To produce the velocity, multiply this by 1024 and divide it by the elapsed time. The 1024 multiplier prevents the loss of accuracy caused by integer division.

Distance as implemented in this algorithm is not true Cartesian distance. This implementation uses an approximation for purposes of efficiency rather than using the square root of the sum of the squares, $(sqrt((x1 - x2)^2 + (y1 - y2)^2))$, which is more computationally expensive.

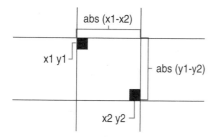

You also predefine a hot zone along the edges of the scrollable area and a scroll time-out value. Use twice the width of a vertical scroll bar or the height of a horizontal scroll bar to determine the width of the hot zone.

During the drag operation, scroll the area if the following conditions are met: the user moves the pointer within the hot zone, the current velocity is below a certain threshold velocity, and the scrollable area is able to scroll in the direction associated with the hot zone it is in. The recommended threshold velocity is 20 pixels per second.

These conventions are illustrated in Figure 6.7.

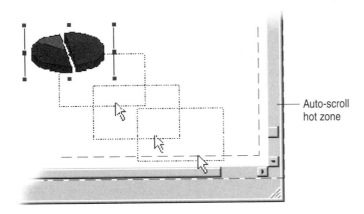

Auto-scroll
hot zone

Figure 6.7 Automatic scrolling based on velocity of dragging

The amount you scroll depends on the type of information and reasonable scrolling distance. For example, for text you typically scroll vertically one line at a time. Consider using the same scrolling granularity that is provided for the scroll bar arrows.

To support continuous scrolling, determine what scroll frequency you want to support — for example, four lines per second. After using a velocity check to initiate auto-scrolling, set a timer — for example, 100 milliseconds. When the timer expires, determine how long it has been since the last time you scrolled. If the elapsed time is greater than your scrolling frequency, scroll another unit. If not, reset your timer and check again when the timer finishes.

Transfer Feedback

Because transferring objects is one of the most common user tasks, providing appropriate feedback is an important design factor. Inconsistent or insufficient feedback can result in user confusion.

For more information about designing transfer feedback, see Chapter 14, "Visual Design."

Command Method Transfers

For a command method transfer, remove the selected object visually when the user chooses the **Cut** command. If there are special circumstances that make removing the object visually impractical, you can instead display the selected object with a special appearance to inform the user that the **Cut** command was completed but that the object's transfer is pending. For example, the system displays icons in a checkerboard dither to indicate this state. You also need to restore the visual state of the object if the user chooses **Cut** or **Copy** for another object before choosing a **Paste** command, effectively canceling the pending **Cut** command. The user will expect **Cut** to remove a selected object, so carefully consider the impact of inconsistency if you choose this alternate feedback.

The **Copy** command requires no special feedback. A paste operation also requires no further feedback than that already provided by the insertion of the transferred object. However, if you did not remove the display of the object and used an alternate representation when the user chose the **Cut** command, you must remove it now.

Direct Manipulation Transfers

During a direct manipulation transfer operation, provide the following visual feedback for the object, the pointer, and the destination:

- Display the object with its selected appearance while the view it appears in has the focus. To indicate that the object is in a transfer state, you can optionally display the object with some additional appearance characteristics. For example, for a move operation, you can use the checkerboard dithered appearance used by the system to indicate when an icon is cut. Change this visual state based on the default completion operation supported by the destination the pointer is currently over. Retain the representation of the object at the original location until the user completes the transfer operation. This not only provides a visual cue to the nature of the transfer operation, it provides a convenient visual reference point.

- Display a representation of the object that moves with the pointer. Use a presentation that provides the user with information about how the information will appear in the destination and that does not obscure the context of the insertion location. For example, when transferring an object into a text context, it is important that the insertion point not be obscured during the drag operation. A translucent or outline representation, as shown in Figure 6.8, works well because it allows the underlying insertion location to be seen while also providing information about the size, position, and nature of the object being dragged.

Figure 6.8 Outline and translucent representations for transfer operations

- The object's existing source location provides the transferred object's initial appearance, but any destination can change the appearance. Design the presentation of the object to provide feedback as to how the object will be integrated by that destination. For example, if an object will be embedded as an icon, display the object as an icon. If the object will be incorporated as part of the native content of the destination, then present the object to reflect it. For example, if a table being dragged into a document will be incorporated as a table, the representation could be an outline or translucent form of the table. On the other hand, if the table will be converted to text, display the table as a representation of text, such as a translucent presentation of the first few words in the table.

- Display the pointer appropriate to the context of the destination, usually the pointer used for inserting objects. For example, when the user drags an object into text where the object will be inserted between characters, display the usual text editing pointer (sometimes called the I-beam pointer).

- Display the interpretation of the transfer operation at the lower right corner of the pointer, as shown in Figure 6.9. No additional glyph is required for a move operation. Use a plus sign (+) when the transfer is a copy operation. Use the shortcut arrow graphic for linking.

Figure 6.9 Pointers for move, copy, and link operations

- Use visual feedback to indicate the receptivity of potential destinations. You can use selection highlighting and optionally animate or display a representation of the transfer object in the destination. You can also indicate when a destination cannot accept an object by using the "no drop" pointer when the pointer is over it, as shown in Figure 6.10.

Figure 6.10 A "no drop" pointer

Specialized Transfer Commands

In some contexts, a particular form of a transfer operation may be so common that introducing an additional specialized command is appropriate. For example, if copying existing objects is a frequent operation, you can include a **Duplicate** command. Following are some common specialized transfer commands.

Common Specialized Transfer Commands

Command	Function
Delete	Removes an object from its container. If the object is a file, the object is transferred to the Recycle Bin.
Clear	Removes the content of a container.
Duplicate	Copies the selected object.
Print	Prints the selected object on the default printer.
Send To	Displays a list of possible transfer destinations and transfers the selected object to the user-selected destination.

The **Delete** and **Clear** commands are often used synonymously. However, they are best differentiated by applying **Delete** to an object and **Clear** to the container of an object.

Shortcut Keys for Transfer Operations

Following are the defined shortcut techniques for transfer operations.

Shortcuts for Transfer Operations

Shortcut	Operation
CTRL+X	Performs a **Cut** command.
CTRL+C	Performs a **Copy** command.
CTRL+V	Performs a **Paste** command.
CTRL+drag	Toggles the meaning of the default direct manipulation transfer operation to be a copy operation (provided the destination can support the copy operation); the modifier may be used with either mouse button.
ESC	Cancels a drag-and-drop transfer operation.

For more information about reserved and recommended shortcut key assignments, see Appendix B, "Keyboard Interface Summary."

Because of the wide use of these command shortcut keys throughout the interface, do not reassign them to other commands.

Creation Operations

Creating new objects is a common user action in the interface. Although applications can provide the context for object creation, avoid considering an application's interface as the exclusive means of creating new objects. Creation is typically based on some predefined object or specification and can be supported in the interface in a number of ways.

Copy Command

Making a copy of an existing object is the fundamental paradigm for creating new objects. Copied objects can be modified and serve as prototypes for the creation of other new objects. The transfer model conventions define the basic interaction techniques for copying objects. **Copy** and **Paste** commands and drag-and-drop manipulation provide this interface.

New Command

The **New** command facilitates the creation of new objects. **New** is a command applied to a specific object, automatically creating a new instance of the object type. The **New** command differs from the **Copy** and **Paste** commands in that it is a single command that generates a new object.

Insert Command

The **Insert** command works similarly to the **New** command, except that it is applied to a container to create a new object, usually of a specified type, in that container. In addition to inserting native types of data, use the **Insert** command to insert objects of different types. By supporting the Microsoft Component Object Model (COM) technology, you can support the creation of a wide range of objects. In addition, objects supported by your application can be inserted into data files created by other applications that support the COM OLE technology.

For more information about inserting objects, see Chapter 12, "Working with OLE Embedded and Linked Objects."

Using Controls

You can use controls to support the automatic creation of new objects. For example, in a drawing application, buttons are often used to specify tools or modes for the creation of new objects, such as drawing particular shapes or controls. Buttons can also be used to insert COM objects.

For more information about using buttons to create new objects, see Chapter 12, "Working with OLE Embedded and Linked Objects."

Using Templates

A *template* is an object that automates the creation of a new object. To distinguish its purpose, display a template icon as a pad that displays a small icon of the type of the object to be created, as shown in Figure 6.11.

Figure 6.11 A template icon

Define the **New** command as the default operation for a template object; this starts the creation process, which can either be automatic or can request specific input from the user. Place the newly created object in the same location as the container of the template. If circumstances make that impractical, place the object in a common location, such as on the desktop, or, during the creation process, include a prompt that allows the user to specify some other destination. In the former situation, display a message box informing the user where the object will appear.

Operations on Linked Objects

A *link* is a connection between two objects that represents or provides access to another object that is in another location in the same container or in a different, separate container. The components of this relationship include the link source (sometimes referred to as the referent) and the link or linked object (sometimes referred to as the reference). A linked object often has operations and properties independent of its source. For example, a linked object's properties can include attributes like update frequency, the path description of its link source, and the appearance of the linked object. The containers in which they reside provide access to and presentation of commands and properties of linked objects.

For information about OLE linked objects, see Chapter 12, "Working with OLE Embedded and Linked Objects." For information about hyperlinks in Help text, see Chapter 13, "User Assistance."

Links can be presented in various ways in the interface. For example, a *data link* propagates a value between two objects, such as between two cells in a worksheet or a series of data in a table and a chart. *Hyperlinks* (also referred to as *jumps*) provide navigational access to another location. A Web link (also known as a URL, or uniform resource locator) is an example of a hyperlink. An *OLE linked object* provides access to any operation available for its link source and also supplies a presentation of the link source. A shortcut icon is a link displayed as an icon.

For information about the use of hyperlinks in Web application design, see Chapter 10, "Window Management." For information about the display of hyperlinks, see Chapter 14, "Visual Design."

When the user transfers a linked object, store both the absolute and relative path to its link source. The absolute path is the precise description of its location, beginning at the root of its hierarchy. The relative path is the description of its location relative to its current container.

The destination of a transfer determines whether to use the absolute or relative path when the user accesses the link source through the linked object. The relative path is the most common default path. However, regardless of which path you use, if it fails, use the alternative path. For example, if the user copies a linked object and its link source to another location, the result is a duplicate of the linked object and the link source. The relative path for the duplicate linked object is the location of the duplicate of the link source. The absolute path for the duplicate linked object is the description of the location of the initial link source. Therefore, when the user accesses the duplicate of the linked object, its inferred connection should be with the duplicate of the link source. If that connection fails — for example, because the user deletes the duplicate of the linked source — use the absolute path, the connection to the original link source.

Optionally, you can make the preferred path for a linked object a field in the property sheet for the linked object. This allows the user to choose whether to have a linked object make use of the absolute or relative path to its link source.

When the user applies an operation to a linked object, apply the operation to the linked object rather than to its linked source. That is, linking a linked object results in a linked object linked to a linked object. If such an operation is not valid or appropriate — for example, because the linked object provides no meaningful context — then disable any link commands or options when the user selects a linked object.

Activation of a linked object depends on the kind of link. For example, a single click navigates a hyperlink. However, a single click results in only selecting a data link or a linked object. If you use a single click to do anything other than select the linked object, distinguish the object by presenting it as a button control, displaying the hand pointer (as shown in Figure 6.12) when the user moves the pointer over the linked object, or both. These techniques provide feedback to the user that the clicking involves more than selection.

Figure 6.12 The hand pointer

Record Processing

Record processing, or transaction-based applications, may require somewhat different structuring than the typical productivity application. For example, rather than opening and saving discrete files, the interface for such applications focuses on accessing and presenting data as records through multiple views, forms, and reports. One of the distinguishing and most important design aspects of record-processing applications is the definition of how the data records are structured. This dictates what information can be stored and in what format.

However, you can apply much of the information in this guide to record-oriented applications. For example, the basic principles of design and methodology are just as applicable as they are to individual file-oriented applications. You can also apply the guide's conventions for input, navigation, and layout when designing forms and report designs. Similarly, you can apply other secondary window conventions for data-entry design, including the following:

- Provide reasonable default values for fields.

- Use the appropriate controls. For example, use drop-down list boxes instead of long lists of option buttons.

- Distinguish text entry fields from read-only text fields.

- Design for logical and smooth user navigation. Order fields as the user needs to move through them. Auto-exit text boxes are often good for input of predefined data formats, such as time or currency inputs.

- Provide data validation as close to the site of data entry as possible. You can use input masks to restrict data to specific types or use list box controls to restrict the range of input choices.

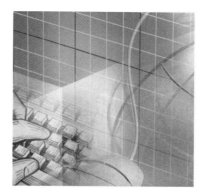

Windows
Interface Components

Windows

Windows provide the fundamental way in which a user views and interacts with data. Consistency in window design is particularly important because it enables users to easily transfer their learning skills and to focus on completing their tasks rather than on learning new conventions. This chapter describes the common window types and presents guidelines for their general appearance and operation.

Common Types of Windows

Because windows provide access to different types of information, they are classified according to common usage. Interaction with objects typically occurs in a primary window where most primary viewing and editing activity takes place. In addition, multiple supplemental secondary windows can be included to allow users to specify parameters or options or to provide more specific details about the objects or actions included in the primary window.

For more information about secondary windows, see Chapter 9, "Secondary Windows."

Primary Window Components

A typical primary window consists of a frame (or border) that defines its extent and a title bar that identifies what is being viewed in the window. If the viewable content of the window exceeds the current size of the window, scroll bars are used. The window can also include other components such as menu bars, toolbars, and status bars.

Figure 7.1 shows the common components of a primary window.

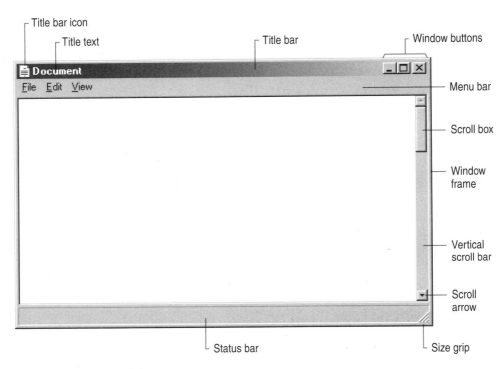

Figure 7.1 A primary window

Window Frames

Every window has a boundary that defines its shape. A sizable window has a distinct border that provides control points (handles) for resizing the window by using direct manipulation. If the window cannot be resized, the border coincides with the edge of the window.

Title Bars

At the top edge of the window, inside its border, is the title bar (also referred to as the caption or caption bar), which extends across the width of the window. The title bar identifies the contents of the window. It also serves as a control point for moving the window and an access point for commands that apply to the window and its associated view. For example, when a user clicks the title bar by using the secondary mouse button, the shortcut menu for the window appears. Pressing the ALT+SPACEBAR key combination also displays the shortcut menu for the window.

Do not place your own buttons or other controls into the title bar area. Doing so may conflict with the special user controls Windows adds for configurations that support multiple languages.

Title Bar Icons

A primary window includes the 16 x 16 pixels version of the object's icon. The small icon appears in the upper left corner of the title bar and represents the object being viewed in the window. If the window contains a tool or utility (that is, an application that does not create, load, and save its own data files), use the small version of the application's icon in its title bar, as shown in Figure 7.2.

For information about how to register icons for your application and data file types, see Chapter 11, "Integrating with the System." For more information about designing icons, see Chapter 14, "Visual Design."

Application icon

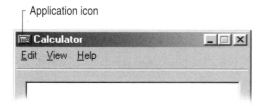

Figure 7.2 A tool title bar

If the application creates, loads, and saves documents or data files and the window represents the view of one of its files, use the small (16 x 16 pixels) icon that represents its document or data file type in the title bar, as shown in Figure 7.3. Even if the user has not yet saved the file, display the data file icon rather than the application icon, and then display the data file icon after the user saves the file.

Document icon

Figure 7.3 A document title bar

When the user clicks the title bar icon with the secondary mouse button, display the shortcut menu for the object. Typically, the menu contains a set of commands similar to the menu for the icon that opened the window, except that **Close** replaces **Open**. Also, define **Close** as the default command, so when the user double-clicks the title bar icon, the window closes. Clicking elsewhere on the title bar using the secondary mouse button displays the shortcut menu for the window.

Title Text

The window title text identifies the name of the object being viewed in the window. It should always correspond to the type of icon that you display in the title bar. It should also match the label of the icon that represents the object in the file system. For example, if the user opens a data file named My Document, then in the resulting window you should display the icon for that document type followed by the name of the data file. You can also include the name of the application in use after the name of the data file, as shown in Figure 7.4.

Figure 7.4 Title text order: document name — application name

If the window contains a tool that does not create or edit its own data files, such as Windows Calculator, then display the application name with the application icon in the title bar, just as you would for the application icon label. If the tool operates as a utility or viewer for files created by other applications, place the name of the application first, then include a dash and the tool specification text. Use this same convention for tools that require an additional specification to indicate context, such as Windows Explorer, which includes the name of the current container displayed in the browser.

When the user opens an application that displays a new data file, supply a name for the file and place it in the title bar, even if the user has not yet saved the file. Use the type name — for example Document (n), Sheet (n), Chart (n), where n is a number, as in Document (1). Make sure that the proposed name does not conflict

When the user clicks the title bar icon using the primary mouse button, the system also displays the shortcut menu for the window. This behavior is supported only for compatibility with previous versions of Windows. Avoid documenting it as the primary way to access the shortcut menu for the window. Instead, document the use of the secondary mouse button as the correct way to display the shortcut menu for the window.

For more information about title bar conventions of multiple document interface (MDI) applications, see Chapter 10, "Window Management."

For more information about type names, see Chapter 11, "Integrating with the System." For more information about the Save As dialog box, see Chapter 9, "Secondary Windows."

with an existing name in the folder. Also use this name as the proposed default file name for the object in the Save As dialog box. If it is impractical or inappropriate to supply a default name, display a placeholder in the title, such as (Untitled).

Follow the same convention if your application includes a **New** command that creates new files. Avoid prompting the user for a name. Instead, you can supply a Save As dialog box that allows the user to confirm or change your proposed name when saving or closing the file or attempting to create a new file.

Display a file name in the title bar exactly as it appears to the user in the file system, using both uppercase and lowercase letters. Avoid displaying the file extension or the path in the title bar. This information is not meaningful for most users and can make it more difficult for them to identify the file. However, because the system provides an option for users to display file name extensions, use the system-supplied functions to format and display a file name appropriately based on the user's preference.

The **GetFileTitle** and **SHGet-FileInfo** functions automatically format names correctly. For more information about these functions, see the Microsoft Platform SDK on the MSDN Online Web site at http://msdn.microsoft.com/ui/guide/sdk.asp.

If your application supports multiple windows for viewing the same file, you can use the title text to distinguish between the views — but use a convention that will not be confused as part of the file name. For example, you may want to append :n, where n represents the instance of the window, as in Document:2. Make sure that you do not include this view designation as part of the file name you supply in the Save As dialog box.

If the name of the displayed object in the window changes — for example, when the user edits the name in the object's property sheet — update the title text to reflect that change. Always try to maintain a clear association between an object and its open window.

The title text and title bar icon should always represent the outermost container — the object that was opened — even if the user selects an embedded object or navigates the internal hierarchy of the object being viewed in the window. If you need an additional specification to clarify what the user is viewing, place this specification after the file name and separate it clearly from the file name, such as enclosing it in parentheses — for example, My HardDisk (C:). Because the system supports long file names, avoid additional text whenever possible. Complex or verbose additions to the title text also make it more difficult for the user to easily read the title and identify the window.

When the width of the window does not allow you to display the complete title text, you can abbreviate the title text, being careful to maintain the essential information that allows the user to quickly identify the window.

For more information about abbreviating names, see Chapter 11, "Integrating with the System."

Avoid drawing directly in the title bar or adding other controls. Such added items can make reading the name in the title bar difficult, particularly because the size of the title bar varies with the size of the window. In addition, the system uses this area for displaying special controls. For example, in some international versions of Windows, the title area provides information or controls associated with the input of certain languages.

Title Bar Buttons

Include command buttons associated with the common commands of the primary window in the title bar. These buttons act as shortcuts to specific window commands. Clicking a title bar button with the primary mouse button invokes the same command as that associated with the command button. Optionally, you can support clicking a title bar command button with the secondary mouse button to display the shortcut menu for the window. All buttons on a primary window's title bar must have equivalent commands on the shortcut menu for that window.

In a typical situation, one or more of the following buttons appear in a primary window (provided that the window supports the respective functions).

Title Bar Buttons

Button	Command	Operation
✕	**Close**	Closes the window
▬	**Minimize**	Minimizes the window
▢	**Maximize**	Maximizes the window
▣	**Restore**	Restores the window

When these buttons are displayed, use the following guidelines:

- When a command is not supported by a window, do not display its command button.

- The **Close** button always appears as the rightmost button. Leave a gap between it and any other buttons.

- The **Minimize** button always precedes the **Maximize** button.

- The **Restore** button always replaces the **Maximize** button or the **Minimize** button when that command is carried out.

The system does not support the inclusion of the context-sensitive **Help** button available for secondary windows. If you want to provide this functionality in your application, include a Help toolbar button. Similarly, avoid including **Maximize**, **Minimize**, and **Restore** buttons in the title bars of secondary windows because the commands do not apply.

Basic Window Operations

The basic operations for a window include activating and deactivating, opening and closing, moving, sizing, scrolling, and splitting. The following sections describe these operations.

Activating and Deactivating Windows

While the system supports the display of multiple windows, the user generally works within a single window at a time. This window is called the active window. The active window is typically at the top of the window Z order. Its title bar, displayed in the active window title color, makes it visually distinct. All other windows are inactive with respect to the user's input; that is, while other windows may be involved in ongoing processes, only the active window receives the user's input. The title bar of an inactive window displays the system inactive window color. Your application can query the system for the current values for the active title bar color and the inactive title bar color, but this should be necessary only if your application draws its own window frames.

The user activates a primary window by switching to it; this inactivates any other primary windows. To activate a window with the mouse, the user clicks any part of the window, including its interior. If the window is minimized, the user clicks the button representing the window in the taskbar. To switch between primary windows using the keyboard, the user can press ALT+TAB. To switch between primary windows in reverse order, the user can press

For more information about using the **GetSysColor** function to access the **COLOR_ACTIVE-CAPTION** and **COLOR_INACTIVE-CAPTION** constants, see the Microsoft Platform SDK on the MSDN Online Web site at http://msdn.microsoft.com/ui/guide/sdk.asp.

SHIFT+ALT+TAB. The system also supports ALT+ESC for switching between windows. The reactivation of a window should not affect any pre-existing selection within it; the selection and focus are restored to the previously active state.

When the user reactivates a primary window, the window and all its secondary windows come to the top of the window order and maintain their relative positions. If the user activates a secondary window, its primary window comes to the top of the window order along with the primary window's other secondary windows.

When a window becomes inactive, hide the selection feedback (for example, display of highlighting or handles) of any selection within it to prevent confusion over which window is receiving keyboard input. A direct manipulation transfer, such as a drag-and-drop operation, is an exception. Here, you can display transfer feedback if the pointer is over the window during the drag operation, but do not activate the window unless the user releases the mouse button in that window.

Opening and Closing Windows

When the user opens a primary window, include an entry for it on the taskbar. If the window has been opened and closed previously, restore the window to its size and position when it was last closed. If possible and appropriate, reinstate the other related view information, such as selection state, scroll position, and type of view. When opening a primary window for the first time, open it to a reasonable default size and position as best defined by the object or application. For details about storing state information in the system registry, see Chapter 11, "Integrating with the System."

An entry on the taskbar should be included only for primary windows, not for secondary windows.

Because display resolution and orientation vary, your software should not assume a fixed display size, but rather adapt to the shape and size defined by the system. If you use standard system interfaces, the system automatically places your windows relative to the current display configuration.

When a window is reopened or restored, always verify that the screen location is valid in the current resolution. If the window's title bar would not be visible based on the current display, move the window until the title bar is visible.

The **SetWindowPlacement** function is an example of a system interface that automatically places windows correctly relative to the current display. For more information about this function, see the Microsoft Platform SDK on the MSDN Online Web site at http://msdn.microsoft.com/ui/guide/sdk.asp.

Opening the primary window activates that window and places it at the top of the window order. If the user tries to open a primary window that is already open on the same desktop, activate the existing window using the following recommendations. If the existing window is minimized, restore it when you activate it.

Recommended Actions for Repeating an Open Operation

File type	Action
Document or data file	Activate the existing window of the object and display it at the top of the window Z order.
Application file	Display a message box indicating that an open window of that application already exists and offer the user the option to switch to the open window or to open another window. Either choice activates the selected window and brings it to the top of the window Z order.

The user closes a window by clicking the **Close** button in the title bar or by clicking the **Close** command on the window's shortcut menu. Although the system supports double-clicking the title bar icon as a shortcut for closing the window to remain compatible with previous versions of Windows, avoid documenting it as the primary way to close a window. Instead, document the **Close** button.

If your application does not automatically save changes, when the user clicks the **Close** command, display a message asking whether to save any changes, discard any changes, or cancel the close operation before closing the window. If there are no pending transactions, just close the window. Follow this same convention for any other command that results in closing the primary window (for example, **Exit** or **Shut Down**).

For more information about supporting the **Close** command, see Chapter 6, "General Interaction Techniques."

When the primary window is closed, you should typically close any of its dependent secondary windows as well. The design of your application determines whether closing the primary window also ends the application processes. For example, closing the window of a text document typically halts any application code or processes remaining for inputting or formatting text. However, closing the window of a printer has no effect on the jobs in the printer's queue. In both cases, closing the window removes its entry from the taskbar.

Moving Windows

The user can move a window either by dragging its title bar with the mouse or by clicking the **Move** command on the window's shortcut menu. On most configurations, an outline representation moves with the pointer during the operation, and the window is displayed again in the new location after the move is completed. (The system also provides a display property setting that redraws the window dynamically as it is moved.) After clicking the **Move** command, the user can use the keyboard to move the window by using the arrow keys, then by pressing ENTER to end the operation and establish the window's new location. Never allow the user to reposition a window so that it is inaccessible.

A window need not be active before the user can move it. The action of moving the window implicitly activates it.

Moving a window may clip or reveal information shown in the window. In addition, activation can affect the view state of the window — for example, the current selection can be displayed. However, when the user moves a window, avoid making any changes to the content being viewed in that window.

Resizing Windows

Make your primary windows resizable unless the information displayed in the window is fixed or cannot be scaled to provide the user with more information, such as in the Windows Calculator program. The system provides several conventions that support user resizing of a window.

Sizing Borders

The user resizes a primary window by dragging the sizing border at the edge of a window with the mouse or by clicking the **Size** command on the window's menu. An outline representation of the window moves with the pointer. (On some configurations, the system may include a display option to dynamically redraw the window as it is sized.) After clicking the **Size** command, the user can use the keyboard to resize the window by using the arrow keys, then pressing the ENTER key.

A window does not need to be active before the user can resize it. The action of sizing the window implicitly makes it active, and it remains active after the sizing operation.

When the user reduces the size of a window, you must determine how to display the information viewed in that window. Use the context and type of information to help you choose your approach. Typically, the best approach is to redisplay the information using the new size. You may want to consider using different methods, such as wrapping or scaling the information, unless readability or maintaining the structural relationship of the information is important. In that case, you may want to fix or clip the information.

Although the size of a primary window can vary based on the user's preference, you can define a window's maximum size. When defining this size, consider the reasonable usage within the window and the size and orientation of the screen. Avoid setting a maximum size smaller than the screen's working area unless there is no benefit to the user in increasing the size of the window.

Maximizing Windows

Although the user can manually resize a window to its maximum size, the **Maximize** command optimizes this operation. Include this command on a window's shortcut menu and as the **Maximize** command button in the title bar of the window.

Maximizing a window increases the size of the window to its largest, optimum size. The system default setting for the maximum size is as large as the display, excluding the space used by the taskbar (or other application-defined desktop toolbars). However, you can define the size to be less than or, in some cases, more than the default dimensions.

When the user maximizes a window, replace the **Maximize** button with a **Restore** button. Then, disable the **Maximize** command and enable the **Restore** command on the shortcut menu for the window.

Minimizing Windows

Minimizing a window reduces it to its smallest size. To support this command, include it on the shortcut menu for the window and as the **Minimize** command button in the title bar of the window.

For primary windows, minimizing removes the window from the screen but leaves its entry on the taskbar. To minimize a window, the user clicks the **Minimize** command from the window's shortcut menu or the **Minimize** command button on the title bar.

When the user minimizes a window, disable the **Minimize** command on the shortcut menu and enable the **Restore** command.

Restoring Windows

Support the **Restore** command to restore a window to its previous size and position after the user has maximized or minimized the window. For maximized windows, enable this command on the window's shortcut menu, and replace the **Maximize** button with the **Restore** button in the title bar of the window.

For minimized windows, enable the **Restore** command on the shortcut menu of the window. The user restores a minimized primary window to its former size and position by clicking the button on the taskbar that represents the window, selecting the **Restore** command on the shortcut menu of the window's taskbar button, or by pressing ALT+TAB (or SHIFT+ALT+TAB).

Size Grip

When you define a sizable window, you can include a size grip. A size grip is a special handle for sizing a window. It is not exclusive to the sizing border. To size the window, the user drags the grip and the window resizes, following the same conventions as the sizing border.

Always locate the size grip in the lower right corner of the window. Typically, this means you place the size grip at the right end of a horizontal scroll bar or the bottom of a vertical scroll bar. However, if you include a status bar in the window, display the size grip at the far corner of the status bar instead. Never display the size grip in both locations at the same time.

For more information about the use of the size grip in a status bar, see Chapter 8, "Menus, Controls, and Toolbars."

Scrolling Windows

When the information viewed in a window exceeds the size of that window, the window should support scrolling. Scrolling enables the user to view portions of the object that are not currently visible in a window. Scrolling typically does not affect the input focus or selection in the window.

Scrolling is commonly supported through the use of a scroll bar. A scroll bar is a rectangular control consisting of scroll arrow buttons, a scroll box, and a scroll bar shaft, as shown in Figure 7.5.

For more information about scrolling, see Chapter 6, "General Interaction Techniques."

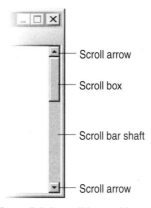

Scroll arrow

Scroll box

Scroll bar shaft

Scroll arrow

Figure 7.5 A scroll bar and its components

You can include a vertical scroll bar, a horizontal scroll bar, or both. Align a scroll bar with the vertical or horizontal edge of the window orientation it supports. If the content is never scrollable in a particular direction, do not include a scroll bar for that direction.

Scroll bars are also available as separate window components. For more information about scroll bar controls, see Chapter 8, "Menus, Controls, and Toolbars."

The common practice is to display scroll bars if the view requires scrolling under any circumstances. If the window becomes inactive or is resized so that its contents do not require scrolling, you should continue to display the scroll bars. Removal of the scroll bars when the window is inactive may display more content and provide feedback about the state of the window, but it also has a drawback. A user must then take an extra step and explicitly activate the window to display the scroll bars and use them. Consistently displaying scroll bars provides a more stable environment.

Scroll Arrows

Scroll arrow buttons appear at each end of a scroll bar, pointing in opposite directions away from the center of the scroll bar. The scroll arrows point in the direction that the window moves over the data. When the user clicks a scroll arrow, the data in the window moves, revealing information in the direction of the arrow in appropriate increments. The granularity of the increment depends on the nature of the content and context, but it is typically based on the size of a standard element. For example, for vertical scrolling you can use one line of text or one row for spreadsheets. You can also use an increment based on a fixed unit of measure. Whichever convention you choose, maintain the same scrolling increment throughout a window. The objective is to include an increment that provides smooth but efficient scrolling. When a window cannot be scrolled any further in a particular direction, disable the scroll arrow for that direction.

When scroll arrow buttons are pressed and held, they exhibit a special auto-repeat behavior. This action causes the window to continue scrolling in the associated direction as long as the pointer remains over the arrow button. If the pointer is moved off the arrow button while the user presses the mouse button, the auto-repeat behavior stops and does not continue unless the pointer is moved back over the arrow button.

The default system support for scroll bars does not disable the scroll arrow buttons when the region or area is no longer scrollable in this direction. However, it does provide support for you to disable the scroll arrow button under the appropriate conditions.

Scroll Box

The scroll box, sometimes referred to as the elevator, thumb, or slider, moves along the scroll bar to indicate how far the visible portion is from the top (for vertical scroll bars) or from the left edge (for horizontal scroll bars). For example, if the current view is in the middle of a document, the scroll box in the vertical scroll bar is displayed in the middle of the scroll bar.

The size of the scroll box can vary to reflect the difference between what is visible in the window and the entire contents of the file, as shown in Figure 7.6.

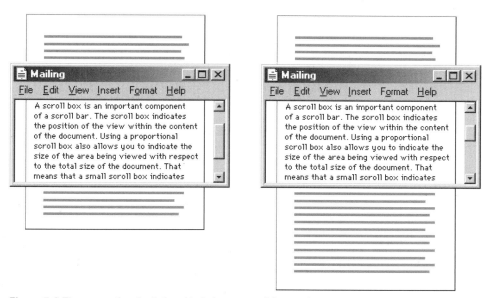

Figure 7.6 The proportional relationship between scroll box and content

For example, if the content of the entire document is visible in a window, the scroll box extends the entire length of the scroll bar, and the scroll arrows are disabled. Make the minimum size of the scroll box no smaller than the width of a window's sizing border.

The user can also scroll a window by dragging the scroll box. Update the view continuously as the user moves the scroll box. If you cannot support scrolling at a reasonable speed, you can scroll the information at the end of the drag operation as an alternative.

If the user starts dragging the scroll box and then moves the pointer outside of the scroll bar, the scroll box returns to its original position. The distance the user can move the pointer off the scroll bar before the scroll box returns to its original position is proportional to the width of the scroll bar. If dragging ends at this point, the scroll action is canceled — that is, no scrolling occurs. However, if the user moves the pointer back within the scroll-sensitive area, the scroll box returns to tracking the pointer movement. This behavior allows the user to scroll without having the pointer remain within the scroll bar and to selectively cancel the initiation of a drag-scroll operation.

Dragging the scroll box to the end of the scroll bar implies scrolling to the end of that dimension, but it does not always mean that the area cannot be scrolled further. If your application's document structure extends beyond the data itself, you can interpret dragging the scroll box to the end of its scroll bar as moving to the end of the data rather than to the end of the structure. For example, a typical spreadsheet extent exceeds the data in it — that is, the spreadsheet may have 65,000 rows, with data only in the first 50 rows. This means you can implement the scroll bar so that dragging the scroll box to the bottom of the vertical scroll bar scrolls to the last row containing data rather than to the last row of the spreadsheet. The user can use the scroll arrow buttons to scroll further to the end of the structure.

This situation also illustrates why disabling the scroll arrow buttons can provide important feedback so that the user can distinguish between scrolling to the end of the data and scrolling to the end of the extent or structure. In the example of the spreadsheet, when the user drags the scroll box to the end of the scroll bar, the arrow would still be shown as enabled because the user can still scroll further, but it would be disabled when the user scrolls to the end of the spreadsheet.

Scroll Bar Shaft

The scroll bar shaft not only provides a visual context for the scroll box, it also serves as part of the scrolling interface. Clicking in the scroll bar shaft should scroll the view in the direction of the click a distance equivalent to the visible area. For example, if the user clicks in the shaft below the scroll box in a vertical scroll bar, scroll the view a distance equivalent to the height of the view. Where possible, allow overlap from the previous view, as shown in Figure 7.7. For example, if the user clicks below the scroll box, the bottom line becomes the top line of the scrolled view. The same conventions apply to clicking above the scroll box and to horizontal scrolling. These conventions provide the user with a common reference point.

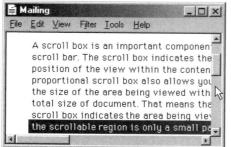 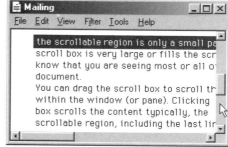

Figure 7.7 Scrolling with the scroll bar shaft

Pressing and holding the primary mouse button with the pointer in the shaft auto-repeats the scrolling action. If the user moves the pointer outside the scroll-sensitive area while pressing the button, the scrolling action stops. The user can resume scrolling by moving the pointer back into the scroll bar area. (This behavior is similar to the effect of dragging the scroll box.)

Automatic Scrolling

The techniques discussed in previous sections describe explicit methods of scrolling. However, the user can also scroll as a secondary result of another action. This type of scrolling is called automatic scrolling. Support automatic scrolling in the following situations:

- When the user begins or adjusts a selection and drags it past the edge of the scroll bar or window, scroll the area in the direction of the drag.

- When the user drags an object and approaches the edge of a scrollable area, scroll the area following the recommended auto-scroll conventions covered in Chapter 6, "General Interaction Techniques." Base the scrolling increment on the context of the destination and, if appropriate, on the size of the object being dragged.

- When the user enters text with the keyboard at the edge of a window or moves or copies an object into a location at the edge of a window, the view should scroll to allow the user to focus on the inserted information. The amount to scroll depends on the context. For example, for text, vertically scroll a single line at a time. When scrolling horizontally, scroll in units greater than a single character to prevent continuous or uneven scrolling. Similarly, when the user transfers a graphic object near the edge of the view, base scrolling on the size of the object.

- If an operation results in a selection or moves the cursor, scroll the view to display the new selection and input focus. For example, for a **Find** command that selects a matching object, scroll the object into view; typically, the user wants to focus on that location. In addition, other forms of navigation may cause scrolling. For example, completing an entry field in a form may result in navigating to the next field. In this case, if the field is not visible, the form can scroll to display it.

- When the user clicks a hyperlink linked to a location within the same document, scroll the document so that the new location (the hyperlink anchor) is in view.

Keyboard Scrolling

Use navigation keys to support scrolling with the keyboard. When the user presses a navigation key, the cursor moves to the appropriate location. For example, in addition to moving the cursor, pressing arrow keys at the edge of a scrollable area scrolls in the corresponding direction. Similarly, the PAGE UP and PAGE DOWN keys are comparable to clicking in the scroll bar shaft, but they also move the cursor.

For more information about using the keyboard for scrolling, see the Microsoft Accessibility Web site at http://microsoft.com/enable/training/keyboard.htm.

Optionally, you can use the SCROLL LOCK key to facilitate keyboard scrolling. In this case, when the SCROLL LOCK key is toggled on and the user presses a navigation key, scroll the view without affecting the cursor or selection.

Placing Adjacent Controls

It is sometimes convenient to locate controls or status bars adjacent to a scroll bar and to position the end of the scroll bar to accommodate them. Take care when placing adjacent elements; too many can make it difficult for users to scroll, particularly if you reduce the scroll bar too much. If you need a large number of controls, consider using a conventional toolbar instead.

For more information about toolbars, see Chapter 8, "Menus, Controls, and Toolbars."

Splitting Windows

A window can be split into two or more separate viewing areas, which are called *panes*. For example, a split window allows the user to examine two parts of a document at the same time. You can also use a split window to display different, yet simultaneous, views of the same information, as shown in Figure 7.8.

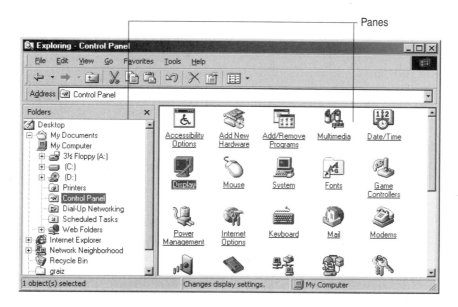

Figure 7.8 A split window

While you can use a split window to view the contents of multiple files or containers at the same time, displaying these in separate windows typically allows the user to better identify the files as individual elements. When you need to present views of multiple files as a single task, consider window management techniques such as those described in Chapter 10, "Window Management."

The panes that appear in a split window can be implemented either as part of a window's basic design or as a user-configurable option. To support splitting a window that is not pre-split by design, include a split box. A split box is a special control placed adjacent to the end of a scroll bar that splits or adjusts the split of a window. The split box should be just large enough for the user to successfully target it with the pointer; the default size of a size handle, such as the window's sizing border, is a good guideline. Locate the split box at the top of the up arrow button of the vertical scroll bar, as shown in Figure 7.9, or to the left of the left arrow button of a horizontal scroll bar.

Figure 7.9 Split box location

The user splits a window by dragging the split box to the desired position. When the user positions the hot spot of the pointer over a split box, change the pointer's image to provide feedback and help the user target the split box. While the user drags the split box, move a representation of the split box and split bar with the pointer, as shown in Figure 7.10.

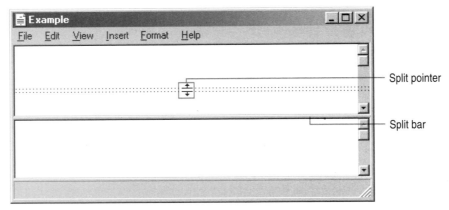

Figure 7.10 Moving the split bar

At the end of the drag, display a visual separator, called the split bar, that extends from one side of the window to the other, defining the edge between the resulting windows. The minimum size for the split bar should be the same as the current setting for the window sizing borders. This allows you to adjust appropriately when a user adjusts size borders. If you display the split box after the split operation, place it adjacent to the split bar.

You can support dragging the split bar (or split box) to the end of the scroll bar to close the split. Optionally, you can also support double-clicking as a shortcut for splitting the window at some default location (for example, in the middle of the window or at the last split location) or for removing the split. This technique works best when the resulting window panes display peer views. It may not be appropriate when the design of the window requires that it always be displayed as split or for some types of specialized views.

To provide a keyboard interface for splitting the window, include a **Split** command on the window or on the menu for the current view. When the user clicks the **Split** command, split the window in the middle or in a context-defined location. Support arrow keys for moving the split box up or down; pressing the ENTER key sets the split at the current location. Pressing the ESC key cancels the split mode. When the window is split, change the **Split** command to **Remove Split**.

You can also use other commands to create a split window. For example, you can define specialized views that, when selected by the user, split a window to a fixed or variable set of panes. Similarly, you can enable the user to remove the split of a window by closing a view pane or by selecting another view command.

When the user splits a window, add scroll bars if the resulting panes require scrolling. In addition, you may need to scroll the information in panes so that the split bar does not obscure the content over which it appears. Use a single scroll bar, at the appropriate side of the window, for a set of panes that scroll together. However, if each pane requires independent scrolling, a scroll bar should appear in each one for that purpose. For example, the vertical scroll bars of a set of panes in a horizontally split window are typically controlled separately.

When you use split window panes to provide separate views, independently maintain each pane's view properties, such as view type and selection state. Display only the selection in the active pane. However, if the selection state is shared across the panes, display a selection in all panes and support selection adjustment across panes.

When a window is closed, you should save the window's split state (that is, the number of splits, the place where they appear, the scrolled position in each split, and its selection state) as part of the view state information for that window so that it can be restored the next time the window is opened. However, if the user's task more frequently uses the non-split view, you can restore the window to its non-split view.

Menus, Controls, and Toolbars

Microsoft Windows includes a number of components to support user input. These interactive components enable users to carry out commands and specify values. They also provide a consistent structure and set of interface conventions for users and for automation utilities. This chapter describes interactive elements, such as menus, controls, and toolbars, and how to use them.

Menus

Menus display a list of commands available to the user. Because menus make commands visible and discoverable, you can use them to leverage the greater capacity people have for recognizing commands than for remembering them.

There are several types of menus, including drop-down menus, shortcut menus, and cascading menus. The following sections cover these menus in more detail.

The Menu Bar and Drop-Down Menus

A *menu bar*, one of the most common forms of a menu interface, is a special area displayed across the top of a window directly below the title bar (as shown in Figure 8.1). A menu bar includes a set of entries called *menu titles*. Each menu title provides access to a *drop-down menu* composed of a collection of *menu items*, or choices.

Figure 8.1 A menu bar

The contents of the menu bar and its drop-down menus are determined by your application's functionality and the context in which the user is interacting with it. You can allow users to configure the menu structure.

A drop-down menu appears as a panel with its list of items arranged in a column. Avoid using multiple columns or scrolling menus. While the system supports these forms of presentation, they typically add complexity to a user's experience with browsing and interacting with the menu.

Drop-Down Menu Interaction Using the Mouse

When a user points to a menu title and clicks the primary mouse button, the menu title is highlighted and the associated drop-down menu appears. When the user moves the pointer over the menu items, the menu tracks the pointer's movement, highlighting each item in the menu as the pointer moves over it. To choose the command associated with a menu item, the user points to that item, then clicks the mouse button. The system then closes the drop-down menu.

Also in the menu bar, the user can press the primary mouse button and drag the pointer into the menu. When the user releases the button with the pointer over a menu item, the corresponding command is chosen and the menu is closed. While this is an efficient method for choosing menu items, document the click method instead.

If the user presses the mouse button, then moves the pointer off the menu and releases the mouse button, the menu is also closed. However, if the user moves the pointer back onto the menu before releasing the mouse button, the pointer tracking resumes and the user can still select a menu item. The user can also close a drop-down menu by clicking its title again or by pointing to a different menu title.

Drop-Down Menu Interaction Using the Keyboard

To use the keyboard to access drop-down menus, the user presses the ALT (or F10) key to activate the menu bar. When the user presses an alphanumeric key while holding the ALT key, or after the ALT key is released, the system displays the drop-down menu whose access key matches the alphanumeric key pressed. (Matching is not case sensitive.)

The user can also use arrow keys to access drop-down menus from the keyboard. When the user presses the ALT key, pressing the LEFT ARROW or RIGHT ARROW keys moves the input focus to the previous or next menu title, respectively. If the user continues to press the arrow key, the input focus wraps to the other end of the menu bar. The user then presses the ENTER key to display the drop-down menu associated with the selected menu title. If a drop-down menu is already displayed on the menu bar, then pressing LEFT ARROW or RIGHT ARROW highlights the next drop-down menu in that direction, unless the drop-down menu spans multiple columns. In this case, the arrow keys move the highlight to the next column in that direction, and then to the next drop-down menu.

To display a drop-down menu if none is currently open, the user can also press the ALT key and then the UP ARROW or DOWN ARROW keys in the menu bar. In an open drop-down menu, pressing these keys moves to the next menu item in that direction and wraps the highlight around at the top or bottom. If the drop-down menu spans multiple columns, then pressing the arrow keys first wraps the highlight around to the next column. To display the window's shortcut menu, the user presses ALT or F10 and then presses the SPACEBAR key.

To close a drop-down menu and deactivate the menu bar, the user can press the ALT key. Pressing the ESC key also closes a drop-down menu. However, pressing the ESC key closes only the current menu level. For example, if a drop-down menu is open, pressing the ESC key closes the drop-down menu but leaves its menu title highlighted. Pressing ESC a second time removes the highlight on the menu title, deactivates the menu bar, and returns input focus to the content in the window. Selecting a menu item within the menu also closes the menu.

You can assign shortcut keys to commands in drop-down menus. When the user presses a shortcut key associated with a command in the drop-down menu, the command is carried out immediately. You can also highlight the title of the menu that contains the command, but do not display the drop-down menu.

Common Drop-Down Menus

This section describes the conventions for drop-down menus commonly used in applications. Although these menus are not required for all applications, follow these guidelines when you use these menus in your application.

The File Menu

The **File** menu provides an interface for the primary operations applied to a file. Your application should include commands such as **New**, **Open**, **Save**, **Send To**, and **Print**. These commands are often included on the shortcut menu of the icon displayed in the title bar of the window.

For more information about the commands in the short-cut menu for a title bar icon, see "Icon Shortcut Menus" later in this chapter.

If your application supports an **Exit** command, place this command at the bottom of the **File** menu preceded by a menu separator. When the user chooses the **Exit** command, close any open windows and files, and stop any further processing. If the object remains active even when its window is closed — for example, a folder or printer — then use the **Close** command instead of **Exit**.

The Edit Menu

Include general-purpose editing commands on the **Edit** menu. These commands include the **Cut**, **Copy**, and **Paste** transfer commands, embedded and linked (OLE) object commands, and the following commands (if they are supported).

For more Information about transfer commands, see Chapter 6, "General Interaction Techniques."

Other Commands Found on the Edit Menu

Command	Function
Undo	Reverses last action
Redo	Redoes the last undo action

Other Commands Found on the Edit Menu *(continued)*

Command	Function
Find and Replace	Searches for and substitutes text
Delete	Removes the current selection

Also include these commands on the shortcut menu of the selected object.

The View Menu

Place commands on the **View** menu that change the user's view of data in the window. Include commands on this menu that affect the view and not the data itself — for example, **Zoom** or **Outline**. Also include commands for controlling the display of particular interface elements in the view — for example, **Show Ruler** or **Show Status Bar**.

You should also include these commands on the shortcut menu for the window or pane.

Help Menu

Use the **Help** menu for commands that provide user access to Help information. Include a **Help Topics** command; this command provides access to the HTML Help Viewer, which displays topics included in your application's Help file. Alternatively, you can provide individual commands that access specific pages of the HTML Help Viewer, such as **Contents**, **Index**, and **Find Topic**. You can include other user assistance commands on this drop-down menu.

For more information about the HTML Help Viewer and support for user assistance, see Chapter 13, "User Assistance."

If you provide user access to copyright and version information for your application, include an **About** *application name* command on this menu. When the user chooses this command, display a window containing the application's name, version number, copyright information, and any other information related to the application. Display this information in a dialog box or as a copyright page of the property sheet for the application's main executable file. Do not

For more information about the use of ellipses, see Chapter 14, "Visual Design."

use an ellipsis at the end of this command because the resulting window does not require the user to provide any further information. (Ellipses are typically used when further input from the user is required to carry out the command.)

Shortcut Menus

Even if you include a menu bar in your software's interface, you should also support shortcut menus. Shortcut menus, also referred to as context or pop-up menus, provide an efficient way for the user to access the operations of objects (as shown in Figure 8.2). Because shortcut menus are displayed at the pointer's current location, they eliminate the need for the user to move the pointer to the menu bar or a toolbar. In addition, because you include on shortcut menus commands that are specific to the object or to its immediate context, shortcut menus reduce the number of commands the user must browse through. Shortcut menus also minimize screen clutter because they are displayed only on demand and do not require dedicated screen space.

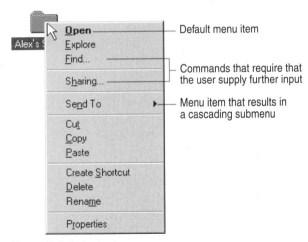

Figure 8.2 A shortcut menu

While a shortcut menu looks similar to a drop-down menu, include only commands that apply to the selected object (or objects) and its context, rather than commands grouped by function. For example, a shortcut menu for a text selection can include commands for moving and copying the text. It could also provide access to the font properties of the text and to the paragraph properties associated with the text.

Keep the length and depth (use of submenus) of a shortcut menu as small as possible. Limit the items you include on the menu to common, frequent actions. For example, to provide access to a large number of properties, it may be better to include a single **Properties** command and allow the user to navigate in a property sheet.

The container of a selection, or the composite object of which a selection is a part, typically provides the shortcut menu for the selection. Similarly, the commands included on a shortcut menu may not always be supplied by the object itself, but rather may be a combination of commands supplied by the object and by its current container. For example, the shortcut menu for a file in a folder includes transfer commands. In this case, the folder (container) supplies the commands, not the files. Shortcut menus for embedded or linked objects follow these same conventions.

Avoid using a shortcut menu as the only way for a user to access a particular operation. At the same time, the items on a shortcut menu need not be limited only to commands that are included in drop-down menus. For example, you can include frequently used commands typically found in a secondary window, such as a specific property setting.

To decide the order of commands on a shortcut menu, use the following guidelines:

- Place the object's primary commands first — for example, **Open**, **Play**, and **Print**.

- Place transfer commands next. Order the transfer commands as follows: **Cut**, **Copy**, **Paste**, and other specialized **Paste** commands.

- Include other commands supported by the object (whether provided by the object or by its context).

- Include the **What's This?** command (when supported).

- Place the **Properties** command, when present, as the last command on the menu.

- Use separators to separate groups of commands.

For more information about transfer commands and the **Properties** command, see Chapter 6, "General Interaction Techniques." For more information about the **What's This?** command, see Chapter 13, "User Assistance."

Shortcut Menu Interaction

With a mouse, the user displays a shortcut menu by clicking an object with the secondary button. When the button is pressed, if the object under the pointer's hotspot is not selected, select the object. When the button is released, display the menu to the right of and below the hot spot of the pointer. Adjust the menu to avoid its being clipped by the edge of the screen.

If the pointer is over an existing selection when the user invokes a shortcut menu, display the menu that applies to that selection. If the pointer is outside a selection but within the same selection scope, then establish a new selection (usually resetting the current selection in that scope) at the point where the user pressed the button. Display the menu for the new selection. If the pointer is over an area that can't be selected but is within the container for the selectable items, such as the white space between icons in a folder, then display that container's shortcut menu.

Close the shortcut menu when the user clicks outside the menu with the primary mouse button or presses the ESC key. Also close the menu if the user clicks with the secondary mouse button in another window.

You can support shortcut menus for objects that are implicitly selected or that cannot be directly selected, such as scroll bars or items in a status bar. When you provide shortcut menus for objects such as controls, include commands for the object that the control represents rather than for the control itself. For example, a scroll bar represents a navigational view of a document, so commands might include **Beginning of Document**, **End of Document**, **Next Page**, and **Previous Page**. But when a control represents itself as an object, as in a forms layout or window design environment, you can include commands that apply to the control — for example, commands to move or copy the control.

To provide keyboard access to shortcut menus, use SHIFT+F10 and the Application key (for keyboards that support the Windows keys specification). In addition, access keys, arrow keys, ENTER, and ESC keys operate in shortcut menus the same way they operate in drop-down menus. However, to enhance spatial efficiency and readability, avoid including shortcut keys in shortcut menus.

When the user presses a system-defined shortcut menu key, the system provides a message, **WM_CONTEXTMENU**. For more information about this message, see the MSDN Online Web site at http://msdn.microsoft.com/ui/guide/sdk.asp.

When the keyboard focus is on an item that can also be selected (such as an item in a list view control), the user presses SHIFT+F10 or the Application key to display the shortcut menu for the selected item or items. In some cases, this may not be the item that has the keyboard focus. If no item is selected, the user presses SHIFT+F10 or the Application key to display the shortcut menu for the container. This is the most common way to provide access to the shortcut menu for a container.

If the keyboard focus is on an object that does not explicitly support selection (such as a command button), the user presses SHIFT+F10 or the Application key to display the shortcut menu for the object with the keyboard focus.

Common Shortcut Menus

The shortcut menus included in any application depend on the objects and context supplied by that application. The following sections describe common shortcut menus for Windows-based applications.

The Window Shortcut Menu

The window shortcut menu is just that: the shortcut menu associated with a window. Do not confuse it with the window drop-down menu found in MDI applications. It is sometimes also referred to as the system or **Control** menu. The shortcut menu for a typical primary window includes the **Close**, **Restore**, **Move**, **Size**, **Minimize**, and **Maximize** commands.

You can include other commands on a window's shortcut menu that apply to the window or to the view within the window. For example, you could do any of the following:

For compatibility with previous versions of Windows, the system also supports accessing a window shortcut menu by clicking the icon in the title bar with the primary mouse button. However, do not document this as the main method for accessing the window shortcut menu. Document only the use of the secondary mouse button.

- Add a **Split** command to the menu to divide the window into panes.

- Add a command that affects the view, such as **Outline**.

- Add commands that add, remove, or filter elements from the view, such as **Show Ruler**.

- Add commands that open certain subordinate or special views in secondary windows, such as **Show Color Palette**.

A secondary window also has a window shortcut menu. Because the range of operations is more limited than in a primary window, a secondary window's shortcut menu usually includes only **Move** and **Close** commands (and a **Size** command if the window is resizable). Palette windows can include an **Always on Top** command that sets the window to always be on top of its parent window and other secondary windows.

The user displays a window shortcut menu by clicking anywhere in the title bar area with the secondary mouse button, excluding the title bar icon. Clicking the title bar icon with the secondary button displays the shortcut menu for the object represented by the icon. To avoid confusing users, if you do not provide a shortcut menu for the title bar icon, do not display the window shortcut menu when the user clicks the title bar icon with the secondary button.

There are other ways to display a window shortcut menu. The user can press ALT+SPACEBAR, or press the ALT key and then the UP ARROW and DOWN ARROW keys to navigate beyond the first or last entry in the menu bar.

Icon Shortcut Menus

A shortcut menu displayed for an icon should contain the operations of the object that the icon represents. To provide user access to the shortcut menu of an application or document icon, follow the standard convention of displaying a shortcut menu when the user clicks the secondary mouse button. You can also display the shortcut menu when the user selects the object's icon and then presses SHIFT+F10 or the Application key.

An icon's container application supplies the shortcut menu for the icon. For example, shortcut menus for icons placed in standard folders or on the desktop are automatically provided by the system. However, your application supplies the shortcut menus for OLE embedded or linked objects placed in it — that is, placed in the document or data files your application supports.

For more information about supporting shortcut menus for OLE objects, see Chapter 12, "Working with OLE Embedded and Linked Objects."

The container populates an icon's shortcut menu with commands the container supplies for its content, such as transfer commands and those registered by the object's type. For example, an application can register a **New** command that automatically generates a new data file of the type supported by the application.

For more information about registering commands, see Chapter 11, "Integrating with the System."

The shortcut menu of an application's icon — for example, the Microsoft WordPad executable file — should include the commands listed in the following table.

Application File Icon Shortcut Menu Commands

Command	Meaning
Open	Opens the application.
Send To	Displays a submenu of destinations to which the application file can be transferred; the content of the submenu is based on the content of the system's Send To folder.
Cut	Marks the application file for moving and registers the file on the Clipboard.
Copy	Marks the application file for duplication and registers the file on the Clipboard.
Paste	Attempts to open a file registered on the Clipboard with the application.
Create Shortcut	Creates a shortcut icon to the application.
Delete	Deletes the application file.
Rename	Allows the user to edit the application file name.
Properties	Displays the properties for the application file.

An icon representing a document or data file typically includes the following common menu items for its shortcut menu.

Document or Data File Icon Shortcut Menu Commands

Command	Meaning
Open	Opens the file's primary window (using the application registered for opening it).
Print	Prints the file on the current default printer (using the application registered for printing it).

Document or Data File Icon Shortcut Menu Commands *(continued)*

Command	Meaning
Quick View	Displays the file (using the application registered for viewing it).
Send To	Displays a submenu of destinations to which the file can be transferred; the content of the submenu is based on the content of the system's Send To folder.
Cut	Marks the file for moving and registers the file on the Clipboard.
Copy	Marks the file for duplication and registers the file on the Clipboard.
Delete	Deletes the file.
Rename	Allows the user to edit the file name.
Properties	Displays the properties for the file.

Except for the **Open** and **Print** commands, the system automatically provides these commands for icons when they appear in system containers, such as on the desktop or in folders. If your application supplies its own containers for files, you need to supply these commands.

For the **Open** and **Print** commands to appear on the shortcut menu, your application must register these commands in the system registry. You can also register additional or replacement commands. For example, you can optionally register a **Quick View** command that displays the content of the file without running the application that created it, and a **What's This?** command that displays a description of your data file type.

For more information about registering commands and the **Quick View** command, see Chapter 11, "Integrating with the System." For more information about the **What's This?** command, see Chapter 13, "User Assistance."

The icon in the title bar of a window represents the same object as the icon the user opens. As a result, the application associated with the icon also should include a shortcut menu with appropriate commands for the title bar's icon. When an application's icon appears in the title bar, include the same commands on its shortcut menu as are included for the icon that the user opens, unless a particular command cannot be applied when the application's window is open. In addition, replace the **Open** command with the **Close** command.

Similarly, when the icon of the data or the document file icon appears on the title bar, you use the same commands as for its file icon as it appears in a folder, with the following exceptions: replace the **Open** command with the **Close** command, and add **Save** if the edits in the document must be saved to a file.

Cascading Menus

A *cascading menu* (also referred to as a *hierarchical menu* or child menu) is a submenu of a menu item. The visual cue for a cascading menu is a triangular arrow displayed adjacent to the label of its parent menu item.

You can use cascading menus to provide user access to additional choices rather than using more space in the parent menu. A cascading menu can also display hierarchically related objects.

However, be aware that cascading menus add complexity to the menu interface by requiring the user to navigate further through the menu structure to get to a particular choice. The navigation also requires more effort on the part of the user. In light of these design trade-offs, use cascading menus sparingly. Minimize the number of levels for any given menu item, ideally limiting your design to a single submenu. Avoid using cascading menus for frequent, repetitive commands.

As an alternative, you can make choices available in a secondary window, particularly when the choices are independent settings; this allows the user to set multiple options with one invocation of a command. You can also support many common options as entries on a toolbar. This is effective unless you overload the toolbar. However, do not use toolbar entries as the only way to access a feature. Commonly used features should also be available through a menu or a keyboard shortcut.

Users interact with a cascading menu similarly to the way they interact with a drop-down menu off the menu bar, except that a cascading menu appears when the user moves the pointer over its parent menu item for a short time-out. The delay avoids displaying the menu unnecessarily if the user is browsing or navigating to another item on the parent menu. If the user moves the pointer to another menu item after the cascading menu appears, the cascading menu does not close immediately but remains displayed for a brief time. This time-out delay enables the user to drag an item directly from the parent menu onto an entry on its cascading menu.

When the user uses the keyboard to interact with a menu, there is no delay in displaying (or closing) a cascading menu. The submenu is displayed immediately when the user chooses its parent menu item.

Menu Titles

All drop-down and cascading menus have a menu title. For drop-down menus, the menu title is the entry that appears in the menu bar. For cascading menus, the menu title is the name of their parent menu item. Menu titles represent the entire menu and should communicate as clearly as possible the purpose of all items on the menu.

Menu Items

Menu items are the individual choices that appear on a menu. Menu items can be text or graphics — such as icons — or graphics and text combinations that represent the actions presented in the menu. Graphics-only or owner-drawn menus without keyboard access are not recommended; these types of menus may not be accessible to all users.

The format for a menu item provides the user with visual cues about the nature of the effect it represents, as shown in Figure 8.3.

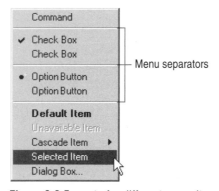

Figure 8.3 Formats for different menu items

Whenever a menu contains a set of related menu items, you can separate those sets with a grouping line known as a *separator*. The standard separator is a single line that spans the width of the menu. Avoid using menu items themselves as group separators, as shown in Figure 8.4.

 — Don't use a menu item as a menu separator

Figure 8.4 An inappropriate separator

Always provide the user with a visual indication about which menu items can be applied. If a menu item is not appropriate or applicable in a particular context, then disable or remove it. Leaving the menu item enabled and presenting a message box when the user selects the menu item is a poor method for providing feedback.

In general, it is better to disable a menu item rather than remove it because this provides more stability in the interface. However, if the context is such that the menu item is no longer or never relevant, remove it. For example, if a menu displays a set of open files and one of those files is closed or deleted, it is appropriate to remove the corresponding menu item.

If all items in a menu are disabled, disable its menu title. If you disable a menu item or its title, the user can still browse to it or choose it. You should include a status bar message, balloon tip, or other context-sensitive Help support indicating that the command is unavailable and why. If you use a status bar message, display it when the input focus moves to the corresponding item.

The system provides a standard appearance for displaying disabled menu items. If you are supplying your own text or graphic for a disabled menu item, follow the visual design guidelines for how to display it. Check the colors for the current system settings, because these can change the appearance of menu items that appear unavailable.

For more information about displaying the unavailable appearance, see Chapter 14, "Visual Design."

Types of Menu Items

Many menu items take effect as soon as they are chosen. If the menu item is a command that requires the user to provide additional information before it can be completed, follow the command with an *ellipsis* (...). For example, the **Save As** command includes an ellipsis because the command is not complete until the user supplies or confirms a file name. However, not every command that opens a window should include an ellipsis.

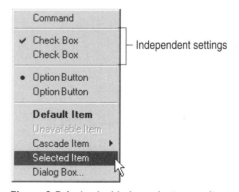 For more information about the use of ellipses, see Chapter 14, "Visual Design."

While you can use menu items to carry out commands, you can also use menu items to switch a mode or set a state or property rather than to initiate a process. For example, choosing an item from a menu that contains a list of tools or views implies changing to that state. If the menu item represents a property value, when the user chooses the menu item, the property setting changes.

Menu items for state settings can be independent or interdependent:

- Independent settings are the menu equivalent of check boxes. For example, if a menu contains commands for text properties, such as **Bold** and **Italic**, they form a group of independent settings. The user can change each setting without affecting the others, even though they both apply to a single text selection. Include a check mark to the left of an independent setting when that state applies, as shown in Figure 8.5.

Figure 8.5 A checked independent menu item

- Interdependent settings are the menu equivalent of option buttons. For example, if a menu contains alignment properties — such as **Left**, **Center**, and **Right** — they form a group of interdependent settings. Because a particular paragraph can have only one type of alignment, choosing one resets the property to the chosen menu item setting. When the user chooses an interdependent setting, place an option button mark to the left of that menu item, as shown in Figure 8.6.

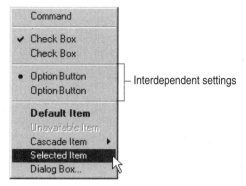

Figure 8.6 Selected option in a set of interdependent menu items

To represent two opposing states of a setting on the menu bar, such as the presence or absence of a property value, you can use a check mark to indicate when the setting applies. For example, a text selection marked bold shows a check mark next to the menu item labeled **Bold**. There is no check mark next to the menu item when the text is normal. If a selection contains mixed states for the setting listed in the menu, display the menu without the check mark applied.

However, if the two states of the setting are not obvious opposites, use similar menu item names to indicate the two states, or choices. For example, a new user might incorrectly guess that the opposite of a menu item named **Full Duplex** is **Empty Duplex**. Because this is not the case, pair the **Full Duplex** command with an altered command name, **Half Duplex**, instead of using a check mark to indicate the different states. Use the following guidelines to display related setting states:

- If there is room on a menu, include both setting states as individual menu items and interdependent choices. This helps to avoid confusion because the user can view both options at once. Use menu separators to group the choices.

Avoid defining menu items that change depending on the state of a modifier key. Such techniques hide functionality from a majority of users.

- If there is not sufficient room on the menu for both choices, use a single menu item and change its name to the related action when selected. In this case, the menu item's name does not reflect the current state; it indicates the state after the user chooses the item. Where possible, define names that use the same access key. For example, the letter D could be used for a menu item that toggles between **Full Duplex** and **Half Duplex**. Carefully consider the trade-offs before using this alternative because it is harder for users to locate and identify the appropriate menu item.

A menu can also have a default item. A default menu item reflects a choice that is supported through a shortcut technique, such as double-clicking or drag-and-drop. For example, if the default command for an application or document file icon is **Open**, define this as the default menu item. Similarly, if the default command for a drag-and-drop operation is **Copy**, display this command as the default menu item on the shortcut menu for a nondefault (secondary mouse button) drag-and-drop operation. The system designates a default menu item by displaying its label in bold text.

Menu Item Labels

Include descriptive text or a graphic label for each menu item. Even if you provide a graphic for the label, consider including text also. Or provide an option to use the text label instead of, or in addition to, the graphic. The text allows you to provide more direct keyboard access to the user and provides support for a wider range of users. When you use graphics, verify that the menu item label can be accessed by user automation and accessibility utilities. For more information, see the Microsoft Accessibility Web site at http://www.microsoft.com/enable/training/keyboard.htm.

Menu Text

Use the following guidelines for defining text for menu titles and menu items:

For more information about writing interface text, see Chapter 14, "Visual Design."

- Use unique menu title text across the menu bar and unique menu items within an individual menu. Item names can be repeated in different menus to represent similar or related actions.

- Keep menu text for a command brief, but clearly represent its functionality. Verbose menu names make it hard for users to scan the menu. Use single words for menu bar menu titles. Multiple-word titles or titles that contain spaces may be indistinguishable from two 1-word titles. However, don't create artificial compound words, such as **Fontsize**, either.

- Designate one character out of each menu title or item as its access key. This character provides keyboard access to the menu. Windows displays the access key for a menu title as an underlined character, as shown in Figure 8.7.

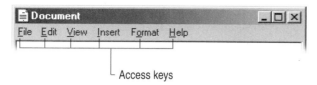

Figure 8.7 Access keys on a menu bar

Choose unique access keys for each menu title. Using the same access key for more than one menu title can eliminate direct access to a menu.

For more information about defining access keys, see Chapter 5, "Input Basics." For more information about common access key assignments, see Appendix B, "Keyboard Interface Summary."

- Use book title capitalization. For English language versions, capitalize the first letter of every word, except for articles, conjunctions, and prepositions that occur other than at the beginning or end of a multiple-word label. For example, the following capitalization is correct for menu text: **New Folder**, **Go To**, **Select All**, and **Table of Contents**.

- Avoid formatting individual menu items with different font properties. Even though these may illustrate a particular text style, they also may make the menu appear cluttered or illegible. For example, access keys might not be visible if you format a menu item using underlined text. If you do use special formatting, also provide users with the option to display elements that use system fonts, such as menus, in normal text.

- Use verbs or verb and noun phrases to label commands that represent actions. Use nouns for menu items that represent an object or group of objects, such as **Headings** or **Revisions**, as shown in the following table.

Suggested Wording for Menu Items

If the menu title is	Use	Example
A verb	A noun or noun phrase	On the **Insert** menu: **Text**, **Table**, **Picture**
A noun	A verb or verb phrase	On the **Table** menu: **Insert Table**, **Select Row**, **Insert Column**

Shortcut Keys in Menu Items

If you define a keyboard shortcut for a command that also appears in a drop-down menu, display the shortcut in the menu. Display the shortcut key next to the item, and align shortcuts with other shortcuts in the menu. Left-align shortcuts to the first tab position after the longest menu item with a shortcut. Do not use spaces for alignment. They may not be displayed properly in the proportional font that the system uses to display menu text or if the user changes the font setting for menu text.

Match *key* names to those inscribed on the *key*caps. For example, display CTRL and SHIFT *key* combinations as Ctrl+*key* (rather than Control+*key* or CONTROL+*key* or ^+*key*) and Shift+*key*. When using function *key*s for menu item shortcuts, display the name of the *key* as F*n*, where *n* is the function *key* number.

Avoid including shortcut keys on shortcut menus. Shortcut menus are already a shortcut form of interaction and are typically accessed with the mouse. In addition, shortcut menus without shortcut keys are easier for users to scan.

For more information about selecting shortcut keys, see Chapter 5, "Input Basics."

Controls

Controls are graphic objects that represent the properties or operations of other objects. Some controls display and allow editing of particular values. Other controls start associated commands.

Each control has a unique appearance and operation designed for a specific form of interaction. The system also provides support for designing your own controls. However, avoid defining your own controls when the system-supplied controls already provide the necessary functionality. This eliminates the possibility of confusing users and introducing incompatibilities or inconsistencies. When you define your own controls, follow the conventions established by the system-supplied controls.

For more information about using standard controls and designing your own controls, see Chapter 14, "Visual Design."

Like most elements of the interface, controls provide feedback to the user indicating when they require input and when they are activated. For example, when the user interacts with controls using a mouse, each control indicates that it is selected when the user presses the mouse button. The control is not activated until the user releases the mouse button, unless the control supports auto-repeat.

Controls are generally interactive only when the hot spot of the pointer is over the control. If the user moves the pointer off the control while pressing a mouse button, the control no longer responds to the input device. If the user moves the pointer back onto the control, it once again responds to the input device. The hot zone, or boundary that defines whether a control responds to the pointer, depends on the type of control. For some controls, such as buttons and scroll bars, the hot zone coincides with the visible border of the control. For others, the hot zone may include the control's graphic and label (for example, check boxes).

Many controls provide labels. Because labels help identify the purpose of a control, always label a control with which you want the user to directly interact, using the appropriate capitalization style defined for that control. If a control does not have a label, you can provide a label using a static text field or a ToolTip control. If you use a static text field as the label, you may need to include a colon to make the control accessible to screen-reader utilities.

Define an access key for a text label so that users have direct keyboard access to a control. Where possible, define consistent access keys for common commands.

For more information about defining access keys, see Chapter 5, "Input Basics."

Although controls provide specific interfaces for user interaction, you can also include shortcut menus for controls. This provides an effective way to transfer the value of the control through **Copy** and **Paste** commands or to provide access to context-sensitive Help. The interface to shortcut menus for controls follows the standard conventions for shortcut menus, except that it does not affect the state of the control; that is, when the user clicks the control with the secondary mouse button, the control itself is not activated. (The control is activated when the user clicks it with the primary mouse button.) The only action is that the shortcut menu is displayed.

A shortcut menu for a control is defined by what the control represents, rather than the control itself. Therefore, avoid commands such as **Set**, **Unset**, **Check**, or **Uncheck**. The exception is in a forms design or window layout context, where the commands on the shortcut menu can apply to the control itself.

Buttons

Buttons are controls that start actions or change properties. There are three basic types of buttons:

- Command buttons

- Option buttons

- Check boxes

Toolbars also contain buttons, but these buttons are typically provided by the toolbar control, not by a separate button control. Similarly, other user interface elements — such as the taskbar, window title bar, spin box, or scroll bar — include buttons, but these are also not exposed as button controls. However, the buttons included in these interface elements generally work the same as command button controls.

Command Buttons

A *command button*, also referred to as a push button, is a control that causes the application to perform some action when the user clicks it. A command button is usually rectangular and includes a label (text, graphic, or both), as shown in Figure 8.8.

Figure 8.8 Command buttons

Interaction

When the user clicks a command button with the primary mouse button, a command is carried out. When the user presses the mouse button, the input focus — a dotted rectangle — moves to the command button, and the command button state changes to its pressed appearance. If the user moves the pointer off the command button while the mouse button remains pressed, the command button returns to its original state but still displays the input focus rectangle. If the user moves the pointer back over the command button while pressing the mouse button, the command button returns to its pressed state.

When the user releases the mouse button with the pointer on the command button, the command associated with the control starts. If the pointer is not on the control when the user releases the mouse button, no action occurs.

You can define access keys and shortcut keys for command buttons. In addition, you can use the TAB key and arrow keys to support user navigation to or between command buttons. The SPACEBAR activates a command button once the user moves the input focus to the button. When the user presses the SPACEBAR, the command button state changes to its pressed appearance. When the user releases the SPACEBAR, the button is activated. If the user presses ESC before releasing the SPACEBAR, the command button returns to its original unactivated state but retains the keyboard focus.

For more information about navigating between and activating controls, see Chapter 9, "Secondary Windows."

The effect of choosing a button is immediate and can vary depending on the button's context. For example, in toolbars, clicking a button carries out the associated action. In a secondary window, such as a dialog box, activating a button may initiate a transaction within the window, or apply a transaction and close the window.

In some cases, a command button can represent an object and its default action. For example, the taskbar buttons represent an object's primary window and the **Restore** or **Minimize** commands. When the user clicks a taskbar button with the primary mouse button, the default command of the object is carried out. When the user clicks a taskbar button with the secondary mouse button, a shortcut menu for the window that the taskbar button represents is displayed.

Label Appearance

The label for a command button should describe the button's action. Aim for the shortest possible label; one word is best. If possible, use label text that makes sense when read out of context — for example, when a user reads or hears only the label of the current control.

When you create a text label, follow book-title capitalization. You can use the button label to reflect other information about the button's operation. For example, if the action represented by the button requires additional information, include an ellipsis (...). If the button expands the window to display additional information, include >>, as shown in Figure 8.9.

For more information about how to design buttons for use in your windows, see Chapter 14, "Visual Design."

Figure 8.9 A button that provides access to additional information

Similarly, if the button provides direct access to a menu, include a triangular arrow similar to the one found in cascading menu titles, as shown in Figure 8.10.

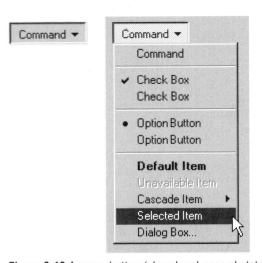

Figure 8.10 A menu button (closed and opened states)

If you use a button to display a menu, create the same type of interaction as with a drop-down menu. Display the menu when the user clicks or presses the button, and allow the user to use arrow keys or drag onto the menu and make menu selections. As with any other menu, use highlighting to track the movement of the pointer, and remove the menu when the user clicks an item on the menu or clicks outside the menu.

A command button typically displays feedback when the user presses the button. When the user releases the button, it returns to its normal "up" state.

Command Button States

Command button appearance	Button state
OK	Normal appearance
OK	Pressed appearance
OK	Input focus appearance
OK	Default appearance
OK	Unavailable appearance

While you can use a command button to reflect a mode, tool, or property value, consider using a toolbar button instead. The toolbar control already includes support for different button states you might use. If you use a command button instead of a toolbar button, its interaction should be generally consistent with toolbar buttons.

Instructional Text

In instructional references, use *click* to indicate how the user interacts with command buttons — for example, "To continue, click Next."

Option Buttons

An *option button*, also referred to as a radio button, represents a single choice within a limited set of mutually exclusive choices. That is, the user can choose only one of a set of options. Accordingly, always group option buttons in sets of two or more, as shown in Figure 8.11.

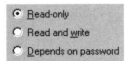

Figure 8.11 A set of option buttons

Limit the set of option buttons to a small number, typically seven or fewer, but always at least two. If you need more choices, consider using a different type of control, such as a single-selection list box or a drop-down list box. For option button functionality in a toolbar, use the toolbar control's button support.

Interaction

Option buttons appear as a set of small circles. When an option button choice is set, a dot appears in the middle of the circle. When the item is not the current setting, the circle next to the current setting is empty.

Avoid using option buttons to start an action other than to set a particular option or value. There is one exception. If the user's primary action is to choose an option button for the window, then you can support double-clicking the option button as a shortcut for setting the value and carrying out the window's default command.

You can use option buttons to represent a set of choices for a particular property. When a set of mixed values exists for a property, display all the option buttons in the group using the mixed-value appearance. The mixed-value appearance for a group of option buttons displays all buttons without a setting dot, as shown in Figure 8.12.

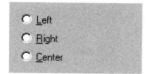

Figure 8.12 Option buttons with mixed-value appearance

If the user chooses any option button in a group with mixed-value appearance, that value becomes the setting for the group; the dot appears in that button and all the other buttons in the group remain empty.

As with command buttons, the mouse interface for choosing an option button requires the user to click the primary mouse button, either on the option button circle or on its label. When the user presses the mouse button, the input focus moves to the option button label, and the option button displays its pressed appearance. If the user moves the pointer off the option button before releasing the mouse button, the option button returns to its original state but retains the input focus. The option is not set until the user releases the mouse button while the pointer is over the control. In addition, repeated mouse clicks on the same option button do not toggle the button's state; the user needs to explicitly select another value in the group to change or restore a setting.

Assign access keys to option button labels to support a keyboard interface for the buttons. You should also support the TAB or arrow keys to allow the user to navigate to and choose a button. Access keys or arrow keys automatically set the input focus to an option and select that button. Use the TAB key to move to the first option button within a group, but do not set that option. Instead, enable the user to press the SPACEBAR to set the option and to press the arrow keys to move to and set an option button within the group. Similarly, enable the user to press the arrow keys with the CTRL modifier key to move the input focus within the group without setting an option.

For more information about the guidelines for defining access keys, see Chapter 5, "Input Basics." For more information about navigating and interacting with option buttons, see Chapter 9, "Secondary Windows."

Label Appearance

Label every option button in a set. Write the label to represent the value or effect for that choice. Also use the label text appearance to indicate when the choice is unavailable. Use sentence-style capitalization, capitalizing the first word in the label and any proper nouns. Write the label as a phrase, not as a sentence, and use no ending punctuation, as shown in Figure 8.13. If you want to use graphic labels for a group of exclusive choices, consider using toolbar buttons or command buttons instead.

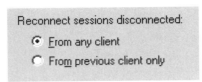

Figure 8.13 Option buttons with no ending punctuation

Write parallel labels of approximately equal length for related option buttons. When you write multiple-line labels, align the top of the text label with the option button unless the context requires a different orientation.

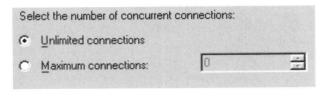
For more information about labeling or appearance states, see Chapter 14, "Visual Design."

Avoid repeating words in option button labels. Repetition makes it harder for the user to scan the text and differentiate among options.

Because option buttons appear as a group, you can use a group box control to visually distinguish the group when they appear with other controls. In a group box, label the option buttons relative to the group box's label. For example, for a group box labeled Alignment, you can label the option buttons as **Left**, **Right**, and **Center**. For more information about layout of options buttons, see Chapter 14, "Visual Design."

If you use an option button to label a control that follows it, end the label with a colon, as shown in Figure 8.14.

Figure 8.14 An option button used to label another control

Instructional Text

In instructional references, use *click* to indicate user interaction with buttons — for example, "Click Left."

Check Boxes

A *check box* represents an independent or non-exclusive choice. As with independent settings in menus, use check boxes only when both states of a choice are opposites and unambiguous. If this is not the case, then use option buttons or some other form of single-selection control instead. For example, if the alternative to the **Print to file** option is understood by your users to be printing on the printer, then you can use a check box; otherwise, list both choices with option buttons.

A check box can have one of three states:

- Checked — the associated value or property is set.

- Cleared — the associated value or property is not set.

- Mixed value — the associated value is set for some, but not all, elements of the selection.

A check box appears as a square box with an accompanying label. When the choice is set, a check mark appears in the box. When the choice is not set, the check box is empty, as shown in Figure 8.15.

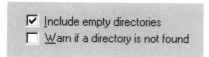

Figure 8.15 A set of check boxes

Limit the number of check boxes included in your application's interface, as you limit the number of option buttons. If you need many choices, consider using a different type of control, such as a multiple-selection list box or list view control. For check box functionality in a toolbar, use button support within the toolbar control.

Interaction

When the user clicks a check box with the primary mouse button, either in the check box or on its label, the check box is selected and its state is toggled. When the user presses the mouse button, the input focus moves to the control and the check box displays its pressed appearance. Like option buttons and other controls, if the user moves the pointer off the check box or its label while pressing the mouse button, the control's appearance returns to its original state and retains the input focus. The state of the check box does not change until the mouse button is released. To change a control's setting, the pointer must be over the check box or its label when the user releases the mouse button.

Define access keys for check box labels to allow users to navigate to and select a check box using a keyboard interface. In addition, you can support the TAB key and arrow keys to allow users to navigate to check boxes. In a dialog box, for example, the user can press SPACEBAR to toggle a check box when the input focus is on the check box.

For more information about the guidelines for defining access keys, see Chapter 5, "Input Basics." For more information about navigating and interacting with option buttons, see Chapter 9, "Secondary Windows."

If you use a check box to display a property that has multiple values (for example, a text selection that is partly in bold style and partly in normal style), display the check box in its mixed-value appearance, as shown in Figure 8.16.

Figure 8.16 A mixed-value check box (magnified)

If the user clicks a check box that is in the mixed-value state, or presses and releases the SPACEBAR when the control has the input focus, set the check box as follows:

- At the first click, set the check box to its selected state (check mark in the check box) and set the associated value it represents. This implies that the property value will be set for all elements in the selection when the operation is applied.

- At the next click, toggle the setting to the unchecked state. When the operation is applied, this toggles the property values of the selected items to their not-set state.

- If the user clicks the check box a third time, toggle the value back to the mixed-value state. When the user applies the operation at this point, all elements in the selection retain their original property values.

This three-state toggling occurs only when the control represents a mixed set of values.

Group related check box choices. If you group check boxes, it does not prevent the user from setting the check boxes on or off in any combination.

While each check box's setting is typically independent of the check boxes and options, you can use a check box's setting to affect other controls. For example, you can use the state of a check box to filter the contents of a list, as shown in Figure 8.17.

Figure 8.17 A check box setting used to filter the contents of a list

If the list contains a large number of choices or if the number of choices varies, use a multiple-selection list box instead of check boxes. Controls that are dependent on the state of a check box should immediately follow that check box in the TAB order, especially when the check box setting can make those controls unavailable.

Label Appearance

Label every check box to express the value or effect of the choice. The label also serves to indicate when the control is unavailable.

A check box label is typically displayed as text. The standard control includes a text label. Use sentence-style capitalization with no ending punctuation. (When you need a non-exclusive choice with only a graphic label, use a toolbar or command button instead of a check box.)

Use a single line of text for the label to make it easier to read. However, if you do use multiple lines, use top alignment unless the context requires a different orientation.

Write parallel labels of approximately equal length for related check boxes. If a check box label also acts as the label for the control that follows it, end the label with a colon, as shown in Figure 8.18.

Figure 8.18 A check box label used to label another control

Instructional Text

In instructional references, use *select* and *clear* to indicate user action in check boxes — for example, "To add a component, select its check box. To remove the component, clear the check box."

List Boxes

A *list box* is a control for displaying a list of choices for the user. The choices can be text, color, icons, or other graphics. The purpose of a list box is to display a collection of items and, in most cases, support selection of an item or items in the list. This section describes several list box controls.

List boxes are best used for displaying large numbers of choices that vary in number or content. If a particular choice is not available, omit the choice from the list. For example, if a point size is not available for the currently selected font, do not display that size in the list.

Order the entries in a list to best represent the content and to facilitate easy browsing by the user. For example, you would typically alphabetize a list of names, but put a list of dates in chronological order. If there is no natural or logical ordering for the content, use ascending or alphabetical ordering — for example, 0–9 or A–Z. You can also provide separate controls or menu items to enable the user to change the sort order or filter items displayed in the list.

Interaction

When the user clicks an item in a list box, it becomes selected. Support for multiple selection depends on the type of list box you use. List boxes can also include scroll bars when the number or width of items in the list exceeds the visible area of the control.

Arrow keys support selection and scrolling in a list box. In addition, list boxes include support for keyboard selection using text keys. When the user presses a text key, the list selects the matching initial character of the first word in a list entry, scrolling if necessary to keep the user's selection visible. Subsequent key presses continue the matching process.

List boxes can also support sequential matches of text keys based on timing. Each time the user presses a key within the system's time-out setting, the control moves the input focus within the list to the next item that matches the typed characters. If the time-out is reached, the control is reset to match the first character of the first word in an entry. If there are multiple entries and the input focus is already on a matched item in the list, the control moves the input focus to the next matching item. For example, if the list contains the entries "properties" and "proposal," the control moves the input focus to "properties" when the P key is pressed and then to "proposal" if the key is pressed again.

Other list box controls, such as combo boxes and drop-down combo boxes, do sequential character matching based on the characters typed into the text box component of the control. These controls may be preferable because they do not require the user to master the timing sequence. However, they do take up more space and potentially allow the user to type in entries that do not exist in the list box.

When the user scrolls the list to its beginning or end, disable the corresponding scroll bar arrow button. If all items in the list are visible, disable both scroll arrows. If the list box never includes more items that can be shown in the list box, so that the user will not need to scroll, remove the scroll bar.

For more information about disabling scroll bar arrows, see Chapter 7, "Windows."

When you incorporate a list box into a window's design, consider whether it is also appropriate to support transfer commands (**Cut**, **Copy**, and **Paste**) and direct manipulation (drag-and-drop) transfers to and from the list box. For example, if the list displays icons or values that the user can move or copy to other locations, such as another list box, support transfer operations for the list. The list view control automatically supports this; however, the system provides support for you to enable this for other list boxes as well.

Label Appearance

List box controls do not include their own labels. However, you should include a label using a static text field; the label enables you to provide a description of the control and keyboard access to the control. Use sentence-style capitalization for a list box label and end the label with a colon, as shown in Figure 8.19.

For more information about navigating to controls in a secondary window, see Chapter 9, "Secondary Windows." For more information about defining access keys for control labels, see Chapter 5, "Input Basics." For more information about static text fields, see "Static Text Fields" later in this chapter.

Figure 8.19 A list-box label with sentence-style capitalization

Make sure that your support for keyboard access moves the input focus to the list box and not to the static text field label. When a list box is disabled, display its label using an unavailable appearance. If possible, display all of the entries in the list as unavailable to avoid confusing the user as to whether or not the control is enabled.

Use sentence-style capitalization for items in the list. The width of the list box should be sufficient to display the average width of an entry in the list. If that is not practical because of space or the variable length of the list's entries, consider one or more of the following options:

- Make the list box wide enough so that the visible portions of the entries are easily distinguished from each other.

- Use an ellipsis (...) in the middle or at the end of long text entries if you need to shorten them, preserving the important characteristics needed to distinguish them. For example, for long paths, usually the beginning and end of the path name are the most critical; you can use an ellipsis to shorten the entire name — for example, \Sample\...\Example. When shortening an item's name in this way, you may want to include a ToolTip that displays the item's full name.

- Include a horizontal scroll bar. This option reduces usability because the scroll bar reduces the number of entries the user can view at one time. In addition, if most entries in the list box do not need to be horizontally scrolled, it is of limited use.

Instructional Text

If you need to add instructional text for the list box, add it above the label. Use complete sentences with ending punctuation, as shown in Figure 8.20.

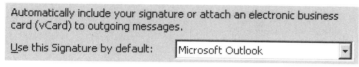

Figure 8.20 Instructional text for a list box

Additional information that is helpful but not necessary should be brief. Place this information either in parentheses between the label and colon or without parentheses below the list box. Use complete sentences and ending punctuation, as shown in Figure 8.21.

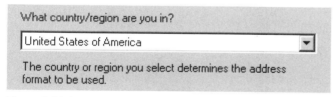

Figure 8.21 Additional information for a list box

Use *select* to indicate user interaction with list box items.

Single-Selection List Boxes

A *single-selection list box* is designed for selecting only one item in a list. Therefore, the control provides a mutually exclusive operation similar to a group of option buttons, except that a list box can handle a large number of items more efficiently.

Define a single-selection list box to be tall enough to show at least three to eight choices, as shown in Figure 8.22, depending on the design constraints of where the list box is used. Always include a vertical scroll bar. If all the items in the list are visible, then follow the window scroll bar guidelines for disabling the scroll arrows and enlarging the scroll box to fill the scroll bar shaft.

Figure 8.22 A single-selection list box

The currently selected item in a single-selection list box is highlighted using selection appearance and the input focus.

The user can select an entry in a single-selection list box by clicking it with the primary mouse button. This also sets the input focus to that item in the list. Because this type of list box supports only a single selection, when the user chooses another entry, the previous selection is canceled. The scroll bar in the list box allows the user to scroll through the list of entries, following the interaction defined for scroll bars.

For more information about the interaction techniques of scroll bars, see Chapter 7, "Windows."

The keyboard interface uses navigation keys, such as the arrow keys, HOME, END, PAGE UP, and PAGE DOWN. It also uses text keys, with matches based on timing; for example, when the user presses a text key, an entry matching that character scrolls to the top of the list and is selected. These keys not only navigate to an entry in the list, but also select it. If no item in the list is currently selected, then when the user chooses a list navigation key, the first item in the list that corresponds to that key is selected. For example, if the user presses the DOWN ARROW key, the first entry in the list is selected instead of the second entry in the list.

If the choices in the list box represent property values of a selection, then make the current value visible and highlight it when displaying the list. If the list box reflects mixed values for a multiple selection, then no entry in the list should be selected.

Drop-Down List Boxes

Like a single-selection list box, a *drop-down list box* allows the selection of only a single item from a list; the difference is that the list is displayed on demand. In its closed state, the control displays the current value for the control. The user opens the list to change the value. Figure 8.23 shows the drop-down list box in its closed and opened states.

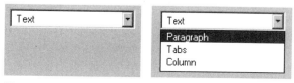

Figure 8.23 A drop-down list box (closed and opened states)

While drop-down list boxes are an effective way to conserve space and reduce clutter, they require more user effort to browse and select an item than does a single-selection list box.

Make the width of a closed drop-down list box a few spaces larger than the average width of the items in its list. The open list component of the control should be tall enough to show three to eight items, following the same conventions as for a single-selection list box. The width of the list should be wide enough not only to display the choices in the list, but also to allow the user to drag items directly onto the list.

The interface for drop-down list boxes is similar to that for menus. For example, the user can click the current setting of the control or the control's menu button to display the list. Choosing an item in the list automatically closes the list.

If the user navigates to the control using an access key, the TAB key or arrow keys, the user can display the list by pressing an UP ARROW or DOWN ARROW or ALT+UP ARROW or ALT+DOWN ARROW keys. Within the list, the user can navigate to and select items in the list by pressing arrow keys or text keys. If the user presses ALT+UP ARROW, ALT+DOWN ARROW, a navigation key, or an access key to move to another control, the list automatically closes. When the list is closed, preserve any selection made while the list was open. The ESC key also closes the list and restores the previous setting.

If the choices in a drop-down list represent values for the property of a multiple selection and the values for that property are mixed, then display no single value in the current setting component of the control.

Extended- and Multiple-Selection List Boxes

Although most list boxes are single-selection lists, some contexts require the user to choose more than one item. *Extended-selection list boxes* and *multiple-selection list boxes* support this functionality.

For more information about contiguous and disjoint selection techniques, see Chapter 6, "General Interaction Techniques."

Extended- and multiple-selection list boxes follow the same conventions for height and width as do single-selection list boxes. The height of the box should display no fewer than three items and generally no more than eight, unless the size of the list varies with the size of the window. Base the width of the box on the average width of the entries in the list.

Extended-selection list boxes support conventional navigation and contiguous and disjoint selection techniques. That is, extended-selection list boxes are optimized for selecting a single item or a single range while still providing for disjoint selections.

When you want to enable the user to select several disjointed entries from a list, but an extended-selection list box is too cumbersome, you can define a multiple-selection list box. While extended-selection list boxes are optimized for individual item or range selection, multiple-selection list boxes are optimized for independent selection.

Because simple multiple-selection list boxes are not visually distinct from extended-selection list boxes, consider designing them to appear similar to a scrollable list of check boxes, as shown in Figure 8.24.

For more information about the flat appearance style for controls in a list box, see Chapter 14, "Visual Design." For more information about keyboard interaction with different kinds of list boxes, see the Microsoft Accessibility Web site at http://www.microsoft.com/enable/training/keyboard.htm.

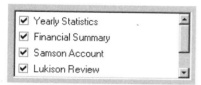

Figure 8.24 A multiple-selection list box

This requires providing your own graphics for the items in the list (using the owner-drawn list box style). This display helps the user see a difference in the list box interface while still using a familiar convention. Because the check box controls are nested, use the flat appearance for check boxes. A list view control is a better alternative for creating this kind of list box. It provides greater flexibility and compatibility with interface and accessibility utilities.

List View Controls

A *list view control* is a special extended-selection list box that displays a collection of items, each consisting of an icon and a label. List view controls can display content in four different views.

List View Controls

View	Description
Large Icon	Each item appears as a full-sized icon with a label below it. The user can drag the icons to any location within the view.
Small Icon	Each item appears as a small icon with its label to the right. The user can drag the icons to any location within the view.
List	Each item appears as a small icon with its label to the right. The icons appear in one or more sorted columns.
Details	Each item appears as a line in a multi-column format with the leftmost column including the icon and its label. The subsequent columns contain information from the application displaying the list view control.

The control supports options for aligning, selecting, and sorting icons and for editing icon labels. It also supports drag-and-drop interaction.

Use this control where an icon representation of objects is appropriate, or to represent items with multiple columns of information. List view controls are generally a better alternative than owner-drawn list boxes and are more compatible with interface and accessibility utilities.

If you use the control to display items represented by icons, provide shortcut menus for the icons displayed in the views. This provides a consistent paradigm for how the user interacts with icons elsewhere in the Windows interface. Also include a shortcut menu and separate controls to enable the user to change the view if you support different control viewing options.

Selection and navigation in this control work similarly to selection and navigation in folder windows. For example, the user clicks an icon to select it. After selecting the icon, the user can use extended selection techniques with the mouse or keyboard, including region selection for contiguous or disjoint selections. Arrow keys, PAGE UP, PAGE DOWN, HOME, END, and text keys (time-out-based matching) support keyboard navigation and selection. Pressing CTRL+PLUS (on the numeric keypad) adjusts the width of all columns to fit their contents.

As an option, the standard control also supports the display of graphics that can be used to represent state information. For example, you can use this functionality to include check boxes next to items in a list.

Tree View Controls

A *tree view control* is a special list box control that displays a set of objects as an indented outline based on their logical hierarchical relationship. The control includes buttons that expand and collapse the outline, as shown in Figure 8.25. You can use a tree view control to display the relationship between a set of containers or other hierarchical elements.

Buttons for expanding and collapsing outline —

Lines illustrate hierarchical relationships —

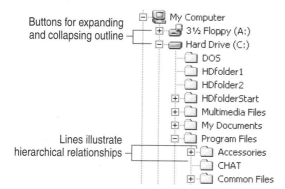

Figure 8.25 A tree view control

You can optionally include icons with the text label of each item in the tree. Different icons can be displayed when the user expands or collapses the item in the tree. You can also include a graphic, such as a check box, that can be used to reflect state information about the item. The control also supports optional display of lines to illustrate the hierarchical relationship of the items in the list and optional display of buttons for expanding and collapsing the outline.

Arrow keys provide keyboard support for navigating through the control. The user presses the UP ARROW and DOWN ARROW keys to move between items and the LEFT ARROW and RIGHT ARROW keys to move along a particular branch of the outline. Pressing the RIGHT ARROW key can also expand the outline at a branch if it is not currently displayed. Pressing LEFT ARROW collapses a branch if the focus is on an item with an expanded branch; otherwise it moves the focus to the current item's parent. Pressing * on the numeric keypad expands the current branch and all its sub-branches. Text keys can also be used to navigate to and select items in the list, using the matching technique based on timing.

When you use this control in a dialog box, if you use the ENTER key or use double-clicking to carry out the default command for an item in the list, make sure that the default command button in your dialog box matches. For example, if the user must double-click an entry in the outline to display the item's properties, then define a **Properties** button to be the default command button in the dialog box when the tree view control has the input focus.

Text Fields

Windows includes a number of controls that facilitate displaying, entering, or editing a text value. Some of these controls combine a basic text-entry field with other types of controls.

When you create a text field for input of a restricted set of possible values — for example, a field where only numbers are appropriate — validate user input immediately, either by ignoring inappropriate characters or by providing feedback such as a balloon tip. Also, play the system error audio tone any time the user enters an invalid value.

For more information about validating input, see Chapter 9, "Secondary Windows."

Label Appearance

Text fields do not include labels as a part of the control. However, you can add a label using a static text field, as shown in Figure 8.26. A label helps the user identify the purpose of a text field and provides a way to indicate when the field is disabled. For multiple-word labels, use sentence-style capitalization ending with a colon.

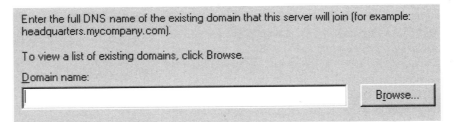

Figure 8.26 Text box label appearance

A text box that follows an option button or check box does not need a label as long as the label of the preceding control describes the text box and ends with a colon.

To provide keyboard access to the text field, you can also define an access key for the text label. Define keyboard access to move the input focus to the text field with which the label is associated rather than to the static text field itself. You can also support keyboard navigation to text fields by using the TAB key (and, optionally, the arrow keys).

For more information about static text fields, see "Static Text Fields" later in this chapter.

Instructional Text

If you need to add instructional text about a text box, add it above the label. Use complete sentences with ending punctuation.

Use *type* or *enter* in instructions for text box input. If the user must type or paste the information into the text box, use *type*. For example, "Type your user name." However, use *enter* if the text box is accompanied by a **Browse** button or a list from which the user can also select. Use *select* when referring to an entry in a text box that the user must choose by clicking or by using the keyboard. For spin boxes, use *enter* when the user can either type or select an option. Use *select* when the spin box does not allow typing.

Additional information that is helpful but not necessary should be kept short. Place this information either in parentheses between the label and colon or without parentheses below the text box. Use complete sentences with ending punctuation, as shown in Figure 8.27.

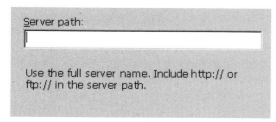

Figure 8.27 Additional information for a text box

Text Boxes

A *text box* (also referred to as an edit control) is a rectangular control where the user enters or edits text, as shown in Figure 8.28. It can be defined to support a single line or multiple lines of text. The outline border of the control is optional, although the border is typically included when the control is displayed in a toolbar or a secondary window.

Figure 8.28 A standard text box

The standard text box control provides basic text input and editing support. Editing includes inserting and deleting characters and the option of text wrapping. Although individual font or paragraph properties are not supported, the entire control can support a specific font setting.

You can also use text boxes to display read-only text that the user can select but cannot edit. When setting this option with the standard control, the system automatically changes the background color of the field to indicate to the user the difference in behavior.

A text box supports standard interactive techniques for navigation and contiguous selection. Horizontal scrolling is available for single-line text boxes, and horizontal and vertical scroll bars are supported for multiple-line text boxes.

You can limit the number of characters accepted as input for a text box to whatever is appropriate for the context. In addition, you can support *auto-exit* for text boxes defined for fixed-length input; that is, as soon as the last character is typed in the text box, the focus moves to the next control. For example, you can define a five-character auto-exit text box to facilitate entering a ZIP code, or three 2-character auto-exit text boxes to support entering a date. Use auto-exit text boxes sparingly; the automatic shift of focus can surprise the user. They are best limited to situations involving extensive data entry.

Rich-Text Boxes

A *rich-text box*, as shown in Figure 8.29, provides the same basic text editing support as a standard text box. In addition, a rich-text box supports font properties, such as typeface, size, color, bold, and italic format, for each character and paragraph format property, such as alignment, tabs, indents, and numbering. The control also supports printing its content and embedded and linked objects.

The Quick Fox
    The quick fox chases the rabbit everyday over the
        hills and through the
        woods and streams.

Figure 8.29 A rich-text box

Combo Boxes

A *combo box* combines a text box with a list box, as shown in
Figure 8.30. This allows the user to type an entry or choose one
from the list.

Figure 8.30 A combo box

The text box and its associated list box have a dependent
relationship. As text is typed into the text box, the list scrolls to the
nearest match. In addition, when the user selects an item in the list
box, it automatically uses that entry to replace the content of the text
box and selects the text.

The interface for the control follows the conventions supported for
each component, except that the UP ARROW and DOWN ARROW keys
move only in the list box. The LEFT ARROW and RIGHT ARROW keys
operate only in the text box.

Drop-Down Combo Boxes

A *drop-down combo box*, as shown in Figure 8.31, combines the
characteristics of a text box with a drop-down list box. A drop-down
combo box is more compact than a regular combo box; it can be
used to conserve space, but it requires additional user interaction to
display the list.

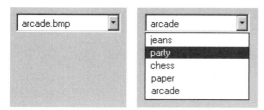

Figure 8.31 A drop-down combo box (closed and opened states)

The closed state of a drop-down combo box is similar to that of a drop-down list, except that the text box is interactive. When the user clicks the control's menu button, the list is opened. When the user clicks the menu button a second time, chooses an item in the list, or clicks another control, the list is closed.

Provide a static text field label for the control. Assign an access key so the user can navigate to the control. You should also support the TAB key or arrow keys for navigation to the control. When the control has the input focus, the list is displayed when the user presses the UP ARROW or DOWN ARROW or ALT+UP ARROW or ALT+DOWN ARROW keys.

When the control has the input focus, the list closes when the user presses ALT+UP ARROW or ALT+DOWN ARROW or a navigation key, such as the TAB key or an access key to navigate to another control. When the list is closed, preserve any selection made while the list was open, unless the user presses a **Cancel** command button. The ESC key also closes the list but restores the previous setting for the control.

When the list is displayed, the interdependent relationship between the text box and list is the same as it is for standard combo boxes when the user types text into the text box. When the user chooses an item in the list, the interaction is the same as for drop-down lists — the selected item becomes the entry in the text box.

Spin Boxes

Spin boxes are text boxes that allow the user to move, or spin, through a fixed set of ascending or descending values such as times or dates. A spin box is a combination of a text box and a special control that incorporates a pair of buttons (also known as an up-down control), as shown in Figure 8.32.

Figure 8.32 A spin box

When the user clicks the text box or the buttons, the input focus is set to the text box component of the control. The user can type a text value directly into the control or use the buttons to increase or decrease the value. The unit of change depends on what you define the control to represent. If you use numbers, left-align them when they appear in the text box.

Use caution in situations where the meaning of the control buttons may be ambiguous. For example, with numeric values such as dates, it may not be clear whether the top button moves forward to the next date or back to the previous date. Define the top button to increase the value by one unit and the bottom button to decrease the value by one unit. Typically, wrap around at either end of the set of values. You may need to provide some additional information to communicate how the buttons apply.

By including a static text field as a label for the spin box and defining an associated access key, you can provide direct keyboard access to the control. You can also use an option button label or check box label. Support keyboard access using the TAB key (or, optionally, the arrow keys). Once the control has the input focus, the user can change the value by pressing the UP ARROW or DOWN ARROW key. In some cases the user can also type the value directly. Position the label either to the left of the box or above it and aligned with the left edge of its text box component.

You can also use a single set of spin box buttons to edit a sequence of related text boxes — for example, time as expressed in hours, minutes, and seconds. The buttons affect only the text box that currently has the input focus.

Static Text Fields

You can use *static text fields* to present read-only information. Unlike read-only text box controls, the user cannot select the text, so avoid using it for any text the user might want to copy to the Clipboard. However, your application can still alter read-only static text to reflect a change in state. For example, you can use static text to display the current folder path or status information, such as page number, key states, or time and date. Figure 8.33 illustrates a static text field.

Static Text Field

Figure 8.33 A static text field

You can also use static text fields to provide labels or descriptions for other controls. Using a static text field as a label for a control allows you to provide access key activation for the control with which it is associated. Make sure that the input focus moves to its associated control and not to the static field. Also remember to include a colon at the end of the text. Not only does this help communicate that the text represents the label for a control, it is also used by screen-review utilities.

For more information about the layout of static text fields, see Chapter 14, "Visual Design." For information about the use of static text fields as labels and about screen-review utilities, see Chapter 15, "Special Design Considerations."

Shortcut Key Input Controls

A *shortcut key input control* (also known as a hot-key control) is a special kind of text box that enables the user to define a shortcut key assignment by entering a key or key combination. Use it when you provide an interface for the user to customize shortcut keys supported by your application. Because shortcut keys carry out a command directly, they provide a more efficient interface for common or frequently used actions.

For more information about the use of shortcut keys, see Chapter 5, "Input Basics."

The control allows you to define invalid keys or key combinations to ensure valid user input; the control will access only valid keys. You also supply a default modifier to use when the user enters an invalid key. The control displays the valid key or key combination including any modifier keys.

When the user clicks a shortcut key input control, the input focus is set to the control. Like most text boxes, the control does not include its own label, so use a static text field to provide a label and assign an appropriate access key. You can also support the TAB key to provide keyboard access to the control.

Other General Controls

The system also provides support for controls designed to organize other controls and controls for special types of interfaces.

Column Headings

You can use a *column heading control*, also known as a header control, to display a heading above columns of text or numbers. You can divide the control into two or more parts to provide headings for multiple columns, as shown in Figure 8.34. The list view control also provides support for a column heading control.

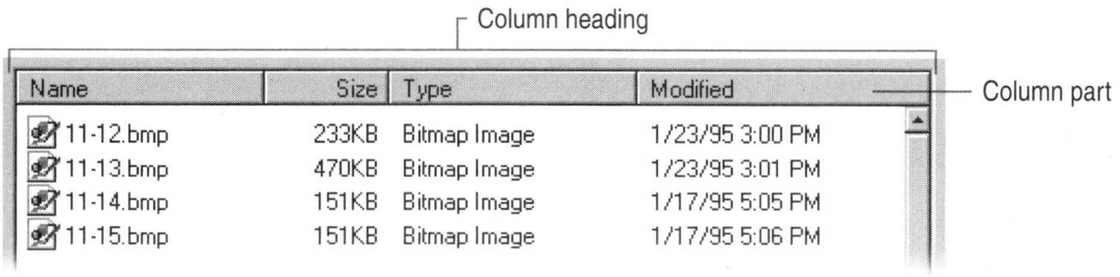

Figure 8.34 A column heading divided into four parts

The width of the column should fit the average size of the column entries.

Interaction

You can configure each part to respond like a command button to support a specific function when the user clicks it. For example, consider sorting the list when the user clicks a particular part of the header with the primary mouse button, and reverse the sort order if the view is already sorted by that field. Also, you can support displaying the shortcut menu when the user clicks the part with the secondary mouse button. The shortcut menu would contain commands specific to that part, such as **Sort Ascending** and **Sort Descending**.

The control also supports the user dragging the divisions that separate header parts to set the width of each column. As an option, you can support double-clicking on a division as a shortcut to a command that applies to formatting the column, such as automatically sizing the column to the largest value in that column.

Column heading controls do not support keyboard access, so you should also include an alternate way for users to resize and sort columns. You can use separate controls in your window or add these commands to the shortcut menu that is displayed when the user presses SHIFT+F10 or the Application key when no item in the list is selected.

Label Appearance

Each header part's label can include text and a graphic image. Keep the text brief and use book title capitalization without ending punctuation. Typically, you should align the title text with the appropriate alignment of the items listed in the column. For example, if there are text items in the column's list, you would left align the text and the column part's title. However, if there are right-aligned numbers in the column, you would right-align the column title. If you use a graphic image instead of text for the title, support a ToolTip for the title so that your users can identify the meaning of the image.

You can also include a graphic image with a text label to illustrate information about column item attributes. When you do, make sure they properly communicate the current state of the column items. For example, a downward pointing arrow graphic used to indicate sort order should indicate descending sort order. When sorting by date on U.S. system configurations, this means that the contents of the column should be sorted with the most recent item first.

Date-Picker

The *date-picker control* provides a calendar month display that enables the user to select a date, as shown in Figure 8.35.

Figure 8.35 A date-picker control

You can use this control directly in a window or as a pop-up window from a drop-down list control.

Group Boxes

A *group box* is a special control you can use to organize a set of controls. A group box is a rectangular frame with an optional label that surrounds a set of controls, as shown in Figure 8.36. Group boxes generally do not directly process any input. However, you can provide navigational access to items in the group by using the TAB key or by assigning an access key to the group label. If you use arrow keys to support user navigation for controls within a group box (for example, option buttons), you should use them to move only between controls in the group box.

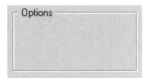

Figure 8.36 A group box

Label Appearance

Use a noun or noun phrase for most group box labels, keeping the text brief (one or two words). Avoid using instructional text as the label. Use sentence-style capitalization, but do not include any ending punctuation.

When you label your group box, also consider the labels for the controls it contains. Where possible, label them relative to the group box's label. For example, a group labeled Alignment can have option buttons labeled **Left**, **Right**, and **Center**.

For more information about the layout of controls in a group box, see Chapter 14, "Visual Design."

Progress Indicators

You can use a *progress indicator*, also known as a progress bar control, to show the percentage of completion of a lengthy operation. It consists of a solid or segmented rectangular bar that "fills" from left to right, as shown in Figure 8.37.

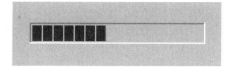

Figure 8.37 A progress indicator

Because a progress indicator only displays information, it is typically not interactive. However, it may be useful to add static text or other information to help communicate the purpose of the progress indicator. If you do include text, place it outside of the progress indicator control.

Use the control as feedback for long operations or background processes to supplement pointer "busy" feedback. The control provides more visual feedback to the user. You can also use the control to reflect the progression of a background process, leaving the pointer to reflect activity in the foreground. To decide whether to use a progress indicator in a message box or status bar, evaluate how modal the operation or process is that the progress indicator represents.

For more information about message boxes, see Chapter 9, "Secondary Windows." For more information about status bars, see "Toolbars and Status Bars" later in this chapter.

The progress indicator control includes an option to display the control as a solid or segmented bar. The solid bar is the default and is most commonly used.

Property Sheet Controls

A *property sheet control* provides the basic framework for defining a property sheet. It includes the common controls used in a property sheet and accepts modeless dialog box layout definitions to automatically create tabbed property pages.

For more information about designing property sheets, see Chapter 9, "Secondary Windows." For details about designing wizards, see Chapter 13, "User Assistance."

The property sheet control also includes support for creating wizards. Wizards are a special form of user assistance that guide the user through a sequence of steps in a specific operation or process. When the property sheet control is used as a wizard, tabs are not included and the standard **OK**, **Cancel**, and **Apply** buttons are replaced with **Back**, **Next** or **Finish**, and **Cancel** buttons.

Scroll Bars

Scroll bars are horizontal or vertical scrolling controls you can use to create scrollable areas other than on the window frame or list box where they are automatically included. Use scroll bar controls only for supporting scrolling contexts. For contexts where you want to provide an interface for setting or adjusting values, use a slider or other control, such as a spin box. Because scroll bars are designed for scrolling through information, using a scroll bar to set values may confuse the user about the purpose or interaction of the control.

When you use scroll bar controls, follow the recommended conventions for disabling the scroll bar arrows. Disable a scroll bar arrow button when the user scrolls to the beginning or end of the data, unless the structure permits the user to scroll beyond the data. For more information about scroll bar conventions, see Chapter 7, "Windows."

While scroll bar controls can support the input focus, avoid defining this type of interface. Instead, define the keyboard interface of your scrollable area so that it can scroll without requiring the user to move the input focus to the scroll bar. This makes your scrolling interface more consistent with the user interaction for window and list box scroll bars.

Sliders

A *slider*, sometimes called a trackbar control, consists of a bar that defines the extent or range of the adjustment and an indicator that shows the current value for the control, as shown in Figure 8.38. Use a slider for setting or adjusting values on a continuous range, such as volume or brightness.

Figure 8.38 A slider

Interaction

The user moves the slide indicator by dragging it to a particular location or by clicking in the hot zone of the bar, which moves the slide indicator directly to that location. To provide keyboard interaction, support the TAB key and define an access key for the static text field you use for its label. When the control has the input focus, the user can also press the arrow keys to move the slide indicator in the directions represented by the keys.

Sliders support a number of options. You can set the slider orientation to be vertical or horizontal, define the length and height of the slide indicator and the slide bar component, define the increments of the slider, and display tick marks for the control.

Label Appearance

Because a slider does not include its own label, use a static text field or a group box label to provide one. Position the label either to the left of the slider or above it and aligned with the left edge of the slider. Use sentence-style capitalization for the slider label. If you use a static text field to label the control, end the label text with a colon, as shown in Figure 8.39.

Figure 8.39 A static text label for a slider

You can also add text and graphics to the control to help the user interpret the scale and range of the control. Make sure these range identifier labels are descriptive and parallel — for example, **Low** and **High**, **Soft** and **Loud**, and so on.

Instructional Text

In instructional text, use *move* to refer to the user's interaction with the slider — for example, "Move the slider to the right."

Tabs

A *tab control* is analogous to a divider in a file cabinet or notebook. You can use this control to define multiple logical pages or sections of information within the same window, as shown in Figure 8.40.

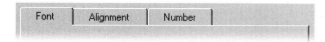

Figure 8.40 A tab control

Interaction

When the user clicks a tab with the primary mouse button, the input focus moves and switches to that tab. When a tab has the input focus, the user can press the LEFT ARROW and RIGHT ARROW keys to move between tabs. The user can also press CTRL+TAB, CTRL+PAGE UP, or CTRL+PAGE DOWN to switch between tabs. If multiple rows of tabs are displayed, the user can press the UP ARROW and DOWN ARROW to move to the corresponding tab in the next or previous row. Optionally, you can also define access keys for navigating between tabs. If there is no appropriate control or field in which to place the tab, leave the input focus on the tab itself.

Label Appearance

In general, use text for your tab labels. Usually, the control automatically sizes the tab to the size of its label; however, you can define your tabs to have a fixed width.

Use the system font for the text labels of your tabs, and use book title capitalization with no ending punctuation or ellipsis. Keep tab text labels brief and of the same general length. Nouns are usually better than verbs.

By default, a tab control displays only one row of tabs. Although the control supports multiple rows or scrolling a single row of tabs, avoid these options because they add complexity to the interface and make it harder for the user to read and access a particular tab. You may want to consider alternatives such as separating the tabbed pages into sets and using another control to move between the sets or using subordinate dialog boxes. However, if scrolling through the tabs seems appropriate, follow the conventions documented in this book.

The tab control supports placement of the tabs at the top, left, right, or bottom of the control. The default and most common placement is at the top of the control.

Instructional Text

In instructional text, use *click* to refer to the user's interaction with a set of tabs — for example, "Click the **Settings** tab, and then select the settings you want to use."

ToolTip Controls

A ToolTip control provides the basic functionality of a ToolTip. A *ToolTip* is a small context window that includes descriptive text displayed when the user moves the pointer over a control, as shown in Figure 8.41.

For more information about ToolTips, see Chapter 13, "User Assistance." For more information about the use of ToolTips in toolbars, see "Toolbars and Status Bars" later in this chapter.

Figure 8.41 A ToolTip control

Interaction

The ToolTip appears after a short time-out and is automatically removed when the user clicks the control or moves the pointer off the control. The system displays a ToolTip control at the lower right of the pointer, but automatically adjusts the ToolTip to avoid displaying it off-screen. However for text boxes, the ToolTip should appear centered under the control it identifies. The control provides an option to support this behavior.

Label Appearance

When used to provide descriptions of toolbar buttons, keep ToolTip text brief, usually one or two words that correspond to the label of the button's action — for example, Insert Object. Use book-title capitalization and no ending punctuation. If you include the shortcut key assigned to the button's function, place the shortcut key text in parentheses.

You can also use ToolTips to provide descriptive or status information about other elements in your interface. For example, you can use ToolTips to provide information about menu commands, the scroll bar position, or a progress indicator in a window. In this situation, use a short phrase that briefly describes the item or status, and use sentence-style capitalization.

Balloon Tips

The ToolTip control also supports a *balloon tip* style. This style presents information in a word balloon and includes support for an icon, a title, and body text, as shown in Figure 8.42. The icon can be one of three message images: information, warning, or critical. (There is no support for defining custom icons.)

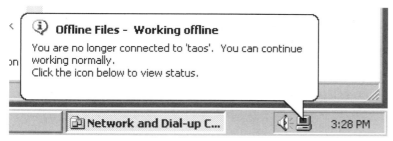

Figure 8.42 A taskbar notification balloon tip

You can use balloon tips for items in the taskbar status notification area. Here, the balloon tip can be used to notify the user of unexpected system behavior, such as the computer going offline. Although a tip can be posted at any time, only one, the last posted, will be visible at any time. Therefore, do not rely on tips to display critical information.

Interaction

Balloon tips appear adjacent to the item to which they apply. Generally, they appear above or to the left of the item; however, the system automatically adjusts their position to remain on-screen. Always point the tip of the balloon to the item it references.

The taskbar notification balloon tip supports a time-out for the length of time you specify. The default time is fixed, but you can set a value that cannot be greater than the tip maximum value or less than the system's minimum value.

You can define a balloon tip with either a notification or a reminder behavior. The notification balloon is displayed and then times out. Use this tip style to notify the user about state changes. The reminder balloon appears at regular intervals. The default interval is 60 minutes. Use the reminder balloon only for state changes that the user might not usually notice.

You can also use a balloon tip for other elements of your interface, although the reminder style is not supported. However, balloon tips are not intended to replace standard ToolTips for items that provide feedback when the user moves the pointer over them. Instead, use a balloon tip for non-critical information, special conditions, or status information that would otherwise require a message box, as shown in Figure 8.43.

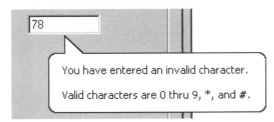

Figure 8.43 Balloon tips in a dialog box

Unlike a message box, a balloon tip does not take focus away from the active element in a window. For example, if the user types an invalid character into a text field, you could display a balloon tip with this information. However, be careful not to overuse balloon tips, as this can decrease their effectiveness.

As with balloon tips used for taskbar notification items, you can set
the length of the time-out for displaying the balloon tip. The tip is
also automatically removed when the user clicks it or clicks
elsewhere. Just like the taskbar notification balloon tip, you define
an icon, a title, and body text for the tip.

ToolTips and balloon tips are mutually exclusive. If a ToolTip is
currently displayed and you attempt to display a balloon tip, the
balloon tip will automatically cause the ToolTip to be removed.
Further, while a balloon tip is displayed, ToolTips will not appear
until the balloon tip is dismissed.

Text Appearance

The notification balloon tip has a text length limit of 100 characters,
including title and body text. Title text automatically appears as bold
text. Body text uses the text style and size of standard ToolTips.

Balloon tip text includes a title and body text. For the title text, if the
balloon tip refers to an icon or other image representing a specific
object, include the object's name using its normal capitalization and
its status using sentence-style capitalization without ending
punctuation. Otherwise, just display the status text.

The body text should include a statement of the problem in one or
two brief sentences, followed by a brief suggestion for correcting
the problem. Use sentence-style capitalization and appropriate
punctuation.

WebBrowser Control

The *WebBrowser control*, shown in Figure 8.44, enables you to add browsing, document viewing, and data downloading capabilities to your applications. You can use this control to allow the user to browse sites on the World Wide Web, as well as folders in the local file system and on a network.

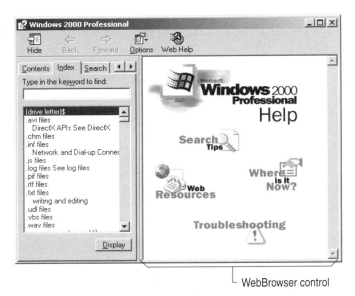

WebBrowser control

Figure 8.44 Example of the WebBrowser control

The WebBrowser control supports Web browsing through both point-and-click hyperlinking and Uniform Resource Locator (URL) navigation. The control maintains a history list that allows the user to browse forward and backward through previously browsed sites, folders, and documents.

The actual parsing and rendering of the HTML documents in the WebBrowser control is handled by the Mshtml.dll component of Microsoft Internet Explorer and provides support for parsing and rendering with the Dynamic HTML (DHTML) object model, as well as for hosting Microsoft ActiveX™ Controls and scripts.

You can also use the WebBrowser control as an Active Document container to host other Active Documents. This means that richly formatted documents, such as a Microsoft Excel spreadsheet or Microsoft Word document, can be opened and edited in-place from within the WebBrowser control.

For situations where you need rich presentations that must respond to mouse actions, or other cases where scripting is easier than a full Win32 implementation, the WebBrowser control may be a good alternative to consider. It gives you greater flexibility since it can be hosted anywhere in your Windows application, and at the same time gives you all of the benefits of writing segments in DHTML. The WebBrowser control also handles scrolling automatically. As a result, it can be a better choice than creating your own custom control.

However, avoid using the WebBrowser control as a replacement for primary functions in your user interface, such as navigating between windows, displaying messages, or supporting menus. It is best used as a supplement, providing better visualization and responsiveness for data and information presented within the Windows environment.

Toolbars and Status Bars

Toolbars and status bars are special interface constructs, like menu bars, for managing sets of controls.

A *toolbar* is a panel that contains a set of controls, as shown in Figure 8.45, designed to provide quick access to specific commands or options. Specialized toolbars are sometimes called ribbons, tool boxes, and palettes.

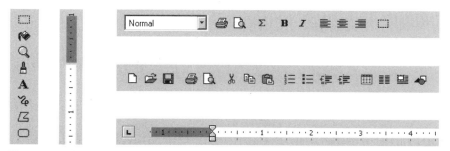

Figure 8.45 Sample toolbars

A *status bar*, shown in Figure 8.46, is a special area within a window, typically at the bottom, that displays information about the current state of what is being viewed in the window or any other contextual information, such as the keyboard state. Although a status bar can contain controls, it typically includes read-only or non-interactive information.

For more information about status bar messages, see Chapter 13, "User Assistance."

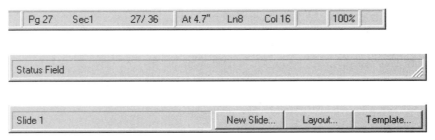

Figure 8.46 Sample status bars

Interaction with Controls in Toolbars and Status Bars

The user can access the controls included in a toolbar or status bar with the mouse. You should also provide keyboard access using either shortcut keys or access keys. If a control in a toolbar or status bar does not have a text label, access keys may not be as effective. Further, if a particular access key is already in use in the primary window, it may not be available for accessing the control in the toolbar. For example, if the menu bar of the primary window is already using a particular access key, then the menu bar receives the key event. In addition, because toolbars and status bars are typically optional display components, avoid including controls whose functionality is not available elsewhere in the interface.

When the user interacts with controls in a toolbar or status bar that represent property settings, apply any change directly to the current selection. For example, if a button in a toolbar changes the property of text to bold, clicking that button immediately changes the text to bold; no further confirmation or action is required. The only exception is if a control, such as a button, requires additional input from the user, such as the selection of an object or input from a dialog box; then the change may not be put into effect until the user provides the necessary information.

Always provide a ToolTip for controls that you include in a toolbar or status bar that do not have a text label. The system provides support for ToolTips in the standard toolbar control and a ToolTip control for use in other contexts.

You can also use a toolbar frame control to support toolbars in your application. For more information about toolbar frames, see "Toolbar Frame Control" later in this chapter.

Support for User Options

To provide maximum flexibility for users and their tasks, design your toolbars and status bars to be user-configurable. Give the user the option to display or hide toolbars and status bars. You can also include options that allow the user to change or rearrange the elements included in toolbars and status bars. Make sure your configuration options are also available from the keyboard to ensure that they are accessible for all users.

Although toolbars are typically *docked* by default — that is, aligned to the edge of a window or pane to which they apply — consider designing your toolbars to be moveable so that the user can dock them along another edge or display them as a floating palette window.

For more information about palette windows, see Chapter 9, "Secondary Windows."

To enable the user to undock the toolbar, provide a toolbar grip handle on the left end of the toolbar, an empty area at the right end of the toolbar, or both, that the user can drag to move the toolbar to its new location. If the new location is within the hot zone of an edge, your application should dock the toolbar at the new edge when the user releases the mouse button. If the new location is not within the hot zone of an edge, redisplay the toolbar in a palette window. To re-dock the window with an edge, the user drags the window by its title bar until the pointer enters the hot zone of an edge. Return the toolbar to a docked state when the user releases the mouse button.

As the user drags the toolbar, provide visual feedback, such as a dotted outline of the toolbar. When the user moves the pointer into a hot zone of a docking location, display the outline in its docked configuration to provide a cue to the user about what will happen when the drag operation is complete. You can support user options, such as resizing the toolbar by dragging its border, docking multiple toolbars side by side, and reconfiguring their arrangement and size as necessary.

When you provide support for toolbar and status bar configuration options, always preserve the current position and size, and other state information, of a toolbar or status bar configuration so that they can be restored when the user reopens the window. When you restore the configuration of a toolbar or status bar, verify that the size and position are appropriate for the current display settings.

Toolbar Control

The toolbar control supports docking and windowing functionality. It also includes a dialog box so that the user can customize the toolbar. You define whether the customization features are available to the user and what features the user can customize.

The system also supports the creation of desktop toolbars. For more information about desktop toolbars, see Chapter 11, "Integrating with the System."

Toolbar Frame Control

The common control system interface also provides support for toolbars through the *rebar control*, as shown in Figure 8.47. This control provides a special area for managing a set of toolbars, similar to the functionality supported by Microsoft Internet Explorer.

Figure 8.47 Sample toolbar frame

Each toolbar band includes a single-grip handle to enable the user to size or rearrange the toolbars. When the user moves the pointer over the grip, it changes to a two-headed arrow. When the user drags the grip, the pointer changes to a split move pointer. To resize the toolbar to its maximum or minimum size, the user clicks the grip.

The control supports including buttons, separators, and owner-drawn controls. You can define a toolbar button to support actions or set state (the button reflects the current state). You can also define a button, sometimes called a split button, to support both a default action and a menu of other related actions. For example, the Internet Explorer **Back** toolbar button both supports the **Back** command and provides a menu of the recent pages to which the user can return.

The control also includes the option to display buttons hidden by a resized toolbar, as shown in Figure 8.48. The toolbar includes a double-chevron button that the user clicks to display the hidden buttons in a shortcut menu.

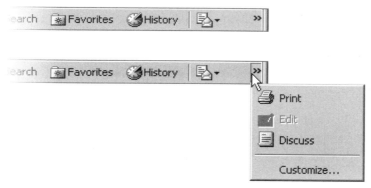

Figure 8.48 The shortcut menu for hidden toolbar items

As the user moves the pointer over the buttons, the control automatically tracks the movement, displaying a 3-D effect around the button's border. If you also include 4-bit monochrome versions of your images, the control supports tracking from monochrome to color as the pointer moves over the button. This makes the toolbar button images less distracting when the user is not interacting with the toolbar.

For more information about designing toolbar button images, see Chapter 14, "Visual Design."

You can also use a toolbar frame control to replace a menu bar. This enables you to provide your users with more flexibility to customize the interface. However, if you use a toolbar frame for menus, make sure you also support the standard keyboard interface for conventional menu bars.

Toolbar Buttons

The toolbar control includes support for buttons. You can make a toolbar button perform specific actions or reflect a state, mode, or property value similar to that of option buttons or check boxes.

The typical interaction for a toolbar button is to return to its normal "up" state, but if you use the button to represent a state, display it in the option-set appearance. When the user clicks a button that represents a tool mode — for example, in drawing or forms-design programs for drawing specific shapes or controls — display the button using the option-set appearance and change the pointer to indicate the change in the mode of interaction.

For more information about designing toolbar buttons, see Chapter 14, "Visual Design."

Provide toolbar buttons in at least two different sizes: 22 x 21 pixels and 28 x 26 pixels. This includes the border. Toolbar buttons should include a graphic image. Provide images in two sizes: 16 x 16 pixels, 16- and 256-colors; and 20 x 20 pixels, 256 colors. For larger buttons on very high-resolution displays, you can proportionally size the button to be the same height as a text box control. This allows the button to maintain its proportion with respect to other controls in the toolbar. You can stretch the image when the button is an even multiple of the basic sizes. Alternatively, you can supply additional image sizes. This may be preferable because it provides better visual results.

For more information about toolbar button image design, see Chapter 14, "Visual Design."

Toolbar buttons can also include text. The text label can appear below or to the right of the button's image. In general, set the text label to appear below the image. However, if you always display a text label for the button, you should display the label to the right of the image. For example, you might use this convention to distinguish between multiple buttons that have the same image — for example, buttons that provide access to particular Web pages or document files that use the same image.

Use book title capitalization for toolbar button text, and follow the conventions for menu and command button text. Keep the text brief, using one or two words.

Set your toolbar default presentation to display the 16 x 16 pixels color images without labels, except for those buttons that should always have labels. A user can always see the label by moving over the button and reading its ToolTip. However, you should also offer users the option of reconfiguring how the toolbar appears, including an option that displays labels for all the buttons. Always restore the user's button size preference.

Status Bar Control

The standard status bar control supports the standard display function of a status bar. It also includes an optional size grip control for sizing the window, described in Chapter 7, "Windows." When the status bar size grip is displayed, if the window displays a size grip at the junction of the horizontal and vertical scroll bars of a window, you should hide that grip so that it does not appear in both locations at the same time. Similarly, if the user hides the status bar, restore the size grip at the corner of the scroll bars.

Secondary Windows

Most primary windows require a set of secondary windows to support and supplement a user's activities in the primary windows. Secondary windows are similar to primary windows but differ in some fundamental aspects. This chapter covers the common uses of secondary windows, such as property sheets, dialog boxes, palette windows, and message boxes.

Characteristics of Secondary Windows

Although secondary windows share many characteristics with primary windows, they also differ from primary windows in behavior and use. For example, a secondary window should typically not appear as an entry on the taskbar. Secondary windows obtain or display supplemental information that is often related to the objects that appear in a primary window.

Appearance and Behavior

A typical secondary window includes a title bar and a frame; a user can move it by dragging its title bar or by clicking the **Move** command on its shortcut menu. However, a secondary window typically does not include **Maximize** and **Minimize** buttons because these sizing operations rarely apply to a secondary window. You can include a **Close** button to dismiss the window.

The title text is a label that describes the purpose of the window; the content of the label depends on the use of the window. The title bar does not include icons.

A typical secondary window is shown in Figure 9.1.

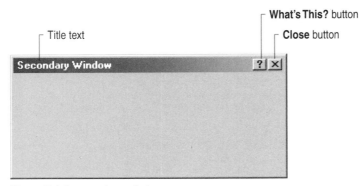

Figure 9.1 A secondary window

You can include status information in secondary windows, but avoid including a status bar control used in primary windows.

Like a primary window, a secondary window includes a shortcut menu with commands that apply to the window. A user can access the shortcut menu the same way as for primary windows, by clicking the title bar with the secondary mouse button.

A secondary window can also include a **What's This?** button in its title bar. This button allows a user to display context-sensitive Help for controls displayed in the window.

Size

A secondary window is typically smaller than its associated primary window and smaller than the minimum display resolution. As a general rule, avoid displaying any secondary window larger than 263 dialog units x 263 dialog units. A *dialog unit* (DLU) is the device-independent measure to use for layout based on the current system font. For example, the recommended sizes for property sheets are as follows:

- 252 DLUs wide x 218 DLUs high

- 227 DLUs wide x 215 DLUs high

- 212 DLUs wide x 188 DLUs high

These sizes keep the window from becoming too large to display at most resolutions. However, they still provide reasonable space to display supportive information, such as Help windows, that apply to the property sheet.

For more information about dialog units, see Chapter 14, "Visual Design."

Layout

Because secondary windows often provide a large part of the user's interaction with your application, spend a significant amount of time on the design and layout of the controls you place in the windows. Consistency and aesthetics contribute to readability and comprehension of operations and tasks. This, in turn, has an impact on the overall usability of your application. In addition to the information in this chapter, you can find information about layout for controls in Chapter 8, "Menus, Controls, and Toolbars," and an overview of layout design in Chapter 14, "Visual Design."

Modeless vs. Modal

A secondary window can be modeless or modal. A *modeless* secondary window allows the user to interact with either the secondary window or the primary window, just as the user can switch between primary windows. It is also well suited to situations where the user wants to repeat an action — for example, finding the occurrence of a word or formatting the properties of text.

A *modal* secondary window requires the user to complete interaction within the secondary window and close it before continuing with any further interaction outside the window. A secondary window can be modal in respect to its primary window.

Because modal secondary windows restrict the user's choice, limit their use to situations when additional information is required to complete a command or when it is important to prevent any further interaction until satisfying a condition.

Interaction with Other Windows

A dependent secondary window is the most common type of secondary window. This kind of secondary window can be displayed only from a command on the interface of its primary window. In general, you should close dependent secondary windows when the primary window closes, and hide them when their primary window is hidden or minimized.

Independent secondary windows are secondary windows that the user can open without opening a primary window — for example, a property sheet displayed when the user clicks the **Properties** command on the menu of a desktop icon. An independent secondary window can typically be closed without regard to the state of any primary window unless there is an obvious relationship to the primary window.

When the user opens or switches from a secondary window, it is activated or deactivated like any other window. For mouse control, activate a secondary window the same way as a primary window. For keyboard control, use the ALT+F6 key combination to support the user switching between a secondary modeless window and its primary window, or between other peer secondary modeless windows related to its primary window. In addition, if you define a shortcut key to open the secondary window, use this key to activate the secondary window when it is already open. If a secondary window appears independently of its parent window, as is the case for property sheets for desktop icons, you can also provide more general access to the secondary window by supporting ALT+TAB for switching to the window.

When the user activates a primary window, bringing it to the top of the window Z order, you should also bring all of its dependent secondary windows to the top, maintaining their same respective Z orders. Similarly, activating a dependent secondary window should bring its primary window and related peer windows to the top.

When activated, a secondary window should appear at the top of the Z order of its peers. When a peer is activated, the previous topmost secondary window appears on top of its primary window but behind the newly activated secondary window. You should always display a dependent secondary window higher in the Z order than its primary window.

You can design a secondary window to appear always at the top, or topmost, of its peer secondary windows. Typically, you should use this technique only for palette windows and, even in this situation, enable users to configure this feature by providing an Always on Top property setting for the window. If you support this technique for more than one secondary window, then the windows should be managed in their own Z order within the collection of topmost windows of which they are a part.

Avoid having a secondary window with the always topmost behavior appear on top of another application's primary window (or any of the other application's dependent secondary windows) when the user activates a window of that application, unless that topmost window can also be applied to the application's windows.

When the user clicks a command that opens a secondary window, use the context of the operation to determine how to present information in that window. In property sheets, for example, set the values of the properties in that window to represent the selection.

In general, display a secondary window in the same state as the user last accessed it. For example, an Open dialog box should preserve the current folder setting between the openings of a window. However, always verify that the settings being restored are appropriate for the current system display settings, and adjust the window settings if necessary. Similarly, if you use tabbed pages for navigating through information in a secondary window, display the last page the user was viewing when the user closed the window. This makes it easier for the user to repeat an operation that is associated with the window and provides more stability in the interface.

However, if a command or task implies or requires that the user begin a process in a particular sequence or state, such as with a wizard window, you should present the secondary window using a fixed or consistent presentation. For example, entering a record into a database may require the user to enter the data in a particular sequence. Therefore, it may be more appropriate to present the input window always displaying the first entry field.

Resizing and Unfolding Secondary Windows

A secondary window's purpose is to provide concise, predefined information. Avoid defining a secondary window to be resizable unless it provides some benefit to the user, such as reconfiguring the arrangement or showing more information. If you support a resizable secondary window, make sure you appropriately adjust the presentation of all its elements.

You can also use an unfold button to expand a window to reveal additional options as a form of progressive disclosure. An *unfold button* is a command button with a label that includes >> as part of its label, as shown in Figure 9.2.

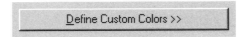

Figure 9.2 An unfold button

When the user clicks the button, the secondary window expands to its alternative size. As an option, you can use the button to "refold" the additional part of the window. This is a good alternative when the interface contains a fixed set of options or controls that seldom need to be accessed.

Cascading Secondary Windows

You can provide the user with access to additional options by including a command button that opens another secondary window. If the resulting window is independent in its operation, close the secondary window from which the user opened it and display only the new window. However, if the intent of the subsequent window is to obtain information for a field in the original secondary window, then keep the original window displayed with the dependent window on top, offset slightly to the right and below the original secondary window. However, limit the number of cascading levels to a single sublevel to avoid creating a cluttered chain of hierarchical windows.

Window Placement

When determining where to place a secondary window, consider a number of factors, including the use of the window, the overall display dimensions, and the reason for the appearance of the window. The first time you open the window, display it in a location that is convenient for the user to navigate to and that fully displays the window. In a multiple-monitor configuration, display the secondary window on the same monitor as its primary window. If neither of these guidelines apply, horizontally center the secondary window within the primary window, just below the title bar, menu bar, and any docked toolbars. If the user then moves the window, display it at this location the next time the user opens the window, adjusted as necessary to the current display configuration.

Default Buttons

When defining a secondary window, you can assign the ENTER key to activate a particular command button, called the *default button*, in the window. The system distinguishes the default button from other command buttons by adding a bold outline around it.

Define the default button to be the most likely action, such as a confirmation action or an action that applies transactions made in the secondary window. Avoid making a command button the default button if its action is irreversible or destructive. For example, in a text search and substitution window, do not use a **Replace All** button as the default button for the window.

You can change the default button as the user interacts with the window. For example, if the user navigates to a command button that is not the default button, the new button temporarily becomes the default. In such a case, the new default button takes on the default appearance and the former default button loses the default appearance. Similarly, if the user moves the input focus to another control within the window that is not a command button, the original default button resumes the default appearance.

Defining one of your command buttons as a default button is a common convention. However, when there is no appropriate button to designate as the default button or you need to apply the ENTER key to another function (for example, entering new lines in a multi-line text control), you do not need to define a default button for the window. In addition, when a particular control has the input focus and requires use of the ENTER key, you can temporarily have no button defined as the default. Then when the user moves the input focus out of the control, you can restore the default button.

Optionally, you can use double-clicking a single-selection control, such as an option button or single-selection list, as a shortcut technique to set or select the option and carry out the action of the default button of the secondary window.

Navigation in Secondary Windows

With the mouse, navigating to a particular field or control is accomplished by the user pointing to the field and clicking it. For button controls, this action also activates that button. For example, for check boxes, it toggles the check box setting; for command buttons, it carries out the command associated with that button.

The keyboard interface for navigation in secondary windows uses the TAB and SHIFT+TAB keys to move between the next and previous controls, respectively. Each control has a property that determines its place in the navigation order. Set this property such that the user can move through the secondary window following the usual conventions for reading: in western countries, left-to-right and top-to-bottom, with the primary control the user interacts with located in the upper left area of the window.

You can use static text fields to provide access to controls that do not have labels. However, when the user navigates to that label, move the input focus to the associated control. Order controls such that the user can progress through the window in a logical sequence, proceeding through groups of related controls. Command buttons for handling overall window transactions are usually at the end of the order sequence.

You do not need to provide TAB key access to every control in the window. For example, because option buttons typically appear as a group, use the TAB key for moving the input focus to the current set choice in that group, but not between individual options — use arrow keys for this purpose. However, for a group of check boxes, provide TAB navigation to each control because their settings are independent of each other. Combination controls such as combo boxes, drop-down combo boxes, and spin boxes are considered single controls for navigational purposes.

Optionally, you can use arrow keys to support keyboard navigation between controls in addition to the TAB navigation technique wherever the interface does not require those keys. For example, you can use the UP ARROW and DOWN ARROW keys to navigate between single-line text boxes or within a group of check boxes or command buttons. Always use arrow keys to navigate between option button choices and within list box controls.

Also define access keys to provide navigation to controls within a secondary window. This allows the user to access a control by pressing and holding the ALT key and an alphanumeric key that matches the access key character designated in the label of the control.

For more information about guidelines for selecting access keys, see Chapter 5, "Input Basics."

Unmodified alphanumeric keys also support navigation if the control that currently has the input focus does not use these keys for input. For example, if the input focus is currently on a check box control and the user presses a key, the input focus moves to the control with the matching access character. However, if the input focus is in a control where an alphanumeric key is used as text input, such as a text box or list box, the user will not be able to use it for navigation within the window without using it in combination with the ALT key.

Access keys not only allow the user to navigate to the matching control, they have the same effect as clicking the control with the mouse. For example, pressing the access key for a command button carries out the action associated with that button. To ensure the user efficient access to all controls, select unique access keys within a secondary window. If two or more controls share the same access key, pressing that key moves the input focus to the next matching control but does not activate it.

You can also use access keys to support navigation to a control, but then return the input focus to the control from which the user navigated. For example, when the user presses the access key for a specific command button that modifies the content of a list box, you can return the input focus to the list box after the command has been carried out.

Avoid assigning access keys to **OK** and **Cancel** command buttons because the ENTER and ESC keys, respectively, should typically provide access to these buttons. Pressing ENTER should always navigate to the default command button, if one exists, and invokes the action associated with that button. If there is no current default command button, then the ENTER key can be used for a control.

Hyperlinks in Secondary Windows

In some situations you may want to include a hyperlink to a Web page in your secondary window. This works best when you use the link to display supplemental or related information about the topics described in the secondary window. Do not use hyperlinks to replace the standard **OK** and **Cancel** buttons or other actions.

You can create hyperlinks in a secondary window by using a text box control without its visible border or by using the WebBrowser control. However you implement hyperlinks, always use display and interaction conventions consistent with the system conventions. For example, display the text for the link using the system's settings for link colors, and display the hand pointer when the user moves the pointer over the link.

When you include a hyperlink in your secondary window, always express what will happen when the link is clicked, or why the user would want to click it. In some cases, connecting to the Web can be expensive, time consuming, or not currently available. Make sure that users have as much information as possible so they can decide whether or not the link is worth clicking. Avoid using the phrase "click here," which takes up valuable room on the screen. Most users understand the concept of links.

For more information about designing hyperlinks, see Chapter 10, "Window Management."

Correct	Incorrect
Register your product online	Click here to register your product
Online Support	For product support, click here

Validation of Input

Validate the user's input for a field or control in a secondary window as closely to the point of input as possible. Ideally, validate the user's input when the user types in text or chooses an option. You can either disallow the input or use audio and visual feedback, such as balloon tips, to alert the user that the data is not appropriate. You can also display a message box, particularly if the user repeatedly tries to enter invalid input. In either case, make sure you provide enough information to help the user enter appropriate data. In any case, avoid requiring that the user enter valid data before navigating away from a control.

You can also reduce invalid feedback by using controls that limit selection to a specific set of choices — for example, check boxes, option buttons, or drop-down lists — or preset the field with a reasonable default value.

If it is not possible to validate input at the point of entry, consider validating the input when the user navigates away from the control. If this is not feasible, then validate it when the transaction is committed or whenever the user attempts to close the window. At that time, leave the window open and display a message; after the user dismisses the message, set the input focus to the control with the inappropriate data.

Property Sheets and Inspectors

You can display the properties of an object in the interface in a number of ways. For example, some folder views display certain file system properties of an object. The image and name of an icon on the desktop also reflect specific properties of that object. You can also use other interface conventions, such as toolbars, status bars, or even scroll bars, to reflect certain properties. Secondary windows provide another technique for displaying properties. There are two basic designs for this purpose: property sheets and property inspectors.

Property Sheet Interface

The most common presentation of an object's properties is a secondary window called a property sheet. A *property sheet* is a modeless secondary window that displays the user-accessible properties of an object — that is, properties that the user can view but not necessarily edit. Display a property sheet when the user clicks the **Properties** command for an object or when the input focus is on the object and the user presses ALT+ENTER.

Title Bar Text

The title bar text of the property sheet identifies the displayed object. Use book title capitalization. If the object has a name, use its name and the word "Properties." If the combination of the name plus "Properties" exceeds the width of the title bar, the system truncates the name and adds an ellipsis. If the object has no name, use the object's type name.

If the property sheet represents several objects, then also use the objects' type name. Where the type name cannot be applied — for example, because the selection includes heterogeneous types — substitute the word "Selection" for the type name.

Property Pages

Because there can be numerous properties for an object and its context, you may need to categorize and group properties as sets within the property window. There are two techniques for supporting navigation to groups of properties in a property sheet. The first is a tabbed *property page*. Each set of properties is presented within the window as a page with a tab labeled with the name of the set. Use tabbed property pages for grouping peer-related property sets, as shown in Figure 9.3.

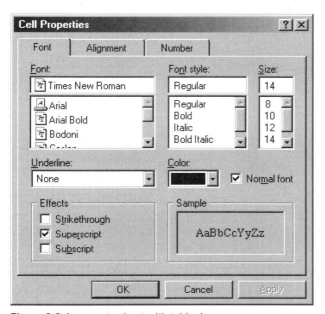

Figure 9.3 A property sheet with tabbed pages

When displaying the property sheet of an object, you can also provide access to the properties of the object's immediate context or hierarchically related properties in the property sheet. For example, if the user selects text, you may want to provide access to the properties of the paragraph of that text in the same property sheet. Similarly, if the user selects a cell in a spreadsheet, you may want to provide access to its related row and column properties in the same property sheet. Although you can support this with additional tabbed pages, better access may be facilitated using another control — such as a drop-down list — to switch between groups of tabbed pages, as shown in Figure 9.4. This technique can also be used instead of multiple rows of tabs. Multiple rows of tabs can create usability problems for users, so don't use this convention.

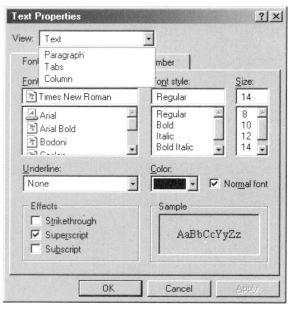

Figure 9.4 A drop-down list for access to hierarchical property sets

Where possible, make the values for properties found in property sheets transferable. For example, you may want to support **Copy** and **Paste** or dragging for text in text boxes or items in a list box.

For more information about transfer operations, see Chapter 6, "General Interaction Techniques."

Property Sheet Commands

Property sheets typically allow the user to change the values for a property and then apply those transactions. Include the following common command buttons for handling the application of property changes.

Common Command Buttons

Command	Action
OK	Applies all pending changes and closes the property sheet window.
Apply	Applies all pending changes but leaves the property sheet window open.
Cancel	Discards any pending changes and closes the property sheet window. Does not cancel or undo changes that have already been applied.

You can optionally support a **Reset** command to cancel pending changes without closing the window.

You can also include other command buttons in property sheets. However, the location of command buttons within the property sheet window is very important. If you place a button on a property page, it implies that the action associated with the button applies only to that page. For command buttons placed outside the page but still inside the window, apply the command to the entire window.

For the common property sheet transaction buttons — **OK**, **Cancel**, and **Apply** — it is best to place the buttons outside the pages because users consider the pages to be just a simple grouping or navigation technique. This means that if the user makes a change on one page, the change is not applied when the user switches pages. However, if the user makes a change on the new page and then clicks the **OK** or **Apply** command buttons, changes on both pages are applied — or, in the case of **Cancel**, discarded.

Avoid including a **Help** command button. If your property sheet needs a **Help** button, this may indicate that you need to simplify the interface. Consider redesigning the layout, the text, or the flow of commands. However, do include support for context-sensitive Help for each control in a property sheet.

For more information about designing Help for your application, see Chapter 13, "User Assistance."

If your design requires groups of properties to be applied on a page-by-page basis, then place **OK**, **Cancel**, and **Apply** command buttons on the property pages, always in the same location on each page. When the user switches pages, any property value changes for that page are applied, or you can prompt the user by displaying a message box that asks whether to apply or discard the changes.

You can include a sample in a property sheet window to illustrate a property value change that affects the object when the user applies the property sheet. Where possible, include the aspect of the object that will be affected in the sample. For example, if the user selects text and displays the property sheet for the text, include part of the text selection in the property sheet's sample. If displaying the actual object — or a portion of it — in the sample is not practical, use an illustration that represents the object's type.

Closing a Property Sheet

If the user closes a property sheet window, follow the same convention as for closing the content view of an object, such as a document. Avoid interpreting the **Close** button as **Cancel**. If there are pending changes that have not been committed, consider prompting the user to apply or discard the changes by displaying a message box, as shown in Figure 9.5. If there are no unsaved changes, just close the window.

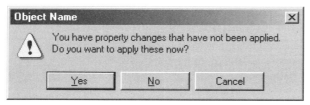

Figure 9.5 Prompting for pending property changes

If the user clicks the **Yes** button, the properties are applied and the message box window and the property sheet window are closed. If the user clicks the **No** button, the pending changes are discarded and the message box and property sheet windows are closed. To allow the user to cancel closing the property sheet window, include a **Cancel** button in the message box.

Property Inspectors

You can also display the properties of an object by using a dynamic viewer or browser that reflects the properties of the current selection. Such a property window is called a *property inspector*. A property inspector is different from a property sheet. Even when a property sheet window is modeless, the window is typically modal with respect to the object for which it displays properties. If the user selects another object, the property sheet continues to display the properties of the original object. A property inspector always reflects the current selection.

You typically use a palette window (described later in this chapter) or toolbar to create a property inspector, as shown in Figure 9.6. An even better alternative is to use a palette window that the user can also configure as a docked toolbar.

For more information about supporting docked and windowed toolbars, see Chapter 8, "Menus, Controls, and Toolbars." For more information about palette windows, see "Palette Windows" later in this chapter.

Figure 9.6 A property inspector

You may also want to include a control in a property inspector that enables the user to display the properties of another object in the primary window. For example, as the first control in the property inspector, you can include a drop-down list box that displays the name of the object being viewed. To view another object's properties within the inspector, the user selects that object in the drop-down list box.

Title Bar Text

For the title text of the window, use the same conventions that you use for a property sheet.

Property Inspector Interaction

Apply property transactions that the user makes in a property inspector dynamically. That is, change the property value in the selected object as soon as the user makes the change in the control reflecting that property value.

Other Alternatives

Property inspectors and property sheets are not exclusive interfaces; you can include both. Each has its advantages. You can choose to display only the most common or frequently accessed properties in a property inspector and the complete set in the property sheet. You also can include multiple property inspectors, each optimized for managing certain types of objects.

As an option, you also can provide an interface for the user to change the behavior between a property sheet and a property inspector form of interaction. For example, you can provide a control on a property inspector that "locks" its view to be modal to the current object rather than tracking the selection.

Properties of a Multiple Selection

When a user selects multiple objects and requests the properties for the selection, reflect the properties of all the objects in a single property sheet or property inspector rather than opening multiple windows. Where the property values differ, display the controls associated with those values using the mixed value appearance — sometimes referred to as the indeterminate state. However, when the user individually selects objects and requests their properties, you can display separate property sheet windows for each object.

> For more information about displaying controls using the mixed value appearance, see Chapter 14, "Visual Design."

If your design still requires access to individual properties when the user displays the property sheet of a multiple selection, consider including a control such as a list box or drop-down list in the property window for switching between the properties of the objects in the set.

Properties of a Heterogeneous Selection

When a multiple selection includes different types of objects, include the intersection of the properties between the objects in the resulting property sheet. If the container of those selected objects treats the objects as if they were of a single type, the property sheet includes properties for that type only. For example, if the user selects text and an embedded object, such as a circle, and in that context an embedded object is treated as an element within the text stream, present only the text properties in the resulting property sheet.

Properties of Grouped Items

When displaying properties, do not equate a multiple selection with a grouped set of objects. A group is a stronger relationship than a simple selection, because the aggregate resulting from the grouping can itself be considered an object, potentially with its own properties and operations. Therefore, if the user requests the properties of a grouped set of items, display the properties of the group or composite object. The properties of its individual members may or may not be included, depending on what is most appropriate.

Dialog Boxes

A *dialog box* provides an exchange of information or dialog between the user and the application. Use a dialog box to obtain additional information from the user that is needed to carry out a particular command or task.

Title Bar Text

Because dialog boxes generally appear after the user clicks a particular menu item (including shortcut menu or cascading menu items) or a command button, define the title text for the dialog box window to be the name of the associated command. Use book title capitalization.

Do not explicitly include an ellipsis in the title text, even if the command menu name includes one. The exception is for title bar text that exceeds the current width of the window. Also, avoid including the command's menu title unless it is necessary to compose a reasonable title for the dialog box. For example, for a **Print...** command on the **File** menu, define the dialog box window's title text as Print, not Print... or File Print. However, for an **Object...** command on an **Insert** menu, you can title the dialog box Insert Object.

Dialog Box Commands

Like property sheets, dialog boxes commonly include **OK** and **Cancel** command buttons. If the user clicks **OK**, apply the values in the dialog box and close the window. If the user clicks **Cancel**, ignore the changes and close the window, canceling the user's chosen operation. **OK** and **Cancel** buttons work best for dialog boxes that allow the user to set the parameters for a particular command. Typically, define **OK** to be the default command button when the dialog box window opens.

You can include other command buttons in a dialog box in addition to or instead of the **OK** and **Cancel** buttons. Label your command buttons to clearly define the button's purpose, but be as concise as possible. Long, wordy labels make it difficult for the user to easily scan and interpret a dialog box's purpose. Follow the design conventions for command buttons.

For more information about command buttons, see Chapter 8, "Menus, Controls, and Toolbars."

Layout

Orient controls in dialog boxes in the direction people read. In countries where roman alphabets are used, this means left-to-right, top-to-bottom. Locate the primary field with which the user interacts as close to the upper left corner as possible. Follow similar guidelines for orienting controls within a group in the dialog box.

For more information about layout of controls in a dialog box, see Chapter 14, "Visual Design."

Lay out the major command buttons either stacked along the upper right border of the dialog box or lined up across the bottom of the dialog box. Position the most important button — typically the default command — as the first button in the set. If you use the **OK** and **Cancel** buttons, group them together. You can use other arrangements if there is a compelling reason, such as a natural mapping relationship. For example, it may make sense to place buttons labeled **North**, **South**, **East**, and **West** in a compass-like layout. Similarly, a command button that modifies or provides direct support for another control may be grouped or placed next to those controls. However, avoid making that button the default button because the user will expect the default button to be in the conventional location.

Common Dialog Box Interfaces

The system provides pre-built interfaces for many common operations. Use these interfaces where appropriate. They can save you time while providing a high degree of consistency. If specific functionality is missing, you can extend the common dialog boxes to include additional controls. When you do, append the new functionality in the toolbars or on the right side or bottom of the common dialog box.

The common dialog box interfaces have been revised from the ones provided in previous releases of Microsoft Windows.

If you customize or provide your own interfaces, maintain consistency with the basic functionality supported in these interfaces and the guidelines for their use. For example, if you provide your own property sheet for font properties, model your design to be similar in appearance and design to the common Font dialog box. Consistent visual and operational styles will allow users to transfer their knowledge and skills more easily.

Open Dialog Box

The Open dialog box, as shown in Figure 9.7, allows the user to browse the file system, including direct browsing of the network, and includes controls to open a specified file. Use this dialog box for commands that open files or browse for a file name, such as the **File Open** menu command or a **Browse** command button. Always set the title text to correctly reflect the command that displays the dialog box.

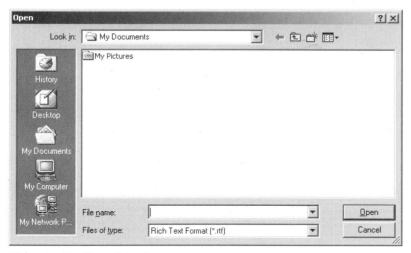

Figure 9.7 The Open dialog box

The system-supplied dialog box automatically handles the display of long file names, direct manipulation transfers — such as drag-and-drop operations — and access to an icon's shortcut menus. The dialog box displays file name extensions only for files of registered types when the user selects this viewing option.

To open a file, the user selects a file from the list in the dialog box or types a name in the **File name** field and then clicks the **Open** command. The user can also display the shortcut menu for the file and click its **Open** command. As a shortcut, double-clicking also opens the file. Clicking the **Cancel** button closes the window without opening the file.

When the user opens a shortcut icon, the dialog box opens the file of the object to which the link refers. In other words, the effect is the same as if the user directly opened the original file. Therefore, the name of the original file — not the name of the file link — should appear in the primary window's title bar.

The files listed in the dialog box reflect the current directory path and the type filter set in the **Files of type** drop-down list box. The list of files also includes shortcut icons in the current directory; these shortcut icons refer to file types that match the type filter.

The **Look in** drop-down list box displays the current directory. Displaying the list allows the user to view the hierarchy of the directory path and to navigate up the path tree. Tool buttons adjacent to the drop-down list box provide the user with easy access to common functions. The dialog box also includes a list of shortcuts to the key places that a user can navigate, such as History, Desktop, and My Documents.

Set the default directory based on context. If the user opened the file directly, either from its location from the file system or using the Open dialog box, set the directory path to that location. If the user opened the application directly, then set the path either directly to the My Documents folder or to a subfolder your application created in the My Documents folder. For example, an application may set up a default directory for its user-generated data files.

The user can change the directory path in a variety of ways:

- Select a different item in the **Look in** list.

- Select a file system container (such as a folder) in the list of files.

- Click an icon in the common places list.

- Enter a valid path in the **File name** field and then click the **Open** button.

Clicking the **Cancel** button should not change the path. Always preserve the latest directory path between subsequent openings of the dialog box. If the application supports opening multiple files, set the directory path to the last file opened, not to the currently active child window. However, for multiple instances of an application, maintain the path separately for each instance.

The **File name** text box supports HTTP addresses (URLs) and FTP path names. It also supports a history list of the most recently entered file names.

The dialog box also includes an optional thumbnail view for a variety of common file types. To support thumbnail views for your own file type, implement a thumbnail extractor. For more information, see the Microsoft Platform SDK on the MSDN Online Web site at http://msdn.microsoft.com/ui/guide/sdk.asp.

Your application determines the default **Files of type** filter for the Open dialog box. This can be based on the last file opened, the last file type set by the user, or always a specific type, based on what most appropriately fits the context of the application.

The user can change the type filter by selecting a different type in the **Files of type** drop-down list box or by typing a filter into the **File name** text box and clicking the **Open** button. Filters can include file name extensions. For example, if the user types *.txt* and then clicks the **Open** button, the list displays only files that have the .txt extension. Typing an extension into this text box also changes the file type setting for the **Files of type** drop-down list box. If the application does not support that file type, display the **Files of type** control with the mixed-case (indeterminate) appearance.

Include the types of files your application supports in the **Files of type** drop-down list box. For each item in the list, use a type description preferably based on the registered type names for the file types. For example, for text files, the type descriptor should be "Text Documents." You can also include an "All Files" entry to display all files in the current directory, regardless of type.

When the user types a file name into the Open dialog box and then clicks the **Open** button, the following conventions apply to the file name string:

- The string includes no extension. The system attempts to use your application's default extension or the current setting in the **Files of type** drop-down list box. For example, if the user types *Sample Document*, and the application's default extension is .doc, then the system attempts to open Sample Document.doc. (The extension is not displayed.) If the user changes the type setting to Text Documents (*.txt), the file specification is interpreted as Sample Document.txt. If using the application's default type or the type setting fails to find a matching file, the system attempts to open a file with the same name (regardless of extension) that appears in the list of files. If more than one file matches, the first one will be selected and the system displays a message box indicating that multiple files match.

- The string includes an extension. The system first checks to see whether it matches the application's default type, any other registered types, or any extension in the **Files of type** drop-down list box. If it does not match, the system attempts to open it using the application's default type or the current type setting in the **Files of type** drop-down list box. For example, Microsoft WordPad will open the file named A Letter to Dr. Jones provided that the file's type matches the .doc extension or the current type setting, and because the characters Jones (after the period) do not constitute a registered type. If this fails, the system follows the same behavior as for a file without an extension, checking for a match among the files that appear in the list of files.

- The string includes double quotation marks at the beginning and end. The system interprets the string exactly, without the quotation marks and without appending any extension. For example, "Sample Document" is interpreted as Sample Document.

- The system fails to find a file. When the system cannot find a file, it displays a message box indicating that the file cannot be found and advises the user to check the file name and path specified. However, you can have your application handle this condition.

- The string includes invalid characters for a file name. The system displays a message box advising the user of this condition.

The Open dialog box handles only matching a name to a file. It is your application's responsibility to ensure that the format of the file is valid, and if not, to appropriately notify the user.

Save As Dialog Box

The Save As dialog box, as shown in Figure 9.8, is designed to save a file using a particular name, location, type, and format. Typically, applications that support the creation of multiple user files provide this command. However, if your application maintains only private data files and automatically updates those files, this dialog box might not be appropriate.

Display this dialog box when the user clicks the **Save As** command or file-oriented commands with a similar function, such as the **Export File** command. Also display the Save As dialog box when the user clicks the **Save** command and has not supplied or confirmed a file name. If you use this dialog box for other tasks that require saving files, define the title text of the dialog box to appropriately reflect that command.

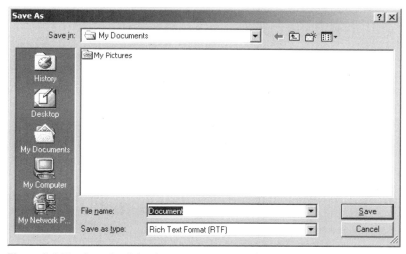

Figure 9.8 The Save As dialog box

The appearance and operation of the Save As dialog box are similar to those for the Open dialog box, except that the type field — the **Save as type** drop-down list box — defines the default type for the saved file; it also filters the list of files displayed in the window.

For more information about naming files, see Chapter 7, "Windows," and Chapter 11, "Integrating with the System."

To save a file, the user clicks the **Save** button and saves the file with the name that appears in the **File name** text box. Although the user can type a name or select a file from the list of files, your application should preset the field to the current name of the file. If the file has not yet been named, propose a name based on the registered type name for the file — for example, Text Document (2). Alternatively, you can use data from the document, such as its first sentence, the subject line, a title property, or other key data.

The **Save in** drop-down list box indicates the immediate container in the directory path (or folder). The user can change the path by using this control and the list of files box. If the file already exists, save it to its original location. This means that the current path for the Save As dialog box should always be set to the path where the file was last saved. If the file has never been saved, save the file with your application's default path setting (which should typically be in the My Documents folder) or to the location defined by the user, either by typing the path or by using the controls in the dialog box.

If the user clicks the **Cancel** button in the Save As dialog box, do not save the file or other settings. Restore the path to its original setting.

Include the file types supported by your application in the **Save as type** drop-down list box. You may need to include a format description as part of a type name description. Although a file's format can be related to its type, a format and a type are not the same thing. For example, a bitmap file can be stored in monochrome, 16-color, 256-color, or 24-color format, but the file's type is the same in all cases. Consider using the following convention for the items you include as type descriptions in the **Save as type** drop-down list box.

Type name [*format description*]

When the user supplies a name for the file, the Save As dialog box follows conventions similar to the Open dialog box. If the new file name does not include an extension, the system uses the setting in the **Save as type** drop-down list or your application's default file type. If the new file name includes an extension, the system checks to see whether the extension matches your application's default extension or a registered extension. If it does, the system saves the file as the type matching that extension. (The extension is hidden unless the system is set to display extensions.) Otherwise, the

Preserve the creation date for files that the user opens and saves. If your application saves files by creating a temporary file, deletes the original, and renames the temporary file to the original file name, be sure you copy the creation date from the original file. System file management functionality may depend on preserving the identity of the original file.

system interprets the user-supplied extension as part of the file name and appends the extension set in the **Save as type** field. Note that this means only that the type (extension) is set. The format may not be correct for that type. Your application must write out the correct format.

If the user types a file name that begins and ends with double quotation marks, the system saves the file without appending any extension. If the string includes a registered extension, the file appears as that type. If the user supplies a file name that contains invalid characters or if the specified path does not exist, the system displays a message box, unless your application handles these conditions.

Here are some examples of how the system saves user-supplied file names. These examples assume .txt as the application's default type or the **Save as type** setting.

How the System Saves Files

What the user types	How the system saves the file	Description
Sample Document	Sample Document.txt	Type is based on the **Save as type** setting or the application's default type.
Sample Document.txt	Sample Document.txt	Type must match the application's default type or a registered type.
Sample Document for Mr. Jones	Sample Document for Mr. Jones.txt	. Jones does not qualify as a registered type or as a type included in the **Save as type** drop-down list box, so the type is based on the **Save as type** setting or the application's default type.
Sample Document for Mr. Jones.txt	Sample Document for Mr. Jones.txt	Type must match a registered type or a type included in the **Save as type** drop-down list box.

How the System Saves Files *(continued)*

What the user types	How the system saves the file	Description
"Sample Document"	Sample Document	Type will be unknown. The file is saved exactly as the string appears between the quotation marks.
"Sample Document.txt"	Sample Document.txt	No type is appended. The file is saved exactly as the string appears between the quotation marks.
Sample Document.	Sample Document..txt	Type is based on the **Save as type** drop-down list box or the application's default type.
"Sample Document."	Sample Document.	Type will be unknown.
"Sample" Document	File is not saved.	System (or application) displays a message box notifying the user that the file name is invalid because quotation marks cannot be used in a file name.

Browse for Folder

This Browse for Folder dialog box, shown in Figure 9.9, enables the user to select a folder. Use it when the user needs to select only a destination, such as with a **Move To** or **Copy To** command. The dialog box includes support for enabling you to specify the default folder.

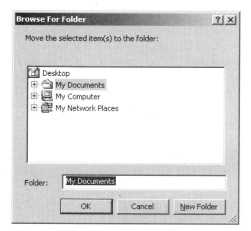

Figure 9.9 The Browse for Folder dialog box

Do not use this dialog box as an interface for general browsing, because the control does not provide access to the contents of a folder. To support creating new folders, you can include the **New Folder** button.

Find and Replace Dialog Boxes

The Find and Replace dialog boxes provide controls that search for a text string specified by the user and optionally replace it with a second text string specified by the user. These dialog boxes are shown in Figure 9.10.

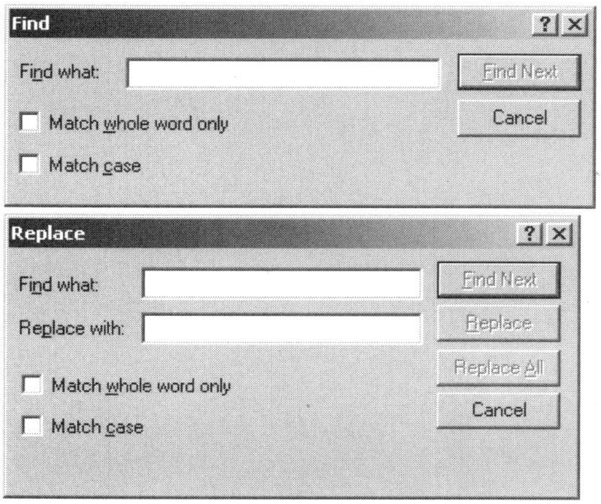

Figure 9.10 The Find and Replace dialog boxes

Print Dialog Box

The Print dialog box, shown in Figure 9.11, allows the user to select what to print, the number of copies to print, and the collation sequence for printing. It also allows the user to choose a printer and contains a command button that provides shortcut access to that printer's properties. This dialog box also includes support for adding new printers and finding other printers on the network.

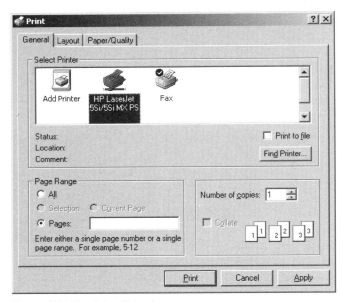

Figure 9.11 The Print dialog box

Page Setup Dialog Box

The Page Setup dialog box, as shown in Figure 9.12, provides controls for specifying properties about the page elements and layout.

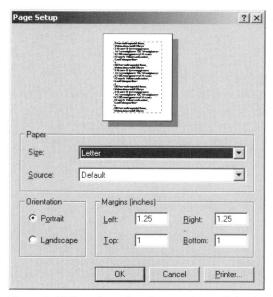

Figure 9.12 Page Setup interface used as a dialog box

In this context, page orientation refers to the orientation of the page and not the printer, which may also have these properties. Generally, the page's properties override those set by the printer, but only for printing that page or document.

The **Printer** button in the dialog box displays a supplemental dialog box, as shown in Figure 9.13, that provides information about the current default printer. Like the Print dialog box, it displays the current property settings for the default printer and a button for access to the printer's property sheet.

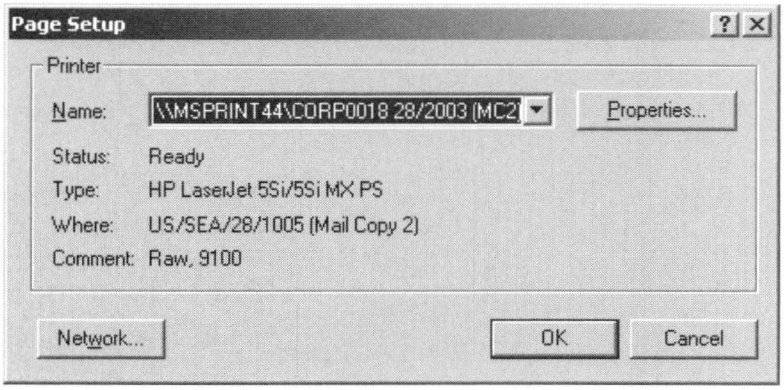

Figure 9.13 The supplemental Printer dialog box

Font Dialog Box

The Font dialog box, shown in Figure 9.14, displays the fonts and point sizes of the available fonts installed in the system. Your application can filter this list to show only the fonts applicable to your application. You can use the Font dialog box to display or set the font properties of a selection of text.

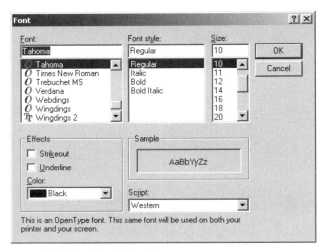

Figure 9.14 The Font dialog box

Color Dialog Box

The Color dialog box, as shown in Figure 9.15, displays the available colors and includes controls that allow the user to define custom colors. You can use this control to provide an interface for users to select colors for an object.

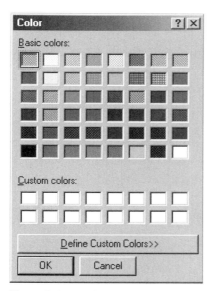

Figure 9.15 The Color dialog box (unexpanded appearance)

The **Basic colors** control displays a default set of colors. The number of colors displayed is determined by the installed display driver. The **Custom colors** control allows the user to define more colors by using the various color selection controls provided in the window.

Initially, you can display the dialog box as a smaller window with only the **Basic colors** and **Custom colors** controls. Then you can allow the user to expand the dialog box to define additional colors, as shown in Figure 9.16.

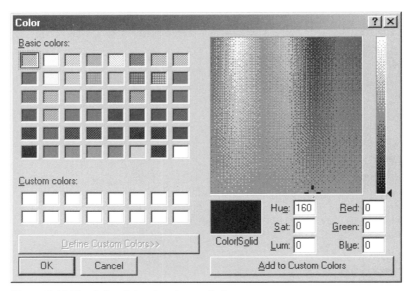

Figure 9.16 The Color dialog box (expanded)

Palette Windows

Palette windows are modeless secondary windows that present a set of controls. For example, when toolbar controls appear as a window, they appear in a palette window. Palette windows are distinguished by their visual appearance. The height of the title bar for a palette window is shorter, but it still includes only a **Close** button in the title area, as shown in Figure 9.17.

For more information about toolbars and palette windows, see Chapter 8, "Menus, Controls, and Toolbars."

Figure 9.17 A palette window

Title Bar Text

Define the title bar text for a palette using the name of the command that displays the window or the name of the toolbar it represents. The system supplies default size and font settings for the title bar and title bar text for palette windows. Use book title capitalization.

The title bar height and font size settings can be accessed by using the **SystemParametersInfo** function. For more information about this function, see the Microsoft Platform SDK on the MSDN Online Web site at http://msdn.microsoft.com/ui/guide/sdk.asp.

Window Design

You can define palette windows as a fixed size, or, more typically, sizable by the user. Two visual cues indicate when the window is sizable: changing the pointer image to the size pointer, and placing a **Size** command in the window's shortcut menu. Preserve the window's size and position so the window can be restored if it or its associated primary window is closed.

Like other windows, the title bar and the border areas provide an access point for the window's shortcut menu. Commands on a palette window's shortcut menu can include **Close**, **Move**, **Size** (if sizable), **Always on Top**, and **Properties**, as shown in Figure 9.18.

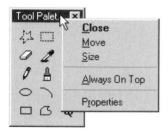

Figure 9.18 A shortcut menu for a palette window

This feature allows the user to configure preferred access to the palette window. If you include the **Always on Top** command or property in the window's property sheet, the user can configure the palette window to always stay at the top of the Z order of its window set. If the user clears this option, the palette window stays within its set of related windows, but the user can have other windows of the set appear on top of the palette window.

You can also optionally include a **Properties** command on the palette window's shortcut menu. This provides an interface for allowing the user to edit properties of the window, such as the **Always on Top** property, or a way to customize the content of the palette window.

Message Boxes

A message box is a secondary window that displays a message about a particular situation or condition. Messages are an important part of the interface for any software product. Messages that are too generic or poorly written frustrate users, increase support costs, and ultimately reflect poorly on the quality of the product. Therefore, it is worthwhile to design effective message boxes.

It is even better to avoid creating situations that require you to display such a message. For example, if the user does not have sufficient disk space to perform an operation, you can check for available disk space before the user attempts the operation and disable the command if necessary. You can use a balloon tip or status bar message to notify the user about why the command is unavailable.

Title Bar Text

Use the title bar of a message box to appropriately identify the source of the message — usually the name of the object. For example, if the message results from editing a document, the title text is the name of that document, optionally followed by the application name. If the message results from a non-document object, then use the application name.

Providing an appropriate identifier for the message is particularly important in the Windows multitasking environment, because message boxes might not always be the result of current user interaction. In addition, because objects supported by different applications can be embedded in the same document, different application code may be running when the user activates the object for editing. Therefore, the title bar text of a message box plays an important role in communicating the source of a message.

Do not use descriptive text — such as "warning" or "caution" — for message box title text. The message symbol already conveys the nature of the message. Also, never use the word "error" in the title text. The word "error" provides no useful information.

Follow the same conventions as for other secondary window title bar text. For example, use book title capitalization.

Message Box Types

Message boxes typically include a graphical symbol that indicates what kind of message is being presented. Most messages can be classified in one of the categories shown in the following table.

Message Types and Associated Symbols

Symbol	Message type	Description
ⓘ	Information	Provides information about the results of a command. Offers no user choices; the user acknowledges the message by clicking the **OK** button.
⚠	Warning	Alerts the user to a condition or situation that requires the user's decision and input before proceeding, such as an impending action with potentially destructive, irreversible consequences. The message can be in the form of a question — for example, "Save changes to MyReport?"
✖	Critical	Informs the user of a serious problem that requires intervention or correction before work can continue.

The system also includes a question mark message symbol, as shown in Figure 9.19. This message symbol was used in earlier versions of Windows for cautionary messages that were phrased as a question.

Figure 9.19 Inappropriate message symbol

However, the question mark message icon is no longer recommended, because it does not clearly represent a specific type of message and because the phrasing of a message as a question could apply to any message type. In addition, users can confuse the message symbol question mark with Help information. Therefore, do not use this question mark message symbol in your message boxes. The system continues to support its inclusion only for backward compatibility.

You can include your own graphics or animation in message boxes. However, limit your use of these types of message boxes and avoid defining new graphics to replace the symbols for the existing standard types.

For more information about how to use the taskbar to notify the user when the application may not be active, see Chapter 11, "Integrating with the System."

Because a message box disrupts the user's current task, it is best to display a message box only when the window of your application is active. If your application's window is not active, then use your application's button entry on the taskbar to alert the user. After the user activates the application, you can display the message box. Display only one message box for a specific condition. Displaying a sequential set of message boxes tends to confuse users.

You can also use message boxes to provide information or status without requiring direct user interaction to dismiss them. For example, message boxes that provide a visual representation of the progress of a particular process automatically disappear when the process is complete, as shown in Figure 9.20.

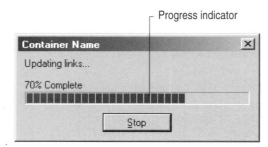

Figure 9.20 A progress message box

Similarly, product start-up windows that identify the product name and copyright information when the application starts can be removed automatically after the application has loaded. In these situations, you do not need to include a message symbol. Use this technique only for noncritical, informational messages, because some users may not be able to read the message within the short time it is displayed. If the window includes information that might be of value at other times, provide another way for users to access this information, such as an About dialog box.

Command Buttons in Message Boxes

Typically, message boxes contain only command buttons as the appropriate responses or choices offered to the user. Designate the most frequent or least destructive option as the default command button. Command buttons allow the message box interaction to be simple and efficient. If you need to add other types of controls, always consider the potential increase in complexity.

If a message requires no choices to be made but only acknowledgment, include an **OK** button — and, optionally, a **Help** button. If the message requires the user to make a choice, include a command button for each option. Include **OK** and **Cancel** buttons only when the user has the option of continuing or stopping the action. Use **Yes** and **No** buttons when the user must decide how to continue, as shown in Figure 9.21.

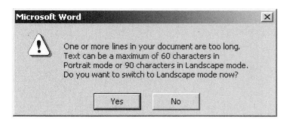

Figure 9.21 Yes and **No** buttons in a message box

If these choices are too ambiguous, label the command buttons with the names of specific actions — for example, **Save** and **Delete**.

You can include command buttons in a message box to correct the action that caused the message box to be displayed. For example, if the message box indicates that the user must switch to another application window to take corrective action, you can include a button that opens that application window. Be sure to clearly label the button and the results the user can expect from clicking it.

When you include **Cancel** as a command button in a message box, remember that to users, **Cancel** implies restoring the state of the process or task that started the message. If you use **Cancel** to interrupt a process and the state cannot be restored, use **Stop** instead.

Some situations may require offering the user not only a choice between performing and not performing an action, but an opportunity to cancel the process altogether. In such situations, include a **Cancel** button, as shown in Figure 9.22. Be sure to clearly label the button and the results the user can expect from clicking it.

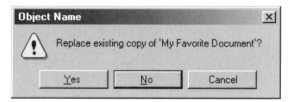

Figure 9.22 Message box choices

Enable the title bar Close box only if the message includes a **Cancel** button. Otherwise, the meaning of the Close operation may be ambiguous.

You can optionally include a **Help** button in a message box for messages that you want to provide more details about. This enables you to keep the message text succinct.

Message Box Text

The message text you include in a message box should be clear, concise, and written in terms that the user understands. This usually means using no technical jargon or system-oriented information. Try not to exceed two or three lines.

For more information about writing interface text, see Chapter 14, "Visual Design."

In addition, observe the following guidelines for your message text.

Presentation

- Use complete sentences with ending punctuation. For example, instead of "Date too far in future," say, "The date is too far in the future."

- Avoid contractions, especially in technical messages. Contractions may slow comprehension.

- State the problem, its probable cause (if known), and what the user can do about it, no matter how obvious the solution.

Correct	Incorrect
There is not enough disk space to save this file. Free additional space on this disk, or save the file to a different disk.	Insufficient disk space.

- Make messages as specific as possible. Avoid combining more than two or three conditions in a single message. For example, if a file cannot be opened for several reasons, provide a specific message for each condition.

- Consider making the solution an option offered in the message. For example, instead of "One or more lines are too long. The text can only be a maximum of 60 characters wide," you might say, "One or more lines are too long. Text can be a maximum width of 60 characters in Portrait mode or 90 characters in Landscape mode. Do you want to switch to Landscape mode now?" Offer **Yes** and **No** as the choices.

- Avoid multi-step solutions. Users have a hard time remembering more than two or three simple steps after a message box closes. If multiple steps are necessary, provide general instructions, or add a **Help** button that displays a relevant Help topic. Always present the steps in the order they should be completed.

For more information about designing Help topics, see Chapter 13, "User Assistance."

Correct	Incorrect
Remove the floppy disk, and then shut down the computer.	Shut down the computer after you remove the floppy disk.

- Provide only as much background information as necessary for the user to understand the message. Include enough information so that an advanced user or support person can help diagnose the problem. To balance the amount of content you include, you can add a command button that calls a Help topic with further information.

- Where possible, replace general system-supplied messages, such as MS-DOS® extended error messages, with your own specific messages.

- You can also include a message identification number as part of the message text for each message for support purposes. However, to avoid interrupting the user's ability to quickly read a message, place such a designation at the end of the message text and not in the title bar text.

- Avoid including support or country-specific information that may not be available to all users.

- Use confirmation messages, such as "Are you sure you want to…" judiciously. A more useful alternative is to describe to the user what the effect of the choice will be.

Terminology

- Use terminology that your audience understands. Avoid unnecessary technical terminology and sentences. For example, "picture" can be understood in context, whereas "picture metafile" is a technical concept.

- Use consistent words and phrasing for similar situations. For example, the following phrases have the same meaning:

  Not enough memory.
  There is not enough memory.
  There is not enough free memory.
  Insufficient memory.
  No memory was available.
  Your computer does not have sufficient memory.
  Memory resource is not enough.
  Ran out of memory.
  You may be out of memory.

The following messages are commonly used in Windows-based products. Consider using or adapting them in your application in similar scenarios.

Sample Messages

Message type	Sample message
Not enough memory	There is not enough memory to display the object. Save your work, close other programs, and then try again.
Not enough disk space	There is not enough disk space to complete the operation. Delete some unneeded files on your hard disk, and then try again.
File not found	The program cannot find the file *filename*.
Re-running setup	The *filename* file is missing. Run Setup again to reinstall the missing file. For more information about running Setup, press F1.

- Avoid using *please* except in the following situations:

  - When the user is asked to wait while the program completes an action. For example, "Please wait while Setup copies files to your computer."

  - When the user is asked to retype information that is required before the user can continue. For example, "The password is incorrect. Please type the correct password."

  - When the user is inconvenienced in some other way.

- Avoid phrasing that blames the user or implies user error. For example, use "Cannot find file name" instead of "File name error." Avoid the word "error" altogether.

- Do not anthropomorphize; that is, do not imply that programs or hardware can think or feel.

Correct	Incorrect
The node cannot use any of the available protocols.	The node does not speak any of the available protocols.

Pop-up Windows

Use pop-up windows to display additional information when an abbreviated form of the information is the main presentation. For example, you could use a pop-up window to display the full path for a field or control when an entire path cannot be presented and must be abbreviated. Pop-up windows are also used to provide context-sensitive Help information, as shown in Figure 9.23.

For more information about using pop-up windows for Help information, see Chapter 13, "User Assistance."

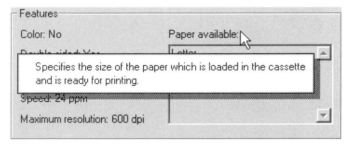

Figure 9.23 A context-sensitive Help pop-up window

ToolTips and balloon tips that provide the names for controls in toolbars are another example of pop-up windows used to display contextual information.

How pop-up windows are displayed depends on how they are used. Typically, the user points at an object, clicks an object or uses its keyboard equivalent, or clicks an explicit command.

If your application uses pointing as the technique for displaying a pop-up window, display the window after a time-out. The system automatically handles time-outs if you use the standard ToolTip controls. If you are providing your own implementation, you can use the current settings for ToolTip controls, which can be retrieved by creating a ToolTip and sending it a **TTM_GETDELAYTIME** message.

For more information about **TTM_GETDELAYTIME**, see the Microsoft Platform SDK on the MSDN Online Web site at http://msdn.microsoft.com/ui/guide/sdk.asp.

If your application uses clicking to display a pop-up window, change the pointer as feedback to the user indicating that the pop-up window exists and requires a click. From the keyboard, you can use the Select key (SPACEBAR) to open and close the window.

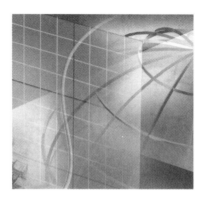

Design Specifications
and Guidelines

Window Management

User tasks often involve working with different types of information contained in more than one window or view. You can use a variety of techniques to manage a set of windows or views. This chapter covers some common techniques and the factors to consider in selecting a particular model.

Selecting a Window Management Model

To present your application's collection of related tasks or processes, consider a number of design factors: your intended audience and its skill level, the objects or tasks to be presented, and the effective use of the display space.

The view or window management models in this chapter are not exclusive design techniques. It may be advantageous to combine them or design others. However, keep these techniques in mind because these models are used frequently.

Presentation of Object or Task

To help you decide how to present an object's view, determine what the object represents, how it is used, and how it is related to other objects. Some objects — such as device objects like the mouse, keyboard, and display — may not even require a primary window; instead, these objects use only a secondary window for viewing and editing their properties.

It is also possible for an object to have no windows and an icon as its only representation. However, in this rare case, make sure that you provide an adequate set of object menu commands to allow a user to control its activity.

More typically, objects require a primary window supplemented with secondary windows. For other scenarios, where the composition of an object requires multiple views or the nature of the user's tasks requires views of multiple objects, you may need a construct that logically groups and supports management of these views.

Display Layout

To design object views for your application, you need to consider how these views will be used; for example, how many simultaneous views does the user need to work most efficiently? You must also determine how much data needs to be shown in the views.

Take into account the type of configuration you recommend to your users. For very high-resolution displays, the presence of menu bars, toolbars, and status bars still allows for information to be adequately displayed in a window. These common interface elements in each window have little impact on the overall presentation. At VGA resolution, however, this many elements on screen can limit the amount of data the user can see.

The interface components for a window or view should not so dominate the user's work area that the user cannot easily view or manipulate data. Consider a design that allows interface components, such as menu commands or other controls, to be shared among multiple views. However, make it clear that a particular interface component applies to a particular view by appropriately enabling or disabling it. Identify which functions are common to all views and present them in a consistent way for interface stability. For example, if multiple views share a **Print** button on the toolbar, place the button in a consistent location. If the button's location changes when the user switches views, the user's efficiency will decrease.

However, shared interfaces can make it harder for users to customize the interface components because your application must indicate whether the customization applies to the current context or across all views. However, when supporting user customization, don't neglect your application's default configuration — most users do not make any changes.

Single-Document Window Interface

In many cases, the interface of an object or application can be established using a single primary window. A single-document (or single-application) window design is sufficient when the object's primary presentation or use is as a single unit, such as a folder or document, even when the object contains different types.

In a single-document window design, the primary window provides the primary view or work area. You can use secondary windows for supplemental or specialized forms of input and to view information about objects in the primary window.

The desktop and taskbar provide the user with ways to manage the primary windows. When the user opens a window, the system puts it at the top of the Z order and places an entry on the taskbar, making it easy for the user to access the contents of the window.

You can support alternative views in the primary window by including commands and controls that enable the user to change the view. The standard folder window offers a good example of multiple viewing options. You can also provide support for simple simultaneous views of the same data by splitting a window into panes, as in Windows Explorer.

If your application includes several viewing options, create a **View** menu for your window that contains the viewing commands. Allow the user to navigate between panes by clicking their contents or pressing CTRL+TAB, or by pressing SHIFT+CTRL+TAB to move in reverse order. If the TAB and SHIFT+TAB keys are not already used by the pane's contents, you can also use those keys to support user navigation between panes.

In addition, Microsoft COM supports the creation of compound documents or other types of information containers. Using these constructs, the user can embed or link objects of different types within a single primary window, eliminating the need to display or edit information in separate windows.

> For more information about designing the interface for embedded and linked objects, see Chapter 12, "Working with OLE Embedded and Linked Objects."

You can also make primary windows more manageable by supporting a single-instance model that activates an existing window (within the same desktop) if the user reopens the object. This approach establishes a data-centered, one-to-one relationship between an object and its window.

Workbooks

A *workbook* is a design for managing a set of views that uses the metaphor of a book or notebook. Within the workbook, you present views of objects as sections within the workbook's primary window rather than in individual child windows. For more information about child windows, see "Mutiple-Document Interface" later in this chapter. Figure 10.1 illustrates one possible way of presenting a workbook.

Sample Workbook

File Edit View Insert Format Tools Data Help

A6 = PMT($E25/12,$D$23*12,-F$23)*1000

	A	B	C	D	E	F	G	H
1				30 Year Mortgage Rates				
2		$135 K	$145 K	$155 K	$165 K	$175 K	$185 K	$195 K
3	7.0%	$898	$965	$1,031	$1,098	$1,164	$1,231	$1,297
4	7.1%	$907	$974	$1,042	$1,109	$1,176	$1,243	$1,310
5	7.2%	$916	$984	$1,052	$1,120	$1,188	$1,256	$1,324
6	7.3%	$926	$994	$1,063	$1,131	$1,200	$1,268	$1,337
7	7.4%	$935	$1,004	$1,073	$1,142	$1,212	$1,281	$1,350
8	7.5%	$944	$1,014	$1,084	$1,154	$1,224	$1,294	$1,363
9	7.6%	$953	$1,024	$1,094	$1,165	$1,236	$1,306	$1,377
10	7.7%	$962	$1,034	$1,105	$1,176	$1,248	$1,319	$1,390
11	7.8%	$972	$1,044	$1,116	$1,188	$1,260	$1,332	$1,404
12	7.9%	$981	$1,054	$1,127	$1,199	$1,272	$1,345	$1,417
13								

Sheet1 / Sheet2 / Sheet3 /

Ready   NUM

Figure 10.1 A sample workbook design

Workbook Design

For a workbook, you can use tabs to serve as a navigational interface to move between different sections. Locate the tabs to fit the content and organization of the information you present. Each section represents a view of data, which could be an individual document. Unlike a folder or workspace, a workbook may be better suited for ordered content — that is, where the order of the sections is significant. In addition, you can include a special section listing the contents of the workbook, like a table of contents. This view can also be included as part of the navigational interface for the workbook.

You can use COM to support transfer operations so the user can move, copy, and link objects in the workbook. You may also want to provide an **Insert** command that allows the user to create new objects and include a new section tab in the workbook. You can also include a **Save All** command to save any uncommitted changes or to prompt the user to save or discard those changes. When the user closes the workbook, follow the normal conventions for handling unsaved edits or unapplied transactions.

Design Trade-offs

A workbook helps save screen real estate by enabling your application to share interface elements across views, including the menu bar and status bar. A workbook also provides quick user navigation to multiple views, but it is not the right choice if you need to provide simultaneous views.

Web-Application Interface

The Web provides a well-established model for moving between multiple views or documents using navigation mechanisms, such as hyperlinks and commands, such as **Back** and **Forward**. The Windows platform enables you to include the richness of the Web in a locally run application.

Web-Style Design

You can incorporate Web access into a Web-style application interface in any of the following ways:

- Run your application within the browser.

- Include the WebBrowser control to display HTML content.

- Mimic the Web form of presentation and navigation.

Consistency

Although Web-style applications allow for greater expression and freedom of design, the need for consistency still applies and should be adhered to, particularly in the following areas:

- Consistency with common operating system interface conventions — for example, in Windows, a navigational hyperlink is indicated when the pointer changes to the pointing hand image as the user moves over the defined link area.

- Consistency with de facto industry Web conventions — for example, the terms "home," "back," and "forward" already have an accepted meaning among users and should be used consistently in your application's design.

- Internal consistency — layout and navigational interfaces need to be consistent from page to page. Common elements such as headers, footers, navigation aids, fonts, color, and general layout conventions should be presented in a manner consistent with their purpose.

Navigation Design

A key success factor of any Web-style design is its support for navigation and organization. Always give users a clear indication of where they are and how they can get to where they want to go.

To design your navigation, begin by dividing the functionality into separate activities and tasks, and determine both their relationships and the paths to them. Then map your navigational design. A central context or home page is a useful and consistent starting point, and an important reference point for user navigation. Try to achieve a good balance between breadth and depth. Avoid a very shallow hierarchy that forces the user to backtrack to a particular page in order to move to others. Such a design makes navigation not only tiresome but annoying. However, making the user navigate through multiple levels of menus before getting to information can also be annoying.

When you provide access to a page from multiple locations, avoid the assumption that the user is coming from a single context. Label all contexts so users know where they are.

When your application is not operating directly in the browser, provide your own navigation bar for the user. Make sure that the **Forward** and **Back** commands work properly, and maintain an internal history log. Users rarely understand exactly what these commands will do other than take them forward or back with respect to the current location.

Avoid relying only on the basic navigation controls. Many users have difficulty predicting what the **Back** command will do because the command sometimes goes back to the same level and sometimes up a level depending on the navigational design. Therefore, you may need to provide additional navigation controls that more directly navigate within a specific level. Be careful not to confuse **Next** and **Previous** with the **Back** and **Forward** commands.

The **Next** and **Previous** commands imply navigation at the same level. In some situations, the user may have difficulty understanding the difference between the **Next** and **Back** commands, so be specific in defining your application's general navigational controls. For example, instead of a **Previous** button, use a descriptive reference label such as "Selecting a Product." You can also use thumbnail graphics (screen miniatures) to represent previous pages.

You must also choose whether to implement supplemental interfaces for gathering parameters as new pages in the navigational stack or in a separate dialog box window. To decide, consider the flow of the task and the importance of maintaining a centralized context.

Page Design

In a Web-style design, a page is the span of information that can be viewed in a window. It often does not correspond to the size of a printed page. Because pages are viewed on-screen, design your pages and their size to take this into account. A good rule of thumb is to limit the page size to a single maximized window. Usability studies have shown that users have difficulty reading and retaining information in documents that require extensive scrolling, or they may not see content located outside the current view.

The screen resolution you design for depends on your target audience. While many users now use an 800 x 600 display, if you want to reach the maximum number of users, target a 640 x 480 display. If you need to provide scrollable information, create an embedded list rather than making the entire page scrollable. Similarly, design your page horizontally to fit within a maximized window.

Because you can embed commands directly into pages, conventional menus — that is, a menu bar on the page's window — might seem extraneous. However, menus are valuable for presenting global commands, supporting primary navigation, and documenting keyboard shortcuts. Similarly, consider including shortcut menus. They can be useful to provide quick access to actions for a single object. Avoid designing menus as part of the content of a page, because they can be difficult for users to find.

Keep in mind that the user can override the formatting of any Web-based application or document you host in the browser. Make sure your application remains usable when the user adjusts the color, font, and accessibility options in Internet Explorer, as these will affect how your application is displayed.

In Web-style applications, you can include both hyperlinks and command buttons in your interface. As a general rule, use hyperlinks for navigating to locations and buttons for carrying out actions.

Because you can include links to other documents, let users know when they will be going outside the local context. Otherwise, users may get disoriented and have difficulty returning to the previous context. You may want to consider placing such links in a separate location or otherwise distinguishing them on the page rather than mixing them with the internal content. For example, you can include a graphic or description that makes a link to another document obvious.

Avoid navigational dead ends. Provide links that allow the user to return to the previous page. At a minimum, consider a link back to a primary navigation page, such as the home page or the table of contents page.

Finally, when you design any Web-based application or content, be sure to follow the standards set by the World Wide Web consortium for accessibility of Web content. This will ensure that your application is accessible to the widest possible range of users and that it is compatible with automation tools. For more information, see the Microsoft Accessibility Web site at http://www.microsoft.com/enable.

Design Trade-offs

Web-style design offers many benefits, including richer visual expression and hyperlink navigation conventions. It also provides for a more document-oriented, rather than application-centered, design. However, like workbooks, a Web-style application design limits views to a single window. It also requires that you provide a secondary navigational interface and offers more cumbersome and restricted keyboard access.

Projects

A *project* is another window management technique that associates a set of objects and their windows. It is similar to multiple-document interface (MDI), but does not visually contain the child windows.

Project Design

A project is similar to a folder in that the objects represented by icons contained within it can be opened into primary windows that are peers with the parent window. As a result, each child window can have its own entry on the taskbar. Unlike a folder, a project provides window management for the windows of its content. For example, when the user opens a document in a folder and then closes the folder, it has no effect on the window of the opened document. However, when the user closes a project window, all the child windows of objects contained in the project also close. In addition, when the user opens a project window, this action should restore the windows of objects contained within it to their previous state.

To facilitate window management, when the user minimizes a project window, you may want to minimize any windows of the objects that the project contains. Taskbar entries for these windows remain. Enable the user to restore a specific child window without restoring the project window or other windows within the project. In addition, enable the user to minimize any child window without affecting the project window. Figure 10.2 shows an example of a project.

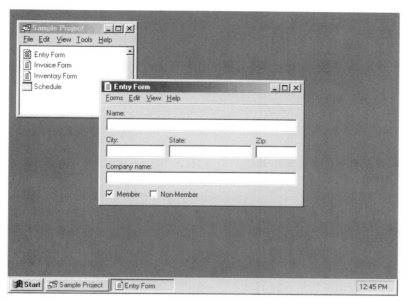

Figure 10.2 A sample project design

The windows of objects stored in the project do not share the menu bar or other areas within the project window. Instead, include the interface elements for each object in the object's own window. However, you can provide toolbar palette windows that can be shared in the windows of the objects in the project.

As with workbooks, a project should include commands for creating new objects within the project, for transferring objects in and out of the project, and for saving any changes to the objects stored in the project. In addition, a project should include commands and properties for the project object itself.

Design Trade-offs

A project provides the greatest flexibility for user placement and arrangement of its windows. It does so, however, at the cost of increasing complexity; it may be more difficult for a user to differentiate the child window of a project from windows of other applications.

Multiple-Document Interface

The multiple-document interface (MDI) technique uses a single primary window, called a *parent window*, to visually contain a set of related *document* or *child windows*, as shown in Figure 10.3. Each child window is essentially a primary window, but it is constrained to appear only within the parent window instead of on the desktop.

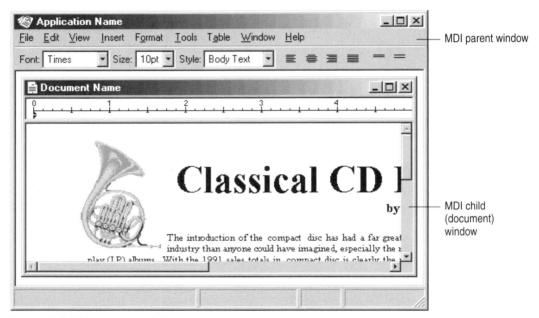

MDI parent window

MDI child (document) window

Figure 10.3 MDI parent and child windows

MDI Design

With MDI, the parent window provides a visual and operational framework for its child windows. For example, child windows typically share the menu bar of the parent window and can also share other parts of the parent's interface, such as a toolbar or status bar. You can change these to reflect the commands and attributes of the active child window.

For more information about the interaction between a primary window and its secondary windows, see Chapter 7, "Windows" and Chapter 9, "Secondary Windows."

Secondary windows displayed as a result of interaction within the MDI parent or child — such as dialog boxes, message boxes, or property sheets — typically are not contained or clipped by the parent window. These windows should activate and display content according to the conventions for secondary windows associated with a primary window, even if they apply to specific child windows.

Window Design

For the title bar of an MDI parent window, include the icon and name of the application or the object that it represents in the work area displayed in the parent window. For the title bar of a child window, include the icon representing the document or data file type and its file name, as shown in Figure 10.4.

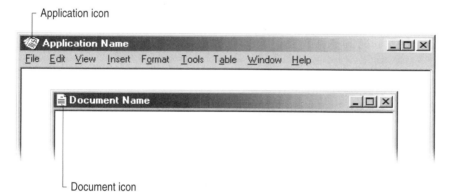

Figure 10.4 MDI application and child (document) window title bars

Supply a shortcut menu for the application icon in the parent window using the conventions for application title bar icons. Include the following commands where they apply.

For more information about window shortcut menus, see Chapter 8, "Menus, Controls, and Toolbars."

Optional Shortcut Menu Commands for MDI Parent Window Title Bar Icons

Command	Meaning
New	Creates a new data file or displays a list of data file types supported by the application from which the user can choose.
Save All	Saves all data files open in the MDI workspace and the state of the MDI window.
Find	Displays a window that allows the user to specify criteria to locate a data file.

In addition, supply an appropriate shortcut menu for the title bar icon that appears in the child window's title bar. You can follow the same conventions for non-MDI data files. Note that although pressing ALT+SPACEBAR should display the shortcut menu for the application's parent window, use ALT+HYPHEN to display the shortcut menu for the active child window.

Opening and Closing MDI Windows

The user starts an MDI application either by opening the application itself or by opening a document (or data file) of the type supported by the MDI application. If an MDI document is opened, the MDI parent window opens first, and then the child window for the document opens within it. To support the user opening other documents associated with the application, include an interface such as an Open dialog box.

If a user opens an MDI document outside the interface of its MDI parent window — for example, by double-clicking the file — and the parent window for the application is already open, open another instance of the MDI parent window. Although opening the child window within the existing parent window can seem more efficient, the new open window can disrupt the task environment already set up in the existing parent window. For example, if the newly opened file is a macro, opening it in the existing parent window could inadvertently affect other open documents in that window. If the user wants to open a file as part of the set in a particular parent MDI window, the commands within that window provide support.

Because an MDI child window is a special form of primary window, support its closure by following the same conventions for primary windows: include a **Close** button in its title bar and a **Close** command on the shortcut menu for the child window. When the user closes a child window, any unsaved changes are processed just as they are for primary windows. Do not automatically close its parent window, unless the parent window provides context or operations only with an open child window.

When the user closes the parent window, close all of its child windows. Where possible, preserve the state of a child window, such as its size and position within the parent window, and restore the state when the user reopens the file.

Moving and Sizing MDI Windows

MDI allows the user to move or hide the child windows as a set by moving or minimizing the parent window. When the user moves an MDI parent window, maintain the relative positions of the open child windows within the parent window.

MDI child windows can support the same window commands as their parent. Therefore, you should create shortcut menus for your application's MDI child windows and include **Move**, **Size**, **Minimize**, **Maximize**, and **Close** commands.

Moving a child window constrains it to its parent window. In some cases, the size of the parent window's interior area may result in clipping a child window. Optionally, you can support automatic resizing of the parent window when the user moves or resizes a child window either toward or away from the edge of the parent window.

A minimized child window in Microsoft Windows should appear sized down to display only part of its title area and its border. This avoids potential confusion between minimized child window icons and icons that represent objects.

Although an MDI parent window minimizes as an entry on the taskbar, MDI child windows minimize within their parent window, as shown in Figure 10.5.

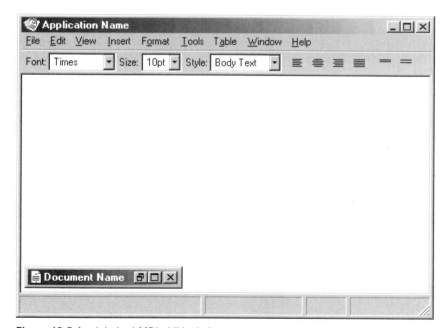

Figure 10.5 A minimized MDI child window

When the user maximizes an MDI parent window, expand the window to its maximum size, like any other primary window. When the user maximizes an MDI child window, also expand it to its maximum size. When this size exceeds the interior of its parent window, merge the child window with its parent window. The child window's title bar icon, **Restore** button, **Close** button, and **Minimize** button (if supported) are placed on the menu bar of the parent window in the same relative positions as in the title bar of the child window, as shown in Figure 10.6. Append the child window title text to the parent window title text.

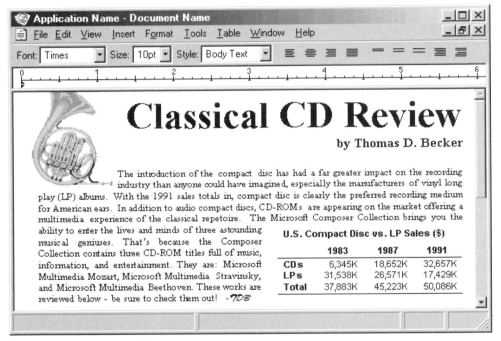

Figure 10.6 A maximized MDI child window

If the user maximizes one child window and it merges with the parent window, and then the user switches to another child window, display that window as maximized. Similarly, when the user restores one child window from its maximized state to its previous size, restore all other child windows to their previous sizes.

Switching Between MDI Child Windows

For MDI child windows, apply common mouse conventions for activating and switching between primary windows. The recommended keyboard shortcuts for switching between child windows are CTRL+F6 and CTRL+TAB (and SHIFT+ modified combinations to move backwards). On the menu bar of the parent window, include a **Window** menu with commands for switching between child windows and managing or arranging the windows within the MDI parent window, such as **Tile** or **Cascade**.

When the user switches child windows, you can change the interface of the parent window — such as its menu bar, toolbar, or status bar — to appropriately reflect the commands that apply to a particular child window. However, provide as much consistency as possible, keeping constant any menus that represent the document files and control the application or overall parent window environment, such as the **File** menu or the **Window** menu.

Design Trade-offs

MDI offers multiple benefits, such as sharing the parent window's interface components (menus, toolbars, and status bars) to make it a very space-efficient interface. It also provides a logical separation of its views from other document or application windows. However, MDI also has a number of limitations. First, MDI supports a more conventional application-centered design. Although the user can start an MDI application by opening one of its document or data files, the application interface must be visible for the user to open and work with multiple documents within the same MDI parent window.

An MDI implementation could also confuse or be frustrating to users who are familiar with switching between documents by using separate taskbar buttons or by pressing ALT+TAB. Similarly, users cannot easily determine what documents they have open because there is only one entry for the parent window on the taskbar.

When the user opens multiple files within the same MDI parent window, the storage relationship between the child windows and the objects being viewed in those windows is not consistent. That is, although the parent window provides visual containment for a set of child windows, it does not provide containment for the files those windows represent. This makes the relationship between the files and their windows more abstract, making an MDI application more challenging for beginning users to learn.

Similarly, because the MDI parent window does not actually contain the objects opened within it, MDI cannot support an effective design for reopening the application's windows to their last state. When the user closes the parent window and then reopens it, the context cannot be restored because the application state must be maintained independently from that of the files last opened in it.

MDI can make some aspects of the COM interface unintentionally more complex. For example, if the user opens a text document in an MDI application and then opens a worksheet embedded in that text document, the task relationship and window management break down. This is because the embedded worksheet's window does not appear in the same MDI parent window.

Finally, the MDI technique of managing windows by confining child windows to the parent window can be inconvenient or inappropriate for some tasks, such as designing with window or form layout tools. Similarly, the nested nature of child windows may make it difficult for the user to distinguish between a child window in a parent window and a primary window that is a peer with the parent window but is positioned on top.

Integrating with the System

Users appreciate seamless integration between the system and their applications. This chapter discusses integrating your software with the system and extending the system's features, including using the registry to store application information. It also includes information about installing your application, using appropriate naming conventions, and supporting shell features, such as the taskbar, Control Panel, and Recycle Bin.

This chapter provides only an overview: details required for some conventions are beyond the scope of this book. For more information about these conventions, see the documentation included in the Microsoft Platform SDK on the MSDN Online Web site at http://msdn.microsoft.com/ui/guide/sdk.asp. In addition, some of the conventions and features discussed may not be supported in all releases.

Using the File System

The file system is one of the most significant application services provided by Windows. Integration with the file system is not only crucial to the smooth operation of your application, but also to the overall usability and reliability of the system.

Location of Files

Store your application's files and the files it generates in system-defined folders such as Program Files, My Documents, and Application Data. Avoid placing any files in the root folder of the user's hard disk unless the user specifies this as the target location. These system-defined locations help keep user data and application code separate. This makes system administration and backup easier and provides better support for shared-use scenarios. Using the prescribed folders also makes the system more robust. Files and folders are organized more predictably. This helps keep users from inadvertently modifying files, which might result in compromising the integrity of your application or the system.

The **SHGetFolderPath()** API, exported from the redistributable Shfolder.dll file, enables you to find the locations (and localized names) of the standard system folders. For more information about shell basics, see the MSDN Online Web site at http://msdn.microsoft.com/ui/guide/shell.asp.

Where to Store Files

Folder	What to store
My Documents	User-created documents or data files
My Documents\My Pictures	User-created images, including those created with cameras or scanners
Program Files*Application Name*	Read-only implementation files and libraries or samples
Program Files\Common Files\ *Company Name*	Shared services or components
Documents and Settings\User Name\ Application Data*Application Name*	User customizable per-user application data available to roaming users
Documents and Settings\User Name\ Application Data\Local Settings\ *Application Name*	Discardable or local per-user application data not necessary for roaming users
Documents and Settings\All Users\ Application Data*Application Name*	Other local-user dynamic data that applies to all users

Program Files

To store your application's read-only files, create a subfolder within the Program Files folder. Include your application's executable (.exe) files as well as any .dll files, Help files, clip art or other fixed library files, and other support files used by your application. You can use the Common Files subfolder for any shared components (such as .dll files). For files that you do not want the user to access directly, set the hidden file attribute.

Also consider the layout of files you provide with your application. In addition to the recommended structure for your main executable file and its support files, you may want to create special folders for documents, templates, conversion tools, or other files that the user accesses directly.

Documents and Other User-Created Data Files

Save all user-created document files in the My Documents folder. Use this as the default location for your application's Save As dialog box. Save all user-generated images in the My Pictures subfolder. Avoid creating your own subfolders in My Documents and My Pictures unless your application generates multiple related files for user-created data. In that case, it may be better to develop a structure that keeps the associated files together.

Application Data

Create other miscellaneous files that the user doesn't directly access in the Application Data folder. For example, include custom dictionaries, mail stores, user history and other caches, index files, and log files. If you provide multiple applications, within the Application Data folder you can create a folder with your company's name that contains subfolders for each product.

The system provides three Application Data folders for the following types of files:

- *User Name* folder (for example, for Windows 2000, C:\Documents and Settings*user name*) — Store per-user customization files.

- Local Settings folder — Store per-user files that do not apply when the user roams, such as discardable data or temporary files.

- All Users folder — Store local application data common to all users, such as log files, hidden databases, and index files.

File Naming Conventions

Avoid cryptic file names, especially names that contain obscure abbreviations. With Windows support for long file names (up to 255 characters), you can define comprehensible names for the files and folders that are available to users.

Always use the long file name when displaying the name of a file. Long file names can include any character except the following:

\ / : * ? < > | "

When your application automatically supplies a file name, use a name that communicates information about its creation. For example, files created by a particular application should use either the application-supplied type name or the short type name as a proposed name — for example, worksheet or document. When a file by that name already exists in the target folder, add a number to the end of the proposed name — for example, Document (2). When adding numbers to the end of a proposed file name, use the first number of an ordinal sequence that does not conflict with an existing name in that folder. When you create a file name, the system automatically creates an MS-DOS file name (alias) for a file.

Do not display file name extensions (the "dot 3 extension") unless the user chooses the option to display extensions or the file type is not registered. To correctly handle when to display extensions, use the system function **SHGetFileInfo()** to display file names. This ensures that the file name is displayed correctly based on user preferences.

The system automatically formats a file name correctly if you use the **SHGetFileInfo** or **GetFileTitle** function. For more information about these functions, see the Microsoft Platform SDK on the MSDN Online Web site at http://msdn.microsoft.com/ui/guide/sdk.asp.

Because the system uses a file's extension (typically three characters) to describe a file type, do not use extensions to distinguish different forms of the same file type. For example, if your application has a function that automatically backs up a file, name the backup file

Backup of file name.ext (using its existing extension) or some reasonable equivalent, not *file name*.bak. The latter implies that the file's type has changed. Similarly, do not use a Windows file name extension unless your file fits the type description.

When your application saves a file, make sure you preserve the file's creation date and other attributes that are stored separately from the file's contents. For simple applications that open and save a file, this happens automatically. However, more sophisticated applications may create a temporary file, delete the original file, and rename the temporary file to the original file name. In this case, the application should copy the creation date, security information, or other external data from the old file to the new file using the standard system functions. For example, the **ReplaceFile()** function in Windows 2000 transfers all of this information. Certain system file management functionality depends on a file's accurate creation date.

When a file is copied, use the words "Copy of" as part of the generated file name — for example, *Copy of Sample* for a file named *Sample*. If the prefix "Copy of" is already assigned to a file, include a number in parentheses — for example, Copy (2) of Sample. You can apply the same naming scheme to links, except the prefix would be "Link to" or "Shortcut to."

It is also important to support UNC paths for identifying the location of files and folders. UNC paths and file names have the following form.

\\ Server\Share\Folder\Filename.ext

Using UNC names enables users to directly browse the network and open files without having to make explicit network connections.

Wherever possible, display the full name of a file (without the extension). The number of characters you can display depends on the font used and the context in which the name is displayed. In any case, supply enough characters that users can reasonably distinguish between names. Take into account common prefixes such as "Copy of" or "Shortcut to." If you don't display the full name, indicate that it has been truncated by adding an ellipsis at the cutoff point.

In cases where a file name is displayed but cannot be edited, you can use an ellipsis to abbreviate path names. In that case, include at least the first two entries of the beginning and the end of the path, using ellipses in place of the middle entries, as shown in the following example.

```
\\My Server\My Share\...\My Folder\My File
```

When you use an icon to represent a network resource, label the icon with the name of the resource. If you need to show the network context rather than using a UNC path, label the resource using the following format.

Resource Name on *Computer Name*

Shared User Data Files

When you store a file in the shared space of the network, the file should be readily accessible to all users. You must design the file to be opened by multiple users at the same time. The level of concurrent access you need to provide depends on the file type; that is, for some files you may support only concurrent access by word, paragraph, section, page, and so on. Provide clear visual cues as to which information can be changed and which cannot. When you cannot easily support access by multiple users, provide the users with an option to open a copy of the file if the original is already open.

Disk Cleaners

If you provide a temporary file cache that the user can empty, register a Disk Cleanup manager with the system. A disk cleaner is a COM object that implements the **IEmptyVolumeCache** interface.

The system provides a standard dialog box that enables the user to manage temporary storage. The system provides access to this dialog box through the low-disk-space message box, the Maintenance Wizard, and the disk properties window. When this dialog box is displayed, it will call your Disk Cleanup manager to reclaim temporarily used disk space. For information about registering a Disk Cleanup manager and integrating your application with the Maintenance Wizard, see the documentation included in the Microsoft Platform SDK on the MSDN Online Web site at http://msdn.microsoft.com/ui/guide/sdk.asp.

Using the Registry

Windows provides a special repository called the *registry* that serves as a central configuration database for user-, application-, and computer-specific information. Although the registry is not intended for direct user access, the information placed in it affects your application's user interface. Registered information determines the icons, commands, and other features displayed for files. The registry also makes it easier for system administrators to manage and support configuration information used by your application and eliminates redundant information stored in different locations.

The example registry entries in this chapter represent only the hierarchical relationship of the keys. For more information about the registry and registry file formats, see the documentation included in the Microsoft Platform SDK on the MSDN Online Web site at http://msdn.microsoft.com/ui/guide/sdk.asp.

An application should never fail to write a registry entry because the entry is already installed. To ensure that this happens, use registry creation functions when adding an entry.

Registering New File Types

Every file your program creates, even if it is hidden or rarely seen by users, should have a registered file type. This is important so that users can understand exactly how any file on the computer was created. Whenever possible, use conventional Windows file types. For other unique file types your application uses, at least make sure to register an icon and a friendly type name. If your program creates files that users should not modify, you can register the corresponding file type with a **NoOpen** option, as described in "Registering Commands" later in this chapter.

For every file type you register, include at least two entries: a file name extension key entry and a file type (class) identifier key entry.

The File Name Extension Key

The file name extension entry maps a file name extension to a file type identifier. To register an extension, create a subkey in the **HKEY_CLASSES_ROOT** key using the three (or more) letter extension (including a period), and set its default value to a file type identifier, as follows:

```
HKEY_CLASSES_ROOT
    .ext = FileTypeIdentifier
```

You may want to consider using a longer (four- to five-character) extension. This may decrease possible file type collisions with other applications.

For the value of the file type identifier (also known as the programmatic identifier or Prog ID), use a string that uniquely identifies a given class. This string is used internally by the system and is not exposed directly to users (unless explicitly exported with a special registry utility); therefore, you do not need to localize this entry.

Avoid assigning multiple extensions to the same file type identifier. To ensure that the user can distinguish each file type, define each extension such that each has a unique file type identifier. If your application contains utility files that the user does not interact with directly, you should still register an extension (and icon) for them, preferably the same extension so that they can be identified. In addition, mark them with the hidden file attribute.

Always try to define unique identifiers for your application's file types, and check the registry to avoid accidentally writing over and replacing existing extension entries, a practice that can seriously affect the user's existing files. More importantly, avoid registering an extension that conflicts with or redefines the common file name extensions used by the system. For common file name extensions, see the Microsoft Platform SDK on the MSDN Online Web site at http://msdn.microsoft.com/ui/guide/sdk.asp. If you want to add support for existing file types, see "Taking Over a File Type" later in this chapter.

The File Type Identifier Key

The second registry entry you create for a file type is its class-definition (Prog ID) key. Using the same string as the file type identifier you used for the extension's value, create a key and assign a type name as the default value of the key, as follows:

```
HKEY_CLASSES_ROOT
    .ext = FileTypeIdentifier
    FileTypeIdentifier = Type Name
```

Under this key, you specify the shell and COM properties of the class. Include this entry even if you do not have any extra information to place under this key; doing so provides a label for users to identify the file type. In addition, you use this entry to register the icon for the file type.

Define the type name (also known as the **MainUserTypeName**) as the human-readable form of its file type identifier or class name. It should convey to the user the object's name, behavior, or capability. A type name can include all of the following elements:

Elements of a File Type Name

Element	Function
Company name	Communicates product identity.
Application name	Indicates which application is responsible for activating a data object.
Data type	Indicates the basic category of the object (for example, drawing, spreadsheet, or sound); limit the number of characters to a maximum of 15.
Version	Distinguishes within multiple versions of the same basic type; you may want to use this for upgrades.

When you define a type name, use book title capitalization. The name can include a maximum of up to 40 characters. Use one of the following recommended forms:

- *Company Name Application Name [Version] Data Type*
  For example, Microsoft Excel Worksheet

- *Company Name-Application Name [Version] Data Type*
  For cases when the company name and application name are the same — for example, ExampleWare 2.0 Document

- *Company Name Application Name [Version]*
  When the application name sufficiently describes the data type — for example, Microsoft Graph

These type names provide the user with a precise language for referring to objects. Because object type names appear throughout the interface, the user becomes conscious of an object's type and its associated behavior. However, because of their length, you may also want to include a short type name. A *short type name* is the data type portion of the full type name. Applications that support COM always include a short type name entry in the registry. Use the short type name in drop-down and shortcut menus. For example, a Microsoft Excel Worksheet is referred to simply as a "Worksheet" on menus.

To provide a short type name, add an **AuxUserType** subkey under the application's registered **CLSID** subkey (which is under the **CLSID** key), as follows:

For more information about registering type names and other information you should include under the **CLSID** key, see the OLE documentation in the Microsoft Platform SDK on the MSDN Online Web site at http://msdn.microsoft.com/ui/guide/sdk.asp.

```
HKEY_CLASSES_ROOT
    .ext = FileTypeIdentifier
...
    FileTypeIdentifier = File Type Display Name
        CLSID = {CLSID identifier}
...
    CLSID
        {CLSID identifier}
            AuxUserType
                2 = Short Type Name
```

If a short type name is not available for an object because the string was not registered, use the full type name instead. For controls that display the full type name, allocate enough space for 40 characters in width. By comparison, you can design for only 15 characters when using the short type name.

Registering Icons

The system uses the registry to determine which icon to display for a specific file. You register an icon for every data file type that your application supports and that you want the user to be able to distinguish easily. Create a **DefaultIcon** subkey entry under the file type identifier subkey you created and define its value as the file name containing the icon. Typically, you use the application's executable file name and the index of the icon within the file. The index value corresponds to the icon resource within the file. A positive number represents the icon's position in the file. A negative number corresponds to the inverse of the resource ID number of the icon. The icon for your application should always be the first icon resource in your executable file. The system always uses the first icon resource to represent executable files. This means that the index value for your data files will be a number greater than 0, as follows:

```
HKEY_CLASSES_ROOT
    FileTypeIdentifier = File Type Display Name
        DefaultIcon = path [,index]
```

Instead of registering the application's executable file, you can register the name of a dynamic-link library file (.dll), an icon file (.ico), or a bitmap file (.bmp) to supply your data file icons. If an icon does not exist or is not registered, the system supplies an icon derived from the icon of the file type's registered application. If no icon is available for the application, the system supplies a generic icon. These icons do not make your files uniquely identifiable, so it is better to design and register icons for both your application and its data file types. Include 16- and 256-color versions in the following sizes: 16 x 16 pixels, 32 x 32 pixels, and 48 x 48 pixels.

For more information about designing icons for your files, see Chapter 14, "Visual Design."

Registering Commands

Many of the commands found on icons, including **Send To**, **Cut**, **Copy**, **Paste**, **Create Shortcut**, **Delete**, **Rename**, and **Properties**, are provided by their container — that is, their containing folder or the desktop. But you must provide support for the icon's primary commands, also referred to as verbs, such as **Open**, **Edit**, **Play**, and **Print**. You can also register additional commands that apply to your file types and even commands for other file types.

To add these commands, in the **HKEY_CLASSES_ROOT** key, you register a **shell** subkey and a subkey for each verb, and a **command** subkey for each menu command name, as follows:

```
HKEY_CLASSES_ROOT
    FileTypeIdentifier = Type Name
        shell [ = default verb [,verb2 [,..]]
            verb [ = Menu Command Name]
                command = pathname [parameters]
```

A verb is a language-independent name of the command. Applications can use it to invoke a specific command programmatically. When you supply verbs other than "open," "print," "find," and "explore," you must provide menu command names localized for the specific version of Windows on which the application is run. (Windows automatically provides menu command names and appropriate access key assignments for "open," "print," "find," and "explore," localized in each international version of Windows.) To assign a menu command name for a verb, make it the default value of the verb subkey. For example, here's how the registry entry for the verb "open" might look:

```
HKEY_CLASSES_ROOT
    txtfile = Text Document
        shell = open
            command = C:\windows\NOTEPAD.EXE /p %1
```

The menu command names corresponding to the verbs for a file type are displayed to the user, either on a folder's **File** menu or on the shortcut menu for a file's icon. These commands appear at the top of the menu. You define the order of the menu commands by ordering the verbs in the value of the **shell** key. The first verb becomes the default command in the menu.

By default, capitalization follows how you format the menu command name value of the verb subkey. Although the system automatically capitalizes the standard commands (**Open, Print, Explore,** and **Find**), you can use the value of the menu command name to format the capitalization differently. Similarly, you use the menu command name value to set the access key for the menu command following normal menu conventions, prefixing the desired access character in the name with an ampersand (&). Otherwise, the system sets the first letter of the command as the access key for that command.

To support user execution of a verb, provide the path for the application (or a DDE command string).

You can include command-line switches. For paths, include a %1 parameter. This parameter is an operational placeholder for whatever file the user selects.

For example, to register an **Analyze** command for an application that manages stock market information, the registry entries might look like the following:

```
HKEY_CLASSES_ROOT
    stockfile = Stock Data
        shell = analyze
            analyze = &Analyze
                command = C:\Program Files\Stock Analysis\Stock.exe /A
```

You can have different values for each command. For example, you can assign one application to carry out the **Open** command and another to carry out the **Print** command, or use the same application for all commands.

If you have a file type that users should not open, register it by adding a **NoOpen** value under the file type identifier key.

```
HKEY_CLASSES_ROOT
    FileTypeIdentifier = File Type Display Name
                    NoOpen = Optional text message to display.
```

If the user attempts to open this file, the system displays a warning message. If you set the value of **NoOpen**, the system uses your text to display in the message box. Marking your files this way does not prevent users from still opening the files, but it does automatically warn the users.

Supporting the New Command

The system supports the creation of new objects in system containers, such as folders and the desktop. Register information for each file type that you want the system to include. The registered type will appear in the **New** command that the system includes on menus for the desktop and folders, and in the Open and Save As common dialog boxes. This provides a more data-centered design because the user can create a new object without having to locate and run the associated application.

To register a file type for inclusion, create a subkey using the **FileTypeIdentifier** under the extension's subkey in **HKEY_ CLASSES_ROOT**. Under it, also create the **ShellNew** subkey, as follows:

```
HKEY_CLASSES_ROOT
    .ext = FileTypeIdentifier
        FileTypeIdentifier
            ShellNew Value Name = Value
```

Assign a value entry to the **ShellNew** subkey with one of the following four methods for creating a file with this extension.

Ways to Support the New Command Using the Registry

Value name	Value	Result
NullFile	" "	Creates a new file of this type as a null (empty) file.
Data	*binary data*	Creates a new file containing the binary data.
FileName	*path*	Creates a new file by copying the specified file.
Command	*file name*	Carries out the command. Use this to run your own application code to create a new file (for example, to run a wizard).

The system also automatically provides a unique file name for the new file using the type name you register.

When you use a **FileName** value, store the file that will serve as the template in the system-managed Templates folder. You can retrieve the path to that folder with **SHGetFolderPath**(), using **CSIDL_TEMPLATES** (or **CSIDL_COMMON_TEMPLATES** on platforms that support it). This way you don't need to specify a fully qualified path name that could potentially break if the user roams from one computer to another.

Enabling Printing

If the files in your application are of a type that can be printed, include a "print" verb entry in the **shell** subkey under **HKEY_CLASSES_ROOT**, following the conventions described in the previous section. This will display the **Print** command on the shortcut menu for the icon and on the **File** menu of the folder in which the icon resides when the user clicks the icon. When the user clicks the **Print** command, the system uses the registry entry to determine which application to run to print the file.

Also register a **Print To** registry entry for the file types your application supports. This entry enables dragging and dropping a file onto a printer icon. Although a **Print To** command is not displayed on any menu, the printer includes **Print Here** as the default command on the shortcut menu displayed when the user drags and drops a file onto the printer icon using the secondary mouse button.

In both cases, it is preferable to print the file without opening the application's primary window. One way to do this is to provide a command-line switch that runs the application for handling the printing operation only (for example, WordPad.exe /p). In addition, display some form of user feedback that indicates whether printing has been initiated and, if so, its progress. For example, this feedback could be a modeless message box that displays, "Printing page m of n on *printer name*" and a **Cancel** button. You can also include a progress indicator control.

Supporting InfoTips

When you create a new file type, also include an InfoTip description for the type. The system automatically displays a ToolTip with this description when the user moves the pointer over an icon of this type. To register the InfoTip description for a specific type, add an **InfoTip** value to the file extension subkey, as follows:

```
HKEY_CLASSES_ROOT
    .ext = FileTypeIdentifier
            InfoTip=Text to display when user hovers over this file type
```

You can also support an InfoTip for a shortcut link to a program that you include in the Programs folder of the **Start** menu. To do so, include a text description in the Comment field for the shortcut's properties.

Setting Other File Type Values

You can also register certain attributes for your file types. For example, you can mark your file type as being safe to download or keep files of a specific type from being included in the Recent Documents folder. To do this, add an **EditFlag** value to your file type identifier key. For information about values you can set, see the Microsoft Platform SDK on the MSDN Online Web site at http://msdn.microsoft.com/ui/guide/files.asp.

Taking Over a File Type

If your application supports the file type of another application or a common file type that might be used by multiple applications, such as text or HTML files, you may want your application to take over that type. Typically this means taking over the "open" verb of that type so that when the user opens or double-clicks a file of that type, the system automatically runs your application to open (and edit) the file. However, it is also possible to take over (or add) other verbs for a particular file type.

Always warn the user during your application's installation before you take over the file type, offering the user the choice. If your application uses a silent install, don't take over the association or prompt for user confirmation until the user runs your application.

Always store the previous association and provide an option in your application interface that enables the user to restore the previous file type association. In addition, restore the previous association automatically when the user uninstalls your application.

Note that in Windows 2000, if the user explicitly changes the file type association, the system maintains the user's choice even if you overwrite the current association.

Registering NoOpenWith

If your application supports only its own unique file type or you have executable (.exe) files that perform very specific functions, you don't want these files to appear in the system's Open With dialog box. To ensure that your application file is not included, add an entry for your application in the Application subkey of **HKEY_CLASSES_ROOT**. Then add a **NoOpenWith** subkey, as follows:

```
HKEY_CLASSES_ROOT
    Applications
        Application.Exe
            NoOpenWith
```

You can also register file types that the user cannot open by adding a **NoOpen** subkey to your Prog ID for your file type. This is especially good for a type of file that the user could accidentally corrupt by attempting to open. Users can still access a file registered with this setting by using the **Open With** command.

Registering Application State Information

Use the registry to store state information for your application. Typically, the data you store here is information you may have stored in initialization (.ini) files in previous releases of Windows. Create subkeys under the **Software** subkey in the **HKEY_LOCAL_MACHINE** and **HKEY_CURRENT_USER** keys that include information about your application, as follows:

```
HKEY_LOCAL_MACHINE
    Software
        CompanyName
            ProductName
                Version
...
HKEY_CURRENT_USER
    Software
        CompanyName
            ProductName
                Version
```

Store computer-specific data in your application's **HKEY_LOCAL_MACHINE** entry, and store user-specific data in your application's **HKEY_CURRENT _USER** entry. The latter key allows you to store settings to tailor your application for individual users working with the same computer. Under your application's subkey, you can define your own structure for the information. Although the system still supports initialization files for backward compatibility, use the registry wherever possible to store your application's state information instead.

Use these keys to save your application's state whenever appropriate, such as when the user closes your application's primary window. In most cases, it is best to restore a window to its previous state when the user reopens it.

When the user shuts down the system with your application's window open, you can optionally store information in the registry so that the application's state is restored when the user starts Windows. (The system does this for folders.) To have your application's state restored, store your window and application state information under its registry entries when the system notifies your application that it is shutting down. Store the state information in your application's entries under **HKEY_CURRENT_USER** and add a value name–value pair to the **RunOnce** subkey that corresponds to your application. When the user restarts the computer, the system runs the command line you supply. When your application runs, you can use the data you stored to restore its state, as follows:

```
HKEY_CURRENT_USER
    Software
        Microsoft
            Windows
                CurrentVersion
                    RunOnce file type identifier = command line
```

If you have multiple instances open, you can include value name entries for each instance, or consolidate them as a single entry and use the command-line switches that are most appropriate for your application. For example, you can include entries like the following:

```
WordPad Document 1 = C:\Program Files\Wordpad.exe Letter to Bill /restore
WordPad Document 2 = C:\Program Files\Wordpad.exe Letter to Paul /restore
Paint = C:\Program Files\Paint.exe Abstract.bmp Cubist.bmp
```

As long as you provide a valid command-line string that your application can process, you can format the entry in a way that best fits your application.

You can also include a **RunOnce** entry under the **HKEY_LOCAL_ MACHINE** key. When using this entry, however, the system runs the application before starting up. You can use this entry for applications that need to query the user for information that affects how Windows starts. Remember that any entry here will affect all users of the computer.

RunOnce entries are automatically removed from the registry after the system starts. Therefore, you do not need to remove or update the entries, but your application must always save the registry's state when the user shuts down the system. The system also supports a **Run** subkey in both the **HKEY_CURRENT_USER** and **HKEY_LOCAL_ MACHINE** keys. The system runs any value

Use **Run** and **RunOnce** capabilities sparingly. Confronting many different windows simultaneously at the beginning of a session creates a bad end-user experience. On Windows 2000, it is possible to serialize **Run** and **RunOnce** options, so that the system waits for each process to finish before launching the next. For more information, see the Microsoft Platform SDK on the MSDN Online Web site at http://msdn.microsoft.com/ui/guide/sdk.asp.

name entries under this subkey after the system starts, but it does not remove those entries from the registry. For example, a virus-check program can be installed to run automatically after the system starts. You can also support this functionality by placing a file or shortcut to a file in the Startup folder. The registry stores the location of the Startup folder as a value in **HKEY_CURRENT_USER \Software\Microsoft\ Windows\CurrentVersion\Explorer\Shell Folders**.

The system's ability to restore an application's state depends on the availability of the application and its data files. If they have been deleted or if the user has logged on over the network where the same files are not available, the system may not be able to restore the state.

Registering Application Path Information

The system supports "per application" paths. If you register a path, Windows sets the PATH environment variable to be the registered path when it starts your application. You set your application's path in the **AppPaths** subkey under the **HKEY_LOCAL_MACHINE** key. Create a new key using your application's executable file name as its name. Set this key's default value to the path of your executable file. The system uses this entry to locate your application if it fails to find it in the current path — for example, if the user chooses the **Run** command on the **Start** menu and includes only the file name of the application, or if a shortcut icon doesn't include a path setting. To identify the location of .dll files placed in a separate folder, you can also include another value entry called **Path** and set its value to the path of your .dll files, as follows:

```
HKEY_LOCAL_MACHINE
    Software
        Microsoft
            Windows
                CurrentVersion
                    App Paths
                        Application Executable Filename = path
                                                    Path = path
```

The system will automatically update the path and default entries if the user moves or renames the application's executable file using the system shell user interface.

Register any system-wide shared .dll files in a subkey under a
SharedDLLs subkey of the **HKEY_LOCAL_MACHINE** key. If
the file already exists, increment the entry's usage count index, as
follows:

```
HKEY_LOCAL_MACHINE
    Software
        Microsoft
            Windows
                CurrentVersion
                    SharedDLLs file name [= usage count index]
```

For more information about the usage count index, see "Installation"
later in this chapter.

Adding Features to File Types

Windows provides interfaces that enable you to add menu items or
property pages for other file types, define instance-specific icons,
enhance drag-and-drop operation support, and monitor file transfer
operations. However, use these shell extensions judiciously because
these add to the user's existing interface. If you use shell extensions
to enhance or extend the interfaces of files other than those your
application creates, inform users during installation, giving them the
choice to accept the change. Also provide users with support to
disable or remove the extension you provide.

Shell extensions are COM objects, implemented as in process-server
.dll files. These objects implement the interfaces that provide the
functionality of the shell extension. The following types of handlers
can be registered.

Types of Shell Extension Handlers

Handler	Function
Shortcut (context)	Adds menu items to the shortcut menu handler menu for a particular file type.
Drag handler	Allows you to support the OLE data transfer conventions for drag-and-drop operations of a specific file type.
Drop handler	Allows you to carry out some action when the user drops objects on a specific type of file.

For more information about
creating COM objects and
shell extensions, see the COM and
ActiveX documentation included in
the Microsoft Platform SDK on the
MSDN Online Web site at http://
msdn.microsoft.com/ui/guide/
sdk.asp.

Types of Shell Extension Handlers *(continued)*

Handler	Function
Nondefault drag-and-drop handler	Shortcut menu handlers that the system calls when the user drags and drops an object by using the secondary mouse button.
Icon handler	Adds per-instance icons for file objects or supplies icons for all files of a specific type.
Property sheet handler	Adds pages to a property sheet that the shell displays for a file object. The pages can be specific to a class of files or to a particular file object.
Copy-hook handler	Called when a folder or printer object is about to be moved, copied, deleted, or renamed by the user. The handler can be used to allow or prevent the operation.
Thumbnail extractor	Shows your file type in thumbnail view and previews it in the Web view preview control.
Details handler	Adds extra columns to the folder details view.

Installation

The following sections provide guidelines for installing your application's files. Applying these guidelines will help you improve system stability and reduce the clutter of irrelevant files when the user browses for a file. In addition, you'll reduce the redundancy of common files and make it easier for the user to update applications or the system software.

Support the Windows Installer or a third-party setup toolkit that supports the Windows Installer. The Windows Installer not only provides support for installing and uninstalling your application's files, it also includes support for on-demand installation of specific features and repair of damaged installations. The Windows Installer also integrates with Add/Remove Programs in Control Panel and with the Windows 2000 Active Directory services. For more information about the Windows Installer, see the Microsoft Platform SDK on the MSDN Online Web site at http://msdn.microsoft.com/ui/guide/sdk.asp.

Copying Files

When the user installs your software, avoid copying files into the Windows folder (directory) or its System subfolder. In highly managed locked-down computer scenarios, you may not be able to write to these folders. Instead, create a single folder, preferably using the application's name, in the Program Files folder (or the location that the user chooses). In this folder, place the executable file. For example, if a program is named My Application, create a My Application subfolder and place My Application.exe in that folder.

In your application's folder, create a subfolder named System and store in it all support files that the user does not directly access, such as .dll files and Help files. For example, place a support file named My Application.dll in the subfolder Program Files\My Application\System. Hide the support files and your application's System folder and register the System folder's location using a **Path** value in the **App Paths** subkey under **HKEY_LOCAL_MACHINE \Software\Microsoft\Windows\CurrentVersion**. Although you can place support files in the same folder as your application, placing them in a subfolder helps avoid confusing the user and makes files easier to manage.

The process for installing shared files includes these steps:

1. Before copying the file, verify whether the file is already present.

2. If the file is already present, compare its date and size to determine whether it is the same version as the one you are installing. If it is, increment the usage count in its corresponding registry entry.

   The system provides support services in Ver.dll for helping you do version verification. For more information about this utility, see the Microsoft Platform SDK on the MSDN Online Web site at http://msdn.microsoft.com/ui/guide/sdk.asp.

3. If the file you are installing is not more recent, do not overwrite the existing version.

4. If the file is not present, copy it to the folder.

Remember that the System folder installed by Windows is intended for system files only. Avoid installing any files here unless they are necessary for compatibility issues.

If you store a new file in the System folder installed by Windows, register a corresponding entry in the **SharedDLL** subkey under the **HKEY_LOCAL_MACHINE** key.

If a file is shared, but only among your applications, create a subfolder in the following location and store the file there:

C:\Program Files\Common Files*Company Name*

Alternatively, for application "suite" installations where multiple applications are bundled together, you can create suite subfolders as follows:

For your executable files:

C:\Program Files*Suite Name*

For your support files shared only within the suite:

C:\Program Files*Suite Name*\System

In either case, register the path using the **Path** subkey under the **App Paths** subkey.

When you install an updated version of a shared file, ensure that it is upwardly compatible before replacing the existing file. Alternatively, you can create a separate entry with a different file name (for example, Vbrun301.dll).

Windows no longer requires the Autoexec.bat and Config.sys files, so make sure that your application also does not require these files. To make your program accessible from the command window or the Run dialog box without registering it in the **PATH** environment variable, use the **App Paths** section of the registry.

In addition, do not make entries in the Win.ini file. Storing information in this file can make it difficult for users to update or move your application. Also, avoid maintaining your application's own initialization file. Instead, use the registry. The registry provides conventions for storing most application and user settings. The registry provides greater flexibility, allowing you to store information on a per-computer or per-user basis. It also supports accessing this information across a network.

Make sure that you register the types supported by your application and the icons for these types along with your application's icons. In addition, register other application information, such as information required to enable printing.

Providing Access to Your Application

To provide easy user access to your application, place a shortcut icon to the application in the Programs folder on the **Start** menu.

However, avoid adding entries to the **Programs** menu for every application you might include in your product; this quickly overloads the menu. Always limit what you include on the **Programs** menu to applications that the user will frequently access. Do not include **Readme**, **Help**, or **Uninstall** entries on the **Programs** menu. If your product includes several applications, include an entry only for the one that the user will most frequently use. If your program includes other important utilities, you can also include a folder on the **Programs** menu that provides access to these other items.

When you install entries on the **Programs** menu, consider whether they should be available to all users or on a per-user basis. Windows supports user profiles so that each user can customize the configuration.

Avoid adding items to the top of the **Start** menu. This area is intended to provide access to key user features provided by the operating system and user customization. Putting an entry here may interfere with the user's preferences and access.

Avoid adding icons to the Windows desktop. If you want to provide access to your application from the desktop, include an option for adding a shortcut icon in your application's interface.

Similarly, avoid using the taskbar Quick Launch or status notification area as a launching point for your application or utility. Quick Launch is intended primarily for system services and user customization. The status notification area is intended for letting users know about events and information they need to respond to, not for providing a more accessible entry point for your programs. Overloading these areas of the taskbar defeats its purpose and in general is not an effective access point for novice and intermediate users.

Designing Your Installation Program

Your installation program should offer the user different installation options such as the following:

- Typical setup (default): Installs using the common defaults, copying only the most common files.

- Compact setup: Installs the minimum number of files necessary to operate your application. This option is best for situations where disk space must be conserved — for example, on laptop computers. You can optionally add a Portable setup option for additional functionality designed especially for configurations on laptop computers, portable computers, and portable computers used with docking stations.

- Custom setup (for experienced users): Allows users to choose where to copy files and which options or features to include. This can include options or components not available for compact or typical setup.

- CD-ROM setup: Installs from a CD-ROM. This option allows users to select which files to install on the hard disk and which files they want to run directly from the CD.

- Silent setup: Installs using a command-line switch. This allows your setup program to run with a batch file and without any visible user interface.

In addition to these setup options, your installation program should be a well-designed, Windows-based application and follow the conventions detailed in this book and in the following guidelines:

- Supply a default response to every option so that users can step through the installation process by confirming the default settings (that is, by pressing the ENTER key).

- Tell users how much disk space they will need before proceeding with installation. In the custom setup option, adjust the figure as users choose to include or exclude certain options. If there is not sufficient disk space, let users know.

- Offer users the option to quit the installation before it is finished. Keep a log of the files copied and the settings made so the canceled installation can be cleaned up easily. Also make sure your installation program can handle a previously failed or incomplete uninstall.

- Ask users to insert a disk only once during the installation. Lay out your files on the disk so that users do not have to reinsert the same disk multiple times.

- Provide a visual prompt and an audio cue when users need to insert the next disk.

- Support installation from any location. Do not assume that installation must be done from a logical MS-DOS drive (such as drive A). Design your installation program to support any valid universal naming convention (UNC) path.

- Provide a progress indicator to inform users about their progress through the installation process.

- Do not require users to restart the computer after installation unless it is unavoidable.

- Avoid including non-essential information in your Setup program. Keep legal statements to a minimum and do not include any Readme information.

- Keep supplemental windows to a minimum. If possible, try to restrict your installation to a single window. If you are creating your own installation program, consider using the wizard control or design. Following the guidelines for wizards will result in a consistent interface for users.

For more information about designing wizards, see Chapter 13, "User Assistance."

Name your installation program Setup.exe or Install.exe (or the localized equivalent). This allows the system to recognize the file. Place the file in the root folder of the disk the user inserts. This allows the system to run your installation program automatically when the user clicks the **Install** button in the Add/Remove Programs utility in Control Panel.

Installing Fonts

When your application installs fonts on a local computer, determine whether the font is already present. If it is, rename your font file — for example, by appending a number to the end of its file name. After copying a font file, register it with the system by calling the appropriate font installation interface so that it will be available for use immediately.

Installing Your Application on a Network

If you create a client-server application so that multiple users access it from a network server, create separate installation programs:

For more information about designing client-server applications, see the Microsoft Platform SDK on the MSDN Online Web site at http://msdn.microsoft.com/ui/guide/sdk.asp.

- An installation program that allows the network administrator to prepare the server component of the application.

- A client installation program that installs the client component files and selects the settings to connect to the server.

Design your client software so that an administrator can deploy it over the network and have it automatically configure itself when the user starts it.

Because Windows may itself be configured to be shared on a server, do not assume that your installation program can store information in the main Windows folder on the server. In addition, do not store shared application files in the "home" folder provided for the user.

Design your installation program to support UNC paths. Also, use UNC paths for any shortcut icons you install in the Start Menu folder.

Uninstalling Your Application

Users may need to remove your application to recover disk space or to move your application to another location. To facilitate this, provide an uninstall program with your application that removes its files and settings. Remember to remove registry entries and shortcuts your application may have placed in the **Start** menu hierarchy. However, when removing your application's folder structure be careful not to delete any user-created files (unless you confirm their removal with the user).

Your uninstall program should follow the conventions detailed in this guide and in the following guidelines:

- Display a window that provides users with information about the progress of the uninstall process. You can also provide an option to allow the program to uninstall "silently" — that is, without displaying any information so that it can be used in batch files.

- Display clear and helpful messages for any errors your uninstall program encounters during the uninstall process.

- When uninstalling an application, decrease the usage count in the registry for any shared component — for example, a .dll file. If the result is zero, give users the option to delete the shared component with the warning that other applications may use this file and will not work if it is missing.

- If you install your application using a CD-ROM, avoid requiring users to insert the disc to start the uninstall program.

- Restore any file associations your application took over.

Your uninstall program should remove all files in the Program Files folder that it uniquely owns. If your application has files stored here that you are not sure whether you should remove, they probably should not have been stored in the Program Files folder. Files that your application shares with other applications are the exception. For more information about using the file system appropriately to store your application's files, see the guidelines earlier in this chapter.

When you register your uninstall program, your application will be listed on the Uninstall page of the Add/Remove Programs utility included with Windows. To register your uninstall program, add entries for your application to the **Uninstall** subkey, as follows:

```
HKEY_LOCAL_MACHINE
    Software
        Microsoft
            Windows
                CurrentVersion
                    Uninstall
                        ApplicationName    DisplayName = Application Name
                                           UninstallString = path [ switches ]
```

You must supply complete names for both the **DisplayName** and **UninstallString** values for your uninstall program to appear in the Add/Remove Programs utility. The path you supply to **Uninstall-String** must be the complete command line used to carry out your uninstall program. The command line you supply should carry out the uninstall program directly rather than from a batch file or subprocess.

Supporting AutoPlay

Windows supports the ability to run a file automatically when the user inserts removable media that support insertion notification, such as CD-ROMs, PC Cards (PCMCIA), hard disks, or flash ROM cards. This feature is named AutoPlay. With AutoPlay, you can include a custom icon for the media type, start a custom program automatically, and provide custom shortcut menu entries for the media icon. For more information about this feature, see the Microsoft Platform SDK on the MSDN Online Web site at http://msdn.microsoft.com/ui/guide/autoplay.asp.

Using System Settings and Notifications

The system provides standard metrics and settings for user interface aspects, such as colors, fonts, border width, and drag rectangle (used to detect the start of a drag operation). The system also notifies running applications when its settings change. When your application starts, query the system to set your application's user interface to match the system parameters. This ensures visual and operational consistency. Also, design your application to adjust itself appropriately when the system notifies it of changes to these settings.

The **GetSystemMetrics**, **GetSysColor**, and **System-ParametersInfo** functions and the **WM_SETTINGCHANGE** message are important to consider when supporting standard system settings. For more information about these system interfaces, see the Microsoft Platform SDK on the MSDN Online Web site at http://msdn.microsoft.com/ui/guide/sdk.asp.

Integrating with the Shell

Windows includes programming interfaces that enable you to integrate and extend the system's operational environment, also known as the *shell*. Some of these interfaces enable you to add features to the shell and the user interface components it provides. Others enable you to build similar conventions for your own application.

Taskbar Integration

The system provides support for integrating your application's interface with the taskbar. The following sections provide information about some of the capabilities and appropriate guidelines.

Taskbar Window Buttons

When an application creates a primary window, the system automatically adds a taskbar button for that window and removes it when that window closes. For some specialized types of applications that run in the background, a primary window may not be necessary. In such cases, make sure you provide reasonable support for controlling the application using the commands available on the application's icon. This type of application should not include an entry on the taskbar. Similarly, the secondary windows of an application should also not appear as a taskbar button.

The taskbar window buttons support drag-and-drop operations, but not in the conventional way. When the user drags an object over a taskbar window button, the system automatically restores the window. The user can then drop the object in the window.

Quick Launch Toolbar

The taskbar includes a toolbar called the Quick Launch toolbar that enables users to start an application quickly. Unless your application replaces a user system service, such as an Internet browser or e-mail service, do not pre-install an icon for your application on the Quick Launch toolbar. This area is designed primarily for users to customize.

Status Notification

The system allows you to add status or notification information to the taskbar. Because the taskbar is a shared resource, the only kind of information you should add to it is information that is global or that needs monitoring by the user while the user works with other applications. Do not automatically install an icon in the status notification area just to provide convenient access to your application's features or properties. Such convenience icons might be useful for advanced users; however, for typical users, they only add clutter to a potentially already cluttered area of the screen. You can include an option for users to display an icon in the taskbar status notification area, but always configure such an option to be off by default.

The **Shell_NotifyIcon** function provides support for adding a status item in the taskbar. For more information about this function, see the Microsoft Platform SDK on the MSDN Online Web site at http://msdn.microsoft.com/ui/guide/sdk.asp.

Present status notification information in the form of a graphic supplied by your application, as shown in Figure 11.1.

Figure 11.1 Status indicator in the taskbar

When you add a status indicator to the taskbar, also support the following interactions:

- Provide a pop-up window that displays further information or controls for the object represented by the status indicator when the user clicks the primary mouse button. For example, the audio (speaker) status indicator displays a volume control. Use a pop-up window rather than a dialog box to supply further information, because the user should be able to dismiss the window by clicking elsewhere. Position the pop-up window near the status indicator so the user can navigate to it quickly and easily. Avoid displaying other types of secondary windows because they require explicit user interaction to dismiss them. If no information or control applies, do not display anything.

- Display a shortcut menu for the object represented by the status indicator when the user clicks the status indicator by using the secondary mouse button. On this menu, include commands that open property sheets or other windows related to the status indicator. For example, the audio status indicator provides commands that display the audio properties as well as the Volume Control mixer application.

- Carry out the default command defined in the shortcut menu for the status indicator when the user double-clicks.

- Display a ToolTip that indicates what the status indicator represents. For example, this could include the name of the indicator, a value, or both.

- Provide an option so that users can choose not to display the status indicator. This option would preferably appear in the property sheet for the object displaying the status indicator. This allows users to determine which indicator to include in this shared space. You may need to provide an alternate way to convey this status information when users turn off the status indicator.

- Use balloon tips to provide message notifications for your taskbar icon. This can help bring users' attention to the taskbar icon or communicate state changes that users may need to be aware of but that don't require immediate user interaction.

For more information about balloon tips, see Chapter 8, "Menus, Controls, and Toolbars."

Message Notification

Sometimes your application's window is inactive but the application needs to display a message. Avoid displaying a message box on top of the currently active window and switching the input focus; instead, flash your application's title bar and taskbar window button to notify the users of the pending message. This avoids interfering with the user's current activity but lets the user know a message is waiting. When the user activates your application's window, the application can display a message box.

To set your flash rate, use the system setting for the cursor blink rate. This allows users to set the flash rate to a comfortable frequency.

Rather than flashing the button continually, you can flash the window button only a limited number of times (for example, three), then leave the button in the highlighted state, as shown in Figure 11.2. This lets users know there is still a pending message.

The **FlashWindow** function supports flashing your title bar and taskbar window button. The **GetCaretBlinkTime** function provides access to the current cursor blink rate setting. For more information about these functions, see the Microsoft Platform SDK on the MSDN Online Web site at http://msdn.microsoft.com/ui/guide/sdk.asp.

Figure 11.2 Flashing a taskbar button to notify a user of a pending message

The taskbar status notification area and balloon tips are alternative ways to alert users about a special condition when your application's window is not active. In the taskbar status notification area, you can create an icon that displays a balloon tip. This is less intrusive than a message box. After the user resolves the condition that required notification, remove the icon and balloon tip.

Control Panel Integration

Windows Control Panel includes special objects that let users configure overall settings or features of their operating environment. Your application can add Control Panel objects or add property pages to the property sheets of existing Control Panel objects.

Adding Control Panel Objects

Before you create an object to be included in Control Panel (also known as a CPL), consider whether the feature and its settings meet the following criteria:

For more information about developing Control Panel objects, see the Microsoft Platform SDK on the MSDN Online Web site at http://msdn.microsoft.com/ui/guide/sdk.asp.

- The settings represent a system component for Windows. It is not appropriate to create a Control Panel object for application-centric settings.

- The settings are user-oriented rather than administrator-oriented. Administrator-oriented features should be implemented as part of the defined policy interfaces.

- The settings are best designed to require manual user interaction. Settings that can be automated should not also appear in Control Panel.

- The settings require high, centralized visibility.

- The settings are pervasive and have significant impact on the user's interaction. For example, the settings for a mouse or keyboard significantly determine how users interact with Windows.

- The settings cannot logically be added as an extension of the existing user interface. Many of the system-supplied CPLs are extensible, allowing you to add extra pages to the existing property sheets. For example, you can extend the Display CPL to support specific settings for a particular graphics adapter. Extending the existing CPLs, instead of adding new ones, results in a simpler experience for users.

- The settings are not intended to provide product support. If your application must expose certain settings to facilitate help desk or product support, include a program in your application's folder or its utilities folder that can be accessed directly.

- The settings provide parameters that users are likely to need or want to change and are not used only to display status information.

When you create a Control Panel object, choose a user-friendly name that generically describes its function rather than the name of a technology. Because Control Panel is a system folder, design the icon for your Control Panel object to be consistent with the Windows guidelines. If the icon relates to a product, the icon can be designed to be more representative of the product (for example, a specific type of mouse or keyboard), but keep its name generic, not product-specific.

If your CPL is an object, such as the keyboard or mouse, the name of the icon in Control Panel should be "[object]," and the title of the resulting window should be named "[object] Properties." For a concept, such as the Regional or Accessibility CPL, use the name of the concept and the word "Options," as in "Regional Options," for both the icon and the title of the window. In general, use a single secondary window, typically a property sheet or wizard, to display the settings of your Control Panel object.

Every Control Panel object is a .dll file. To ensure that the file can automatically be loaded by the system, give the file name a .cpl extension and install the file in the Windows System folder.

Recycle Bin Integration

The Recycle Bin provides a repository for deleted files. If your application includes a facility for deleting files, support the Recycle Bin using the system file operation programming interfaces.

Your application can support OLE drag-and-drop transfers into the Recycle Bin. This is done by using the standard drag-and-drop mechanism. Because the Recycle Bin cannot store application data, you should support an **Undo** command to enable users to restore the data after a drag-and-drop transfer to the Recycle Bin. You can also generate a warning message box in this situation so that users are aware that the data will be deleted permanently.

The **SHFileOperation** function supports deletion using the Recycle Bin interface. For more information about this function, see the Microsoft Platform SDK on the MSDN Online Web site at http://msdn.microsoft.com/ui/guide/sdk.asp.

Creating Active Desktop Items

Windows includes support for users to optionally configure the desktop to display dynamic objects called Active Desktop items. Active Desktop items enable you to deliver content directly to the user without the need for a window. However, creating an Active

Desktop item requires special design considerations. For example, Active Desktop items are not visible or accessible to many users, so avoid making this type of item the sole interface to your application or data.

Keep It Simple, Small, and Unobtrusive

Design Active Desktop items to be simple and unobtrusive. Remember that desktop real estate is limited and that the desktop is an active work area for the user. Even if the Active Desktop item is intended to provide continuous updated content, such as a stock ticker or news ticker, limit the size of the update area. This avoids distracting the user and minimizes system performance impact. When an Active Desktop item is obtrusive, the user often removes the item.

Avoid Relying on an Active Connection

An Active Desktop item will often be viewed when the system is not connected to the Internet. Therefore, you may want to support caching the updated content so that users can still browse the information. Also, consider indicating when the content was last updated.

Make It Personal

Whenever possible, enable users to customize the content presented by an Active Desktop item. For example, for a stock ticker or news ticker, users should be able to personalize the item with specific stocks or types of news items.

Creating Folder Web Views

Windows includes support for creating *Web views*, HTML-authored pages that provide a backdrop for folders. You can use a Web view to create a graphical, interactive view to customize any folder. However, keep your design simple and relatively passive to avoid distracting users.

For example, you can use Web views for corporate branding; that is; add graphical elements that identify your product, as shown in Figure 11.3.

Figure 11.3 Example of a Web view

Use branding only in Web view folders, not in dialog boxes (such as Add/Remove, Search, Printer, Organize Favorites, or Http Errors). Corporate branding uses up valuable screen real estate, especially in smaller formats. Branding graphics could also be replaced by Windows Plus Pack themes, leading to unforeseen problems.

Creating Themes

Windows supports installation and user selection of themes. A theme is a collection of visual and audio system settings designed to enhance the user's experience and help provide a consistent design across the Windows environment. More specifically, a theme consists of the following elements:

- Wallpaper – a visual image for the desktop

- Icons – including at least images for My Computer, My Documents, Network Neighborhood, and Recycle Bin (full and empty)

- Pointers – including the fourteen standard system pointers

- System sounds – including the 20 system sounds (for more information, see "Creating System Sounds" later in this chapter)

- Web views

- Screen saver – one or more

- Palette settings (color settings)

- Display scheme – including fonts, font sizes, icon spacing, system color scheme, and desktop background colors

When you design a theme, consider the following aesthetic and functional guidelines:

- Set all your sounds to the same reasonable volume and make sure they fit together as a collection.

- Use sounds that are pleasant and natural. Select sounds that users will not find irritating or annoying after continued use.

- Consider the impact of multiple-monitor display configuration and password protection for your screen-saver definition.

- Make sure your color scheme provides sufficient contrast, especially so that fonts are readable.

- Avoid designing wallpapers with too much clutter. Keep things simple enough so that screen-saver content and desktop content do not conflict.

- Define pointers with obvious hotspots.

- Include icons for all recommended sizes and color palettes.

- Make sure that there is some level of consistency between the screen saver and the wallpaper.

For more information about icon design, see Chapter 14, "Visual Design."

To support your theme, install all of its elements in a single folder. Define and register a theme file (stored as ASCII text) that includes the path names to all the theme elements.

Creating System Sounds

In general, Windows system sounds should be subtle to avoid annoying users. Since there is no overall system amplitude control, set the relative amplitude for each sound so that, for example, critical notification sounds are slightly louder than frequently occurring window open and close sounds. Individual sounds should not be normalized. When you design custom system sounds, it is useful to compare new sound amplitudes with the associated default Windows event sound amplitude.

Windows defines the following standard system sound events.

Windows Standard System Sound Events

Name	Description
Asterisk	Plays when an information message box is displayed that provides information about the results of a command.
Close program	Plays when users quit a program.
Critical Stop	Plays when a critical message box is displayed that informs users about a serious problem that requires intervention or correction before work can continue.
Default sound	Plays whenever a program uses a sound to indicate that a process has finished, a user has clicked in an invalid location, or a generic system notification is needed.
Empty Recycle Bin	Plays when users empty the Recycle Bin.
Exclamation	Plays when a warning message box is displayed that alerts the user to a condition or situation that requires user input before proceeding.
Exit Windows	Plays when users shut down Windows.
Maximize	Plays when a window is maximized.
Menu command	Plays when a command is chosen from a menu.
Menu popup	Plays when a menu or submenu appears.
Minimize	Plays when a window is minimized.
New Mail Notification	Plays when a new mail message arrives.

Windows Standard System Sound Events *(continued)*

Name	Description
Open program	Plays when users start a program.
Program error	Plays when a program has a General Protection fault and a message is displayed.
Question	Plays when a message box with a question mark appears. This kind of message box was used in previous versions of Windows to display cautionary messages phrased as a question.
Restore Down	Plays when a window is restored from a maximized state.
Restore Up	Plays when a window is restored from a minimized state.
RingIn	Plays when users receive an incoming call.
Ringout	Plays when users place an outgoing call.
Start Windows	Plays when users log on to Windows.

You can also add your own application-defined sound events. For more information, see "Registering Sound Events" later in this chapter.

Format

Sounds must be in .wav file format. They can be 8-bit or 16-bit files, have up to a 44K sample rate, play in mono or stereo, and can be compressed.

The recommended format for sounds is as follows:

- 16-bit

- 22kHz

The sound format you choose to use in your application depends on your target platform. Because sounds can be processed through only one translation before being played, not all sounds are compatible with all hardware. For example, a 16-bit stereo file compressed with

ADPCM cannot be played on an 8-bit sound card. If you plan to compress your sound files to save disk space, use 16-bit files with mono sounds. If you do not plan to compress them, then 16-bit stereo sounds will work on most systems.

Many applications are available for creating and editing .wav files, including the Sound Recorder program included with Windows. Although Sound Recorder is adequate, it is recommended that you use commercially available tools that offer good down-sampling functions for creating final sounds.

Guidelines for Sounds

In general, sounds should be designed to complement their associated graphical or functional event. The most common system or application sounds should be designed to convey functional or navigational information to users about what they are doing.

The more often the sound is played, the less obtrusive the sound should be. Unless you are designing a sound for an infrequently used novelty application or theme, sounds should be subtle, even barely noticeable. Most well-designed sound schemes are barely noticeable, but if they were absent, the user would miss them.

Appropriate sound design generally reflects the physics of the dominant interface metaphor being used. For example, playing a .wav file of a bird chirping every time the user opens a new Window may be appropriate as a novelty children's theme, but for everyday use, it would eventually become annoying to the average user.

For the most common notification and alert sounds, shorter sounds work best. For example, a sound that plays for five seconds would not be appropriate for the Menu popup event, but a five-second sound might work for the Exit Windows event.

In addition to using shorter sounds for the more frequent sound events, the audio frequency of each sound plays a significant role in user fatigue. It is best to avoid repetitive use of sounds that contain too much low-frequency information. For example, if you use a swish sound for the Open Program or Close Program event, it is much more pleasant and less annoying to use a swish sound that does not sound like a stormy wind gust. In the majority of cases, selecting the appropriate equalization (frequency-based filtering) for the sound to cut back the low frequencies will help users tolerate repetitive sounds.

Registering Sound Events

Your application can register specific events to which the user can assign sound files. When those events are triggered, the assigned sound file is played. To register a sound event, create a key under the **HKEY_CURRENT_USER** key, as follows:

```
HKEY_CURRENT_USER
    AppEvents
        Event Labels
            EventName = Event Name
```

Set the value for **EventName** to a name that users can read. This is what will appear in Control Panel.

Registering a sound event makes it available in Control Panel so that users can assign a sound file to it. Your application must provide the code to trigger that event when appropriate.

Defining as many sound events as possible for your application can be especially helpful for users who need additional feedback — for example, users with visual and some types of cognitive impairments. This does not mean that your application must generate sounds for all events. You can simply not assign sounds to an event by default. This way, users who want additional feedback can use Control Panel to add appropriate sounds.

Always specify sounds to be played by using registry entries. Avoid specifying sounds by file name or resource, because these cannot be customized through Control Panel, and because accessibility aids cannot determine the meaning of these sounds.

In addition, always trigger standard sound events when carrying out equivalent actions. For example, if you display the equivalent of a critical message box, play the **SND_ALIAS_SYSTEMEXCLAMATION** event sound.

For more information about system sound events, see the Microsoft Platform SDK on the MSDN Online Web site at http://msdn.microsoft.com/ui/guide/sdk.asp.

Creating Application Desktop Toolbars

The system supports applications supplying their own desktop
toolbars, also referred to as access bars or appbars, that operate
similarly to the Windows taskbar. Before you include a desktop
toolbar, consider whether your application's tasks really require one.
Remember that a desktop toolbar potentially reduces the visible
work area for all applications. Therefore, you should include a
desktop toolbar only for frequently used interfaces that can be
applied across applications. If a toolbar applies only to a specific
application or set of applications, consider removing it when those
applications are closed. Also, design a desktop toolbar to be optional
so that users can close it or otherwise specify that it not appear.

When you create your own desktop toolbar, design its behavior to be
consistent with the system taskbar. For example, support auto-hide.
This allows the desktop toolbar to be visible only when the user
moves the pointer to the edge of the screen. The system supports the
same auto-hide behavior for application desktop toolbars as it does
for the taskbar; but only for one desktop toolbar on each edge of the
display. Support drag-and-drop transfers to your desktop toolbar if it
includes objects that support transfer operations.

Support undocking and redocking of the desktop toolbar. Display an
undocked toolbar as a palette window that no longer constrains other
windows. However, if the toolbar supports the Always on Top
property, it should remain on top of other application windows.

For more information about
the recommended behavior
for undocking and redocking toolbars, see Chapter 8, "Menus, Controls, and Toolbars."

Provide a shortcut menu to give users access to commands that apply
to the toolbar as a whole, such as **Close**, **Move**, **Size**, and **Properties**.
Do not include on the shortcut menu any commands — such as
Minimize All Windows — that are included on the desktop toolbar.
If the system-supplied customization does not fit your design, be sure
to provide your own property sheet for setting these attributes for
your desktop toolbar.

You can choose to display a desktop toolbar when the user runs a specific application, or you can create a separate application and include a shortcut icon to it in the system's Startup folder. Set the initial size and position of your desktop toolbar so that it does not interfere with other desktop toolbars or with the taskbar. The system supports docking multiple desktop toolbars along the same edge of the display screen. When you dock a toolbar on the same edge of the display screen as the taskbar, the system places the taskbar on the outermost edge.

Supporting Full-Screen Display

Although the taskbar and application desktop toolbars normally constrain or clip windows displayed on the screen, you can define a window to the full extent of the display screen. Because this is not the typical form of interaction, consider using full-screen display only for very special circumstances, such as a slide presentation, and only when users explicitly choose a command for this purpose. Make sure you provide an easy way for users to return to normal display viewing. For example, you can display an on-screen button that users can click to restore the display. In addition, keyboard interfaces, such as ALT+TAB and ESC, should automatically restore the display.

Remember that desktop toolbars, including the taskbar, should support auto-hide options that allow users to reduce toolbars' visual impact on the screen. Consider whether this auto-hide capability may be sufficient before designing your application to require a full-screen presentation. Advising users to close or hide desktop toolbars may provide you with sufficient space without having to use the full display screen.

Some users rely on accessibility aids that must be visible at all times for them to interact with the computer. For example, an on-screen keyboard allows users to simulate keystrokes using a pointing device. When your application is in full-screen mode, such utilities may attempt to position themselves on top of your window. Do not prevent this by requiring that your window always be on top.

Using the Folder Metaphor

Windows also includes interfaces that enable you to create your own folder-like containers. However, if you intend to use the folder metaphor for collections of objects, ensure that you provide consistent support for the full range of folder behaviors. Users have certain expectations about what can be done with objects that express the folder metaphor. For example, a Windows folder includes support for the following functions:

For more information about the **IShellFolder** interfaces, see the MSDN Online Web site at http://msdn.microsoft.com/ui/guide/shellfolder.asp.

- Drag-and-drop operations

- Property sheets on objects contained in the folder

- Large icon, small icon, list, and details view

- Web view of contents

- Common commands for contents, such as **Cut**, **Copy**, **Paste**, **Rename**, **Delete**, and **Create Shortcut**

- Standard verbs used for files, such as Open and Edit

If your design cannot provide reasonable consistency, you may be better off using a list box or list view control in a dialog box.

Supporting Network Computing

Windows provides an environment that allows users to communicate and share information across the network. When designing your software, consider the special needs that working in such an environment requires.

Conceptually, the network is an expansion of the user's local space. The interface for accessing objects from the network should not differ significantly from or be more complex than the user's desktop.

When you design for network access, support standard conventions and interfaces, including the following:

- Use universal naming convention (UNC) paths to refer to objects stored in the file system. This convention provides transparent access to objects on the network.

- Use system-supported user identification that allows you to determine access without including your own password interface.

- Adjust window sizes and positions based on the local screen properties of the user.

- Avoid assuming the presence of a local hard disk. It is possible that some of your users work with diskless workstations.

Supporting Hardware Devices

Hardware devices often include special software to support installation and configuration options. Avoid creating your own setup and configuration user interface and instead use the system-supplied interfaces and conventions. For example, the system automatically supports basic property settings in Device Manager. You can extend this for specialized configuration options by defining an **Advanced** tab for the system-supplied property sheet.

Similarly, avoid adding objects to Control Panel, taskbar notification, or the **Start** menu to support your hardware device except as recommended otherwise in this chapter.

Additional information about designing drivers and hardware for Windows can be found in the PC Design Guide on the Microsoft Windows Driver and Hardware Development Web site at http://www.microsoft.com/hwdev.

Supporting Multiple-Monitor Configuration Devices

Windows 98 and Windows 2000 enable users to display windows across multiple monitors. To properly support multiple monitors, make sure that your application handles an arbitrarily large coordinate space. Unless a user explicitly moves a window to another monitor, display the window on the primary monitor. Similarly, always open secondary windows on the same monitor as their associated primary window, unless the user moves the window to another monitor.

It is also recommended that your application always open its window in the location, size, and position it was in the last time it was opened, unless the task represented by the window always needs to begin in a specific state. In addition, because the user can change the configuration, always check the system settings and adjust your windows to the latest configuration.

Supporting Plug and Play

Plug and Play is a feature of Windows that, with little or no user intervention, automatically installs and configures drivers when their corresponding hardware peripherals are plugged into a PC. This feature applies to peripherals designed according to the Plug and Play specification. Supporting and appropriately adapting to Plug and Play hardware can make your application easier to use. The following are some examples of how you can support Plug and Play:

- Resize your windows and toolbars as the screen size changes.

- Prompt users to shut down and save their data when the system issues a low-power warning.

- Warn users about open network files when they undock their computers.

- Save and close files appropriately when users eject or remove removable media or storage devices or when network connections are broken.

Working with OLE Embedded and Linked Objects

The Microsoft Object Linking and Embedding technology (OLE) makes objects created in a document in one application available to a document created in another application. For example, a user can store a table created in a spreadsheet application in a word processing document. This chapter discusses guidelines for designing the interface for embedded and linked objects implemented with OLE. However, you can apply many of these guidelines to any implementation of a container.

The Interaction Model

As data becomes the major focus of interface design, its content is what occupies the user's attention, not the application managing it. In such a design, data is not limited to its native creation and editing environment; that is, the user is not limited to creating or editing data only within its associated application window. Instead, data can be transferred to other types of containers where it can still be displayed and edited in the window of the container application. Compound documents are a common example of the interaction between containers and their components, but they are not the only expression of this kind of object relationship.

Figure 12.1 shows an example of a compound document. The document includes word-processing text, tabular data from a spreadsheet, a sound recording, and pictures created in other applications.

Classical CD Review

by Thomas D. Becker

The introduction of the compact disc has had a far greater impact on the recording industry than anyone could have imagined, especially the manufacturers of vinyl long play (LP) albums. With the 1991 sales totals in, compact disc is clearly the preferred recording medium for American ears. In addition to audio compact discs, CD-ROMs are appearing on the market offering a multimedia experience of the classical repetoire. The Microsoft Composer Collection brings you the ability to enter the lives and minds of three astounding musical geniuses. That's because the Composer Collection contains three CD-ROM titles full of music, information, and entertainment. They are: Microsoft Multimedia Mozart, Microsoft Multimedia Stravinsky, and Microsoft Multimedia Beethoven. These works are reviewed below - be sure to check them out! -*TDB*

U.S. Compact Disc vs. LP Sales ($)

	1983	1987	1991
CDs	6,345K	18,652K	32,657K
LPs	31,538K	26,571K	17,429K
Total	37,883K	45,223K	50,086K

Multimedia Mozart: The Dissonant Quartet

The Voyager Company
Microsoft

In the words of author and music scholar Robert Winter, the string quartet in the eighteenth century was regarded as one of the "most sublime forms of communication." The String Quartet in C Major is no exception. Discover the power and the beauty of this music with Microsoft Multimedia Mozart: *The Dissonant Quartet,* and enter the world in which Mozart created his most memorable masterpieces. Sit back and enjoy *The Dissonant Quartet* in its entirety, or browse around, exploring its themes and emotional dynamics in depth. View the entire piece in a single-screen overview with the *Pocket Audio Guide.*

Multimedia Stravinsky: The Rite of Spring

The Voyager Company
Microsoft

Multimedia Stravinsky: *The Rite of Spring* offers you an in-depth look at this controversial composition. Author Robert

Winter provides a fascinating commentary that follows the music, giving you greater understanding of the subtle dynamics of the instruments and powerful techniques of Stravinsky. You'll also have the opportunity to discover the ballet that accompanied *The Rite of Spring* in performance. Choreographed by Sergei Diaghilev, the ballet was as unusual for its time as the music. To whet your appetite, play this audio clip.

Multimedia Beethoven: The Ninth Symphony

The Voyager Company
Microsoft

Multimedia Beethoven: The Ninth Symphony is one of a series of engaging, informative, and interactive musical explorations from Microsoft. It enables you to examine Beethoven's world and life, and explore the form and beauty of one of his foremost compositions. You can compare musical themes, hear selected orchestral instruments, and see the symphonic score come alive. Multimedia Beethoven: *The Ninth Symphony* is an extraordinary opportunity to learn while you listen to one of the world's musical treasures. Explore this inspiring work at your own pace in *A Close Reading.* As you listen to a superb performance of Beethoven's

The Audiophile Journal, June 1994   **12**

Figure 12.1 A compound document

How was this music review created? First, a user created a document and typed the text, then moved, copied, or linked content from other documents. Data objects that retain their native full-featured editing and operating capabilities when they are moved or copied and stored into another container (document) are called *embedded objects*.

A user can also link information. A *linked object* represents or provides access to another object that is stored in another location in the same container or in a different, separate container.

This distinction is important for reasons other than the storage location. Embedded data no longer has any association with its source; that is, if you change the source data, the change is not reflected in the embedded object. Similarly, if you change the data in the embedded object, the change is not reflected in the source. With linked objects, the data is being displayed *from the source document,* so a change in either place is propagated to the other.

Generally, containers support nesting of embedded and linked objects to any level. For example, a user can embed a chart in a worksheet, which, in turn, can be embedded in a word-processing document. The model for interaction is consistent at each level of nesting.

Creating Embedded and Linked Objects

Embedded and linked objects are the result of transferring existing objects or creating new objects of a particular type directly in the container document.

Transferring Objects

Transferring objects into a document follows basic command and direct manipulation interaction methods. The following sections provide additional guidelines for these commands when you use them to create embedded or linked objects.

For more information about command transfer and direct manipulation transfer methods, see Chapter 6, "General Interaction Techniques."

The Paste Command

Generally, when the user clicks the **Paste** command, the pasted object should be inserted as an embedded object. However, if the destination container can handle the native format of the pasted object, the container can optionally embed the object as native data instead of embedding it as a separate object. The destination container can also optionally transform the object to a form that it supports or transfer only the salient aspects of the object, such as the object's properties.

Use the format of the **Paste** command to indicate to the user how a transferred object will be incorporated by a container.

Several different things can happen when a user copies a file object:

- If the container can embed the object, include the object's file name as a suffix to the **Paste** command.

- If the object is only a portion of a file, use the short file type name — for example, **Paste Worksheet** or **Paste Recording** — as shown in Figure 12.2. A short type name can be derived from information stored in the registry.

- If the **Paste** command has no name, the data will be pasted as native information.

For more information about type names and the system registry, see Chapter 11, "Integrating with the System," and the OLE documentation included in the Microsoft Platform SDK on the MSDN Online Web site at http://msdn.microsoft.com/ui/guide/sdk.asp.

Figure 12.2 The **Paste** command with short type name

The Paste Special Command

To give the user explicit control over pasting in the data as native information, an embedded object, or a linked object, include the **Paste Special** command. The Paste Special dialog box, as shown in Figure 12.3, includes a list box showing the possible formats that the data can assume in the destination container.

For more information about the Paste Special dialog box and other OLE-related dialog boxes that are described in this chapter, see the Microsoft Platform SDK on the MSDN Online Web site at http://msdn.microsoft.com/ui/guide/sdk.asp.

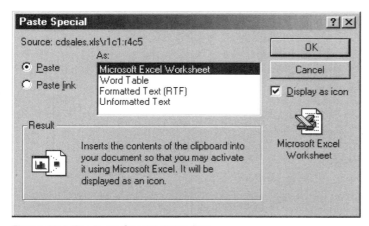

Figure 12.3 The Paste Special dialog box

In the formats listed in the Paste Special dialog box, include the object's full type name first, followed by other appropriate native data forms. When a linked object has been cut or copied, precede its object type by the word "Linked" in the format list. For example, if the user copies a linked Microsoft Excel worksheet, the Paste Special dialog box shows "Linked Microsoft Excel Worksheet" in the list of format options because it inserts a copy of the link; that is, a link to the original linked worksheet. For native data formats, begin with the destination application's name and express the format in the same terms the destination identifies in its own menus. Set the format initially selected in the list to correspond to the default format that the **Paste** command uses. For example, if the **Paste** command is displayed as **Paste** *Object File Name* or **Paste** *Short Type Name* because the data to be embedded is a file or portion of a file, set the same format in the Paste Special list box.

To support creating a linked object, the Paste Special dialog box includes a **Paste link** option, as shown in Figure 12.4.

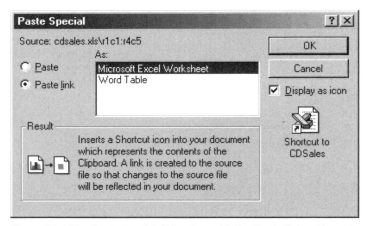

Figure 12.4 The Paste Special dialog box with the **Paste link** option set

If users want to display the embedded or linked object as an icon, they can select the **Display as icon** check box. The text and pictures at the bottom of the dialog box describe the result of the operation. The following table lists the descriptive text to use in the Paste Special dialog box.

Text for Paste Special Dialog Box

Function	Resulting text
Paste as an embedded object	"Inserts the contents of the Clipboard into your document so that you can activate it using *CompanyName ApplicationName*."
Paste as an embedded object so that it appears as an icon	"Inserts the contents of the Clipboard into your document so that you can activate it using *CompanyName ApplicationName*. It will be displayed as an icon."
Paste as native data	"Inserts the contents of the Clipboard into your document as *Native Type Name*. *[Optional additional Help sentence.]*"
Paste as a linked object	"Inserts a picture of the contents of the Clipboard into your document. The picture is linked to the source file so that changes to the file will be reflected in your document."

Text for Paste Special Dialog Box *(continued)*

Function	Resulting text
Paste as a linked object	"Inserts a shortcut icon into your document so that it appears as a shortcut which represents the contents of the Clipboard. The shortcut created is linked to the source file so that changes to the file will be reflected in your document."
Paste as linked native data	"Inserts the contents of the Clipboard into your document as *Native Type Name*. A link is created to the source file so that changes to the source file will be reflected in your document."

The Paste Link, Paste Shortcut, and Create Shortcut Commands

If linking is a common function in your application, you can optionally include a command that optimizes this process. Use a **Paste Link** command to support creating a linked object or linked native data. When the user chooses to create a linked object, the command should include the name of the object preceded by the word "to" — for example, "**Paste Link to Latest Sales**." Omitting the name implies that the operation results in linked native data.

Use a **Paste Shortcut** command to support creation of a linked object that appears as a shortcut icon. You can also include a **Create Shortcut** command that creates a shortcut icon in the container. Apply these commands to containers where icons are commonly used.

Direct Manipulation

You should also support direct manipulation interaction techniques, such as drag-and-drop transfers, for creating embedded or linked objects. When the user drags a selection into a container, the container application interprets the operation using information supplied by both the source (such as the selection's type and format) and the container's own context (such as the container's type and its default transfer operation). For example, dragging a spreadsheet cell selection into a word-processing document can result in an embedded table object. Dragging the same cell selection within the

For more information about using direct manipulation for moving, copying, and linking objects, see Chapter 6, "General Interaction Techniques."

spreadsheet, however, would probably result in simply transferring the data in the cells. Similarly, the container in which the user drops the selection can also determine whether the dragging operation results in a linked object.

In a nondefault drag-and-drop transfer, the container application displays a shortcut menu with appropriate transfer commands at the end of the drag. The choices may include multiple commands that transfer the data in a different format or presentation. For example, as shown in Figure 12.5, a container application could offer the following choices for creating links:

- **Link Here**, which would result in a native data link.

- **Link *Short Type Name* Here**, which would result in a linked object displayed as content.

- **Create Shortcut Here**, which would result in a linked object displayed as an icon.

The choices depend on what the container can support.

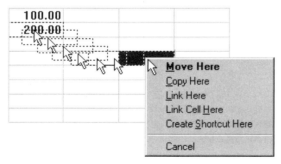

Figure 12.5 A container with different link options

The default appearance of a transferred object also depends on the destination container application. For most types of documents, make the default command one that results in the object being presented as data or content rather than as an icon. If the user clicks **Create Shortcut Here** as the transfer operation, display the transferred object as an icon. If the object cannot be displayed as content — for example, because it does not support OLE — always display the object as an icon.

Transfer of Data to the Desktop

If the application supports the transfer protocol, the system allows the user to transfer selected data within a file to the desktop or to a folder. For move or copy operations — using the **Cut**, **Copy**, and **Paste** commands or direct manipulation — the transfer operation results in a file icon called a *scrap*. A link operation also results in a shortcut icon that represents a link to data in a document.

When the user transfers a scrap into a container supported by your application, integrate it as if it were being transferred from its original source. For example, if the user transfers a selected range of cells from a spreadsheet to the desktop, it becomes a scrap. If the user transfers the resulting scrap into a word-processing document, the document should incorporate the scrap as if the cells were transferred directly from the spreadsheet. Similarly, if the user transfers the scrap back into the spreadsheet, the spreadsheet should integrate the cells as if they had been transferred within that spreadsheet. Typically, internal transfers of native data within a container result in repositioning the data rather than transforming it.

Inserting New Objects

In addition to transferring objects, you can support user creation of new embedded or linked objects in a container document.

The Insert Object Command

Include an **Insert Object** command on your application's menu that contains the commands for creating or importing new objects into a container, such as an **Insert** menu. If no such menu exists, use the **Edit** menu. When the user selects the **Insert Object** command, display the Insert Object dialog box, as shown in Figure 12.6. This dialog box allows the user to generate new objects based on their object type or the format of an existing file.

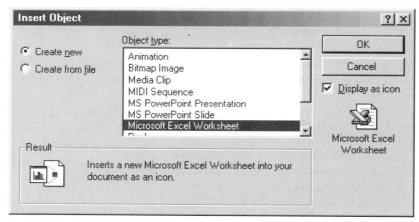

Figure 12.6 The Insert Object dialog box

The type list is composed of the names of registered object types. When the user selects a type from the list box and clicks **OK**, an object of the selected type is created and embedded.

For more information about type names and the registry, see Chapter 11, "Integrating with the System."

The user can also create an embedded or linked object from an existing file by using the **Create from file** and **Link** options. When the user chooses these options and clicks **OK**, the result is the same as directly copying or linking the selected file.

When the user chooses the **Create from file** option, the **Object type** list is removed, and a text box and **Browse** button appear in its place, as shown in Figure 12.7. Ignore any selection formerly displayed in the **Object type** list box.

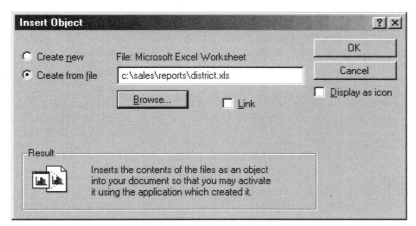

Figure 12.7 Creating an embedded object from an existing file

The text box initially includes the current folder as the selection. The user can edit the current folder path when specifying a file. As an alternative, the **Browse** button displays an Open dialog box that allows the user to navigate through the file system to select a file. Use the file's type to determine the type of the resulting object.

Use the **Link** check box to support the creation of a link to the file specified. The Insert Object dialog box displays this option only when the user chooses the **Create from file** option. This means that a user cannot insert a linked object when choosing the **Create new** option, because linked objects can be created only from existing files.

The **Display as icon** check box in the Insert Object dialog box enables the user to specify whether to display the object as an icon. When the user chooses this option, the icon appears below the check box. A linked object displayed as an icon is the equivalent of a shortcut icon. It should appear with the link symbol over the icon.

If the user chooses to insert a non-OLE file, it can be inserted only as an icon. The result is a package. A *package* is an encapsulation of a file so that it can be embedded in a container. Because packages support limited editing and viewing capabilities, support OLE for all your object types so they will not be converted into packages.

At the bottom of the Insert Object dialog box, text and pictures describe how the object will be inserted. The following table outlines the syntax of descriptive text to use in the Insert Object dialog box.

Text for Insert Object Dialog Box

Function	Resulting text
Create a new embedded object based on the selected type.	"Inserts a new *Type Name* into your document."
Create a new embedded object based on the selected type and display it as an icon.	"Inserts a new *Type Name* into your document as an icon."
Create a new embedded object based on a selected file.	"Inserts the contents of the file as an object into your document so that you can activate it using the application that created it."
Create a new embedded object based on a selected file (copies the file) and display it as an icon.	"Inserts the contents of the file as an object into your document so that you can activate it using the application that created it. It will be displayed as an icon."
Create a linked object that is linked to a selected file.	"Inserts a picture of the file contents into your document. The picture will be linked to the file so that changes to the file will be reflected in your document."
Create a linked object that is linked to a selected file and display it as a shortcut icon.	"Inserts a shortcut icon into your document that represents the file. The shortcut icon will be linked to the original file, so that you can quickly open the original from inside your document."

You can also use the context of the current selection in the container to determine the format of the newly created object and the effect of its being inserted into the container. For example, if the user selects data in a table and then inserts a graph, you could use the selected data to format the graph. Use the following guidelines to support predictable insertion:

- If an inserted object is not based on the current selection, follow the same conventions as for a **Paste** command and add or replace the selection depending on the context. For example, in text or list contexts, where the selection represents the location at which the object is to be inserted, replace the active selection. For non-ordered or Z-ordered contexts, where the selection does not

For more information about the guidelines for inserting an object with a **Paste** command, see Chapter 6, "General Interaction Techniques."

represent an explicit insertion point, add the object. Use the destination's context to determine where to place the object.

- If the new object is automatically connected (linked) to the selection (for example, an inserted graph based on selected table data), insert the new object in addition to the selection and make the inserted object the new selection.

After inserting an embedded object, activate it for editing. However, if the user inserts a linked object, do not activate the object.

Other Techniques for Inserting Objects

The **Insert Object** command provides support for inserting all registered objects. You can include additional commands tailored to provide access to common or frequently used object types. You can implement these as additional menu commands or as toolbar buttons or other controls. These buttons provide the same functionality as the Insert Object dialog box, but perform more efficiently. Figure 12.8 illustrates two examples. The user clicks the drawing button to insert a new blank drawing object; the user clicks the graph button to create a new graph that uses the data values from a currently selected table.

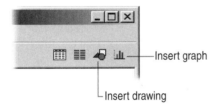

Figure 12.8 Using toolbar buttons to create new objects

Displaying Objects

While a container can control whether to display an embedded or linked object in its content or icon presentation, the container requests the object to display itself in the area the object supplies. In the content presentation, the object may visually be indistinguishable from native objects, as shown in Figure 12.9.

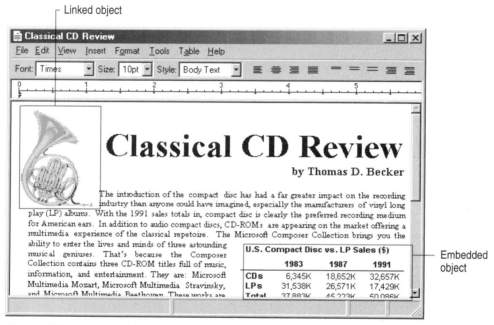

Figure 12.9 A compound document containing objects

You can also enable the user to visually identify embedded or linked objects without interacting with them. To do so, you can include a **Show Objects** command. When the user clicks this command, draw a solid one-pixel-wide border, in the window text color, around the embedded object. Use a dotted border around linked objects (shown in Figure 12.10). If your container (application) cannot guarantee that a linked object is up-to-date with its source because of an unsuccessful automatic update or a manual link, draw a dotted border using the system grayed-text color to show that the linked object may be out of date. The border should be drawn around a container's first-level objects only, not objects nested below this level.

The **GetSysColor** function provides the current settings for window text color (**COLOR_WINDOWTEXT**) and grayed text color (**COLOR_GRAY-TEXT**). For more information about this function, see the Microsoft Platform SDK on the MSDN Online Web site at http://msdn.microsoft.com/ui/guide/sdk.asp.

Border for linked object

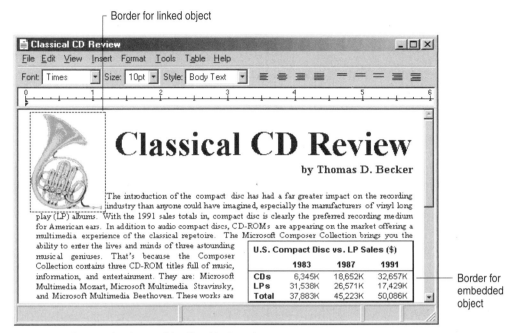

Border for embedded object

Figure 12.10 Using borders to identify objects

If these border conventions are not adequate to distinguish embedded and linked objects, you can include additional distinctions; however, make them clearly different from the appearance of any standard visual states and distinguish between embedded and linked objects.

Whenever the user creates a linked or embedded object by clicking the **Display as icon** check box, display the icon for the original object type (not the destination type), unless the user explicitly changes it. If the object is a link, include the shortcut graphic with the icon. If an icon is not registered in the registry for the object type, use the system-generated icon.

An icon includes a label. When the user creates an embedded object, define the icon's label to be one of the following, based on availability:

- The name of the object, if the object has an existing human-readable name, such as a file name without its extension.

- The object's registered short type name (for example, Picture, Worksheet), if the object does not have a name.

- The object's registered full type name (for example, a bitmap image, a Microsoft Excel Worksheet), if the object has no name or registered short type name.

- "Document" if an object has no name, a short type name, or a registered type name.

When a linked object is displayed as an icon, define the label using the source file name as it appears in the file system, preceded by the words "Shortcut to" — for example, "Shortcut to Annual Report." The path of the source is not included. Avoid displaying the file name extension unless the user chooses the system option to display extensions or the file type is not registered.

When the user creates an object linked to only a portion of a document (file), follow the same conventions for labeling the shortcut icon. However, because a container can include multiple links to different portions of the same file, you may want to provide further identification to differentiate linked objects. You can do this by appending a portion of the end of the link path (moniker). For example, you may want to include everything from the end of the path up to the last or next to last occurrence of a link path delimiter. Applications should use the exclamation point (!) character for identifying a data range. However, the link path may include other types of delimiters. When you derive an identifier from the link path, be careful to format the additional information using only valid file name characters. That way, if the user transfers the shortcut icon to a folder or to the desktop, the name can still be used.

> The system provides support to automatically format the name correctly if you use the **GetIconOfFile** function. For more information about this function, see the OLE documentation included the Microsoft Platform SDK on the MSDN Online Web site at http://msdn.microsoft.com/ui/guide/sdk.asp.

Selecting Objects

A linked or embedded object should support the same keyboard and mouse selection techniques and appearance that are available for selecting native objects. The container of the object supplies the specific appearance of the object when it is selected. For example, Figure 12.11 shows how the linked drawing of a horn is handled as part of a contiguous selection in the document.

> For information about object selection, see Chapter 6, "General Interaction Techniques." For information about selection appearance, see Chapter 14, "Visual Design."

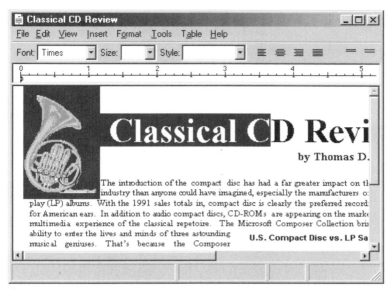

Figure 12.11 A linked object as part of a multiple selection

When the user selects just the object, display it with an appropriate selection appearance. For example, for the content view of an object, display it with handles, as shown in Figure 12.12.

Figure 12.12 An individually selected linked object

For a linked object, overlay the content view's lower left corner with the shortcut graphic. In addition, if your application's window includes a status bar that displays messages, display an appropriate description of how to activate the object (see the table "Descriptive Text for Convert Dialog Box" later in this chapter).

When the object is displayed as an icon, use the same selection appearance as for selected icons in folders and on the desktop, as shown in Figure 12.13.

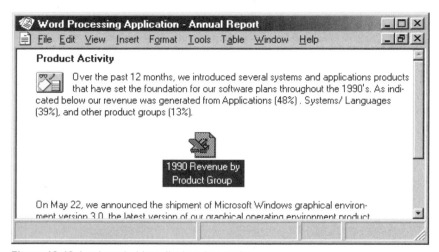

Figure 12.13 A selected object displayed as an icon

Accessing Commands for Selected Objects

A container application always displays the commands that can be applied to its objects. When the user selects an embedded or linked object as part of the selection of native data in a container, enable commands that apply to the selection as a whole. When the user selects just the object, enable only commands that apply specifically to the object. The container application retrieves these commands from registry information about the object's type and displays these commands in the object's menus. If your application includes a menu bar, include the selected object's commands on a submenu of the **Edit** menu, or as a separate menu on the menu bar. Use the name of the object as the text for the menu item. If you use the short type name that you defined in the registry as the name of the object, add the word "Object." For a linked object, use the short type name preceded by the word "Linked." Figure 12.14 shows these variations.

You can also support operations based on the selection appearance. For example, you can support operations, such as resizing, using the handles you supply. When the user resizes a selected object, however, scale the presentation of the object, because there is no method by which another operation, such as cropping, can be applied to the object.

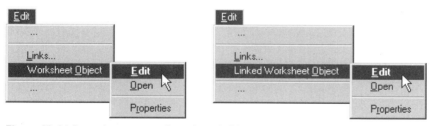

Figure 12.14 Drop-down menus for selected object

Define the first letter of the word "Object," or its localized equivalent, as the access character for keyboard users. When no object is selected, display the command with just the text — "Object" — and disable it.

Your container application should also provide a shortcut menu for a selected object (shown in Figure 12.15). The shortcut menu is displayed when the user clicks the object using the secondary mouse button (the standard interaction technique), or selects the object and presses SHIFT+F10 or the Application key. Include menu commands that apply to the object as a whole, such as transfer commands and the object's registered commands. Display the object's registered commands as individual menu items rather than in a cascading menu. It is not necessary to include the object's name or the word "Object" as part of the menu item text.

Multimedia Mozart: The Dissonant Quartet

...ger Company

In the words ... scholar Robert Winter, the ... the eighteenth century wa... of the "most sublime for... ...n." The String Quartet in C... ...n. Discover the power and ... is music with Microsoft Multimedia Mozart: *The Dissonant Quartet,* and enter the world in which Mozart created his most memorable masterpieces. Sit back and enjoy *The Dissonant Quartet* in its entirety, or browse around, exploring its themes and emotional dynamics in depth. View the entire piece in a single-screen overview with the *Pocket Audio Guide.*

Winter provides a fascinating commentary that follows the music, giving you greater understanding of the subtle dynamics of the instruments and powerful techniques of Stravinsky. You'll also have the opportunity to discover the ballet that accompanied *The Rite of Spring* in performance. Choreographed by Sergei Diaghilev, the ballet was as unusual for its time as the music. To whet your appetite, play this audio clip.

Multimedia Beethoven: The Ninth Symphony

The Voyager Company
Microsoft

Figure 12.15 The shortcut menu for an embedded picture

In both the drop-down menu and the shortcut menu, include a **Properties** command. You can also include commands that depend on the state of the object. For example, on a menu for a media object that supports Play and Rewind operations, you would disable the **Rewind** command when the media is already rewound.

When an object's type is not registered, you still supply any commands that can appropriately be applied to the object as content, such as transfer commands, alignment commands, and **Edit** and **Properties** commands. When the user clicks the **Edit** command, display the system-supplied message box. From this message box, the user can open the File Types dialog box and choose from a list of applications or convert the object's type.

Activating Objects

Although selecting an object provides access to commands applicable to the object as a whole, it does not enable editing the content of the object. The object must be activated in order to provide user interaction with the internal content of the object. There are two basic models for activating objects: outside-in activation and inside-out activation.

Outside-in Activation

Outside-in activation requires that the user choose an explicit activation command. Clicking, or some other selection operation, performed on an object that is already selected simply reselects that object and does not constitute an explicit action. The user activates the object by using a particular command such as **Edit** or **Play**, usually the object's default command. Shortcut actions that correspond to these commands, such as double-clicking or pressing a shortcut key, can also activate the object. Most container applications use this model because it allows the user to easily select objects and reduces the risk of inadvertently activating an object whose underlying code may take a significant amount of time to load and dismiss.

When supporting outside-in activation, display the standard pointer (northwest arrow) over an outside-in activated object within your container when the object is selected but inactive. This indicates to the user that the outside-in object behaves as a single, opaque object. When the user activates the object, the object's application displays the appropriate pointer for its content. Use the registry to determine the object's activation command.

Inside-out Activation

With *inside-out activation*, interaction with an object is direct; that is, the object is activated as the user moves the pointer over the extent of the object. From the user's perspective, inside-out objects are indistinguishable from native data because the content of the object is directly interactive and no additional action is necessary. Use this method for the design of objects that benefit from direct interaction, or when activating the object has little effect on performance or use of system resources.

Inside-out activation requires closer cooperation between the container and the object. For example, when the user begins a selection within an inside-out object, the container must clear its own selection so that the behavior is consistent with normal selection interaction. An object supporting inside-out activation controls the appearance of the pointer as it moves over its extent and responds immediately to input. Therefore, to select the object as a whole, the user selects the border, or some other handle, provided by the object or its container. For example, the container application can support selection techniques, such as region selection, that select the object.

Container Control of Activation

The container application determines how to activate its component objects: either it allows the inside-out objects to handle events directly or it intercedes and activates them only upon an explicit action. This is true regardless of the capability or preference setting of the object. That is, even though an object may register inside-out activation, it can be treated by a particular container as outside-in. Use an activation style for your container that is most appropriate for its specific use and in keeping with its own native style of activation so that objects can easily be assimilated.

Regardless of the activation capability of the object, a container should always activate its content objects of the same type consistently. Otherwise, the unpredictability of the interface is likely to impair its usability.

Visual Editing of Embedded Objects

One of the most common uses for activating an object is editing its content in its current location. Supporting this type of in-place interaction is called *visual editing*, because the user can edit the object within the visual context of its container.

Unless the container and the object both support inside-out activation, the user activates an embedded object for visual editing by selecting the object and choosing its **Edit** command from either a drop-down menu or a shortcut menu. You can also support shortcut techniques. For example, by making **Edit** the object's default operation, the user can double-click to activate the object for editing. Similarly, you can support pressing the ENTER key as a shortcut for activating the object.

When the user activates an embedded object for visual editing, the user interface for its content becomes available and is blended into its container application's interface. The object can display its frame *adornments*, such as row or column headers, handles, or scroll bars, outside the object boundaries, temporarily covering neighboring material. The object's application can also change the menu interface, which can range from adding items to existing drop-down menus to replacing entire drop-down menus. The object can also add toolbars, status bars, and supplemental palette windows, and can display shortcut menus for selected content.

The container application always determines the degree to which an embedded object's interface can be blended with its own, regardless of the capability or preference of the embedded object. A container application that provides its own interface for an embedded object can suppress an embedded object's own interface. Figure 12.16 shows how the interface might appear when its embedded worksheet is active.

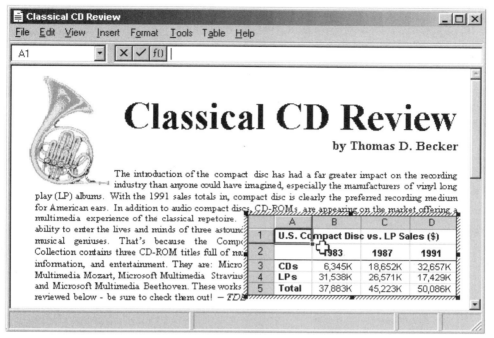

Figure 12.16 An embedded worksheet activated for visual editing

When the user activates an embedded object, avoid changing the view and position of the rest of the content in the window. Although it may seem reasonable to scroll the window and thereby preserve the content's position, doing so can disturb the user's focus, because the active object shifts down to accommodate a new toolbar and shifts back up when it is deactivated. Activation does not affect the title bar. Always display the top-level container's name. For example, when the worksheet shown in Figure 12.16 is activated, the title bar continues to display the name of the document in which the worksheet is embedded and not the name of the worksheet. You can provide access to the name of the worksheet by supporting property sheets for your embedded objects.

A container can contain multiply-nested embedded objects. However, only a single level is active at any one time. Figure 12.17 shows a document containing an active embedded worksheet with an embedded graph of its own. Clicking the graph merely selects it as an object within the worksheet.

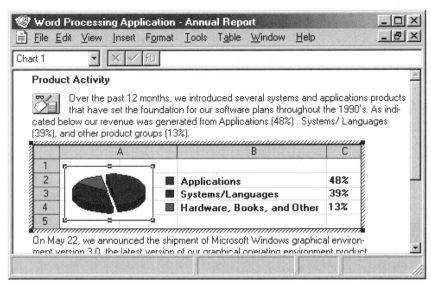

Figure 12.17 A selected graph within an active worksheet

If the user activates the embedded graph by choosing, for example, the graph's **Edit** command, the object is activated for visual editing, and the graph's menus are displayed in the document's menu bar. This is shown in Figure 12.18. At any given time, only the interface for the currently active object and the topmost container are displayed; intervening parent objects do not remain visibly active.

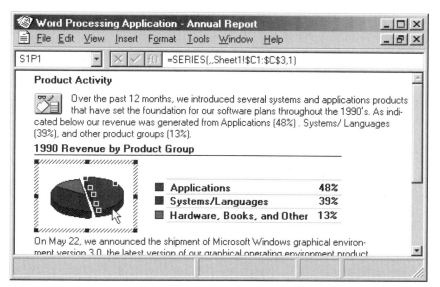

Figure 12.18 An active graph within a worksheet

An embedded object should support visual editing at any view magnification level because the user can scale its container's view arbitrarily. If an object cannot accommodate visual editing in its container's current view scale, or if its container does not support visual editing, open the object in a separate window for editing.

For more information about opening embedded objects, see "Opening Embedded Objects" later in this chapter.

If the user selects or activates another object in the container, deactivate the current object and give the focus to the new object. This is also true for an object that is nested in the currently active object. You should also deactivate the object when the user presses the ESC key; the object will remain selected. If the object already uses the ESC key for an internal operation, support SHIFT+ESC to deactivate the object.

When a user edits an active object, the edits become part of the container immediately and automatically, just like edits made to native data. Consequently, do not display an "Update changes?" message box when the object is deactivated. Remember that the user can abandon changes to the entire container, embedded or otherwise, if the topmost container includes an explicit command that prompts the user to save or discard changes to the container's file.

While **Edit** is the most common command for activating an embedded object for visual editing, other commands can also activate the object. For example, when the user clicks the **Play** command for a video clip, you can display a set of commands that allow the user to control the clip (**Rewind**, **Stop**, and **Fast Forward**). In this case, the **Play** command provides a form of visual editing.

The Active Hatched Border

If the container allows an embedded object to change the container's user interface, then the application that supports editing of the embedded object displays a hatched border around the object's boundary (as shown in Figure 12.19). For example, if an active object places its menus in the topmost container's menu bar, you would surround the object with the active hatched border. The hatched pattern is made up of 45-degree diagonal lines.

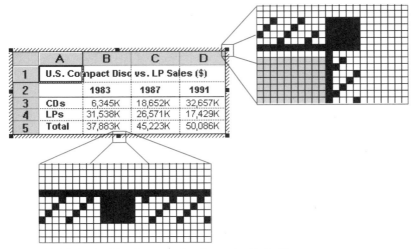

Figure 12.19 Hatched border around active embedded objects

The active object takes on the appearance that is best suited for its own editing; for example, the object may display frame adornments, table gridlines, handles, and other editing aids. Because the hatched border is part of the object's territory, the active object defines the pointer that appears when the user moves the mouse pointer over the border.

When the user clicks within the hatched pattern (and not on the handles) of an active object, the object should respond as if it were clicked just inside the edge of the border. The hatched area is effectively a hot zone that prevents inadvertent deactivations and makes it easier for the user to select the content of the embedded object.

Menu Integration

When the user activates different objects, different commands must be available in the window's user interface. Menus can be grouped into the following broad classifications:

- Primary container menus

- Active object menus

Primary Container Menus

The topmost or primary container viewed in a primary window controls the work area of that window. If the primary container includes a menu bar, it should provide at least one menu whose commands apply to the primary container as a whole. For example, for document file objects, use a **File** menu for this purpose, as shown in Figure 12.20. This menu includes document and file level commands such as **Open**, **Save**, and **Print**. Display the primary container menu in the menu bar at all times, regardless of which object is active.

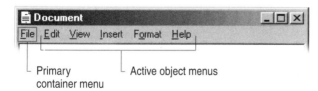

Figure 12.20 Visual editing menu layout

Object Menus

When an object is active, it can add new menus to the primary container's menu bar. These menus contain commands for working directly with the active object's content. Place commands for moving, deleting, searching and replacing, creating new items, applying tools, styles, and Help on these menus. If no embedded objects are active, but the window is active, the primary container should be considered the active object.

An active object's menus typically occupy the majority of the menu bar. Organize these menus the same way they would appear when the user opens the object in its own window. Avoid naming your active object menus **File** or **Window**, because primary containers often use those titles. If an object uses direct manipulation as its sole interface, you do not need to provide an active object menu for it.

If an active object provides a **View** menu, it should include only commands that apply to that object. If the object's container application requires that its own document or window-level "viewing" commands be available while an object is active, place them on the container window's shortcut menu and on the **Window** menu, if one is present.

When you design how selected objects interact within an active object, display the commands of the selected object (as registered in the registry) either as submenus or as separate menus. The active object should also provide a shortcut menu for any selected content within it, containing the common commands needed for working with that selection. Figure 12.21 shows an example of a shortcut menu for a selection within an active bitmap image.

Selection within the active object

Multimedia Mozart: The Dissonant Quartet

The Voyager Company

Inverse
Zoom In

Cut
Copy
Paste

Delete
Properties

In the words [...] scholar Robert Winter, the [...] the eighteenth century wa: [...] of the "most sublime fon [...] h." The String Quartet in C [...] n. Discover the power and [...] s music with Microsoft Micro-soft subtitle to *The Dissonant Quartet*, and enter the world in which Mozart created his most memorable masterpieces. Sit back and enjoy *The Dissonant Quartet* in its entirety, or browse around, exploring its themes and emotional dynamics in depth. View the entire piece in a single-screen overview with the *Pocket Audio Guide.*

Winter provides a fascinating commentary that follows the music, giving you greater understanding of the subtle dynamics of the instruments and powerful techniques of Stravinsky. You'll also have the opportunity to discover the ballet that accompanied *The Rite of Spring* in performance. Choreographed by Sergei Diaghilev, the ballet was as unusual for its time as the music. To whet your appetite, play this audio clip.

Multimedia Beethoven: The Ninth Symphony

The Voyager Company
Microsoft

Figure 12.21 A shortcut menu for a selection in an active object

Keyboard Interface Integration

In addition to integrating the menus, you must also integrate the access keys and shortcut keys used in these menus.

Access Keys

The access keys assigned to the primary container's menu and an active object's menus should be unique. Following are guidelines for defining access keys for integrating these menu names:

- Use the first letter of the menu of the primary container as its access key character. Typically, this is "F" for **File**. Use "W" for a workspace's **Window** menu. Use the appropriate equivalent for localized versions.

- Use characters other than those assigned to the primary container and workspace menus for the menu titles of active embedded objects. (If an embedded object existed previously as a stand-alone document, its corresponding application already avoids these characters.)

- Define unique access keys for an object's registered commands, and avoid using characters that could already be access keys for common container-supplied commands, such as **Cut**, **Copy**, **Paste**, **Delete**, and **Properties**.

Despite these guidelines, if the same access character is used more than once, pressing an ALT+*letter* combination cycles through each command, selecting the next match each time it is pressed. To carry out the command, the user must press the ENTER key when it is selected. This is standard system behavior for menus.

Shortcut Keys

For primary containers and active objects, follow the shortcut key guidelines covered in this book. In addition, when you define shortcut keys for active objects, avoid using keys that could already be assigned to the container. For example, include the standard editing and transfer (**Cut**, **Copy**, and **Paste**) shortcut keys, but avoid **File** menu or system-assigned shortcut keys. There is no provision for registering shortcut keys for a selected object's commands.

If a container and an active object both use the same shortcut key, the shortcut key for the active object is processed first. That is, if the user activates an embedded object, then presses a shortcut key, the active object's application processes the shortcut key. If the active object does not process the shortcut key, the shortcut key becomes available to the container application. This applies to any level of nested embedded objects. If the user wants to use the shortcut key in the container application, the user must first click outside of or otherwise deactivate the embedded object.

For more information about defining shortcut keys, see Chapter 5, "Input Basics," and Appendix B, "Keyboard Interface Summary."

Toolbars, Frame Adornments, and Palette Windows

Integrating drop-down and shortcut menus is straightforward because they are confined within a particular area and follow standard conventions. Toolbars, frame adornments (as shown in Figure 12.22), and palette windows can be constructed less predictably, so it is best to follow a replacement strategy when integrating these elements for active objects. That is, toolbars, frame adornments, and palette windows are displayed and removed as entire sets rather than integrated at the individual control level — just like menu titles on the menu bar.

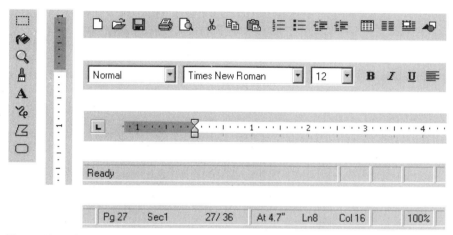

Figure 12.22 Sample toolbars, status bars, and frame adornments

When the user activates an object, the object's application requests a specific area in the container application in which to post its tools. The container application determines whether to:

- Replace its tool with the tools needed by the object, if the requested space is already occupied by a container application tool.

- Add the tools needed by the object if a container application tool does not already occupy the requested space.

- Refuse to display the tools needed by the object. This is the least desirable method.

Toolbars, frame adornments, and palette windows are all basically the same interfaces — they differ primarily in their location and the degree of shared control between container and object. These types of controls reside in four locations in the interface, as shown in the following table.

Locations for Controls

Location	Description
Object frame	Place object-specific controls, such as a table header or a local coordinate ruler, directly adjacent to the object itself for tightly coupled interaction between the object and its interface. An object (such as a spreadsheet) can include scrollbars if its content extends beyond the boundaries of its frame.
Pane frame	Locate view-specific controls at the pane level. Rulers and viewing tools are common examples.
Document (primary container) window frame	Attach tools that apply to the entire document just inside any edge of its primary window frame. Popular examples include ribbons, drawing tools, and status lines.
Windowed	Display tools in a palette window; this allows the user to place them as desired. A palette window typically floats above the primary window and any other windows of which it is part.

You determine their location by their scope. Figure 12.23 shows possible positions for interface controls.

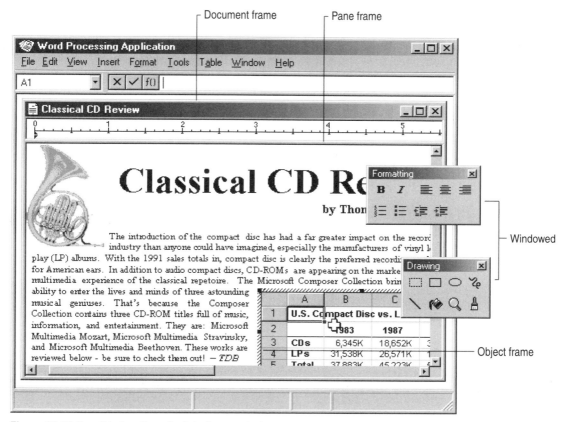

Figure 12.23 Possible locations for interface controls

When determining where to locate a tool area, avoid situations that cause the view to shift up and down as different-sized tool areas are displayed or removed when the user activates different objects. This can be disruptive to the user's task.

Because container tool areas can remain visible while an object is active, they are available to the user simply by interacting with them — this can reactivate the container application. The container determines whether to activate or leave the object active. If the toolbar buttons of an active object represent primary container or workspace commands — such as **Save**, **Print**, or **Open** — disable them.

For more information about the negotiation protocols used for activation, see the Microsoft Platform SDK on the MSDN Online Web site at http://msdn.microsoft.com/ui/guide/sdk.asp.

As the user resizes or scrolls a container's area, an active object and its toolbar or frame adornments placed on the object frame are clipped, as is all container content. These interface control areas lie in the same plane as the object. Even when the object is clipped, the user can still edit the visible part of the object in place and while the visible frame adornments are operational.

Some container applications scroll at certain increments that may prevent portions of an embedded object from being visually edited. For example, consider a large picture embedded in a worksheet cell. The worksheet scrolls vertically in complete row increments; the top of the pane is always aligned with the top edge of a row. If the embedded picture is too large to fit within the pane at one time, its bottom portion is clipped and consequently never viewed or edited in place. In cases like this, the user can open the picture in its own window for editing.

When a window is split into panes, the frame of a pane should clip the frame adornments of nested embedded objects, but not by the extent of any parent object. Objects at the very edge of their container's extent or boundary can display adornments that extend beyond the bounds of the container's defined area. In this case, if the container displays items that extend beyond the edge, display all the adornments; otherwise, clip the adornments at the edge of the container. Do not temporarily move the object within its container just to accommodate the appearance of an active embedded object's adornments. A pane-level control can potentially be clipped by the primary window frame, and a primary window adornment or control is clipped by other primary windows.

Opening Embedded Objects

The previous sections have focused on visual editing — editing an embedded object in its current location within its container. Alternatively, the user can open an embedded object into its own window. This gives the user the opportunity of seeing more of the object or seeing the object in a different view state. To support this operation, register an **Open** command for the object. When the user clicks the object's **Open** command, the object opens in a separate window for editing, as shown in Figure 12.24.

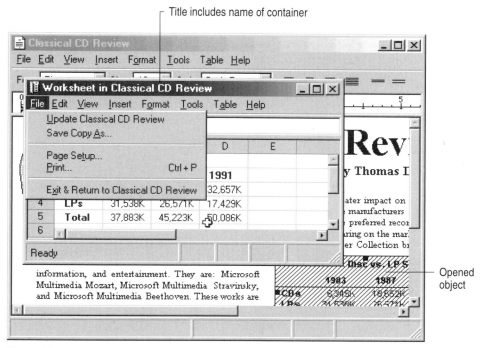

Figure 12.24 An opened embedded worksheet

When the user opens an object in its own window, the container application should display the object masked with an "open" hatched pattern (lines at a 45-degree angle), as shown in Figure 12.25.

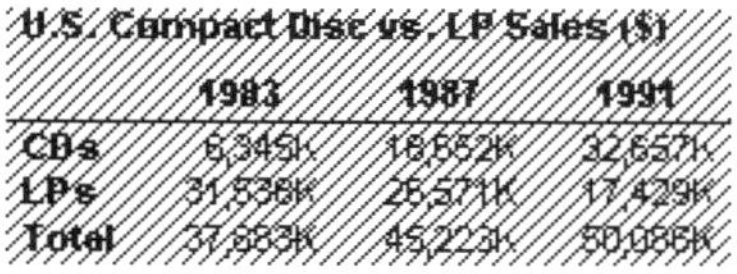

Figure 12.25 An opened embedded object

Format the title text for the open object's window as "*Object Name* in *Container Name*" (for example, "Sales Worksheet in Classical CD Review"). Including the container's name emphasizes that the object in the container and the object in the open window are considered the same object.

This convention for the title bar text applies only when the user opens an embedded object. When the user activates an embedded object for visual editing, do not change the title bar text.

An embedded object that is opened in another window is considered to be a different view of the same object that is in the container application. Therefore, when a user edits the embedded object, the edits should appear immediately and automatically in both the object window and in the container application. You do not need to display an update confirmation message when the user closes the open window. Nevertheless, you can still include an **Update Container File Name** command in the window of the open object to allow the user to request an update explicitly. This is useful if you cannot support frequent "real-time" image updates because of operational performance. In addition, when the user closes an open object's window, automatically update its presentation in the container's window. Provide commands to **Close & Return to Container File Name** or **Exit & Return to** *Container File Name* on the **File** menu to replace the **Close** and **Exit** commands.

If the object's application normally contains file operations, such as **New** or **Open**, remove these in the resulting window or replace them with commands, such as **Import**, to avoid severing the object's connection with its container. The objective is to present a consistent conceptual model; the object in the opened window is always the same as the one in the container. You can replace the **Save As** command with a **Save Copy As** command that displays the Save As dialog box, but unlike **Save As**, **Save Copy As** does not make the copied file the active file.

When the user opens an object, it is the selected object in the container; however, the user can change the selection in the container afterwards. Like any selected embedded object, the container supplies the appropriate selection appearance together with the open appearance, as shown in Figure 12.26.

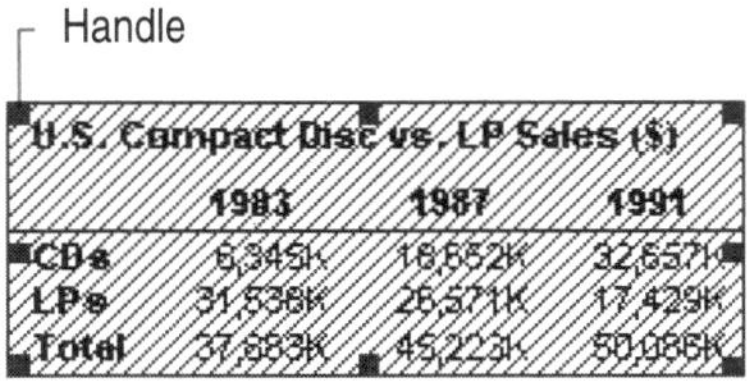

Handle

Figure 12.26 A selected open embedded object

The selected and open appearances apply only to the object's appearance on the display. If the user chooses to print the container while an embedded object is open or active, use the presentation form of objects; neither the open nor active hatched pattern should appear in the printed document because neither pattern is part of the content.

While an embedded object is open, it is still a functioning component of its container. It can still be selected or unselected, and can respond to appropriate container commands. At any time, the user can open any number of embedded objects. When the user closes its container window, deactivate and close the windows for any open embedded objects.

Editing a Linked Object

A linked object can be stored in a particular location, moved, or copied, and it has its own properties. Container actions can be applied to the linked object as a unit of content. So a container supplies commands, such as **Cut**, **Copy**, **Delete**, and **Properties**, and interface elements such as handles, drop-down and shortcut menu items, and property sheets, for the linked objects it contains.

The container also provides access to the commands that activate the linked object, including the commands that provide access to content represented by the linked object. These commands are the same as those that are registered for the link source's type. Because a linked object represents and provides access to another object that resides elsewhere, editing a linked object always takes the user back to the link source. Therefore, the command used to edit a linked object is the same as the command of its linked source object. For example, the menu of a linked object can include both the **Open** and **Edit** commands if its link source is an embedded object. The **Open** command opens the embedded object, just as carrying out the command on the embedded object does. The **Edit** command opens the container window of the embedded object and activates the object for visual editing.

Figure 12.27 shows the result of opening a linked bitmap image of a horn. The image appears in its own window for editing. Note that changes made to the horn are reflected not only in its host container, the "Classical CD Review" document, but also in every other document that contains a linked object linked to that same portion of the "Horns" document. This illustrates both the power and the potential danger of using links in documents.

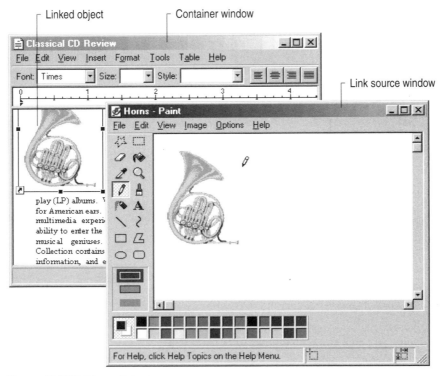

Figure 12.27 Editing a link source

At first glance, editing a linked object appears similar to editing an opened embedded object; a separate primary window opens displaying the data. However, when a linked object is activated, it does not appear with the open hatched pattern. This is because the link source is in a different location. The linked object is not the real object, only a stand-in that enables the source to be visually present in other locations. Editing the linked object is functionally identical to opening the link source. Similarly, the title bar text of the link source's window does not use the convention as an open embedded object because the link source is an independent object. Therefore, the windows operate and close independently of each other. If the link source's window is already visible, the linked object notifies the link source to activate, bringing the existing window to the top of the Z order.

Note that the container of the linked object does display messages related to opening the link source. For example, the container displays a message if the link source cannot be accessed.

Automatic and Manual Updating

When the user creates a link, by default it is an automatic link; that is, whenever the source data changes, the link's visual representation changes. The user does not need to provide any additional information. Therefore, do not display a message box asking the user whether to "Update Automatic Links Now?" If the update takes a significant time to finish, you can display a message box indicating the progress of the update.

If users want to control when links are updated, they can set the linked object's update property to manual. Users must then explicitly choose a command each time they want to update a linked object. The link can also be updated as a part of the link container's **Update Fields**, **Recalc**, or other command that implies updating the presentation in the container's window.

Operations and Links

The operations available for a linked object are supplied by its container and its source. When the user chooses a command supplied by its container, the container application handles the operation. For example, the container processes commands such as **Cut**, **Copy**, or **Properties**. When the user chooses a command supplied (registered) by its source, the operation is conceptually passed back to the link source for processing. In this sense, activating a linked object activates its source.

In some cases, the linked object shows the result of an operation; in other cases, the link source can be brought to the top of the Z order to handle the operation. For example, some commands on a link to a sound recording, such as **Play** or **Rewind**, appear to operate on the linked object. However, if the user chooses a command that could change the source's content (such as **Edit** or **Open**), the operation takes place in the link source.

A link can play a sound in place, but it cannot support editing in place. For a link source to properly respond to editing operations, you must fully activate the source object (with all of its containing objects and its container). For example, when the user double-clicks a linked object whose default operation is **Edit**, the source (or its container) opens, displaying the linked source object ready for editing. If the source is already open, the window displaying the source becomes active. This follows the standard convention for activating a window already open; that is, the window comes to the top of the Z order. You can adjust the view in the window, scrolling or changing focus within the window as necessary to make the source object easily available. The linked source window and the linked object window operate and close independently of each other.

If a link source is contained within a read-only document, display a message box advising the user that edits cannot be saved to the source file.

Types and Links

A linked object includes a cached copy of its source's type at the time of the last update. When the type of a linked source object changes, all links derived from that source object contain the old type and operations until either an update occurs or the linked source is activated. Because out-of-date links can potentially display obsolete operations to the user, a mismatch can occur. When the user chooses a command for a linked object, the linked object compares the cached type with the current type of the linked source. If they are the same, the linked object forwards the operation on to the source. If they are different, the linked object notifies its container. In response, the container can either:

- Carry out the new type's operation, if the operation issued from the old link is syntactically identical to one of the operations registered for the source's new type.

- Display a message box, if the original operation is no longer supported by the link source's new type.

In either case, the linked object adopts the source's new type, and subsequently the container displays the new type's operations in the linked object's menu.

Accessing Properties of Objects

A linked object includes properties, such as the name of its source, its source's type, and the link's updating basis (automatic or manual). A linked object also includes a set of commands related to these properties. The linked object's container gives the user access to these properties and commands by providing a property sheet. You can also include a Links dialog box so that users can view and change the properties of several links simultaneously.

For more information about linked objects, see "The Links Command" later in this section.

The following sections describe how to provide user access to the properties of objects.

The Properties Command

Design a container to include a **Properties** command and property sheets for any objects it contains. If the container application already includes a **Properties** command for its own native data, you can also use it to support selected embedded or linked objects. Otherwise, add the command (preceded by a menu separator) to the drop-down and shortcut menus that you provide for accessing the other commands for the object, as shown in Figure 12.28. You should also display the properties of an object when the user selects the object and then presses ALT+ENTER.

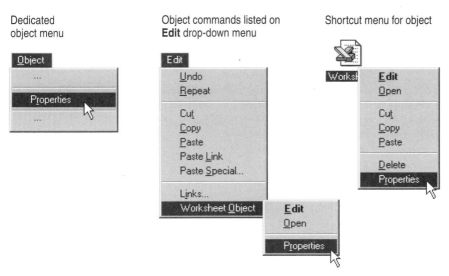

Dedicated object menu

Object commands listed on **Edit** drop-down menu

Shortcut menu for object

Figure 12.28 The **Properties** command

When the user clicks the **Properties** command, the container displays a property sheet containing all the salient properties and values, organized by category, for the selected object. Figure 12.29 shows example property sheet pages for an object.

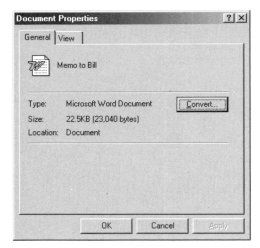
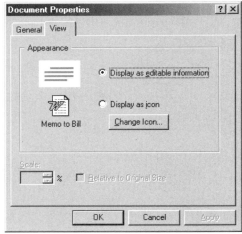

Figure 12.29 Embedded object property sheets

Follow the format the system uses for property sheets and the conventions outlined in this book. Use the short type name in the title bar; for a linked object, precede the name with the word "Linked" — for example, "Linked Worksheet." Include a General property page that displays the icon, name, type, size, and location of the object. Also include a **Convert** button to provide access to the type conversion dialog box. On a **View** page, display properties associated with the view and presentation of the object within the container. These include properties for scaling or position and for displaying the object as content or as an icon. The **Display as icon** field includes a **Change Icon** button that allows the user to customize the icon for the object. The Change Icon dialog box is shown in Figure 12.30.

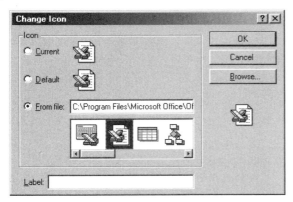

Figure 12.30 The Change Icon dialog box

On the property sheet for linked objects, also include a **Link** page that contains the essential link parameters and commands, as shown in Figure 12.31.

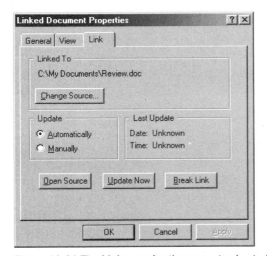

Figure 12.31 The **Link** page for the property sheet of a linked object

For the typical link, include the source name, the **Update** setting (automatic or manual), the **Last Update** time stamp, and buttons that provide the following link operations:

- The **Break Link** command effectively disconnects the selected link.

- The **Update Now** command forces the selected link to connect to its sources and retrieve the latest information.

- The **Open Source** command opens the link source for the selected link.

- The **Change Source** command opens a dialog box similar to the common Open dialog box to allow the user to change the link source.

The Links Command

In addition to property sheets, containers can include link information in the form of a **Links** command. This command opens a dialog box that enables users to display and manage the properties for multiple links, as shown in Figure 12.32. The list box displays the links in the container.

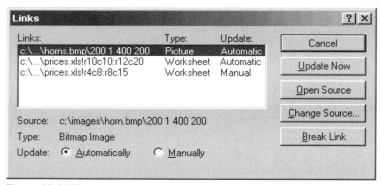

Figure 12.32 The Links dialog box

Each line in the list contains the link source's name, the link source's object type (short type name), and whether the link updates automatically or manually. If a link source cannot be found, "Unavailable" appears in the update status column.

If the user clicks the **Links** command when the current selection includes a linked object (or objects), display that link (or links) as selected in the Links dialog box and scroll the list to display the first selected link at the top of the list box.

Allow 15 characters for the short type name field, and enough space for the words "Automatic" and "Manual" to appear completely. As the user selects each link in the list, display the link's type, name, and updating basis at the bottom of the dialog box. The dialog box also includes the following link management command buttons: **Update Now**, **Open Source**, **Change Source**, and **Break Link**.

Define the **Open Source** command to be the default command when the input focus is within the list of links. Support double-clicking an item in the list as a shortcut for opening the link source.

When the user clicks the **Change Source** button, a version of the Open dialog box appears that enables the user to change the source of a link. If the user enters a source name that does not exist and clicks the default button, display the message box shown in Figure 12.33.

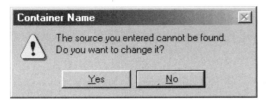

Figure 12.33 A message box for an invalid source

If the user clicks **Yes**, display the Change Source dialog box to correct the string. If the user clicks **No**, store the unparsed display name of the link source until the user links successfully to a newly created object that satisfies the dangling reference. The container application can also choose to allow the user to connect only to valid links.

If the user changes a link source or its folder, and other linked objects in the same container are connected to the same original link source, the container may offer the user the option to change the other references. To support this option, use the message box shown in Figure 12.34.

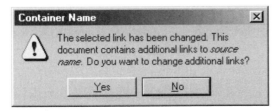

Figure 12.34 Changing additional links with the same source

Converting Types

Users may want to convert an object's type so they can edit the object by using a different application. To support this function, provide a Convert dialog box, as shown in Figure 12.35. To provide access to the Convert dialog box, include a **Convert to** button beside the **Object type** field in an object's property sheet.

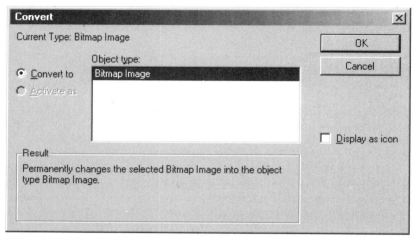

Figure 12.35 The Convert dialog box

This dialog box displays the current type of the object and a list box that contains all possible conversions. This list is composed of all types registered as capable of reading the selected object's format, but this does not necessarily guarantee the possibility of reverse conversion. If the user selects a new type from the list and then clicks **OK**, the selected object is converted immediately to the new type. If the object is open, the container closes it before beginning the conversion.

Make sure the application that supplies the conversion does so with minimal impact in the user interface. That is, avoid displaying the application's primary window, but do provide a progress indicator message box with appropriate controls so that the user can monitor or interrupt the conversion process.

Previous guidelines recommended including a **Convert** command on the menu for a selected object. You can continue to support this; however, the current preferred method is to provide access through a button on the object's property sheet.

If the conversion of the type could result in any lost data or information, the application you use to support the type conversion should display a warning message box indicating that data will be lost and request confirmation by the user before continuing. Make the message as specific as possible about the nature of the information that might be lost; for example, "Text properties will not be preserved."

In addition to converting a type, the Convert dialog box offers the user the option to change the type association for the object by choosing the **Activate as** option. When the user chooses this option, selects a type from the list, and then clicks **OK**, the object's type is treated as the new type. This differs from type conversion in that the object's type remains the same, but its activation command is handled by a different application. It also differs in that converting a type affects only the object that is converted. Changing the activation association of a specific type of single object changes it for all embedded objects of that type. For example, converting a rich-text format document to a text document affects only the converted document. However, if the user clicks the **Activate as** option to change the activation association for the rich-text format object to a text format application, all embedded rich-text format objects would also be affected.

At the bottom of the Convert dialog box, text describes the outcome of the choices the user selects. The following table outlines the syntax of the descriptive text to use in the Convert dialog box.

Descriptive Text for Convert Dialog Box

Function	Resulting text
Convert the selected object's type to a new type.	"Permanently changes the selected *Existing Type Name* object to a *New Type Name* object."
Convert the selected object's type to a new type and display the object as an icon.	"Permanently changes the selected *Existing Type Name* object. The object will be displayed as an icon."
No type change (the selected type is the same as its existing type).	"The *New Type Name* you selected is the same as the type of the selected object, so its type will not be converted."

Descriptive Text for Convert Dialog Box *(continued)*

Function	Resulting text
Change the activation association for the selected object's type.	"Every *Existing Type Name* object will be activated as a *New Type Name* object, but will not be converted to the new type."
Change the activation association for the selected object's type and display the object as an icon.	"Every *Existing Type Name* object will be activated as a *New Type Name* object, and will be converted to the new type. The selected object will be displayed as an icon."

For linked objects, disable the **Convert to** command. The conversion for a link must occur on the link source. If no types are registered for alternative activation, also disable the **Activate as** command. If the user can neither convert nor change the activation association, disable the **Convert to** command that displays this dialog box.

Using Handles

A container displays handles for an embedded or linked object when the object is selected individually. When an object is selected and not active, only the scaling of the object (its cached metafile) can be supported. If a container uses handles for indicating selection but does not support scaling of the image, use the hollow form of handles.

For more information about the appearance of handles, see Chapter 14, "Visual Design."

When an embedded object is activated for visual editing, it displays its own handles. Display the handles within the active hatched pattern, as shown in Figure 12.36.

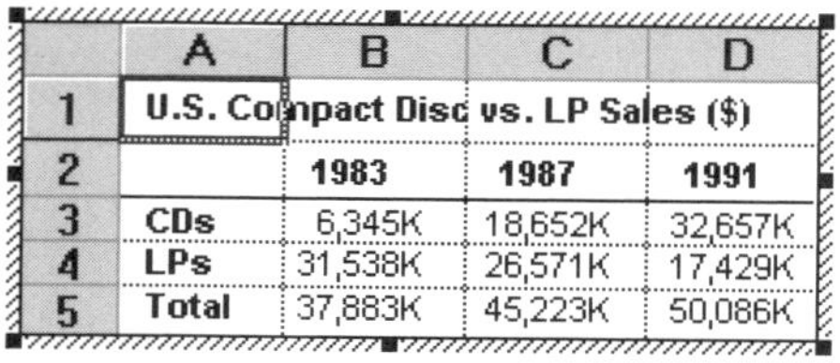

Figure 12.36 An active embedded object with handles

How the object is changed when the user drags the handle is defined by the embedded object's application. The recommended operation is cropping, where you expose more or less of the embedded object's content and adjust the viewing portion of the object. If cropping is inappropriate or unsupportable, use an operation that better fits the context of the object or simply support scaling of the object. If no operation is meaningful, but handles are required to indicate active selection, use the hollow handle appearance.

Displaying Messages

This section includes recommendations for displaying message boxes and status line messages for OLE interaction. Use the following messages in addition to those described earlier in this chapter.

The system supplies most of the message boxes described in this chapter. For more information about how to support message boxes, see the OLE documentation included in the Microsoft Platform SDK on the MSDN Online Web site at http://msdn.microsoft.com/ui/guide/sdk.asp.

Object Application Messages

Display the following messages to notify the user about situations where an object's application is inaccessible.

Notifying Users About Inaccessible Applications

Message	When to use
ApplicationName can be run only from within an application.	When the user attempts to open an object that can be opened only within a container.
This action cannot be completed because *ApplicationName* is busy. Click **SwitchTo** to activate *ApplicationName* and correct the problem.	When the object's application is running but busy, such as printing, waiting for user input to a modal message box, or has stopped responding to the system.
The application necessary to activate this *long type name* is unavailable. You can activate it as, or convert it to, another type of object.	When the user attempts to activate an object and the container cannot locate the object's application. For example, this could happen because the object's type is not registered or because the network server where the application resides is unavailable.

Notifying Users About Inaccessible Applications *(continued)*

Message	When to use
Some links could not be updated because their sources are currently unavailable.	When the container requests an update for its linked objects and the link source files are unavailable to provide the update.
This action cannot be completed because the selected link's source is currently unavailable.	When the user chooses a command on a linked object and the source is unavailable.
The link is no longer an *old object type* and cannot respond to the *verb* command. You may choose a different command.	When the link's source type changed but it is not reflected for the linked object, and the user chooses a command that is not supported by the new type.
Updating links... *#%* complete.	When links are being updated.

Status-Line Messages

The following table lists suggested status-line messages for commands on the primary container menu (commonly the **File** menu) of an opened object.

Container Menu Status-Line Messages

Command	Status line message
Update *Container-Document*	Updates the appearance of this *Type Name* in *Container-Document*.
Close and return to *Container-Document*	Closes *Object Name* and returns to *Container-Document*.
Save Copy As	Saves a copy of *Type Name* in a separate file.
Exit and return to *Container-Document*	Exits *Object Application* and returns to *Container-Document*.

If the open object is within an MDI application with other open documents, the **Exit and Return to** command should simply be **Exit**. There is no guarantee of a successful **Return to** *Container-Document* after exiting, because the container might be one of the other documents in that MDI instance.

The following table lists the recommended status-line messages for the **Edit** menu of containers of embedded and linked objects.

Menu Status-Line Messages

Command	Status-line message
Paste *Object Name**	Inserts the content of the Clipboard as *Object Name*.
Paste Special	Inserts the content of the Clipboard with format options.
Paste Link [to *Object Name**]	Inserts a link to *Object Name*.
Paste Shortcut [to *Object Name**]	Inserts a shortcut icon to *Object Name*.
Insert Object	Inserts a new object.
[Linked] *Object Name** **[Object]**	Applies the following commands to *Object Name*.
[Linked] *Object Name** **[Object]** *Command*	Varies based on command.
[Linked] *Object Name** **[Object]** **Properties**	Allows properties of *Object Name* to be viewed or modified.
Links	Allows links to be viewed, updated, opened, or removed.

**Object Name* can be either the object's short type name or its file name.

The following table lists other related status messages.

Other Status-Line Messages

Command	Status-line message
Show Objects	Displays the borders around objects (toggle).
Select Object (when the user selects an object)	Enables the user to double-click or press ENTER to *Default Command Object Name*.

The default command stored in the registry contains an ampersand character (&) and the access key indicator; these must be stripped out before the verb is displayed on the status line.

User Assistance

Online user assistance is an important part of a product's design. It can be supported in a variety of ways, from automatically displaying information based on context to providing troubleshooters that interactively walk through a process with the user. Its content can be composed of contextual, procedural, explanatory, reference, or tutorial information. This chapter provides a description of the common online forms of user assistance and guidelines for implementation.

User Assistance Road Map

User assistance really begins with a good design methodology where you understand your users, how they work, and the problems they encounter. As much as possible, you follow the basic design principles and processes to create an interface that users can learn easily and operate efficiently.

However, to supplement ease of use and support efficient and complex operations, you will inevitably need to provide some form of user assistance. The ideal form of user assistance integrates seamlessly into your application's overall design. Its interface should be simple, efficient, and relevant; the interface should enable the user to get help easily and then return to a task.

Context-sensitive or What's This? Help is the most commonly encountered form of user assistance. Context-sensitive Help provides brief descriptions about the purpose of a control or other object in the interface. Because this form of on-demand user assistance is provided throughout the interface, users come to depend on its availability. Therefore, support this form of user assistance where possible in your application's windows.

There are many other forms of user assistance. The following table describes other common methods and where they can apply:

Common User Assistance Methods

Method	When to use it	Typical audience
What's This? Help	All screen items; limited screen real estate prevents detailed descriptions	All users
Help buttons	Complex user interface	All users
Status bar messages	Complex user interface	Intermediate to expert users
ToolTips	Complex user interface	Novice users
Reference Help	Technical applications (such as languages, syntaxes, or definitions)	Technical users
Procedural Help	Moderate to complex user interfaces	Novice and intermediate users
Conceptual Help	Processes that span several tasks, complex ideas or concepts	Novice and intermediate users
Wizards	Complex, low-frequency tasks; tasks that require a user to walk through a complicated sequence of steps; often requires data entry by the user	All users
Tour	General feature capabilities; feature highlights	Novice users
Tutorial	Complicated user interface for novices; no user assistance support available for user	Novice users and self-taught users

These techniques are described in more detail throughout this chapter.

Contextual Help

Contextual Help provides immediate assistance to users without their having to leave the context in which they are working. It provides information about a particular object and its context. It answers questions such as "What is this?" and "Why would I use it?" Some of the basic ways to support contextual user assistance in your application include:

- Context-sensitive Help

- ToolTips

- Status bar messages

- Help command buttons

Context-Sensitive Help

The **What's This?** command allows users to obtain contextual Help information about objects on the screen, including controls in property sheets and dialog boxes. As shown in Figure 13.1, you can support user access to this command by including the following in your application:

- A **What's This?** command from the Help drop-down menu of a primary window

- A **What's This?** button on a toolbar

- A **What's This?** button on the title bar of a secondary window

- A **What's This?** command on the shortcut menu for a specific object

- Support for the **What's This?** shortcut key when a control has the input focus

- Support for the **What's This?** mode shortcut key

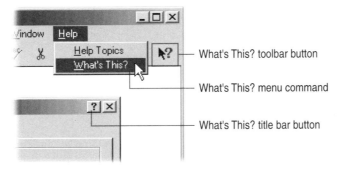

Figure 13.1 Different methods of accessing What's This mode?

Design your application so that the system is set to a temporary mode when the user chooses the **What's This?** command from the Help drop-down menu or clicks **a What's This?** button. Change the pointer's shape to reflect this mode change, as shown in Figure 13.2.

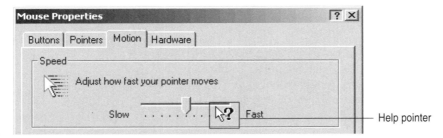

Figure 13.2 A context-sensitive Help pointer

Display the context-sensitive Help pointer only over the window that provides context-sensitive Help; that is, only over the active window from which the **What's This?** command was chosen.

In this mode, display a context-sensitive Help window for an object that the user clicks with the primary mouse button. The context-sensitive Help window provides a brief explanation about the object and how to use it, as shown in Figure 13.3. After the context-sensitive Help window is displayed, return the pointer and pointer operation to the usual state.

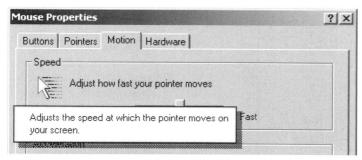

Figure 13.3 A pop-up window for context-sensitive Help

If the user presses a shortcut key that applies to a window in contextual Help mode, display a contextual Help pop-up window for the command associated with that shortcut key.

There are some exceptions to this interaction. First, if the user chooses a menu title either in the menu bar or in a cascading menu, maintain the What's This? mode and pointer until the user chooses a menu item; then display the context-sensitive Help window. Second, if the user clicks the item with the secondary mouse button and the object supports a shortcut menu, maintain the mode until the user chooses a menu item or cancels the menu. If the object does not support a shortcut menu, the interaction should be the same as clicking it with the primary mouse button. Finally, if the object or location chosen does not support context-sensitive Help or is otherwise an inappropriate target for context-sensitive Help, cancel the context-sensitive Help mode.

If the user chooses the **What's This?** command a second time, clicks outside the window, or presses the ESC key, cancel context-sensitive Help mode. Restore the pointer to its usual image and operation in that context.

When the user chooses the **What's This?** command from a shortcut menu (as shown in Figure 13.4), the interaction is slightly different. Because the user has identified the object by clicking the secondary mouse button, there is no need for entering context-sensitive Help mode. Instead, immediately display the context-sensitive Help pop-up window for that object.

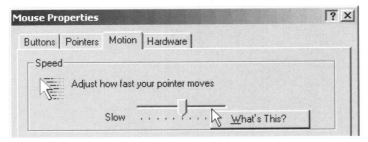

Figure 13.4 A shortcut menu for a control

The F1 and SHIFT+F1 keys are the shortcut keys for this form of interaction. The F1 key displays the most context-sensitive Help available based on the current context. In primary windows, pressing F1 typically displays the HTML Help viewer with an appropriate topic. In secondary windows, pressing F1 typically displays the context-sensitive pop-up window for the control that has the input focus. However, if you support context-sensitive Help for elements of your primary window, use SHIFT+F1 to begin context-sensitive Help mode, changing the pointer and enabling the user to click a menu or control in the window to provide the context. In secondary windows, use SHIFT+F1, like F1, to display the context-sensitive Help pop-up window for the control that has the input focus.

Guidelines for Writing Context-Sensitive Help

When writing text for context-sensitive Help, you are answering the questions "What is this?" and "Why would I want to use it?" Indicate the action associated with the item. In English versions, begin the description with a verb; for example, "Adjusts the speed of your mouse," or "Provides a place for you to type a name for your document." For command buttons, you can use an imperative form — for example, "Click this to close the window." When describing a function or object, use words that explain the function or object in common terms instead of technical terminology or jargon. For example, instead of using "Undoes the last action," use "Reverses the last action."

When describing several option buttons in a group, try to compare and contrast the options together in one topic to answer the question "Which option should I choose?" However, if the options are complex, each option may require a separate topic.

Use sentence-style capitalization and ending punctuation. Also use the system-defined Help font, but avoid the use of italic text because it is hard to read on the screen.

In the explanation, you might want to include "why" information. You can also include "how to" information, but if the procedure requires multiple steps, consider using procedural Help to support this information. Keep your information brief but as complete as possible so that the Help window can be read quickly and is easy to understand.

While you can provide context-sensitive Help for any item in your application's windows, always provide it for the following elements:

• All editable elements or labels for editable elements

• Status bar items that do not have text labels

• All toolbar buttons and controls

• All menu items

Avoid creating context-sensitive Help for parts of the interface that do not do anything, such as group box labels or static descriptive text fields. You can create a common Help topic for group labels such as the following: "Help is available for each item in this group. Click **?** at the top of the dialog box, and then click the specific item you want information about."

ToolTips

ToolTips are another form of contextual user assistance. ToolTips are small pop-up windows that display the name of a control when the control has no text label. The most common use of ToolTips is for toolbar buttons that have graphic labels, as shown in Figure 13.5, but they can be used for any control.

For more information about ToolTips, see Chapter 8, "Menus, Controls, and Toolbars."

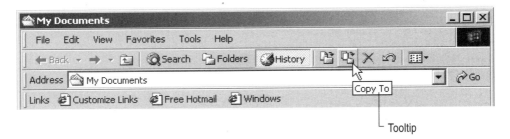

Tooltip

Figure 13.5 A ToolTip for a toolbar button

Display a ToolTip after the pointer (or pointing device) remains over the button for a short period of time. The ToolTip is displayed until the user presses the button or moves the pointer off the control, or after another time-out. If the user moves the pointer to another control that supports a ToolTip, ignore the time-out and display the new ToolTip immediately, replacing the former ToolTip. If you use the standard toolbar control, the system automatically provides support for ToolTips. It also includes a ToolTip control that can be used in other contexts. If you create your own ToolTip controls, make them consistent with the system-supplied controls.

In addition to providing ToolTips for elements in your application window, you should also provide support for ToolTips for your application file and its file types. This form of ToolTip is also known as an *InfoTip*. For information about supporting InfoTips, see Chapter 11, "Integrating with the System."

Status Bar Messages

You can use the status bar to provide contextual Help. However, because the user should be able to hide the status bar, avoid using the status bar to display information or access to functions that are essential to basic operation and are not provided elsewhere in the application's interface. In addition, because the status bar might not be located near the user's area of activity, the user might not notice it. It is best to consider status bar messages as a secondary or supplemental form of Help.

In addition to displaying information about the state of a window, you can display descriptive messages about menu and toolbar buttons, as shown in Figure 13.6. As with ToolTips, the window typically should be active to display these messages. When the user moves the pointer over a toolbar button or menu item, presses or clicks the primary mouse button when the pointer is over a menu or button, or uses the keyboard to move the input focus over a menu or toolbar button, display a short message describing the use of the associated command.

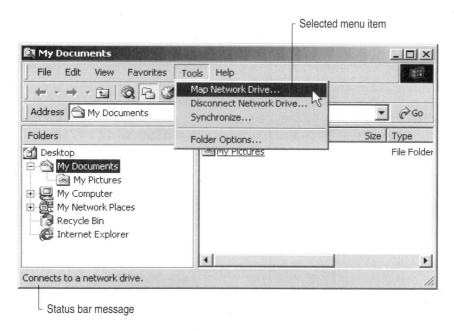

Figure 13.6 A status bar message for a selected menu command

A user can invoke a status bar message for a progress indicator control or other forms of feedback about an ongoing process, such as printing or saving a file. You can display progress information in a message box, but you may want to use the status bar for background processes so that the window's interface is not obscured by the message box.

If your application enables the user to control whether the status bar is displayed, or you want to provide information about other parts of your interface that may not have a status bar, consider using balloon tips.

Guidelines for Writing Status Bar Messages

To write status bar messages, use familiar terms but avoid jargon. Start with a verb in the present tense. For example, use "Cuts the selection and places it on the Clipboard." Try to be as brief as possible so the text can be read easily, but avoid making the text so short that it is cryptic.

Be constructive, not just descriptive, and inform the user about the purpose of the command. To describe a command with a specific function, use words specific to the command. If the command has multiple functions, try to summarize them — for example, "Contains commands for editing and formatting your document."

When you define messages for your menu and toolbar buttons, don't forget their unavailable, or disabled, state. Provide an appropriate message to explain why the item is not currently available. For example, when the user selects a disabled **Cut** command, you could display the message "This command is not available because no text is selected."

The Help Command Button

You can also provide contextual Help for a property sheet, dialog box, or message box by including a **Help** command button in that window, as shown in Figure 13.7.

Figure 13.7 A **Help** command button in a secondary window

When the user clicks the **Help** command button, display an overview, summary, or explanatory topic for a page or for the entire window. For example, for a message box, the Help message can provide more information about causes and remedies for the reason the message was displayed

Placement of a **Help** command button is important. If you include the **Help** command button with the **OK** and **Cancel** buttons, it implies that Help applies to the entire window. If you use the **Help** command button to display Help for a specific page within the window, place the button on that page.

The user assistance provided by a **Help** command button differs from the What's This? form of Help. In this form of Help, you should provide more general assistance rather than information specific to the control that has the current input focus. In addition, display the information in the HTML Help viewer, described later in this chapter, rather than in the context-sensitive Help pop-up window.

Consider the **Help** command button an optional, secondary form of contextual user assistance. Do not use it as a substitute for context-sensitive What's This? Help. Also avoid relying on it as a substitute for clear, understandable designs for your secondary windows.

Procedural Help

Procedural Help provides the steps for carrying out a task. Procedural Help should focus on "how" information rather than "what" or "why." You provide access to procedural Help by defining contents and index entries for the HTML Help Viewer (described later in this chapter).

As with contextual Help, write complete but brief procedural Help topics. Try to limit a procedure to four or fewer steps so the user will not have to scroll the window.

Also, take advantage of the context of a procedure. For example, if a property sheet includes a slider control that is labeled "Slow" at one end and "Fast" at the other, be concise. Say, "Move the slider to adjust the speed," instead of "To increase the speed, move the slider to the right. To decrease the speed, move the slider to the left." If you refer to a control by its label, bold each word in the label to match the user interface. This helps distinguish the label from the rest of your text.

Design procedural Help to help the user complete a task, not to document everything there is to know about a subject. If there are multiple ways to do a task, pick one method — usually the simplest, most common method for a specific procedure. If you want to include information about alternate methods, include it in a Notes section or in a related topic. A link to Related Topics in your window provides access to other topics that are related in some way, as shown in Figure 13.8. This is a good way to reference alternative techniques and conceptual information.

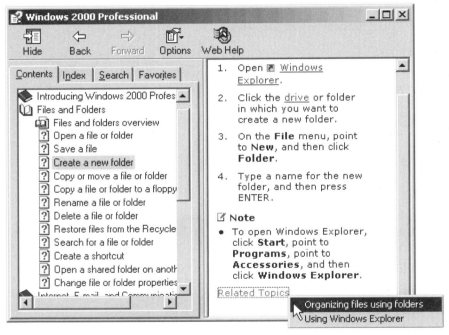

Figure 13.8 Related Topics in a procedural Help topic

Reference Help

Reference Help serves as an online reference book. You can use reference Help to document a programming language or programming interfaces. Reference Help can also be used to provide a user's guide to a product. The use determines the balance of text and graphics in the reference Help file.

Reference-oriented documentation typically includes more text and follows a consistent presentation of information, as shown in Figure 13.9.

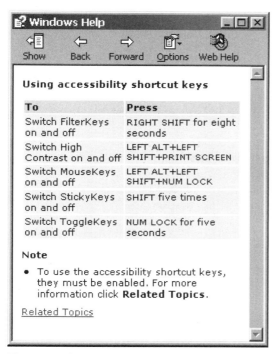

Figure 13.9 Sample reference Help text

Although the reference Help style can provide information similar to that in contextual and procedural Help, these forms of Help do not exclude each other. Often the combination of all three provides the best help for the user.

Conceptual Help

Conceptual Help provides background information, feature overviews, or processes. It provides "what" or "why" information beyond that needed to complete a task. Background information may describe a specific concept or feature, such as security, or how information is stored on your computer, and include links to one or two procedures.

A process overview may describe several separate procedures that are required in order to complete the process. For example, an overview about sending an e-mail message could describe several tasks: opening a new message window, specifying who to send the message to, composing and formatting the message, and then sending the message. The overview might describe each of these tasks and provide links to procedural topics for each task.

A feature overview may highlight features and provide links to tasks associated with using each feature. For example, you might describe accessibility features in the product, and then provide links to topics for setting each specific feature.

Because these topics provide much greater detail than a procedural topic, you may have more text than will fit in the topic window. Longer topics are typically organized under subheadings. A process or feature overview may be organized by bullets with links to related tasks at the end of each bullet.

Include all conceptual Help topics in the index, and include them in the table of contents where appropriate. The top level of the table of contents usually contains one or two conceptual topics, such as a product overview or a getting-started topic. When users read the table of contents, they are generally looking for help on accomplishing tasks. For this reason, any conceptual topics included in a table of contents generally follow the tasks. Most tasks provide Related Topics links to overview topics, if they exist.

HTML Help

Windows provides support for creating Help interfaces using standard HTML. HTML Help replaces the WinHelp support included in previous versions of Windows. While Windows 98 and Windows 2000 still include this support for backward compatibility, HTML Help is a better choice. HTML Help uses common Web conventions, providing a familiar and consistent way for users to learn to navigate through Help information. You can use HTML Help to support Help interfaces for both conventional and Web-style applications. It also enables you to easily include local Help topics as well as HTML pages on Web sites.

Use HTML Help Workshop to compile and compress your HTML Help files. You can also use it to create contents and index files for those files. For more information about Windows HTML Help Workshop, see the MSDN Online Web site at http://msdn.microsoft.com/workshop/author/htmlhelp/.

The HTML Help Viewer

HTML Help includes a special window called the HTML Help Viewer to display the Help topics that you write. Open the HTML Help Viewer to display a window and a toolbar. Below the toolbar, the window is split. The navigation pane is on the left and the topic pane is on the right, as shown in Figure 13.10.

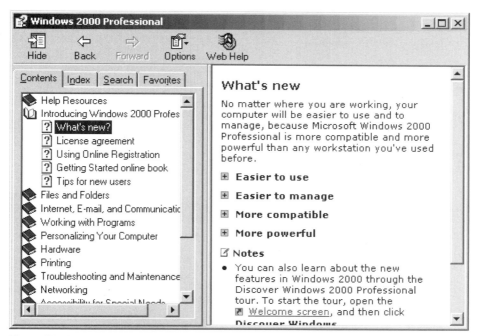

Figure 13.10 HTML Help Viewer

You provide primary access to Help topics through the **Contents**, **Index**, or **Search** tabs. You can also include access to specific topics through other interfaces, such as navigation links placed in other Help topics.

For information about authoring HTML Help files, see the MSDN Online Web site at http://msdn.microsoft.com/workshop/author/htmlhelp/.

To support user access to the HTML Help Viewer window, include a **Help Topics** menu entry on your primary window's Help menu. When the user clicks the **Help Topics** command, open the HTML Help Viewer and display it the last way it was viewed by the user. Alternatively, you can include commands that open the Help Viewer to a particular tabbed page.

You can define the size and location of a Help Viewer window to the specific requirements of your application. It is best to size and position the window so as to cover a minimum amount of space, yet be large enough to allow the user to read the topic, preferably without having to scroll. This makes it easier for the novice user who may be unfamiliar with scrolling. Keep in mind, however, that the user can override the font sizes and other formatting specified by the author. Make sure your Help screens remain usable when the user adjusts the color, font, and accessibility options in Internet Explorer, as these will affect how your content is displayed.

When designing your HTML Help topics, follow the standards set by the World Wide Web consortium for accessibility of Web content. Following these guidelines will ensure that your application is accessible to the widest possible range of users and compatible with automation tools. For more information, see the Microsoft Accessibility Web site at http://www.microsoft.com/enable/.

The Toolbar

The HTML Help Viewer toolbar includes a set of buttons that enable users to navigate, print a topic, and change the view of the window.

Toolbar Buttons in HTML Help Viewer

Button	Purpose
Back	Displays the previously viewed topic.
Forward	Displays the topic viewed before the user selected **Back**.
Hide	Hides the navigation pane.
Home	Displays the designated home topic (page).

Toolbar Buttons in HTML Help Viewer *(continued)*

Button	Purpose
Jump 1	Displays an author-defined URL location. The button label is customizable.
Jump 2	Displays an author-defined URL location. The button label is customizable.
Locate	Synchronizes the navigation pane with the currently displayed topic.
Options	Displays a menu of commands and viewing options.
Print	Displays the Print dialog box to support printing a topic.
Refresh	Updates the content in the topic pane with information stored on a Help Web site.
Show	Displays the navigation pane.
Stop	Stops downloading information.

The default toolbar buttons that appear in the HTML Help Viewer are **Back**, **Hide** (and **Show**), **Options**, and **Print**. You can include any others by defining them in your HTML Help files. For example, if your users access topics from the Web, you could add the **Home**, **Stop**, and **Refresh** buttons. You can also add your own customizable buttons. Avoid adding too many buttons, which can cause the toolbar buttons to wrap. You can also include the **Back**, **Forward**, **Stop**, **Home**, **Refresh**, and **Print** commands on the **Options** menu.

The Navigation Pane

When the user opens HTML Help, a navigation pane is displayed that contains tabbed pages for **Contents**, **Index**, **Search**, and **Favorites**. This provides a starting point for users to find Help information.

The Contents Page

The Contents page displays the list of topics organized by category, as shown in Figure 13.11. You can hide the navigation pane when the HTML Help Viewer displays your Help topics.

Figure 13.11 The Contents page of the Help topics browser

A book icon represents a category or group of related topics, and a page icon represents an individual topic. You can nest topic levels, but do not create more than three levels, as this makes access cumbersome, especially for novice or beginning users. Also try to limit the number of top-level entries to avoid making the user scroll excessively to see all the topics. Similarly, try to limit the number of topic titles you include under a top-level entry to 10 to 12 entries.

If the information in your Help system is targeted for most users, provide single-click access from the Contents page. Most users prefer this. Requiring users to double-click to access topics may provide more flexibility but at a tradeoff of simplicity. If you do support access methods other than single-clicking, consider changing the appearance of the Contents page. For example, you could include plus and minus buttons for expanding and collapsing the tree, or you could use different icons.

You can also customize the icons used for books and topics, either by choosing the ones that come with HTML Help or by creating your own. You might want to use different icons for different types of topics. Always usability test any icons you create, as well as the text that appears with them. Also consider the impact of your icon designs for international users.

You do not have to include all topics on the Contents page. Some topics, especially advanced or seldom-used topics, can be made available as links from other topics or through the **Index** and **Search** tabs. This keeps the table of contents simpler for users. Topics that are not essential should be removed from the table of contents. For example, if the subject is backing up a database, you might move topics about networking out of the table of contents.

Guidelines for Writing Contents Entries

The entries listed on the Contents page are based on the topics included in a set of Help files. Organize them to enable users to see the relationship between topics. Add titles that are brief but descriptive, and make sure the Contents entries correspond to the actual topic titles.

Shorter topic titles are more effective because they can be viewed fully in the navigation pane without scrolling, and usability testing has shown that shorter phrases result in better user comprehension. To improve readability of long topic titles, you can enable ToolTips.

It is generally a good idea to separate procedural Help from conceptual Help. Users who simply want to perform the steps of a task appreciate not having to wade through a lot of conceptual information. Within a procedural Help topic, you can link to Related Topics that contain conceptual information, as shown in Figure 13.12.

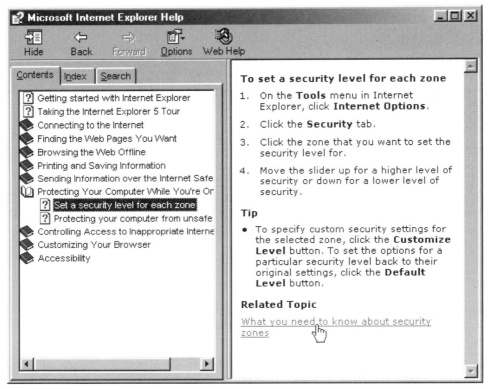

Figure 13.12 Link to conceptual information

The Index Page

The Index page of the HTML Help Viewer organizes topics by keywords that you create for each topic, as shown in Figure 13.13.

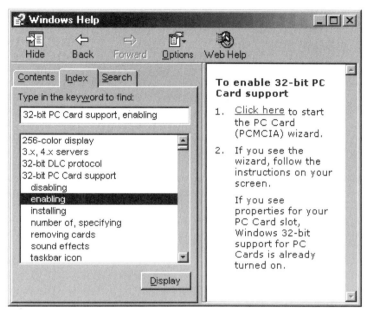

Figure 13.13 The Index page of the Help topics browser

The user can type a keyword or select one from the list. When the user clicks the **Display** button, the topic associated with that keyword is displayed. If multiple topics use the same keyword, then another window is displayed that allows the user to choose from that set of topics, as shown in Figure 13.14.

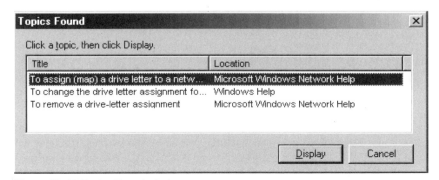

Figure 13.14 Topics Found window

It is never a good idea to reference a specific index entry from a Help topic or from any part of the user interface. A modification to the Help index might not be propagated to the entire software system. There is no good mechanism for searching for references to a particular index entry throughout a product.

Guidelines for Writing Help Index Keywords

Since many users access Help information through the index, it is important to provide a thorough and effective list of keywords in your Help system. A keyword index should include terms for both novice and advanced users, should offer information at as many entry points as possible, and should provide thorough cross-referencing. When deciding what keywords to provide for your topics, consider the following categories:

- Actions the user might want to take (for example, copying, routing, saving)

- Subjects that might be in the user's mind when tackling a problem for which the topic is helpful (for example, files, networks, projects)

- Synonyms for the action and subject terms

- Software industry terms that might be familiar to the user

Another important part of the indexing process is to ensure that the same topics are referenced by related keywords. For example, if the keyword term "network connections" references seven topics, the keyword term "connections, network" should reference the same seven topics. Because checking for this type of consistency can be very time-consuming, it may be simpler to include a cross-reference, in this case "connections, network See network connections."

The following are the recommended guidelines for writing index entries:

- Keywords should be lowercase unless they are proper nouns (for example, use "files" and "File menu").

- Nouns should be plural unless the singular form is more correct (for example, use "programs" but not "Start menus").

- Verbs should be in the gerund form (for example, use "copying files," not "copy files").

- Keyword indexes should have no more than two or three levels of indentation.

Cross-reference keywords can be formatted to either display a certain topic or topics or jump within the index to the *target keyword*. For example, if the user clicks the "See network protocols" cross-reference, the Help system might display a topic that gives an overview of network protocols. Or, the keyword can be set up to actually move the user to the "network protocols" entry in the index. Usability testing indicates that users prefer the latter convention. This style decision should be made for the whole index; users should be able to count on consistent functionality from the cross-references in the index.

When an index keyword has more than one level, as in the example below, user expectations about the behavior of the first level vary.

device drivers
    configuring
    installing
    removing

Some users, especially those more familiar with WinHelp, expect the first level to display a comprehensive list of the topics found below the subentries. These lists, though, were often unwieldy, so HTML Help displays the subentries and their topics in a more manageable form. Setting the first level to jump to itself (inserting the keyword itself as the target keyword) creates a keyword that, when selected, instructs the user to choose one of the subentries below. Again, this is a style decision that should be made early and followed consistently to avoid user confusion.

The Search Page

The Search page, as shown in Figure 13.15, provides a full-text search capability that allows the user to search for any word or phrase in Help. This capability requires a full-text index file that you can create when building Help or that the user can create when using the Search page.

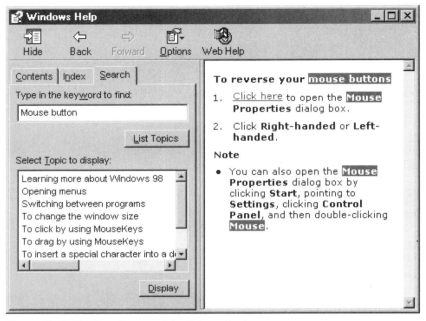

Figure 13.15 The Search page of the Help topics browser

You can offer simple or advanced search support. Use simple search for most consumer applications and advanced search to support Boolean-style queries for programming references or other technical documentation. Advanced search also enables the user to sort the Topics Found dialog box by clicking the Title, Location, or Rank columns.

You can also exclude words from being searchable. This allows you, the Help author, to exclude words from the search results that are inappropriate. For example, you could define the word "the" to be excluded so that a search for the word "the" returns nothing, but a search for "the device" returns the topics that contain both words.

A location column also appears in the search results. This column displays the title of the Help file. This is the word or phrase you author between the <title> and <\title> tags. In this way, users can differentiate between similarly worded topics that refer to different features. For example, if the topic "Adding Hardware" is listed twice in the search results, the two listings might be for "Plug and Play" and "Modems."

The Favorites Page

This page allows the user to create a personalized list of favorite Help topics. When the Topics pane displays a topic the user would like to keep for future reference, the user can switch to the Favorites page and add it.

The Topics Pane

The Topics pane displays the topics in your Help system. The HTML Viewer supports authoring in HTML to add a rich graphical presentation to your Help topics. In addition, the HTML Help Viewer provides other features to support the design of your Help content.

Help Topic Features

HTML Help also provides additional features that you can include in your Help topics.

Links

You can use a link to move from one topic to another within the same window, to another topic in the same Help file, or to a topic in another Help file. You should provide local alternate URLs for links for non-local (Internet) sites when the Internet connection is not available.

You can also link to a pop-up window. As with pop-up windows for context-sensitive Help, use this convention to display a definition or provide an explanation about the word or object the user clicks.

Links can also carry out particular commands; for example, a user could click a link to open a folder or a dialog box.

Always provide some visual indication to distinguish a link from non-interactive areas of the window. You can do this in the presentation of the link and by changing the mouse pointer to indicate an interactive element.

For more information about formatting links, see Chapter 14, "Visual Design."

Shortcut Buttons

The HTML Help window can include a shortcut or "do it" button that provides the user with an automated way to perform a particular step, as shown in Figure 13.16. Use a shortcut to open a dialog box, property sheet, or other object so that the user does not have to search for it.

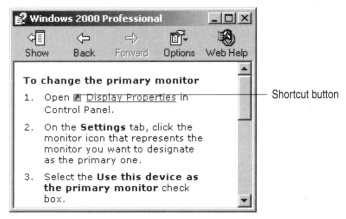

Figure 13.16 A task Help topic with a shortcut button

Shortcut buttons not only improve efficiency for the user, they also reduce the amount of information you need to present. However, do not use the buttons as a substitute for doing the task or a specific step in the task, particularly if you want the user to learn how to perform the task without using Help in the future. For common tasks, you may want to include information that tells the user how to do the task, and shortcut buttons that make stepping through the task easier. For example, you might include text that reads "Show the Display properties" and a shortcut button, and then add a note at the end of the Help topic detailing the steps.

Pop-up Help

Pop-up Help can provide glossary definitions within a topic. By providing hot text within a topic, the user knows clicking it will result in an action. Pop-up Help streamlines the content so that only users who need the extra information view it.

Related Topics

Related Topics links provide access to topics of additional interest based upon the current topic. This feature corresponds to WinHelp Alinks and has the same dynamic characteristics of that feature. For example, a Related Topics link to a topic that is not present on the user's local disk will not show up in the Topics Found list. A Related Topics link for HTML Help displays a pop-up window if multiple topics are related. If only one topic is related, that topic is immediately displayed.

The Related Topics feature provides a key feature for a well-designed Help system. You should include entries for the most basic and useful information on the Contents page, then make less frequently used procedures and concepts available only through Related Topics. Define these topics to cover more in-depth information about a subject.

Topic Titles

Always provide a title for each topic. The title, defined by the HTML <title> and <\title> tags, identifies the topic and serves the user as a landmark within the Help system. Titles should be concise and fit on one line, if possible. The title is displayed when you search for a topic and in the Related Topics list. Try to make your topic titles closely match their titles listed in the Contents page. A user should not be surprised by the topic that appears after clicking a Contents entry.

Topics that appear in the Topics Found dialog box and Index page get their display entries from the topic title you define with the <title> tag. For example, suppose a topic is titled "Installing Plug-and-Play Hardware." Its Contents entry title might be "Installing Hardware." When the Topics Found dialog box appears, the title displayed to the user should be "Installing Plug-and-Play Hardware."

Outlining Buttons

Outlining buttons (plus and minus signs) provide organizational information within a topic. These buttons are used to represent a hierarchical organization, such as can be found in the Tree control, or a progressive revelation of information as the user wants to see it.

The Common Tasks topic in Figure 13.17 shows an example of progressive revelation. The Common Task topic contains general task titles that users can click to view task details.

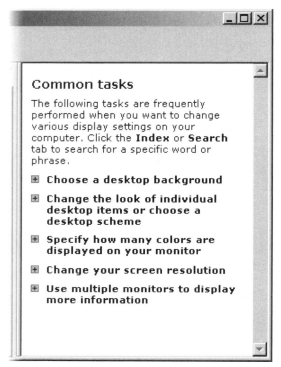

Figure 13.17 Outlining buttons

Browsing Buttons

Although the HTML Help Viewer does not provide explicit browse buttons, you may want to create your own buttons to support the display of Help topics in a sequential order that you determine. This is useful for print books that are being ported to online versions. Users can click the browse buttons to move forward and backward through the material as if turning pages in a book. This technique can also apply to other types of sequential ordering of specific Help sections. For example, you might want to create a troubleshooter in Help and use browse buttons to let users navigate to the next or previous related Help topic.

Wizards

A *wizard* is a special form of user assistance that automates a task through a dialogue with the user. Wizards help the user accomplish tasks that can be complex and require experience. Wizards can automate almost any task, such as creating new objects and formatting a set of objects like a table or paragraph. They are especially useful for presenting complex and infrequent tasks that the user may have difficulty learning or doing.

However, wizards are not well-suited to teaching a user how to do something. Although wizards help the user accomplish a task, they should be designed to hide many of the steps and much of the complexity of a given task.

Similarly, do not use wizards for tutorials; wizards should operate on real data. For instructional user assistance, consider procedural Help or tutorial-style interfaces. Do not rely on wizards as a solution for ineffective designs. If your users must rely too much on wizards, your application's interface might be overly complicated.

Use a wizard to supplement rather than replace the user's direct ability to perform a specific task. Unless the task is fairly simple or is done infrequently, experienced users may find that a wizard can be inefficient or does not provide them with sufficient access to all functionality.

Wizards may not always appear as an explicit part of the Help interface. You can provide access to them in a variety of ways, such as from toolbar buttons or by using specific objects (such as **Add Printer**).

The system provides support for creating a wizard using the standard property sheet control. For more information about this control, see Chapter 8, "Menus, Controls, and Toolbars."

For more information about templates, see Chapter 6, "General Interaction Techniques."

Guidelines for Designing Wizards

A wizard is a series of steps or pages that help the user perform a task. The pages include controls that you define to gather input from the user. The input is then used to complete the task for the user.

You can define a wizard as a series of secondary windows that the user navigates through, but this can lead to increased modality and screen clutter. Instead, design a wizard using a single secondary window. The system supports two wizard designs: simple and advanced, as shown in Figure 13.18.

Simple wizard

Advanced wizard

Figure 13.18 Sample simple and advanced wizard designs

Use the simple wizard design to present a single task that requires minimal explanation. Typically, a simple wizard would consist of three or fewer pages.

Use the advanced wizard design to present longer, more complex tasks that require multiple decision points (multiple paths). The advanced wizard design includes Welcome and Completion pages.

Window Design

Use the title bar of the wizard window to clearly identify the purpose of the wizard. Because wizards are secondary windows, they should not appear in the taskbar. You can optionally also include a context-sensitive **What's This?** Help button on the title bar to clearly identify the wizard and its purpose.

At the bottom of the window, include the following command buttons that allow the user to navigate through the wizard.

Commands for Navigating Through a Wizard

Command	Action
< Back	Returns to the previous page. (Remove or disable the button on the first page.)
Next >	Moves to the next page in the sequence and maintains settings the user provided in previous pages.
Finish	Applies user-selected or default settings from all pages and completes the task.
Cancel	Discards any user-selected settings, terminates the process, and closes the wizard window.

Wizard Pages

Design wizard pages to be easy to understand. It is important that users immediately understand what a wizard is about so they don't feel like they have to read it very carefully to know what is required of them. It is better to have a greater number of simple pages with fewer choices than a smaller number of complex pages with too many options or text. In addition, follow the conventions outlined in this guide and consider the following guidelines when designing a wizard:

- Always include a statement of purpose for the wizard on the first page and include a graphic on the left side of the page. The purpose of this graphic is to establish a reference point, or theme, such as a conceptual rendering, a snapshot of the area of the display that will be affected, or a preview of the result. You can continue to include a graphic on the interior pages for consistency or, if space is critical, use the entire width of the window to display instructional text and controls that require user input.

- Minimize the number of pages that require the display of a secondary window. Novice users are often confused by the additional complexity of secondary windows.

- Avoid a wizard design that requires a user to leave the wizard to complete a task. Less-experienced users rely heavily on wizards. Asking the user to leave a wizard to perform a task can lead to confusion. Instead, design your wizard so that the user can do everything from within it.

- Make it visually clear that the user interface elements in a graphic illustration on a wizard page are not interactive. You can do this by varying elements from their normal sizes or rendering them more abstractly.

- Include default values or settings for all controls where possible.

- Avoid advancing pages automatically. The user may not be able to read the information before a page advances. In addition, wizards are intended to allow the user to be in control of the process that the wizard automates.

- Display a wizard window so that the user can recognize it as the primary point of input. For example, if you display a wizard from a control that the user chooses in a secondary window, you may need to position the wizard window so that it partially obscures that secondary window.

- Make sure that the design alternatives offered by your wizard provide the user with positive results. You can use the context, such as the selection, to determine which options are reasonable to provide.

- Make sure that it is obvious how the user can proceed when the wizard has been completed. This can be accomplished in the text on the last page of the wizard.

You can include the **Finish** button at any point that the wizard has enough information to complete the task. For example, if you can provide reasonable defaults, you can even include the **Finish** button on the first page. Place the **Finish** button to the right and adjacent to the **Next** button. This allows users to step through the entire wizard or only the page on which the users wants to provide input. If the user needs to step through each page of the wizard, replace the **Next** button with the **Finish** button on the last page of the wizard. On the last page of the wizard, indicate to the user that the wizard is prepared to complete the task and instruct the user to click the **Finish** button.

Advanced Wizard Welcome Page

The advanced wizard design includes a Welcome page as its first page. Use the Welcome page to state the purpose of the wizard, as shown in Figure 13.19.

Figure 13.19 Advanced wizard Welcome page

At the top right of the wizard window, title the Welcome page "Welcome to the *Wizard Name* Wizard," using book-title capitalization and no ending punctuation. Also provide a short paragraph that welcomes the user to the wizard and explains in general terms what it does. Begin the text with the phrase "This wizard helps you *task description*." If the wizard performs several tasks or particularly complicated tasks, use a bulleted list of tasks that the user can accomplish. End the Welcome page text with "To continue, click Next."

For frequently used administrative wizards, place a check box with the text "Do not show this Welcome page again" at the bottom of the page before the "To continue..." line.

Advanced Wizard Interior Pages

For advanced wizard interior pages, include a header area at the top of the wizard window. Begin the header area with a title and a subtitle that describe the task that the user can accomplish on that page. For the title, use book title-capitalization with no ending punctuation, as shown in Figure 13.20.

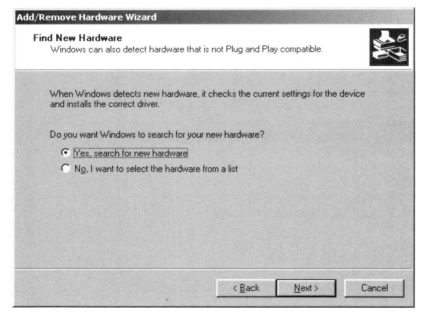

Figure 13.20 Advanced wizard interior page

The subtitle should explain the purpose of the page. If the purpose is self-evident, use the subtitle to provide additional information about the step being performed, to define a term or component mentioned in the title or elsewhere on the page, or to ask a question that helps clarify the purpose of the page. Use a complete sentence and sentence-style capitalization, including appropriate ending punctuation.

Sample Page Subtitles

Subtitle style	Example
Description of purpose	You can choose a sound scheme and then preview different sound events.
Description of step	During the installation, the program files are copied to your computer.
Definition of a term	Upgrade packs are files that help your programs work with Windows 2000 Professional.

Use a complete sentence and sentence-style capitalization, including appropriate ending punctuation. Avoid repeating subtitles within a wizard.

Advanced Wizard Completion Page

After the user completes an advanced wizard, use this page to inform the user that the wizard was completed successfully and to summarize the changes that were made, as shown in Figure 13.21.

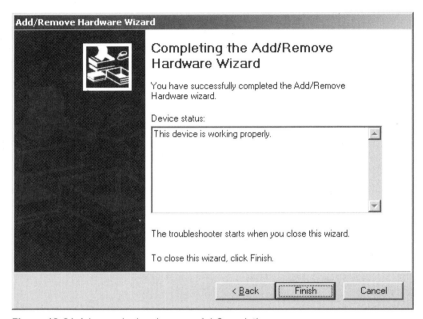

Figure 13.21 Advanced wizard successful Completion page

Title the page "Completing the *Wizard Name* Wizard." In the descriptive text of the page, state that the user has successfully completed the wizard and describe in general terms the task or tasks the user has accomplished. End the Completion page with "To close this wizard, click Finish."

If you include an optional action to be performed after the wizard closes, include a check box with one of the following text selections before the last line of the Completion page:

- "When I click Finish, perform *action* for the first time."

- "Perform *action* when this wizard closes."

- "Begin *action* when this wizard closes."

If the wizard was unsuccessful, use this page to inform the user that the wizard was not successfully completed, as shown in Figure 13.22.

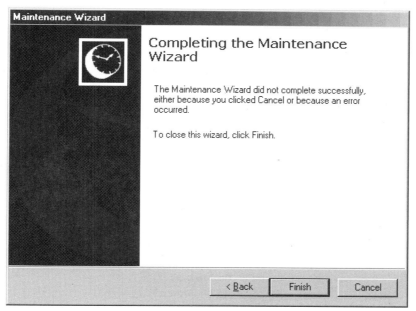

Figure 13.22 Advanced wizard unsuccessful Completion page

In the descriptive text for the page, tell the user that the wizard did not successfully complete the task, and then suggest a solution, if appropriate. For example: "The wizard did not successfully complete *task* because *reason*. *Perform solution*, and then run this wizard again.

Do not use the words "failed" or "failure" to indicate that the completion was unsuccessful. End the Completion page with "To close this wizard, click Finish."

Guidelines for Writing Text for Wizard Pages

Use a conversational rather than instructional writing style for the text you provide on the screens. The following guidelines can assist you in writing the text:

- Use words like "you" and "your."

- Start most questions with phrases like "Which option do you want..." or "Would you like to...." Users respond better to questions that enable them to do a task than to being told what to do. For example, "Which layout do you want?" works better in wizards than "Choose a layout."

- Use contractions and short, common words. In some cases, it may be acceptable to use slang, but you must consider localization when doing so.

  For more information about localization design, see Chapter 15, "Special Design Considerations."

- Avoid using technical terminology that may be confusing to novice users.

- Try to use as few words as possible. For example, the question, "Which style do you want for this newsletter?" could be written simply as "Which style do you want?"

- Keep the writing clear, concise, and simple, but not condescending.

Visual Design

What we see influences how we feel and what we understand. Visual information communicates nonverbally, but very powerfully. It can include cues that motivate, direct, or distract, so you want to ensure that every element in your application's user interface communicates effectively. This chapter contains presentation guidelines that you can apply to enhance the design, style, and layout of graphics and text in your application interface.

Visual Communication

Visual design serves a purpose greater than decoration; it is an important tool for effective communication. The organization of information on the screen can make the difference between a message users understand and one that leaves users feeling puzzled or overwhelmed.

Even the best application functionality can suffer and be underused if the visual presentation does not communicate it well. If you are not trained in visual or information design, it is a good idea to work with a designer who has education and experience in one of these fields. Include that person as a member of the design team early in the development process. Good designers know how best to take advantage of the screen and use the concepts of shape, color, contrast, focus, and composition effectively. Moreover, graphic designers understand how to design and organize information and can assess the impact of fonts and colors on perception.

Keep in mind that visual design should complement, not replace, the structural design of your application. In particular, avoid relying only on visual design to convey important information about what's on the screen. Users who have visual impairments may not be able to interpret this presentation. For example, make sure that controls have labels that communicate their relationship to other items, not strictly their physical location.

Composition and Organization

We choose what we read and how we think about information by its appearance and organization. We read a screen in the same way we read other forms of information. The eye is always attracted to colored elements before black-and-white elements, to isolated elements before elements in a group, and to graphics before text. We even read text by scanning the shapes of groups of letters. Consider the following principles when you design the organization and composition of visual elements of your interface:

- Hierarchy of information

- Focus and emphasis

- Structure and balance

- Relationship of elements

- Readability and flow

- Unity of integration

Hierarchy of Information

The principle of hierarchy of information addresses the placement of information based on its relative importance to other visual elements. The outcome of this ordering affects all of the other composition and organization principles. It also determines which information a user sees first and what a user is encouraged to do first. To further consider this principle, answer these questions regarding your application:

- Which information is most important to the user?

- What are the user's priorities when your application is started?

- What does the user want or need to do first, second, third, and so on?

- Will the order of information support or hamper the user's progression through the interface?

- What should the user see on the screen first, second, third, and so on?

Whenever possible, the visual display should match the user's priorities, but it can also be shaped by other elements you want to emphasize.

Focus and Emphasis

The related principles of focus and emphasis guide you in the placement of priority items. Once you identify the central idea, you can determine the focus, or focal point, for activity. You determine the emphasis by choosing the prominent element and isolating it from others, or by making it stand out in other ways.

Culture and interface design decisions largely determine where the user looks first for information. People in western cultures, for example, look at the upper left corner of the screen or window for the most important information. It makes sense to put a top-priority item there, giving it emphasis.

Structure and Balance

Structure and balance are two of the most important visual design principles. Without an underlying structure and a balance of visual elements, there is a lack of order and meaning that encompasses all other parts of the visual design. More importantly, a lack of structure and balance makes it more difficult for the user to clearly understand the interface.

Relationship of Elements

The relationship of elements is important in reinforcing the previous principles. The placement of a visual element can communicate a specific relationship to other elements. For example, if a button in a dialog box affects the content of a list box, there should be a spatial relationship between the button and the list box. This helps the user make the connection clearly and quickly just by looking at the placement. Similarly, the spatial layout should communicate information consistent with the interactive relationship of the elements, such as keyboard navigation.

Readability and Flow

This principle calls for ideas to be communicated directly and simply with minimal visual interference. Readability and flow can determine the usability of a dialog box or other interface component. When you design the layout of a window, consider the following questions:

- Could the idea or concept be presented more simply?

- Can the user easily step through the interface?

- Do all the elements have a reason for being there?

Unity and Integration

Unity and integration, the last set of principles, reflect how to evaluate a design in relation to its larger environment. Users find an application easier to use when its interface is visually unified with the Windows interface to present a consistent and predictable work environment. For design unity and integration, consider the following questions:

- How do all of the different parts of the screen work together visually?

- How does the visual design of the application relate to the system's interface or to other applications with which it is used?

Color

Color is very important in the visual interface. You can use it to identify elements in the interface to which you want to draw the user's attention — for example, the current selection. Color also has an associative quality; we often assume there is a relationship between items of the same color. Color also carries with it emotional or psychological qualities — for example, a color can be categorized as cool or warm.

However, when color is used indiscriminately, it can have a negative or distracting effect. Misuse of color can cause an unfavorable user reaction to your application and can hinder productivity by making it difficult for users to focus on a task.

Here are a few more things to consider about using color in your application's interface:

- Although you can use color to reinforce relatedness or grouping, it is not always obvious to the user to associate a color with a particular meaning.

- Color appeal is subjective. Everyone has different tastes in color. What is pleasing to you may be distasteful or unusable to someone else.

- Some percentage of your users may work with monitors that support only monochrome.

- Interpretation of color can vary by culture. Even within a single culture, individual associations with color can differ.

- Some percentage of the population may have color-identification problems. This can affect the accessibility of your software to the widest possible audience. For example, about 9 percent of the adult male population have some form of color confusion.

- Some users rely on software utilities that alter the appearance of the screen or replace the screen altogether. For example, some users with low vision run screen programs, such as the Magnifier accessory included with Windows 98, that alter the colors on the screen. Users who are blind rely on software that reads the contents of the screen out loud.

For more information about accessibility issues, see Chapter 15, "Special Design Considerations."

The following sections summarize guidelines for using color as a secondary form of information, using a limited set of colors, and providing the option to change colors.

Color as a Secondary Form of Information

Use color as an additional, reiterative, or enhanced form of information. Avoid relying on color as the only means of expressing a particular value or function. You can also convey information by text labels and by the shape, pattern, and location of items in the interface. It is also a good practice to design visuals in black and white or monochrome first, then add color. This helps you focus on key aspects of the visual information and use color only to enhance that information.

Use of a Limited Set of Colors

Although the human eye can distinguish millions of different colors, the use of too many colors results in visual clutter and makes it difficult for the user to discern the purpose of the color information. The colors you use should fit their purpose. Muted, subtle, complementary colors are often better than bright, highly saturated ones unless you are looking for a carnival-like appearance where bright colors capture the user's attention.

One color affects another. Adjacent or background colors affect the perceived brightness or shade of a particular color. A neutral color (for example, light gray) is often the best background color. Opposite colors, such as red and green, can make it difficult for the eye to focus. Dark colors tend to recede in the visual space, whereas light colors come forward.

Options to Change Colors

Because the choice of color is highly subjective and a matter of personal preference, allow the user to change colors where possible. For interface elements, Windows provides standard system interfaces and color schemes. If you base your software on these system properties, you can avoid including additional controls, and your application's visual elements are more likely to coordinate effectively when the user changes system colors. This is particularly important if you are designing your own controls or screen elements to match the style reflected in the system.

Your application should also support High Contrast Mode. For more information, see Chapter 15, "Special Design Considerations."

When providing your own application interface for changing colors, consider the complexity of the task and the skill of the user. It may be more helpful if you provide palettes, or limited sets of colors, that work well together rather than providing the entire spectrum. You can always supplement the palette with an interface that allows the user to add or change a color in the palette.

Fonts

Fonts have many functions in addition to providing letterforms for reading. Like other visual elements, fonts are used to organize information or to create a particular mood. When you vary the size and weight of a font, the user sees text as more or less important and perceives the order in which it should be read.

At conventional resolutions of computer displays, fonts are generally less legible online than on a printed page. Avoid italic and serif fonts, as these are often hard to read, especially at low resolutions. Figure 14.1 shows various font choices.

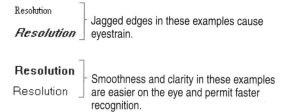

Resolution
Resolution ⎤ Jagged edges in these examples cause eyestrain.

Resolution
Resolution ⎤ Smoothness and clarity in these examples are easier on the eye and permit faster recognition.

Figure 14.1 Effective and ineffective font choices

Limit the number of fonts and styles you use in your software's interface. As with too many colors, using too many fonts usually results in visual clutter.

Use bold fonts sparingly. While bold text attracts attention, overusing it can distract the user and make it difficult to focus on what is important. Too much bold text also lessens its impact. Limit its use to titles, headings, and key items that should have the user's attention.

Similarly, limit your use of italic text. Used in isolation, italics may attract attention, but in general it can decrease the emphasis on the information and make the text less readable.

Wherever possible, use the standard system font for common interface elements for visual consistency between your interface and the system's interface. This standard system font also makes your interface more easily scalable. Since the user can customize many interface elements, check the system settings for the default system font and set the fonts in your interface accordingly. For more information about system font settings, see "Layout" later in this chapter.

For elements other than common interface elements, such as your application's window content, make the fonts adjustable so that users can change them to suit their preferences. You can do this by using commands that display a font selection dialog box, such as the one the system provides, or by including commands that automatically scale the presentation.

Dimensionality

Many elements in the Windows interface use perspective, high-lighting, and shading to provide a three-dimensional appearance. This emphasizes function and provides real-world feedback to the user's actions. For example, the command buttons' appearance provides the user with natural visual cues that help communicate their functionality and differentiate them from other types of information.

Windows bases its three-dimensional effects on a common theoretical light source, the conceptual direction that light would be coming from to produce the lighting and shadow effects used in the interface. The light source in Windows comes from the upper left.

Be careful not to overdo the use of dimensionality when designing your own visual elements. Avoid unnecessary nesting of visual elements and the use of three-dimensional effects for an element that is not interactive. Introduce only enough detail to provide useful visual cues, and use designs that blend well with the system interface.

Design of Visual Elements

All visual elements influence each other. Effective visual design depends on context. In a graphical user interface, a graphic element and its function are completely interrelated. A graphical interface must function intuitively — it should look the way it works and work the way it looks. These are the cornerstones to building a strong user experience with your application.

Basic Border Styles

Windows provides a unified visual design for building visual components based on the border styles shown in Figure 14.2.

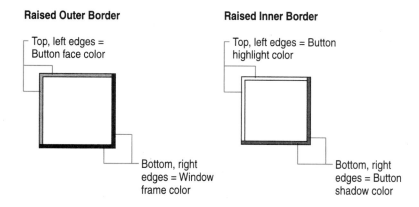

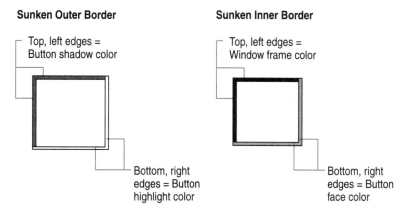

Figure 14.2 Basic border styles

The following table describes each of these border styles.

Border Styles

Border style	Description
Raised outer border	Uses a single line in the button face color for its top and left edges, and the window frame color for its bottom and right edges.
Raised inner border	Uses a single line in the button highlight color for its top and left edges, and the button shadow color for its bottom and right edges.
Sunken outer border	Uses a single line in the button shadow color for its top and left borders, and the button highlight color for its bottom and right edges.
Sunken inner border	Uses a single line in the window frame color for its top and left edges, and the button face color for its bottom and right edges.

If you use standard windows and Windows controls, these border styles are supplied for your application automatically. If you create your own controls, your application should map the colors of those controls to the appropriate system colors so that the controls fit in the overall design of the interface when the user changes the basic system colors.

The **DrawEdge** function automatically provides these border styles using the correct color settings. For more information about this function, see the Microsoft Platform SDK on the MSDN Online Web site at http://msdn.microsoft.com/ui/guide/sdk.asp.

Avoid using fixed widths to define the borders of your own controls. Instead, use the system's **GetSystemMetrics** function to determine the appropriate thickness of a line. These values are defined appropriately for the resolution of the display.

Window Border Style

The borders of primary and secondary windows, except for pop-up windows, use the window border style. Menus, scroll arrows, and other elements where the background color may vary also use this border style. The border style is composed of the raised outer and raised inner basic border styles, as shown in Figure 14.3.

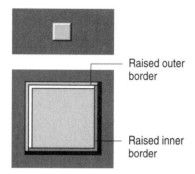

Raised outer border

Raised inner border

Figure 14.3 Window border style

Button Border Style

Command buttons use the button border style. The button border style uses a variation of the basic border styles, where the colors of the top and left outer and inner borders are swapped when combining the borders, as shown in Figure 14.4.

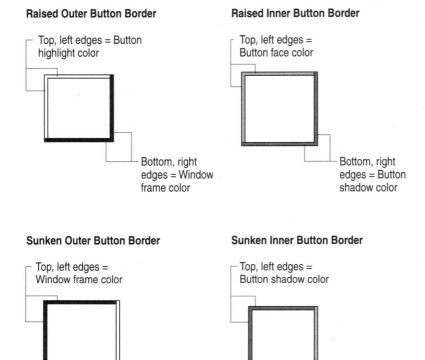

Raised Outer Button Border

Top, left edges = Button highlight color

Bottom, right edges = Window frame color

Raised Inner Button Border

Top, left edges = Button face color

Bottom, right edges = Button shadow color

Sunken Outer Button Border

Top, left edges = Window frame color

Bottom, right edges = Button highlight color

Sunken Inner Button Border

Top, left edges = Button shadow color

Bottom, right edges = Button face color

Figure 14.4 Button border styles

The normal button appearance combines the raised outer and raised inner button borders. When the user presses the button, the sunken outer and sunken inner button border styles are used, as shown in Figure 14.5.

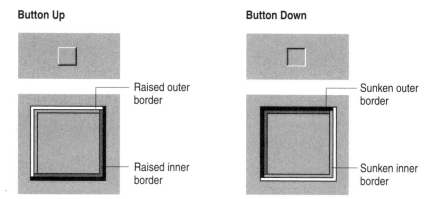

Figure 14.5 Button-up and button-down border styles

Toolbar button borders differ slightly from command button borders. Toolbar buttons show no visible border unless the user moves the pointer over them. In the button-up state, a toolbar button uses the raised inner border, but uses button highlights for the top and left edges and the button shadow color for the bottom and right edges. In the button-down state, a toolbar button uses the button shadow color for the top and left edges and the button highlight color for the bottom right edges. Unlike command button borders, toolbar buttons do not have a secondary edge border.

Field Border Style

Text boxes, check boxes, drop-down combo boxes, drop-down list boxes, spin boxes, and list boxes use the field border style, as shown in Figure 14.6. You can also use the style to define the work area within a window. It uses the sunken outer and sunken inner basic border styles.

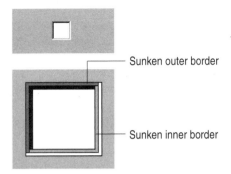

Figure 14.6 Field border style

For most controls, the interior of the field uses the button highlight color. For text fields, such as text boxes and combo boxes, the interior uses the button face color when the field is read-only or disabled.

Status Field Border Style

Status fields use the status field border style, as shown in Figure 14.7. This style uses only the sunken outer basic border style.

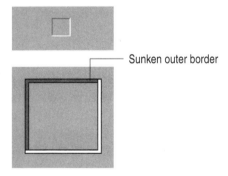

Figure 14.7 Status field border style

You use the status field style in status bars and any other read-only fields where the content of the file can change dynamically.

Grouping Border Style

Group boxes and menu separators use the grouping border style, as shown in Figure 14.8. The style uses the sunken outer and raised inner basic border styles.

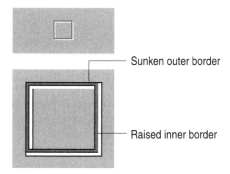

Sunken outer border

Raised inner border

Figure 14.8 Group border style

Visual States for Controls

The visual design of controls includes the various states supported by the control. If you use standard Windows controls, Windows automatically provides specific appearances for these states. If you design your own controls, use the information in the previous section for the appropriate border style. Use the information in the following sections to make your controls consistent with standard Windows controls.

Pressed Appearance

When the user presses a control with the primary mouse button, the control provides visual feedback on the downward stroke of the button (for the keyboard, on the downward stroke of the key).

For standard Windows check boxes and option buttons, the background of the button field is drawn using the button face color, as shown in Figure 14.9.

For more information about standard control behavior and appearance, see Chapter 8, "Menus, Controls, and Toolbars," and the Microsoft Platform SDK on the MSDN Online Web site at http://msdn.microsoft.com/ui/guide/sdk.asp.

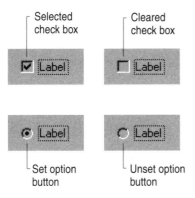

Figure 14.9 Pressed appearance for check boxes and option buttons

For command buttons, the button-down border style is used and the button label moves down and to the right by one pixel, as shown in Figure 14.10.

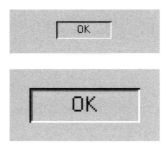

Figure 14.10 Pressed appearance for a command button

The pressed appearance for a toolbar button is similar, but it is slightly different because of the differences in its border design, as shown in Figure 14.11.

Figure 14.11 Pressed appearance for toolbar buttons

Option-Set Appearance

To indicate when a button's associated value or state applies or is currently set, the controls provide an *option-set appearance*. The option-set appearance is set for the up transition, or release, of the primary mouse button and the downward stroke of a key. It is visually distinct from the pressed appearance.

Standard check boxes and option buttons provide visual indicators that the option corresponding to that control is set. A check box uses a check mark, and an option button uses a dot that appears inside the button, as shown in Figure 14.12.

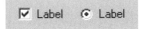

Figure 14.12 Option-set appearance for check boxes and option buttons

For toolbar buttons that represent properties or other state information, the button face reflects when the option is set. The button uses the button-down border style, but a checkerboard pattern (dither) consisting of the button face color and button highlight color is displayed in the background, as shown in Figure 14.13.

Figure 14.13 Option-set appearance for a toolbar button

For configurations that support 256 or more colors, if the button highlight color setting is not white, then the button background is a halftone between the button highlight color and the button face color. The image on the button does not otherwise change from the pressed appearance.

Mixed-Value Appearance

When a control represents a property or other setting that reflects a set of objects where the values are different, the control is displayed with a *mixed-value appearance* (also referred to as an indeterminate appearance), as shown in Figure 14.14.

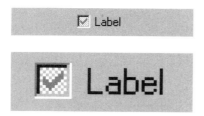

Figure 14.14 Mixed-value appearance for a check box

For most standard controls, leave the field with no indication of a current set value if it represents a mixed value. For example, for a drop-down list, the field is blank.

Standard check boxes support a special appearance for the mixed-value state. The check mark, in the button shadow color, is displayed against a checkerboard background that uses the button highlight color and button face color. For configurations that support 256 or more colors, if the button highlight color setting is not white, then the interior of the control is drawn in a halftone between the button highlight color and the button face color.

For buttons like those used on toolbars, the checkerboard pattern, or halftone composed of the button highlight color and the button face color, is drawn on the background of the button face, as shown in Figure 14.15. The image is converted to monochrome and drawn in the button shadow color.

The system defines the mixed-value states for check boxes as constants **BS_3STATE** and **BS_AUTO3STATE** when using the **CreateWindow** and **CreateWindowEx** functions. For more information about these functions, see the Microsoft Platform SDK on the MSDN Online Web site at http://msdn.microsoft.com/ui/guide/sdk.asp.

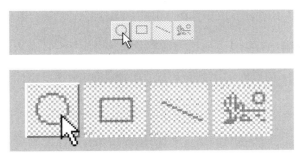

Figure 14.15 Mixed-value appearance for buttons

For check box and command button controls displaying a mixed-value appearance, the property value or state is set when the user clicks the button. Clicking a second time clears the value. As an option, you can support a third click to return the button to the mixed-value state.

Unavailable Appearance

When a control is unavailable, or disabled, its normal functionality is no longer available to the user (although it can still support access to contextual Help) because it does not apply or is inappropriate under the current circumstances. To reflect this state, the label of the control is rendered with a special *unavailable appearance*, as shown in Figure 14.16.

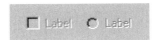

Figure 14.16 Unavailable appearance for check boxes and option buttons

For graphical or text buttons, create the engraved effect by converting the label to monochrome and draw it in the button highlight color. Then overlay it, at a small offset, with the label drawn in the button shadow color, as shown in Figure 14.17.

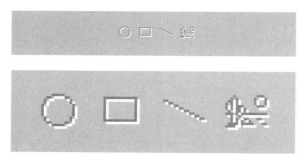

Figure 14.17 Unavailable appearance for buttons

If a check box or option button is set but the control is unavailable, then the control's label is displayed with an unavailable appearance, and its mark appears in the button shadow color, as shown in Figure 14.18.

Figure 14.18 Unavailable appearance for check boxes and option buttons (when set)

If a graphical button needs to reflect both the set and unavailable appearance (as shown in Figure 14.19), omit the background checkerboard pattern and combine the option-set and the unavailable appearance for the button's label.

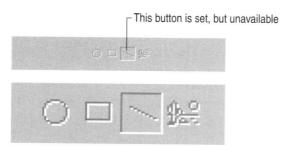

Figure 14.19 Unavailable and option-set appearance for buttons

Input Focus Appearance

You should provide a visual indication so the user knows where the input focus is. For text boxes, the system provides a blinking cursor, or insertion point. For other controls a dotted outline is drawn around the control or the control's label, as shown in Figure 14.20.

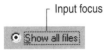

Figure 14.20 Input focus in a control

The system provides the input focus appearance for standard controls. To use it with your own custom controls, specify a rectangle with at least one border width of space around the border of the control. If the input focus indicator would be intrusive, you can instead include it around the text label for the control. Display the input focus when the mouse button is pressed and the cursor is over a control; for the keyboard, display the input focus when a navigation or access key for the control is pressed.

The system provides support for drawing the dotted outline input focus indicator using the **DrawFocusRect** function. For more information about this function, see the Microsoft Platform SDK on the MSDN Online Web site at http://msdn.microsoft.com/ui/guide/sdk.asp.

Whenever you provide a visual indication of the focus location, you should make sure this information is exposed to other software, such as the Magnifier accessory provided with Windows. For details about how to accomplish this, see the Microsoft Accessibility Web site at http://www.microsoft.com/enable/.

Hot-Tracked Appearance

Controls such as toolbar buttons provide visual feedback when the user moves the pointer (hotspot) over the boundary of the control. The system automatically provides support for menus and toolbars.

The convention for toolbar images is to display a border (one border width in thickness) and to change the image of the button from a neutral or grayscale to a color representation. However, if the image is already in color, then only the border presentation appears. The various modes of hot-tracked toolbar buttons are shown in Figure 14.21.

Figure 14.21 Hot-tracked toolbar buttons

If the button represents an option that the user can set, the hot-tracked appearance does not use the border. Instead, the button background changes from the button set color to the normal button face color.

The menu bar uses the same single-pixel border hot-tracked appearance that is used for toolbar buttons. Items in drop-down menus and context-menus use the same hot-tracked appearance that is used for selection highlighting.

Flat Appearance

When you use controls such as check boxes and option buttons in a list box control, you should use the control's flat (as opposed to three-dimensional) appearance, as shown in Figure 14.22.

⊙ Option1   ☑ Check1

Figure 14.22 Displaying check boxes and option buttons using the flat appearance

User Interface Text

User interface text in your application is text that appears on screen in both primary windows and secondary windows, such as dialog boxes, property sheets, wizards, message boxes, or controls. Clear, consistent, informative, and well-written text in these elements is essential for a usable interface. This section provides guidelines for writing and displaying interface text.

Font and Size

The default system font is a key element in the presentation of visual information. The default font used for interface elements in the U.S. releases of Windows 98 and Windows NT 4.0 is MS® Sans Serif 8 point. For applications that will run on Windows 2000, it is recommended you use Tahoma 8 point. For compatibility reasons, this font is not set by default in Windows 2000; you must explicitly select it. The Tahoma 8 point font offers improved readability and globalization support; in Windows 2000, it is the default font used by most of the interface elements in the operating system.

The menu bar titles, menu items, control labels, and other interface text in each operating system use one of these two fonts. The title bar text also uses the bold setting for these fonts, as shown in Figure 14.23. However, because the user can change the system font, make sure you check this setting and adjust the presentation of your interface appropriately rather than assume a fixed size for fonts and other visual elements. Also adjust the presentation when the system notifies your application that these settings have changed.

The **GetSystemMetrics** (for standard window elements), **SystemParametersInfo** (for primary window fonts), and **GetStockObject** (for secondary window fonts) functions provide current system settings. The **WM_SETTINGCHANGE** message notifies applications when these settings change. For more information about these APIs, see the Microsoft Platform SDK on the MSDN Online Web site at http://msdn.microsoft.com/ui/guide/sdk.asp.

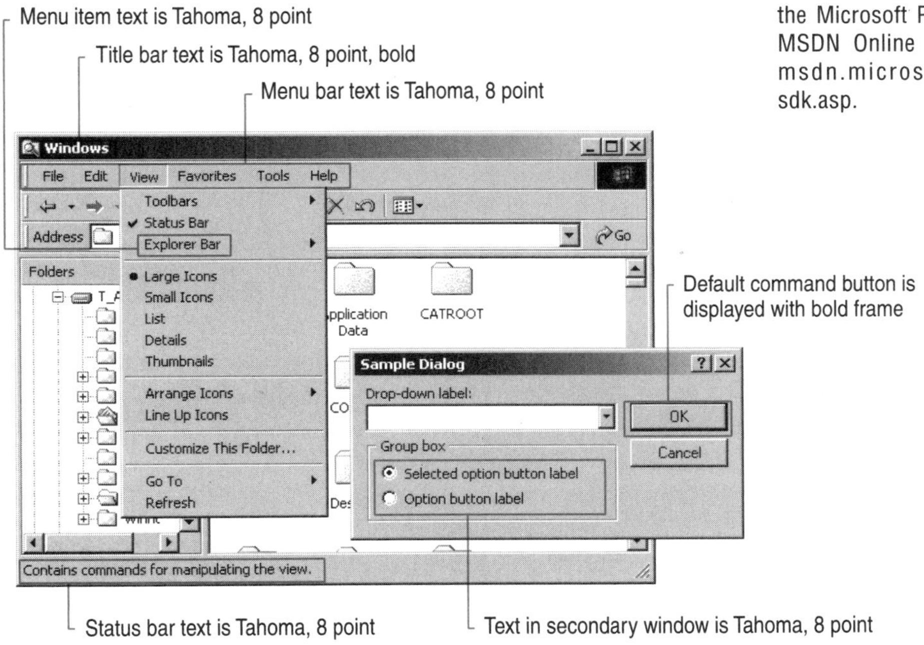

Figure 14.23 Default font usage in windows

The system provides settings for the font and size of many system components including title bar height, menu bar height, border width, title bar button height, icon title text, and scroll bar height and width. When you design your window layouts, take these settings into account so that your interface will scale appropriately. In addition, use the standard system settings to determine the size of your custom interface elements.

Except for title bars, avoid using bold or italic for interface text. In menus, bold text implies that the command is a default action.

The Basics of Writing Interface Text

The wording you use in your interface is a primary form of communication with the user. This section provides basic guidelines for writing effective user interface text.

Abbreviations

Avoid using abbreviations unless the abbreviated form is as familiar to your users as the full word or phrase. If you use an abbreviation, follow these guidelines:

- Always use the spelled-out term the first time it appears in any part of the user interface and include the abbreviation in parentheses. Use the abbreviation alone in subsequent references within the same screen, on subsequent pages of a wizard, or in nested dialog boxes that the user can get to only after seeing the screen, page, or dialog box where the term is spelled out.

- Avoid using abbreviations in headings.

- Do not abbreviate product or feature names without approval from your legal and marketing representatives.

Access Keys

Always define an access key for the label of any control or menu item. The only exceptions are the **OK** and **Cancel** buttons because the ENTER and ESC keys typically serve as the access keys to these buttons. Also, avoid having the same access key used by more than one control in a single context or more than one item on the same menu.

Acronyms

You can use an acronym for a term that is not trademarked or for a well-known industry standard. At its first mention, if a term is an industry standard acronym — for example, HTTP — there is no need to spell it out. But for the first mention of most other acronyms, spell out the full term with the acronym in parentheses directly following — for example, Internet Control Message

For more information about text conventions for particular interface elements, see Chapter 7, "Windows," Chapter 8, "Menus, Controls, and Toolbars," and Chapter 9, "Secondary Windows." *The Microsoft Manual of Style for Technical Publications* is also a useful resource for terminology guidelines.

Protocol (ICMP). You can then use just the acronym in subsequent references on the same screen, on subsequent pages of a wizard, or in nested dialog boxes that the user can get to only after seeing the screen, page, or dialog box where the term is spelled out.

If you use an acronym in a heading, do not spell out its meaning. Instead, use and spell out the full term in the first sentence after the heading, if it hasn't been spelled out previously. You may be able to link to a separate glossary entry or spell out the term in the status bar instead of using the spelled-out term in the text.

Check with your marketing and legal representatives before you create acronyms specific to your product. Also, search your intranet and the Internet for the acronym to make sure it isn't already used for another purpose in your customers' industry.

Capitalization

Correct capitalization helps readers identify important words and breaks in text, as shown in Figure 14.24. Two styles of capitalization are used for interface text: book title capitalization (also referred to as title caps) and sentence-style capitalization (also known as sentence caps).

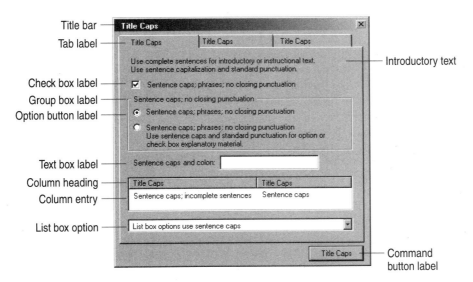

Figure 14.24 Capitalization and punctuation of user interface text

For book title capitalization, capitalize the first letter of the first and last words. Also capitalize all words in between, with the exception of articles (such as a, an, and the); coordinate conjunctions (such as and, but, for, not, or, so, and yet); and prepositions of four letters or fewer (such as at, for, with, and into). For example:

Insert Object
Paste Link
Save As
Go To
Always on Top
By Name

Use book title capitalization for the following elements:

- Column headings

- Command button labels

- Icon labels

- Menu names and menu commands

- Palette titles

- Tab titles

- Title bar text

- Toolbars and toolbar button labels

- ToolTips

- Web page titles and Web navigational elements (unless otherwise defined by your page design)

For sentence-style capitalization, capitalize only the first letter of the initial word and other words normally capitalized in sentences, such as proper nouns. For example:

Working folder
Print to
Use Postscript driver

Use sentence-style capitalization for the following elements:

- Alternate text (alt text) used to describe images on Web pages

- Check box labels

- File names

- Group box labels

- List box entries

- Messages

- Option (radio) button labels

- Status bar text

- Text box labels

If the user supplies a name for an object, always display the name as the user specifies it, regardless of case, wherever the name appears, including in the title bar for a window.

Contractions

Contractions lend an often-desirable informal tone to the user interface and also save space. However, never form a contraction from a subject and its verb:

Correct	Incorrect
Windows 2000 Professional is the latest version of the operating system.	Windows 2000 Professional's the latest version of the operating system.
The company will develop a new product line.	The company'll develop a new product line.

Ellipses

If a command requires additional information to complete its intended action, and you use a dialog box to supply that information, follow the command with an ellipsis (...). The ellipsis provides a visual cue that the command requires additional information.

Here are examples of when to use an ellipsis as part of a command's text:

- Include an ellipsis for a **Save As** command because the command is not complete until the user supplies or confirms a file name. Similar common examples include **Browse**, **Open**, **Find**, **Add**, and **Customize**.

- Include an ellipsis for a **Print** command when it opens the Print dialog box, where the user must confirm the print settings before printing.

However, not every command that results in the display of a window should include an ellipsis. Do not include an ellipsis for commands that simply display a window or view or change the existing view within a window. Similarly, do not use ellipses for commands that display a collection of objects or options, unless the intended action requires that the user select or confirm the selection of one or more elements of the collection. Also, do not include an ellipsis for commands that may result in a confirming message box.

Here are examples of when not to use an ellipsis as part of the command's text:

- Do not include ellipses for commands such as **Cut**, **Copy**, **Paste**, **Undo**, or **Refresh**. These commands perform direct actions; the user is not required to supply any information.

- Do not include ellipses for viewing commands such as **Details**, **Outline**, **Print Preview**, and **Show Toolbar**. Even if these views offer options, the intended action is complete when the view changes.

- Do not include ellipses for Help commands such as **Index** or **Contents**. The user can use these commands to select a Help topic, but the intended action is to display the HTML Help Viewer using a particular view.

- Do not include an ellipsis for an **About** command. This command typically displays copyright and version information about an application. Therefore, its intended action is complete when the window containing this information is displayed.

- Do not include an ellipsis for a **Properties** command. The user does not have to indicate what object to show properties for or what property to show. Even though the user can use this command to change options, the command's intended primary action is to display those options. Similar common examples include **Options**, **Settings**, **Advanced**, and **Preferences**.

- Do not include ellipses for commands such as **Macros**, **Help Topics**, and **Fonts**. The dialog boxes that display these collections may support additional actions, but the primary intended action of the command is to display the collection.

- Do not include an ellipsis for a **Toolbox** command or similar commands that display a palette of tools or options. The command's intended action to display the palette window is complete when the window appears.

- Do not include an ellipsis for a **Close** command, even though it may result in the display of a message box that prompts the user whether to save changes.

Keep in mind that the decision about whether or not to use an ellipsis can depend on the context of the command. You must take into consideration the command's intended action, the wording of the command, or, for menu items, the wording of the command's parent menu item. For example, a **Print** command that prints a document without displaying the **Print** dialog box should not include an ellipsis. A **Font** command on a **Format** menu should include an ellipsis because its intended action is to format the current selection with specific font settings, and the user must use the dialog box to define those settings.

If the object of the intended action is already defined, the **Open** command typically does not take an ellipsis. Contrast the command for a selected file icon in a standard folder window with the same command for the **File** menu in Notepad. In the first case, the user's selection before choosing the command supplies the necessary parameter of what to open, so no ellipsis is used. However, in the second case, the user must type or select the file to open, so an ellipsis should appear with the command. As a general rule, include an ellipsis if a command requires the user to supply "what," "where," or "how" information for the command to complete its intended action.

You can also use ellipses in other forms of interface text. For example, you can use ellipses to abbreviate path names or other information that may extend beyond the size of the field. Do not use an ellipsis in the title bar text of a window when the command that opened it included an ellipsis. Use an ellipsis in the title bar text only when you need to truncate the text. Whenever you use an ellipsis to abbreviate interface text, try to display as much information as possible to still enable the user to identify the item. Also, use other techniques such as ToolTips to display the full text.

Introductory or Instructional Text

Introductory or instructional text helps reduce or eliminate the text for online Help. Use introductory or instructional text in dialog boxes, Web views, and wizard pages to provide additional information about the task that the user wants to accomplish. Follow these guidelines for writing useful introductory or instructional text:

- Write text that is brief and to the point.

- Complement and expand on informative control labels but don't duplicate them.

- Position the text so that any relationship with a particular control is clear.

- Use sentence-style capitalization and ending punctuation.

For more information about instructional text for specific controls, see Chapter 8, "Menus, Controls, and Toolbars." For information about designing wizard pages, see Chapter 13, "User Assistance."

Numbers

Align numbers at the decimal point (or imaginary decimal point). Right-align a block or column of whole numbers or of whole numbers and text, as shown in Figure 14.25.

```
┌─ I/O status ──────────────────────────────────┐
│              Incoming        Outgoing          │
│  Bytes:        62711          253358           │
│  Frames:         733             490           │
│  Bytes/frame:     85             517           │
│  Frame errors:    15               6           │
│  % Frame errors: 0.02           0.01           │
│  Timeout errors:   5             n/a           │
│  Compression ratio: n/a         0.95           │
└────────────────────────────────────────────────┘
```

Figure 14.25 Right-alignment for block or columns of numbers

Punctuation

Follow normal rules of punctuation for your interface text. End a question with a question mark, but avoid phrasing control labels as questions. Separate sentences with one blank space, not two.

In a bulleted or numbered list, introduce the list with a sentence or sentence fragment that ends with a colon. Begin each entry in the list with a capital letter. End each entry with ending punctuation if all entries are complete sentences or complete the introductory phrase, as shown in Figure 14.26. Entries in a list should be parallel (have the same grammatical structure).

For more information about punctuating text for specific types of controls, see Chapter 8, "Menus, Controls, and Toolbars."

Figure 14.26 Punctuation for bulleted lists

Writing Style

Before you begin writing, research your audience to determine the most useful writing style. For example, text in a program intended for novice users should be different from text in a program designed for network administrators. Style, which includes brevity, language, parallel construction, sentence structure, and voice, affects the readability and comprehensibility of text.

Brevity

Keep text in the user interface as brief as possible. Usability studies indicate that users are more likely to read short blocks of text than long ones. Review your work to eliminate wordiness, and keep user interface text short without sacrificing clarity and ease of localization:

- Focus on what the user must know. Do not include extraneous or optional information.

- Use simple and direct words and phrases, especially for the most prominent and often-used interface elements. Introduce more specific and advanced technical terms in dialog boxes.

- Use specific verbs. Watch for helping verbs, such as "make" and "be." These terms may indicate that a more specific verb is available. For example, instead of "...to make the window appear," say "...to display the window."

- Try to limit instructions for correcting an error to three simple steps.

- Replace several words with one whenever you can. Some examples are shown in the following table.

Sample Simplified Phrases

Replace	With
By means of	By
For the purposes of	For
In many cases	Often
In the event that	If
Is able to	Can

Sample Simplified Phrases *(continued)*

Replace	With
On the basis of	Based on
The way in which	The way, how
In order to	To
Prior to	Before
Is required to	Must

- Eliminate words that do not add value. For example:

  Actually
  Basically
  More or less
  To a certain degree
  Various

Language

Clear and consistent use of language can improve usability and ease localization. Use good, standard grammar. Grammar provides important clues to the meaning of terms in a sentence. Keep the following guidelines in mind:

- Write positive statements. Avoid using negative words, such as problem, bad, wrong, fail, error, fatal, terminate, and trouble. Instead, tell the user what the problem is, what to do, and why.

- Avoid redundancy. For example:

  Surrounding environment
  Absolutely complete
  Exactly identical
  Repeat again
  Final conclusion
  Basic and fundamental
  Knowledge and awareness
  Each and every
  Complete overview
  Advance planning
  Full and complete
  Informative message

- If you state the correct condition, do not also state that the incorrect condition should not exist. For example, if you say "The computer must be running," do not also say "It must not be shut off."

- Use consistent phrasing for similar situations. This avoids users assuming that a different meaning may be intended by a change in wording.

- Use the plural form of a word rather than using "(s)" (or use both the singular and plural forms).

Correct	Incorrect
File names	File name(s)

Parallel Construction

Use the same grammatical structure for elements of sentences or phrases that provide the same kind of information. For example, use parallel construction for items in lists and groups of check box labels or option button labels. In the following example, all the items in the Correct list begin with verbs in the active voice and are phrased in the imperative mood. Items in the Incorrect list are in a mix of voice and mood.

Correct	Incorrect
Get up-to-date information about upgrades and new products.	Up-to-date information about upgrades and new products will be sent to you.
Use Windows Update to download product updates.	Using Windows Update you can download product updates.
Receive the best possible customer support.	The best possible customer support is available.
Gain access to the latest files and drivers.	You can gain access to the latest files and drivers.

Sentence Construction

Use sentences in the interface to explain concepts, introduce features, and discuss controls. Follow these guidelines when writing sentences:

- Write short, simple sentences. Break long sentences into two or more shorter sentences.

- Use lists or tables to break up text.

- Use the present tense.

Correct	Incorrect
Windows cannot find the file.	Windows could not find the file.

- Write affirmative statements, telling the user what to do rather than what to avoid (unless there is a reason the user should not perform a particular action).

Correct	Incorrect
To restart your computer, click Restart.	Do not use CTRL+ALT+DEL to restart your computer.

- When a sentence describes a sequence of actions, describe the actions in the order in which the user performs them.

Correct	Incorrect
Reinstall the program and then restart your computer.	You'll need to restart your computer after you reinstall the program.

- Avoid using a control within a sentence or phrase if the text will be localized. Instead, place it at the end of the sentence or phrase.

Correct	Incorrect
Number of concurrent connections per server: *Control*	Per server for *Control* concurrent connections.

For more information about localization, see Chapter 15, "Special Design Considerations."

Voice

Use the active voice to clarify who or what is performing the action in a sentence.

Correct	Incorrect
Windows cannot find the configuration file.	The configuration file cannot be found.

Terminology

You can help users learn your product more quickly by using terminology that is familiar to them and by using the same terminology for a particular concept throughout the interface. If your product will be localized, create a list of defined terms to localize.

Use familiar wording on menus, commands, control labels, and toolbars. Avoid technical jargon. Write so that the least skilled user of the application will understand.

Correct	Incorrect
Send and receive sound at the same time.	Use full-duplex audio.

Define terms that are unfamiliar or are used more narrowly or broadly in your product than in common use. For example, you can sometimes use descriptors to identify a term's meaning or purpose. This can help users understand the context of the term.

Correct	Incorrect
You have to specify the parameter InfID when the option Detect is set to "No."	You have to specify InfID when detect is set to No.
The value CiDialect specification for webhits is not valid.	The CiDialect specified for webhits is not valid.

In general, use "click" to describe selecting command buttons, option buttons, hyperlinks, tabs, menus, and menu items. Use "select" to describe selecting items in a list box or gallery.

Correct	Incorrect
Click OK.	Press OK.
On the Edit menu, click Copy.	On the Edit menu, select Copy.
To remove any temporary files, click Remove.	To remove any temporary files, choose Remove.

Use "press" to describe pressing a key on the keyboard. Use "type" when referring to typing words.

Correct	Incorrect
To continue, press ENTER.	To continue, hit ENTER
Type your name in the space provided.	Key your name into the space provided.

Use "select" and "clear" in instructions for a check box.

Correct	Incorrect
To add a component, select its check box.	To add a component, click its checkbox.
To remove the component, clear the check box.	To remove the component, uncheck it.
Select the appropriate check boxes.	Enable the appropriate options.
Clear the Bookmarks check box.	Click to uncheck the Bookmarks option.

However, use "click to remove the check mark" rather than "clear" to describe removing a check mark from a menu item.

Take care to avoid using words or phrases that may offend some users. The following guidelines can help writers and editors recognize terms that may inadvertently cause offense or convey an inappropriate message.

For the correct usage of Microsoft trademarks, copyrights, and product names, see the Microsoft Copyright Permission Web site at http://www.microsoft.com/permission.

- In general, consider the person first, not the label. Use "a person with [*kind of disability*]," not "the disabled person."

- When you refer to a user interface element or command, use "unavailable" or use "make unavailable" rather than "disabled" or "disable." The word "disable" is acceptable in technical documentation in the context of a programmer setting the guidelines for making a command unavailable.

- Use the following terms to describe people with disabilities or the disabilities themselves.

Use these terms	Instead of
Blind, has low vision, visually impaired	Sight-impaired, vision impaired
Deaf or hard-of-hearing	Hearing-impaired
Has limited dexterity, has motion disabilities	Crippled, lame
Without disabilities	Normal, able-bodied, healthy
One-handed, people who type with one hand	Single-handed
People with disabilities	The disabled, disabled people, people with handicaps, the handicapped
Cognitive disabilities, developmental disabilities	Slow learner, retarded, mentally handicapped
TTY/TDD (to refer to the telecommunication device)	TT/TTD

Title Bars

Include a title for all primary and secondary windows. The only exceptions are as follows:

- Windows that automatically remove themselves at start-up, such as application title or splash screens

- Windows that time-out to avoid obscuring user interaction, such as balloon tips and pop-up windows for context-sensitive Help

- The volume control window that appears when a user clicks the volume icon in the taskbar notification area

Use book title capitalization unless you are displaying a user-defined name. In that case, use the capitalization that the user provides.

For more information about title bars, see Chapter 7, "Windows" and Chapter 9, "Secondary Windows."

The following table summarizes title bar text usage guidelines.

Guidelines for Title Bar Text

For the title bar in a	Use this style	Example
Dialog box	Name of the related command (or slight modification)	Browse for Folder
Document window	Document title	Letter to Bill
Message box	Name of document or program	Letter to Bill –WordPad
Palette window	Name of objects displayed on palette	Color
Program window	Product or program name*	Calculator
Property sheet	*Feature or object name* Properties	Recycle Bin Properties
Toolbar	Toolbar name	Formatting
Web page	Page title – *browser name*	Web Directory – Microsoft Internet Explorer
Wizard	Full wizard name	Maintenance Wizard

* If the application does not explicitly store user data (such as Calculator), then use just the application's product name. If the application is not the primary viewer of user data (such as QuickView) or the object more logically presents itself as a tool rather than as a representation of the user data (such as Find File), then display the program's name, followed by the data file.

Layout

Size, spacing, and placement of information are critical in creating a visually consistent and predictable environment. Visual structure is also important for communicating the purpose of the elements displayed in a window. In general, follow the layout conventions for how information is read. In western countries, this means left-to-right, top-to-bottom, with the most important information located in the upper left corner.

The system defines the size and location of user interface elements in a window based on dialog units (DLUs), not pixels. A *dialog unit* is the device-independent measure to use for layout. One horizontal dialog unit is equal to one-fourth of the average character width for the current system font. One vertical dialog unit is equal to one-eighth of an average character height for the current system font. The default height for most single-line controls is 14 DLUs. Be careful if you use a pixel-based drawing program, because it may not provide an accurate representation when you translate your design into dialog units. If you do use a pixel-based drawing tool, you may want to take screen snapshots from a development tool that supports dialog units and use those images.

> Your application can retrieve the number of pixels per base unit for the current display using the **GetDialogBaseUnits** function. For more information about this function, see the Microsoft Platform SDK on the MSDN Online Web site at http://msdn.microsoft.com/ui/guide/sdk.asp.

Size

The following table lists the typical height and width of common dialog box controls.

Size of Common Dialog Box Controls

Control	Height (DLUs)	Width (DLUs)
Dialog boxes and property sheets	263 max. (for 640 x 480 screen resolution)	263 max. (for 640 x 480 screen resolution)
	218	252
	215	227
	188	212

(For property sheets, heights include 25 DLUs for property sheet button bars.)

> To support localization, you should make controls wider than just enough to display the labels. For more information, see Chapter 15, "Special Design Considerations."

Size of Common Dialog Box Controls *(continued)*

Control	Height (DLUs)	Width (DLUs)
Command buttons	14	50
Check boxes	10	As wide as needed
Drop-down combo box and drop-down list	10	Size to match other drop-down combo boxes and text boxes
Option buttons	10	As wide as needed
Text boxes	14	Size to match other drop-down combo boxes and text boxes
Text labels	8 per line of text	As wide as needed
Other screen text	8 per line of text	As wide as needed

Toolbars and their buttons use pixels instead of dialog units for their measurement. The recommended sizes are shown in the following table.

Size of Toolbars and Toolbar Buttons

Control	Height (pixels)	Width (pixels)
Toolbars in small button mode	23	Width of toolbar area or window
Toolbars in large button mode	28	Width of toolbar area or window
Small toolbar buttons	21	Depends on content; 22 if the button includes only an image
Large toolbar buttons	26	Depends on content; 28 if the button includes only an image

When you cannot reasonably apply the size guidelines for secondary windows, try to maintain a width within a task. This can provide a smooth transition, making it easier for a user to focus on the task. Also, always check to make sure that the window will fit in the minimum screen resolution set by your application's users. Typically, this means using a 640 x 480 resolution screen to ensure that it fits completely. You must also take into account the possible space taken up by the task bar and other desktop toolbars.

Make buttons a consistent length for readability. However, if maintaining this consistency greatly expands the space required for a set of buttons, it may be reasonable to have one button larger than the rest.

Similarly, if you use tabs, try to maintain a consistent width for all tabs in the same window (and in the same dimension). However, if a particular tab's label makes this unworkable, size it larger and maintain a smaller, consistent size for the other tabs. If a tab's label contains variable text, you can size the tab to fit the label, up to some reasonable maximum, after which you truncate the text and add an ellipsis.

Try to maintain a consistent width between text boxes and the list boxes they appear near, using only one or two different widths per group or window. If you localize your application, you should extend text, option button labels, and check box labels to be as wide as the group or window, where possible. This will reduce the work necessary to localize your interface.

Spacing and Positioning

Maintain a consistent margin from the edge of the window — seven dialog units is recommended. Use spacing between groups within the window, as shown in Figure 14.27.

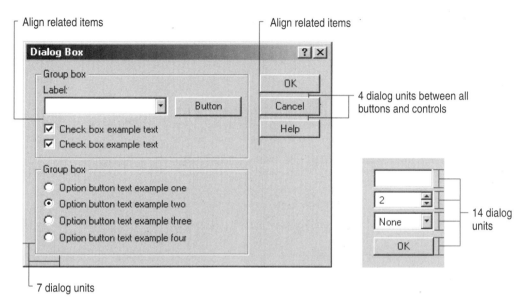

Figure 14.27 Recommended layout and spacing of controls and text

The following table lists the typical items found in an interface and the recommended spacing between them.

Spacing Between Interface Items

Interface items	Use this spacing (DLUs)
Dialog box margins	7 on all sides
Between paragraphs of text	7
Between text labels and their associated controls (for example, text boxes and list boxes)	3
Between related controls	4
Between unrelated controls	7

Spacing Between Interface Items *(continued)*

Interface items	Use this spacing (DLUs)
First control in a group box	11 down from the top of the group box; align vertically to the group box title
Between controls in a group box	4; align vertically to the group box title
Between horizontally or vertically arranged buttons	4; align vertically to the group box title
From the left edge of a group box	9; if the group box is left-aligned, controls are 16 from the left edge of the dialog box or property page
Last control in a group box	7 above the bottom of the group box
Smallest space between controls	2
Text label beside a button	3 down from the top of the button
Check box, list box, or option button beside a button	2 down from the top of the button

Toolbars and their buttons use pixels instead of DLUs. The following table provides spacing for toolbar buttons.

Spacing for toolbar buttons

Button Size	Spacing
Small (16 x 16 pixel image) toolbar buttons	3 pixels between a button and its text label
	2 pixels above the toolbar image
	3 pixels below the toolbar image
Large (20 x 20 pixel image) toolbar buttons	3 pixels between a button and its text label
	2 pixels above the toolbar image
	2 pixels below the toolbar image

In general, for controls that do not contain their own labels, place the label to the left or above the related control. This makes it easier for users to associate the label with the corresponding control.

When a text box is the first item in the group box, use a smaller measurement so the visual spacing above and to the right looks equal. In cases where there are controls below a group box, align the controls to the edge of the group box above and use seven DLUs between the bottom edge of the group box and the control (or text), as shown in Figure 14.28.

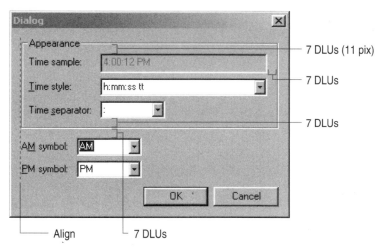

Figure 14.28 Example of group box spacing

Position controls in a toolbar so that there is at least a window's border width from the edges of the toolbar, as shown below.

Use at least 4 DLUs between controls, except for between a set of related toolbar buttons. There should be no space between adjacent toolbar buttons, such as a set of related option buttons.

For wizard design, Figure 14.29 shows suggested positioning and spacing.

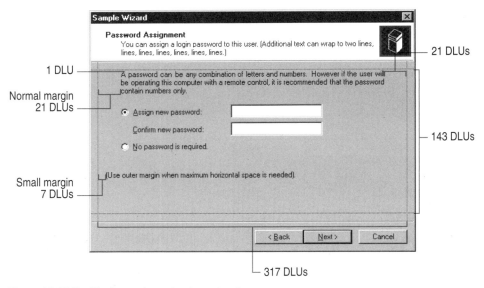

Figure 14.29 Positioning and spacing in a wizard

Grouping

Group related components — you can use group box controls, separator lines, or spacing. Although you can also use color to visually group objects, it is not a common convention and could result in undesirable effects if the user changes color schemes.

A group box provides a strong visual element for related items. However, avoid using a group box when you have only one set of related items or where the group box may take too much space or add visual clutter rather than structure. Instead, consider using separators to group related items. Property sheets for files and folders are a good illustration of the use of separators rather than group boxes.

Stack the main command buttons in a secondary window in the upper right corner or in a row along the bottom, as shown in Figure 14.30. If there is a default button, it is typically the first button in the set. Place **OK** and **Cancel** buttons next to each other. If there is no

For more information about button placement in secondary windows, see Chapter 9, "Secondary Windows."

OK button but there are command buttons that initiate action, place the **Cancel** button at the end of the buttons but before a **Help** button. If a particular command button applies only to a particular field, group it with that field.

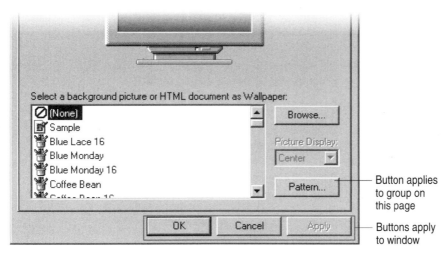

Figure 14.30 Layout of buttons

Group controls so that their location helps users understand the associated context or scope. For tabbed pages, follow these guidelines:

• When command buttons and other controls apply only to that page, place them within the border of the tabbed page.

• When command buttons and other controls apply to the entire window, place them outside the tabbed page.

Alignment

When information is positioned vertically, align fields by their left edges (in western countries). This usually makes it easier for the user to scan the information. Text labels are usually left-aligned and placed above or to the left of the areas to which they apply. When placing text labels to the left of text box controls, align the top of the text with text displayed in the text box.

In group boxes, controls should be left-aligned with the text label of the group. However, command buttons in the group should be right-aligned.

Align command buttons in most secondary windows at the top right or right-align them with the bottom. The exception is for message boxes, where command buttons should be centered. In toolbar arrangements, buttons and other controls are typically left- or top-aligned, depending on the layout of the area.

Required and Optional Input

For input form design, you may want to require certain input fields or controls and make others optional. To help users distinguish required input from optional input, provide some form of visual differentiation. The best way to do this is to separate the two sets of input into separate windows, panes, or groups and label the fields accordingly. However, this may not always work with the type of information you are presenting. The next best way is to label the individual fields with the words "required" or "optional" in parentheses. You can also use fonts, symbols, or graphics; however, such conventions require the user to learn the convention in order to use the application effectively. In scenarios where you cannot rely on training the user, use a more obvious form of identification. Do not use color unless you are using some other form of feedback as well. Color may attract the user's attention, but the perception of color can vary. Therefore, do not rely on it as the only means of identification.

Preview and Sample Boxes

In some situations, you may want to provide an area for a visual example of changes a user is making to an item, as shown in Figure 14.31.

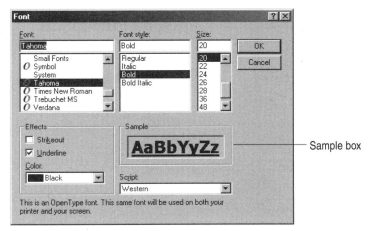

Sample box

Figure 14.31 Preview or sample box

A *sample* is a representation of what might show up on screen, but it does not show the actual data that the user is working on. In contrast, a *preview* shows the user's actual data.

Include text, graphics, or both in your preview or sample boxes. The preview can be illustrative and interactive. If the preview is interactive, include instructions or some visual cue to let the user know that it is interactive.

Include a label for your preview or sample box, and keep the wording for the label brief. A one- or two-word label (often Preview or Sample) is usually sufficient unless the user needs to interact with the preview to update it. Use sentence-style capitalization for the label, but do not include ending punctuation unless the user can interact with the preview, in which case end the label with a colon.

Design of Graphic Images

To design pictorial representations, such as icons or other graphics, begin by defining the graphic's purpose and use. How will the graphics help the users finish a task? Graphics are used to support or illustrate the user's task rather than to compete with or distract from the task.

Consistency is important in the design of graphic images. Make the scale, orientation, and color consistent with other related objects, and fit the graphics into the overall environment in which they appear. In addition, make sure you provide sufficient contrast for your images so that users can identify different elements or details of the images.

Graphics for symbolic purposes, such as icons or toolbar images, are most effective when you use real-world metaphors, so you may need to brainstorm to come up with viable representations. It is often difficult to design icons that define operations or processes — activities that rely on verbs. Consider nouns instead. For example, scissors can represent the action to cut.

Avoid using a triangular arrow graphic similar to the one used in cascading menus, drop-down controls, and scroll arrows, except where user interaction results in additional information being displayed. For example, such an arrow on a button implies that a menu will appear when the user clicks it.

For graphics that represent interactive content, provide a visual cue that the item is interactive and a text description of what it does. Use techniques such as changing the pointer or display a ToolTip or text label to communicate its purpose.

Consider the cultural impact of your graphics. What may have a certain meaning in one country or culture may not have the same meaning in another. Avoid letters or words in graphics where possible, as they may not work in or adapt to other cultures.

For more information about designing for international audiences, see Chapter 15, "Special Design Considerations."

Also consider your entire potential user audience. Users who have visual impairments may not be able to perceive the information in an image. Therefore, use images only to reinforce information that is already conveyed through text.

Finally, hire a good graphic designer to create your images, especially one with experience in designing for computer screen displays. Good visual design requires experience and skill.

Icon Design

Icons are used throughout the Windows interface to represent objects or tasks. The system uses icons to represent your software's objects, so it is important to design effective icons that communicate their purpose.

Design icons as a set and consider their relationship to each other and to the user's tasks. Do several sketches or designs and test them for usability.

Sizes and Types

Supply icons for your application in 16-color and 256-color versions and in three sizes: 16 x 16 pixels, 32 x 32 pixels, and 48 x 48 pixels, as shown in Figure 14.32. The 256-color icons are used in 16- and 24-bit color display modes.

To display icons at 48 x 48 pixel resolution, the registry value **Shell Icon Size** must be increased to 48. To display icons in color resolution depth higher than 16 colors, the registry value **Shell Icon BPP** must be set to 8 or more. These values are stored in **HKEY_ CURRENT_USER\Desktop\ WindowMetrics.**

256 color

48 x 48   32 x 32   16 x 16

16 color

48 x 48   32 x 32   16 x 16

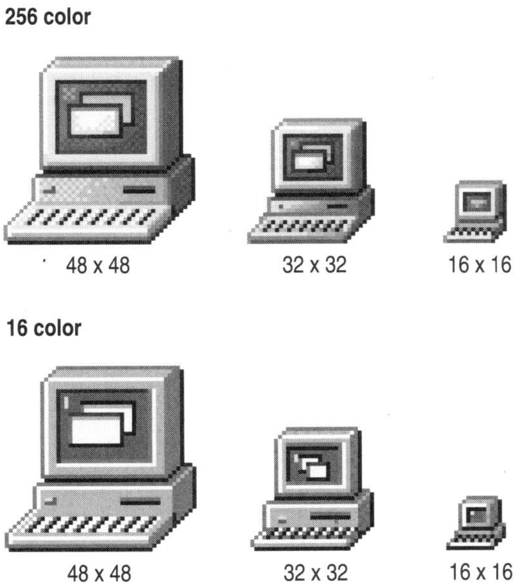

Figure 14.32 Two color versions in three sizes of icons (zoomed)

Use colors drawn from the system palette to make sure that icons look correct in all color configurations.

The system automatically maps colors in your icon design for monochrome configurations. However, check your icon design in a monochrome configuration. If the result is not satisfactory, include monochrome icons as well.

Define icons not only for your application's executable file, but also for all data file types supported by your application, as shown in Figure 14.33.

Application icons

Document icons

Figure 14.33 Application icons and supported document icons

Icons for documents and data files should be distinct from the application's icon. Include some common element of the application's icon, but focus on making the document icon recognizable and representative of the file's content.

Register the icons you supply in the system registry. If your software does not register any icons, the system automatically provides one for your application, as shown in Figure 14.34. However, it is unlikely to be as detailed or distinctive as one you supply.

For more information about registering your icons, see Chapter 11, "Integrating with the System."

48 x 48   32 x 32   16 x 16

Figure 14.34 System-generated icons for a file type without a registered icon

Icon Style

Use a common design style across all icons. Repeat common characteristics, but avoid repeating unrelated elements.

An illustrative style tends to communicate metaphorical concepts more effectively than abstract symbols. However, if you design an image based on a real-world object, use only the amount of detail necessary for user recognition and recall. Where possible and appropriate, use perspective and dimension (lighting and shadow) to better communicate the real-world representation, as shown in Figure 14.35.

Figure 14.35 Graphic improved with perspective and dimension

Design icon images using a light source from the upper left. To reinforce the light source effect, use a black edge on the bottom and right and a dark gray edge on the left and top. An alternative is to use a dark color in place of the dark gray.

User recognition and recollection are two important factors to consider in icon design. Recognition means that the user can identify the icon and easily associate it with a particular object. Support user recognition by using effective metaphors. Use real-world objects to represent abstract ideas so that the user can draw from previous learning and experiences. Exploit the user's knowledge of the world and allude to the familiar.

To facilitate recollection, design your icons to be simple and distinct. Apply the icon consistently to build recognition; therefore, design your small icons to be as similar as possible to their larger counterparts. Try to preserve their general shape and any distinctive detail. Icons that are 48 x 48 pixels can be rendered in 256 colors to create very realistic-looking icons, but focus on simplicity and a careful use of color. If your software is targeted for computers that can display only 256 colors, make sure you only use colors from the system's standard 256-color palette. If your software is targeted for computers configured for 65,000 or more colors, you can use any combination of colors.

Avoid using people, stereotypes, faces, gender, or body parts as icons. This is particularly important for an international audience, as such images may not easily translate or could be offensive. When you must represent people or users, depict them as generically as possible; avoid realistic depictions.

Consider how overlay images — such as a shortcut icon, an offline icon, or other visual annotations — might affect the appearance of icons, as shown in Figure 14.36. Make sure they don't cover up the most important parts of your images.

Normal icon   Shortcut   Sharing
               overlay   overlay

Figure 14.36 Icon overlays and annotations

One solution to avoid covering critical information is to flip your icon image horizontally. If you do, remember to adjust the light source.

Reuse established concepts where possible. For example, if there are existing images for illustrating objects such as documents, you may want to extend that idea, including other details to help differentiate the image for your specific use. However, check on copyright usage before explicitly duplicating any images.

Draw your ideas by using an icon-editing utility or pixel (bitmap) drawing package. Drawing icons directly on the screen provides you with immediate feedback about their appearance. It is a good idea to begin the design in black and white. Consider color as a property enhancement. Test your images on different backgrounds, because they may not always be visible against white or gray backgrounds.

Icon Usage

Icons are primarily intended to represent objects with which users can interact. Therefore, be careful in the use of icons and follow these guidelines:

- Use an icon as the representation of an object — for example, a folder icon in a folder's properties window.

- Use an icon to reinforce important information — for example, a warning icon in a message dialog box.

- Use an icon to provide visual anchors to help users quickly navigate through a task.

Avoid using icons in lower level dialog boxes, as this creates visual clutter.

Toolbar Button Image Design

When you design graphic images for toolbar buttons, create 16-x-16 pixel and 20-x-20 pixel images in 16 colors and 256 colors. If you support additional tracking feedback when the pointer is over the toolbar button, include 16-color grayscale and 256-color grayscale monochrome versions of your images. For examples of toolbar graphics, see Figure 14.37.

256-color large icons

256-color small icons

16-color large icons

16-color small icons

Figure 14.37 Toolbar image sets

Keep the following guidelines in mind when you design toolbar images:

General guidelines for toolbar images

- Use the system's common toolbar images as a resource to maintain consistency.

- Use the same hue and color saturation as in the existing set of toolbar icons for consistency.

- Make sure the visual transition between the default and hot-tracked state is smooth.

Guidelines for 16-color toolbar images

- Use the Windows 16-color palette.

- Place a black border around the image for both the default and active states, except for arrows or X's.

- Images should be fairly flat in appearance with little dimension or shading.

Guidelines for 256-color toolbar images

- Use the Windows halftone palette.

- For both the default and pointer-over states, use icon-style borders with gray or color as the top and left borders and black as the bottom and right borders.

- Images should be more dimensional. Use a light source from the upper left and shading where appropriate.

Common Toolbar Buttons

The following table illustrates the button images for common functions.

Common Toolbar Buttons

16 x 16 button	24 x 24 button	Function
		New
		Open
		Save
		Print
		Print Preview
		Undo
		Redo
		Cut
		Copy
		Paste
		Delete
		Find

Common Toolbar Buttons *(continued)*

16 x 16 button	24 x 24 button	Function
		Replace
		Properties
B	**B**	Bold
		Italic
U	**U**	Underline
		What's This? (context-sensitive Help mode)
		Show Help Topics
		Back (previous document)
		Forward (next document)
		Stop
		Refresh
		Home
		Search
		Favorites

Common Toolbar Buttons *(continued)*

16 x 16 button	24 x 24 button	Function
		History
		Full screen
		Mail
		Edit
		Open parent folder
		View as large icons
		View as small icons
		View as list
		View as details
		Region selection tool

If you use these images, use them only for the functions described. Consistent use of these common tool images allows the user to transfer learning and skills from product to product. If you use one of the standard images for a different function, you may confuse the user.

For licensing information on the use of toolbar images, see the Microsoft Copyright Permission Web site at http://www.microsoft.com/permission/.

Pointer Design

Use a pointer's design to help the user identify objects and to provide feedback about certain conditions or states. However, use pointer changes conservatively so as not to distract the user with multiple pointer changes on screen. One remedy is to use a time-out before making a non-critical pointer change. Similarly, when the user types into a text field, it is appropriate to turn off the pointer so that it does not obscure the input text. However, avoid turning the pointer back on after the user stops typing, because it can flicker on and off. Instead, restore the image only after the pointer has been moved.

For more information about some of the common pointers, see Chapter 5, "Input Basics." For information about displaying pointers for drag-and-drop operations, see Chapter 6, "General Interaction Techniques."

Use a pointer to provide feedback only over areas where that state applies. For example, the hourglass pointer indicates that a window is temporarily non-interactive. If the user moves the pointer over a window that is interactive, then change the pointer to its interactive image. If a process makes the entire interface non-interactive, display the hourglass pointer wherever the user moves the pointer.

Pointer feedback may not provide enough information for lengthy operations. For example, for processes that last longer than a few seconds, it is better to use a progress indicator that indicates progressive status, elapsed time, estimated completion time, or some combination of these to provide the user with more information about the state of the operation. In other situations, use command button states to reinforce feedback — for example, when the user chooses a drawing tool.

Use a pointer that best fits the context of the activity. The I-beam pointer is best used to select text. The standard arrow pointer works best for most drag-and-drop operations, modified when appropriate to indicate copy and link operations.

The location for the hot spot of a pointer (shown in Figure 14.38) is important to help the user target an object. The pointer's design should make the location of the hot spot intuitive. For example, for a cross-hair pointer, the implied hot spot is the intersection of the lines.

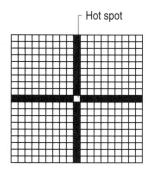 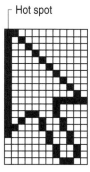

Figure 14.38 Pointer hot spots

Pointer animation can be a very effective way of communicating information. However, remember that the goal is to provide feedback, not to distract the user. In addition, pointer animation should not restrict the user's ability to interact with the interface. Animated pointers can be very distracting for some users. Therefore, always supply non-animated pointers that the user can choose.

Selection Appearance

Provide visual feedback when the user selects an item to enable the user to distinguish it from items that are not selected. Selection appearance generally depends on the object and the context in which the selection appears.

Display an object with its selection appearance as the user performs a selection operation. For example, display the selection appearance when the user clicks the primary mouse button to select an object.

For more information about selection techniques, see Chapter 6, "General Interaction Techniques."

It is best to display the selection appearance only for the scope, area, or level (window or pane) that is active. This helps the user recognize which selection currently applies and the extent of the scope of that selection. Therefore, avoid displaying selections in inactive windows or panes, or at nested levels.

However, in other contexts, it may still be appropriate to display the selection appearance simultaneously in multiple contexts. For example, when the user selects an object and then selects a menu item to apply to that object, the selection appearance is always displayed for both the object and the menu item because it is clear where the user is directing the input. In some cases, you need to show simultaneous selection, but with the secondary selection distinguished from the active selection. In these cases, you can draw an outline in the selection highlight color around the secondary selection or use some similar variant of the standard selection highlight technique.

Highlighting

For many types of objects, you can display the object, its background, or some distinguishing part of the object using the system highlight foreground and background colors. Figure 14.39 shows examples of selection appearances.

The **GetSysColor** function provides access to the current setting for the system selection highlight color (**COLOR_HIGHLIGHT-TEXT**) and selection background color (**COLOR_HIGHLIGHT**). Always use these two system colors in their proper foreground and background combination. For more information about this function, see the Microsoft Platform SDK on the MSDN Online Web site at http://msdn.micro-soft.com/ui/guide/sdk.asp.

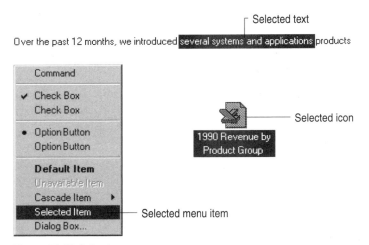

Figure 14.39 Selection appearance

In a secondary window, it may be appropriate to display selection highlighting when the highlight is also being used to reflect the setting for a control. For example, in list boxes, highlighting often indicates a current setting. In cases like this, provide an input focus indication as well so the user can distinguish when input is being directed to another control in the window. You can also use check marks instead of highlighting to indicate the setting.

Handles

Handles provide access to operations for an object, but they can also indicate selection for some kinds of objects. The typical handle is a solid, filled square box that appears on the edge of the object, as shown in Figure 14.40.

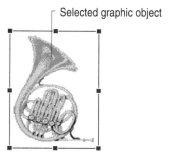

┌ Selected graphic object

Figure 14.40 Selected graphic object with handles

The handle is hollow when it indicates selection but is not a control point by which the user can manipulate the object. Figure 14.41 shows a solid handle and a hollow handle.

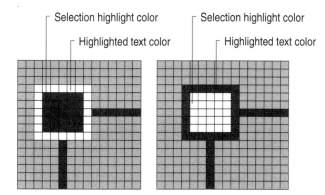

┌ Selection highlight color   ┌ Selection highlight color

┌ Highlighted text color   ┌ Highlighted text color

Figure 14.41 Solid and hollow handles

The system settings for window border and edge metrics can be accessed using the **Get-SystemMetrics** function. For more information about this function, see the Microsoft Platform SDK on the MSDN Online Web site at http://msdn.microsoft.com/ui/guide/sdk.asp.

Base the default size of a handle on the current system settings for resizable window border thickness and on the thickness of the lines in the current system setting for an edge. Then your handles will be sized appropriately to be visible, and will be easily targeted with the mouse when the user changes window border widths or resolutions. Similarly, the colors you use to draw handles should be based on system color metrics so that when the user changes the default system colors, handles change appropriately.

When you use a handle to indicate selection, display the handle in the system highlight color. To help distinguish the handle from the variable background, draw a border around the edge of the handle using the system's setting for highlighted text. For hollow handles, use the opposite: the selection highlight color for the border and the highlighted text color for the fill color. If you display handles for an object even when it is not selected, display the handles in a different color, such as the window text color, so that the user does not confuse it as part of the active selection.

For more information about drag-and-drop transfer operations, see Chapter 6, "General Interaction Techniques."

Transfer Appearance

When the user drags an object to perform an operation — for example, move, copy, or print — display a representation of the object that moves with the pointer. In general, do not simply change the pointer to be the object, as this may obscure the insertion point at some destinations. Instead, use a translucent or outline representation of the object that moves with the pointer, as shown in Figure 14.42.

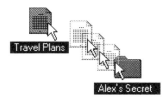

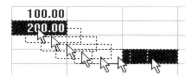

Figure 14.42 Translucent and outline representation (drag transfer)

You can create a translucent representation by using a checkerboard mask made up of 50 percent transparent pixels or use the new alpha blending support in Windows 2000. When used together with the object's normal appearance, this provides a representation that allows part of the destination to show through. An outline representation should also use a translucent or transparent interior and a gray or dotted outline.

The presentation of an object being transferred is always defined by the destination. Use a representation that best communicates how the transferred object will be incorporated when the user completes the drag transfer. For example, if the object being dragged will be displayed as an icon, then display an icon as its representation. If, on the other hand, it will be incorporated as native content, then display an appropriate representation. For example, you could display a graphic object as an outline or translucent image of its shape, a table cell as the outline of a rectangular box, and text selection as the first few characters of a selection with a transparent background.

Set the pointer image to be whatever pointer the target location uses for directly inserting information. For example, when the user drags an object into normal text context, use the I-beam pointer. In addition, include the copy or link image at the bottom right of the pointer if that is the interpretation for the operation.

For more information about the use of open appearance for embedded objects, see Chapter 12, "Working with OLE Embedded and Linked Objects."

Open Appearance

Open appearance is most commonly used for an embedded object, but it can also apply in other situations where the user opens an object into its own window. To indicate that an object is open, display the object in its container's window overlaid with a set of hatched (45 degree) lines drawn every four pixels, as shown in Figure 14.43.

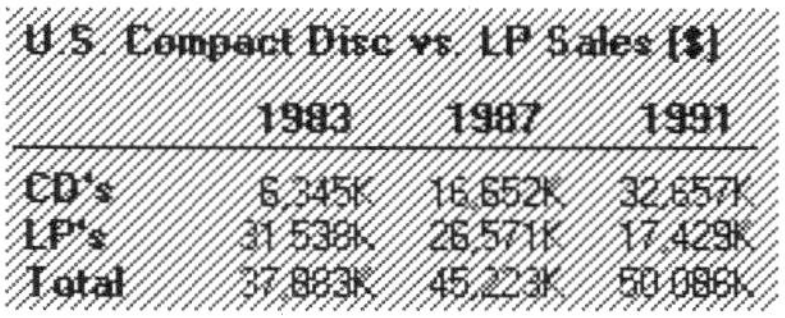

U.S. Compact Disc vs. LP Sales [$]			
	1983	1987	1991
CD's	6,345k	16,652k	32,657k
LP's	31,538k	28,571k	17,429k
Total	37,883k	45,223k	50,086k

Figure 14.43 An object with an open appearance

If the opened object is selected, display the hatched lines using the system highlight color. When the opened object is not selected, display the lines using the system's setting for window text color.

Link Appearance

A link's appearance depends on its type. A shortcut link to another file is represented by a small arrow image that is automatically overlaid on the icon of the original file. Therefore, design your file icons with this overlay in mind.

A hyperlink may appear as text, graphics, or both. A hyperlink differs from a Windows shortcut link in that a shortcut appears as an icon and represents a link to an object. Its location does not typically depend on its context; that is, a shortcut is generally not used to represent a readable form of content.

On the other hand, hyperlinks are references to other locations and appear to blend in with the context in which they appear. Deleting a hyperlink would typically disrupt the context in which it appears. A hyperlink also typically presents information itself, but a shortcut displays only the iconic representation of the object to which it provides access. Also, shortcuts always have names, but a hyperlink may or may not have a name.

Text hyperlinks are typically underlined and in color. Use the system link colors to indicate new and previously visited links. Avoid making the text bold because this can interfere with readability.

Use descriptive definitions to define text hyperlinks. Avoid using the words "Click here" to identify a link.

Correct	Incorrect
For more information about choosing the right product for your needs, see Selecting a Product.	For more information about choosing the right product, click here.

Also, avoid unnecessary navigation information in your reference.

Correct	Incorrect
The tutorial provides more information.	You can read more about this in the tutorial, which is linked to the home page.

Make graphic hyperlinks visually distinct. Users often have difficulty differentiating graphic links from content. Always display the hand pointer when the user moves the pointer over the graphic link, just as you do for text hyperlinks. You may also want to include a redundant text hyperlink for any graphic hyperlinks you include.

If you support links outside the local context of your document or application, provide a visual cue to users. For example, use a unique graphic and place it in a consistent location, or incorporate it into a text link.

A data link is visually indistinguishable unless the user explicitly clicks it or selects a specific command to display the links. For more information about displaying data links, see Chapter 12, "Working with OLE Embedded and Linked Objects."

For more information about hyperlinks, see Chapter 6, "General Interaction Techniques," and Chapter 10, "Window Management."

Animation

Animation can be an effective way to communicate information. For example, it can illustrate the operation of a particular tool or reflect a particular state. It can also be used to include an element of fun in your application's interface. You can use animation effects for objects within a window and interface elements, such as icons, buttons, and pointers. However, do not use animation as the only way to convey essential information.

Effective animation involves many of the same design considerations as other graphic elements, particularly with respect to color and sound. Fluid animation requires presenting images at 16 (or more) frames per second.

When you add animation to your software, make sure that it does not affect the interactivity of the interface. Do not force the user to remain in a specific mode until the animation has finished. Unless animation is part of a process, make sure the user can interrupt it or that it is independent of the user's primary interaction.

Avoid gratuitous use of animation. When animation is used only for a decorative effect, it can distract or annoy the user. To use animation most effectively, use it for a specific purpose or condition. Avoid repeating the animation unless the condition persists or reoccurs. You should provide the user with the option of turning off the animation or otherwise customizing the animation effects.

Special Design Considerations

To create a well-designed application for Microsoft Windows, you must consider factors that appeal to the widest possible audience. This chapter covers special user interface design considerations, such as support for sound, accessibility, and localization.

Sound

You can incorporate sound as part of an application in several ways — for example, music, speech, or sound effects. You can use this auditory information for a variety of purposes:

For information about creating standard system sounds or registering your own sound events, see Chapter 11, "Integrating with the System."

- Provide users with information, such as a particular piece of music or a voice message.

- Enhance the presentation of written or graphical information.

- Notify users about a particular condition.

When used appropriately, sound can be an effective form of information and can enhance your interface. However, avoid using sound as the only means of conveying information. Some users may have hearing loss. Others may work in a noisy environment or in a setting that requires that they turn off sound or maintain it at a low volume. In addition, like color, the benefit of adding sound to an interface is subjective.

As a result, your best use of sound is as a redundant or secondary form of information. You can also supplement sound with alternative forms of communication. For example, if a user turns off the sound, consider flashing the window's title bar or taskbar button, displaying a message box, or using other ways to bring the user's attention to a particular situation. Even when sound is the primary form of information, you can supplement the audio portion by adding a visual representation of the information, such as captioning or animation, to indicate that audio is playing.

The taskbar can also provide visual status or notification information. For more information about using the taskbar for this purpose, see Chapter 11, "Integrating with the System."

Always allow the user to customize sound support. Provide support for the standard system interfaces for controlling volume and associating particular sounds with application-specific sound events. You can also register your own sound events for your application.

Users can indicate that they want a visual representation of audio information by selecting the **Use ShowSounds** check box. Your software should query the status of this setting and provide captioning for the output of any speech or sounds. Captioning should provide as much information visually as is provided in the audible format. It is not necessary to caption ornamental sounds that do not convey useful information.

The **GetSystemMetrics** function provides access to the **ShowSounds** and **SoundSentry** settings. For more information about this function and the settings, see the Microsoft Platform SDK on the MSDN Online Web site at http://msdn.microsoft.com/ui/guide/sdk.asp.

Windows Media Player provides support for closed captioning using the Synchronized Accessible Media Interchange (SAMI) standard. This makes it easy for anyone to enhance multimedia content with closed captions for people who are deaf or hard-of-hearing, and with descriptive narration for users who are blind.
For more information about Windows Media Player, see http://www.microsoft.com/windows/mediaplayer/. For information about SAMI, see http://www.microsoft.com/enable/.

Do not confuse **ShowSounds** with the system's **SoundSentry** option. When the user sets the **SoundSentry** option, the system automatically supplies a visual indication whenever a sound is produced. Avoid relying on **SoundSentry** alone if the **ShowSounds** option is set. **SoundSentry** provides only rudimentary visual indications, such as flashing the display or screen border, and it does not convey the meaning of the sound to the user. The system provides **SoundSentry** primarily for applications that do not provide support for **ShowSounds**. The user sets either of these options in Accessibility Options in Windows Control Panel.

In Microsoft Windows 98, **SoundSentry** works only for audio output directed through the internal PC speaker and does not support multimedia audio output.

Accessibility

Accessibility means making your software usable and accessible to a wide range of users, including those with disabilities. Many users require special accommodation because of temporary or permanent disabilities, the natural effects of aging, or the environment in which they work.

The issue of software accessibility in the home and workplace is becoming increasingly important. Nearly one in five Americans have some form of disability — and it is estimated that more than 30 million people in the U.S. alone have disabilities that may be affected by the design of your software. In addition, between seven and nine out of every ten major corporations employ people with disabilities who may need to use computer software as part of their jobs. As the population ages and more people become functionally limited, accessibility for users with disabilities will become increasingly important to the population as a whole. Legislation, such as the Americans with Disabilities Act, requires that most employers provide reasonable accommodation for workers with disabilities. Section 508 of the Rehabilitation Act is also bringing accessibility issues to the forefront in government businesses and organizations receiving government funding.

Designing software that is usable for people with disabilities does not have to be time-consuming or expensive. However, it is much easier if you take accessibility issues into consideration during planning and design rather than after the software is finished. Following the principles and guidelines in this book will help you design software for most users. Most of these recommendations, such as the conservative use of color or sound, can benefit all users, not just those with disabilities. In addition, keep the following basic objectives in mind:

- Provide a customizable interface to accommodate a wide variety of user needs and preferences.

- Provide compatibility with accessibility utilities that users install.

- Avoid creating unnecessary barriers that make your software difficult or inaccessible to certain types of users.

The following sections provide information about types of disabilities and additional recommendations about how to address the needs of customers with those disabilities. For more information about designing for accessibility, see *The Microsoft Windows Guidelines for Accessible Software Design* on the Microsoft Accessibility Web site at http://www.microsoft.com/enable/.

Types of Disabilities

There are many types of disabilities, but they are often grouped into several broad categories. These include visual, hearing, physical movement, speech or language impairments, and cognitive and seizure disorders.

Visual Disabilities

Visual disabilities range from slightly reduced visual acuity to total blindness. Those with reduced visual acuity may require only that your software support larger text and graphics. For example, the system provides scalable fonts and controls to increase the size of text and graphics. To accommodate users who are blind or have severe impairments, make your software compatible with speech or Braille utilities, described later in this chapter.

Color blindness and other visual impairments may make it difficult for users to distinguish between certain color combinations. This is one reason why color is not recommended as the only way to convey information. Always use color as an additive or enhancing property.

Hearing Disabilities

Users with hearing loss are generally unable to detect or interpret auditory output at normal or maximum volume levels. The best way to support users who have this disability is to avoid using auditory output as the only way to communicate information. Instead, use audio output only in addition to visual output. For more information about supporting sound, see "Sound" earlier in this chapter.

Physical Movement Disabilities

Some users have difficulty performing or are unable to perform certain physical tasks — for example, moving a mouse or pressing two keys simultaneously on the keyboard. Others have a tendency to inadvertently strike multiple keys when targeting a single key. It is important that you consider physical ability not only for users with disabilities, but also for beginning users who need time to master the motor skills necessary to interact with the interface. The best way to support these users is to support all your basic operations by using simple keyboard and mouse interfaces.

Speech or Language Disabilities

Users with language disabilities, such as dyslexia, find it difficult to read or write. Spell-check and grammar-check utilities can help children, users with writing impairments, and users whose first language is not English, including many individuals who are deaf and whose native language is American Sign Language. Some accessibility tools and utilities designed for users who are blind can also help those with reading impairments. Most design issues affecting users with oral communication difficulties apply only to utilities specifically designed for speech input.

Cognitive Disabilities

Cognitive disabilities can take many forms, including perceptual differences and memory impairments. You can accommodate users with these disabilities by allowing them to modify or simplify your application's interface, such as customizing menus and dialog boxes or hiding graphics. Similarly, using icons and graphics to illustrate objects and choices can be helpful for users with some types of cognitive impairments.

Seizure Disorders

Some users are sensitive to visual information that alternates its appearance or flashes at particular rates — often the greater the frequency, the greater the problem. However, there is no perfect flash rate, so base modulating interfaces on the system's cursor blink rate. Users can customize this value to avoid particular frequencies. If that is not practical, provide your own interface for changing the flash rate.

The **GetCaretBlinkTime** function provides access to the current cursor blink rate setting. For more information about this function, see the Microsoft Platform SDK on the MSDN Online Web site at http://msdn.microsoft.com/ui/guide/sdk.asp.

Types of Accessibility Aids

A number of accessibility aids are available to assist users with certain types of disabilities. To allow these users to effectively interact with your application, make sure your application is compatible with these utilities. This section briefly describes the types of accessibility utilities and how they work.

One of the best ways to accommodate accessibility in your application's interface is to use standard Windows conventions wherever possible. Windows already provides a certain degree of customization for users, and most accessibility aids work best with applications that follow standard system conventions.

Screen Enlargement Utilities

Screen enlargers (also referred to as screen magnification utilities or large-print programs) allow users to enlarge a portion of their screen. They effectively turn the computer monitor into a viewport showing only a portion of an enlarged virtual display. Users then use the mouse or keyboard to move this viewport to view different areas of the virtual display. Enlargers also attempt to track where users are working, following the input focus and the activation of windows, menus, and secondary windows, and can automatically move the viewport to the active area.

Windows 98 and Windows 2000 include a low-end screen enlarger, called Magnifier. Magnifier is intended to provide a minimum level of functionality for users with slight visual impairments. Most users with visual impairments will need a magnification utility program with higher functionality for daily use. For a list of Windows-based screen enlargement utilities, see the Microsoft Accessibility Web site at http://www.microsoft.com/enable/.

Screen-Review Utilities

People who cannot use the visual information on the screen can interpret the information with the aid of a screen-review utility (also referred to as a screen-reader program or speech-access utility). Screen-review utilities take the information displayed on the screen and direct it through alternative media, such as synthesized speech or a refreshable Braille display.

Because both of these media present only text information, the screen-review utility must render other information on the screen as text; that is, it must determine the appropriate text labels or descriptions for graphical screen elements. It must also track users' activities to provide descriptions of what the user is doing.

Windows Media Player provides support for closed captioning using the Synchronized Accessible Media Interchange (SAMI) standard. This makes it easy for anyone to enhance multimedia content with closed captions for people who are deaf or hard-of-hearing, and with descriptive narration for users who are blind. For more information about Windows Media Player, see http://www.microsoft.com/windows/mediaplayer/. For information about SAMI, see http://www.microsoft.com/enable/.

These utilities often work by monitoring the system interfaces that support drawing on the screen. They build an off-screen database of the objects on the screen, their properties, and their spatial relationships. They also use information available through Microsoft Active Accessibility, a standard programming interface for Windows and applications to actively cooperate with accessibility aids. Some of this information is presented to users as the screen changes, and other information is maintained until users request it. Screen-review utilities often include support for configuration files (also referred to as set files or profiles) for particular applications.

For more information about Microsoft Active Accessibility, see the Microsoft Accessibility Web site at http://www.microsoft.com/enable/msaa/.

Voice-Input Systems

Users who have difficulty typing can choose a voice-input system (also referred to as a speech recognition program) to control software with their voice instead of with a mouse and keyboard. Like screen-reader utilities, voice-input systems identify objects on the screen that users can manipulate. Users activate an object by speaking the label that identifies the object. Many of these utilities simulate keyboard interfaces, so if your application includes a keyboard interface, it can be adapted to take advantage of this form of input.

On-Screen Keyboards

Some individuals with physical disabilities cannot use a standard keyboard, but can use special devices designed to work with an on-screen keyboard. These switching devices display groups of commands that appear on the screen, and the user employs one or more switches to choose a selected group, then a command within the group. Another technique allows a user to generate keystroke input by using a special mouse or headpointer (a device that lets users manipulate the mouse pointer on the screen through head motion).

Windows 2000 includes a low-end on-screen keyboard. Most users with motion impairments will need an on-screen keyboard utility with higher functionality for daily use. For a list of Windows-based on-screen keyboard utilities, see the Microsoft Accessibility Web site at http://www.microsoft.com/enable/.

Keyboard Filters

Filtering out inappropriate keystrokes can sometimes compensate for users with impaired physical abilities, such as erratic motion, tremors, or slow response. The Accessibility Options in Windows Control Panel support a wide range of keyboard filtering options.

These are generally independent of the application users are interacting with and therefore require no explicit support except for the standard system interfaces for keyboard input. However, users relying on these features may type slowly.

Compatibility with Screen-Review Utilities

You can use the following techniques to ensure that your application is compatible with screen-review utilities. The system allows your application to determine whether the system has been configured to provide support for a screen-review utility, allowing your application to enable or disable certain capabilities.

You can check the **SM_SCREENREADER** setting using the **GetSystemMetrics** function. For more information about this function and other information about supporting screen-review utilities, see the Microsoft Platform SDK on the MSDN Online Web site at http://msdn.microsoft.com/ui/guide/sdk.asp and the Microsoft Accessibility Web site at http://www.microsoft.com/enable/.

Controls

Use standard Windows controls wherever possible. Most of these have already been implemented to support screen-review and voice-input utilities. However, the custom controls you create may not be usable by screen-review utilities.

Include a label for every control, even if you do not want the control's label to be visible. This applies regardless of whether you use standard controls or your own specialized controls, such as owner-drawn controls or custom controls. If the control does not provide a label, you can create a label using a static text control that you can define as hidden.

Follow the standard layout conventions by placing the static text label before the control (above or to the left of the control). Also, set the keyboard TAB navigation order appropriately so that tabbing to a label navigates to the associated control it identifies instead of to a label.

To make sure that the label is recognized correctly, include a colon (:) at the end of the label's text string, as shown in Figure 15.1, unless you are labeling a button, tab, or group box control. Screen-review utilities often use a colon to identify the control. In cases where a label would be visually distracting, provide the label but do not make it visible. Although the label is not visible, it will still be accessible to a screen-review utility.

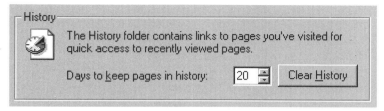

Figure 15.1 Colon in static text label

Text labels are also effective for choices within a control. For example, you can enhance menus or lists that display colors or line widths by including some form of text representation, as shown in Figure 15.2.

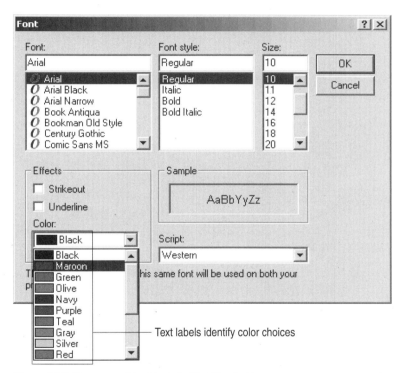

Figure 15.2 Clear use of text to help identify choices

If providing a combined presentation is too difficult, offer users the choice between text and graphical representation, or choose one of them based on the system's screen-review utility setting.

Text Output

Screen-review utilities usually interpret text — including properties such as font, size, and face — that is displayed with standard system interfaces. However, text displayed as graphics (for example, bitmapped text) is not accessible to a screen-review utility. To make it accessible, use the Microsoft Active Accessibility programming interfaces to expose the text. Or you can create an invisible text label and associate it with the graphical representation by drawing the text over the graphic with a null operator (NOP). However, Active Accessibility is strongly recommended; invisible text should be used only as a last resort. Screen-review utilities can read standard text representations in a metafile, so you can also use metafiles instead of bitmap images for graphics information that includes text.

Graphics Output

Users with normal sight may easily be able to distinguish different elements of graphic or pictorial information, such as a map or chart, even if they are drawn as a single image; however, a screen-review utility must distinguish between different components. There are a number of ways to do this. Any of these methods can be omitted when the system's screen-review setting is not selected. One way to help users identify images is to label them. Like labels for controls, labels for images can help screen-review utilities uniquely identify an image or the parts of an image.

Microsoft Active Accessibility supports special programming interfaces that you can use to identify graphics or portions of graphics. Using these interfaces is the best way to support accessibility of graphic images.

However, you can also consider drawing bitmap images that need to be identified separately by users. If performance is an issue, combine the component images in an off-screen bitmap using separate drawing operations, then display the bitmap on the screen with a single operation. You can also draw multiple bitmap images with a single metafile. Although these methods do not identify the nature of each image to the screen reader, they do allow the screen reader to recognize that the image is made up of different components. This is especially important when the user can interact with these different areas.

Alternatively, you can redraw each component separately, or draw a separate image to identify each region using a null operator. This has no effect on the visible image, but it allows a screen-review utility to identify the region. You can also use this method to associate a text label with a graphic element.

When you draw graphics, use standard Windows drawing functions wherever possible. If you change an image directly — for example, clearing a bitmap by writing directly into its memory — a screen-review utility will not be able to recognize the content change and will describe it to users incorrectly. Avoid using such techniques when a screen-reader utility is running.

Icons and Windows

Icons that represent objects should be accompanied by a text label (title) of the object's name. Use the system font and color for icon labels, and follow the system conventions for placement of the text relative to the icon. This allows a screen-review utility to identify the object without special support.

Similarly, make sure that all your windows have titles. Even if the title is not visible, it is still available to access utilities. The more specific your window titles, the easier users can differentiate between them, especially when using a screen-review utility. Using unique window class names is another way to provide for distinct window identification, but providing appropriate window titles is preferred.

The User's Point of Focus

Many accessibility aids must follow where the user is working. For example, a screen-review utility conveys to users where the input focus is; a screen enlarger pans its viewport to ensure that the user's focus is always kept on the visible portion of the screen. Most utilities give users the ability to manually move the viewport, but this becomes laborious, especially if it has to be repeated each time the input focus moves.

When the system handles the move of the input focus — such as when the user selects a menu, navigates between controls in a dialog box, or activates a window — an accessibility utility can track the change. However, the utility may not detect when an application

The **SetCaretPos** function is an example of a system function you can use to indicate focus location. For more information about this function, see the Microsoft Platform SDK on the MSDN Online Web site at http://msdn.microsoft.com/ui/guide/sdk.asp. You can also indicate the focus location using Active Accessibilty. For more information about Microsoft Active Accessibility, see the Microsoft Active Accessibility Web site at http://www.microsoft.com/enable/msaa/.

moves the input focus within its own window. Therefore, whenever possible, use Microsoft Active Accessibility or the standard system functions to place the input focus, such as the text insertion point. Even when you provide your own implementation of focus, you can use the system functions to indicate focus location without making the standard input focus indicator visible.

Timing and Navigational Interfaces

Some users read text or press keys very slowly and do not respond to events as quickly as the average user. Avoid briefly displaying critical feedback or messages and then automatically removing them, because many users cannot read or respond to them. Similarly, limit your use of time-based interfaces. If you do include a time-based interface, always provide a way for users to configure the length of the time-out.

Also, avoid displaying or hiding information based on the movement of the pointer, unless it is part of a standard system interface (for example, ToolTips). Although such techniques can benefit some users, the techniques may not be available for those using accessibility utilities. If you do provide such support, consider making these features optional so that users can turn them on or off when a screen-review utility is installed.

Similarly, avoid using general navigation to trigger operations, because users of accessibility aids may need to navigate through all controls. For example, do not use basic TAB keyboard navigation in a dialog box to activate actions associated with a control, such as selecting a check box or clicking a command button. However, you can use navigation to facilitate further user interaction, such as validating user input or opening a drop-down control.

Color

Base the color properties of your interface elements on the system colors for window components rather than defining specific colors. Remember to use appropriate foreground and background color combinations. If the foreground of an element is rendered with the button text color, use the button face color as its background rather than the window background color. If the system does not provide standard color settings that can be applied to some elements, you can include your own interface that allows users to customize colors. In addition, you can provide graphical patterns as an optional substitute for colors as a way to distinguish information.

For more information about the use of color and how it is used for interface elements, see Chapter 14, "Visual Design."

The system also provides a global setting called **High Contrast** that users can set through the Accessibility Options in Control Panel. The setting provides contrasting colors for foreground and background visual elements. Your application should check the status of this setting when it starts and whenever it receives notification of system setting changes. When set, adjust your interface colors based on those set for the high-contrast color scheme. In addition, whenever **High Contrast** is set, hide any images that are drawn behind text (for example, watermarks or logos) to maintain the legibility of the information on the screen. You can also display monochrome versions of bitmaps and icons using the appropriate foreground color.

The **GetSystemMetrics** function provides access to the **SM_HIGHCONTRAST** setting. For more information about this function, see the Microsoft Platform SDK on the MSDN Online Web site at http://msdn.microsoft.com/ui/guide/sdk.asp.

Scalability

Another important way to provide visual accessibility is to allow for scalability of screen elements. Sometimes this simply means allowing users to change the font for the display of information. The system allows users to change the size and font of standard Windows components. Use these same metrics for appropriately adjusting the size of other visual information you provide. For your own custom elements, you can provide scaling by including a TrueType font or metafiles for your graphics images.

For more information about the system metrics for font and size, see Chapter 14, "Visual Design."

It may also useful to provide scaling features within your application. For example, many applications provide a **Zoom** command that scales the presentation of the information displayed in a window, or other commands that make information easier to read. You may need to add scroll bars if the scaled information exceeds the current size of the window.

Keyboard and Mouse Interface

Providing a good keyboard interface is an important step in accessibility because it affects users with a wide range of disabilities. For example, a keyboard interface may be the only option for users who are blind or who use voice-input utilities, and for those who cannot use a mouse. The Accessibility Options in Control Panel often compensate for users with disabilities related to keyboard interaction; however, it is more difficult to compensate for problems related to pointing device input.

Follow the conventions for keyboard navigation techniques presented in this guide. For specialized interfaces within your software, model your keyboard interface on conventions that are familiar and appropriate for that context. Where they apply, use the standard control conventions as a guide for defining your interaction. For example, support TAB and SHIFT+TAB keys and access keys as ways to navigate to controls.

Make sure that users can navigate to all objects. Avoid relying only on navigational design that requires users to understand the spatial relationship between objects. Accessibility utilities may not be able to convey such relationships.

Providing a well-designed mouse interface is also important. Pointing devices may be more efficient than keyboards for some users. When designing the interface for pointing input, avoid making basic functions available only through multiple clicking, drag-and-drop manipulation, and keyboard-modified mouse actions. These actions are best regarded as shortcut techniques for more advanced users. Make basic functions available by single-clicking.

The system also allows your application to determine when the user relies on the keyboard rather than on pointing device input. You can use this to present special keyboard interfaces that might otherwise be hidden.

To determine whether a user relies on keyboard rather than pointing device input, check the **SM_KEYBOARD PREF** setting using **GetSystemMetrics**. For more information about this function, see the Microsoft Platform SDK on the MSDN Online Web site at http://msdn.microsoft.com/ui/guide/sdk.asp.

Where possible, avoid creating basic functions that depend on the user installing a particular device. This is critical for supporting users with physical disabilities and users who may not wish to use or install a particular device.

Accessible HTML Pages

When you design Web-style applications, there are additional considerations. While HTML provides power and flexibility in presenting information, it can also create barriers for some users. For example, graphic images are inaccessible to users with vision impairments. Careful design and coding of information can minimize these barriers. Here are some guidelines to keep in mind:

For more information about accessible web design, see http://msdn.microsoft.com/ui/guide/webstyle.asp.

- Include a short textual description for all images or audio files using the ALT attribute. For a .jpg image, include a description of the image in the file's comment field. For an illustrative image, be sure to use descriptions that convey the relevant information. For images like bullets, use simple text such as "*". Because text descriptions may wordwrap, preview your page with images turned off to ensure that it looks correct. Avoid arrangements that display text descriptions in multiple columns.

- If an image needs a lengthy description that doesn't fit into the ALT attribute, provide a link to a separate page that contains a complete description. For a .jpg image, also include the description in the file's comment field.

- Provide equivalent text menus for all image maps. Similarly, provide alternative ways to access items in a table, because it may be difficult for a sight-impaired user to navigate through a table using a screen-reader utility.

- For audio files, provide text transcriptions or description files. If the text is lengthy, you can provide a link to a separate page.

- If you provide online forms that cannot be read by screen-review utilities, provide alternate methods of communication. For example, you can include instructions for supplying information by phone, mail, or e-mail.

- Avoid proprietary file formats or use them as alternatives rather than replacements for ASCII or HTML files.

Finally, when you design any Web-based application or content, follow the standards set by the World Wide Web Consortium for accessibility of Web content. This will ensure that your application is accessible to the widest possible range of users and is compatible with automation tools. For more information, see the Microsoft Accessibility Web site at http://www.microsoft.com/enable/.

Documentation, Packaging, and Support

Although this guide focuses primarily on the design of the user interface, a design that provides for accessibility needs takes into consideration other aspects of a product. For example, consider the documentation needs of your users. For users who have difficulty reading or handling printed material, provide online documentation for your product. If the documentation or installation instructions are not available online, you can provide documentation separately in alternative formats, such as ASCII text, large print, Braille, or audiotape. For a list of organizations that can help you produce and distribute such documentation, see the Accessibility section of the Bibliography in this book.

When possible, choose a format and binding for your documentation that makes it accessible for users with disabilities. As in the interface, information in color should be a redundant form of communication. Bindings that allow a book to lie flat are usually better for users with limited dexterity.

Packaging is also important because many users with limited dexterity can have difficulty opening packages. Consider including an easy-opening overlap or tab that helps users remove shrink-wrapping.

Finally, although support is important for all users, it is difficult for users with hearing impairments to use standard support lines. Consider making these services available to customers using text telephones (also referred to as "TT" or "TDD"). You can also provide support through public bulletin boards or other networking services.

Usability Testing

Just as it is important to test the usability of your software, it is a good idea to test its accessibility. There are a variety of ways to do this. One is to include users with disabilities in your prerelease or usability test activities. Another way is to establish a working relationship with companies that provide accessibility aids. Information about accessibility vendors or potential test sites is included in the Bibliography.

You can also try running your software the way a person with disabilities would. Try some of the following ideas for testing:

- Test your application against the accessibility recommendations checklist. Have one or more people go through your application, comparing against the checklist of recommendations in *The Microsoft Windows Guidelines for Accessible Software Design* (available to download at http://www.microsoft.com/enable/dev/). You can methodically test all of your major features, but informal testing can also find many of the most obvious problems.

- Test your application using large, high-contrast appearance schemes. To set up your test computer, click the **Accessibility Options** icon in Control Panel. Click the **Display** tab, and then click **Use High Contrast**. Click the Settings button, and then click **White on black**.

  Next try using your computer. Are there any parts of your application that become invisible or are difficult to use or recognize? Do any areas still appear as black on a white background? Are any elements improperly sized or truncated? Make sure that you repeat this test with the **Black on white** option selected.

- Test your application's keyboard interface. Try using your computer for a week without a mouse. Are there operations you cannot perform? Is anything especially awkward to use? Are the keyboard mechanisms adequately documented? Do all controls and menu items have underlined access keys?

- Test how your application exposes its screen elements. Use the Inspect Objects tool included in the Active Accessibility SDK, or the Narrator accessory included in Windows 2000. Using the mouse pointer, hover over portions of your application and see if the tool can display a proper description. Also try using your application and see how these utilities behave. Compare it with standard windows and controls and see if they match.

- Test how your application exposes the input focus. Use the Magnifier accessory included in Windows 98 and Windows 2000. Use your application with the keyboard and make sure that the place where you are working appears, magnified, in the Magnifier window.

- Test your application's compatibility with accessibility utilities. In addition to the testing tools described here, you should try accessibility aids to see whether they work properly with your application. Many utilities are available at no charge or in trial versions. For a catalog of these tools, see the Microsoft Accessibility Web site at http://www.microsoft.com/enable/.

- Test how your application handles large fonts. To increase the size of your system font in Control Panel, click the **Display** icon and then click the **Appearance** tab. Does your application look good despite the changes? Can you adjust all of the fonts in your application to be at least as large as the system font?

- Test how your application handles custom font sizes. To change the custom font sizes in Control Panel, click the **Display** icon and then click the **Appearance** tab. When you use a custom font size, does your application appear consistent, or do various elements of the user interface appear disproportionately large or small?

Localization

To successfully compete in international markets, your software must easily accommodate differences in language, culture, and hardware. This section summarizes some of the key design considerations regarding the localization of software.

The process of making a software product linguistically and culturally appropriate for use in a different country or region and its language is called *localization*. Like any part of the interface, include international considerations early in the design and development process. This helps cut costs and speeds up the localization process. In addition to adapting screen information

For more information about the technical details for localizing your application, see the Microsoft Global Software Development site at http://www.microsoft.com/globaldev/. Another useful reference is the online book, *Developing International Software*, by Nadine Kano, available on the MSDN Online Web site at http://msdn.microsoft.com/library/.

and documentation for international use, remember that your Help files, scenarios, templates, models, and sample files should also be a part of your localization planning. For example, a scenario or example involving gourmet dog food or styles of birdbaths would be inappropriate in many countries.

Even if you don't plan to localize your application into other languages, you still need to consider how your application will operate with other language configurations. For example, if you use U.S. English names and locations for standard system directories, your application may not install or run.

Language is not the only relevant factor to consider when you localize an interface. Several countries can share a common language but have different conventions for expressing information. In addition, some countries can share a language but use a different keyboard convention.

A subtler factor to consider when preparing software for international markets is cultural differences. For example, users in the U.S. may recognize a rounded mailbox with a flag on the side as an icon for a mail program, but this image may not be recognized by users in other countries. Sounds and their associated meanings may also vary from country to country.

Similarly, consider the implications on brand and trademark decisions. An untranslated, trademarked U.S. term can sound like a vulgar or otherwise undesirable term in another language, and certain colors or color combinations may produce undesirable associations in some countries.

Text

A major aspect of localizing an interface is translating the text used by the software in its title bars, menus and other controls, messages, and some registry entries. To make localization easier, store interface text as resources in your application's resource file rather than including it in the source code of the application. Remember also to translate the menu commands that your application stores in the system registry for its file types.

Translation does not always result in one-to-one correspondence. A single word in English can have multiple translations in another language. Adjectives and articles sometimes change spelling according to the gender of the nouns they modify. Therefore, be careful when re-using a text string in multiple places. Similarly, several English words may have only a single meaning in another language. This is particularly important to remember when you create keywords for your application's Help index.

When text is translated, it is often expanded. For more information, see the "Layout" section later in this chapter.

When you are careful and consistent in your use of terminology, users can learn to use your application more quickly, and it can more easily be translated into other languages. For example, "traveling" and "travelling" are both correct in English, but to ensure ease of translation, use only one variation. This is particularly important if you use automatic translation tools, because the utility may not handle the variation. The first spelling offered in a dictionary is usually preferable to alternate spellings.

Similarly, where possible, use consistent phrasing for text that appears repeatedly in your application, such as messages. This not only makes localization easier, it avoids confusing users who may interpret different words as having a different intended meaning.

Avoid words that can have several meanings in different contexts. These can require extra translation work. For example, time can mean time of day or duration; map can be a noun or a verb.

Similarly, avoid technical jargon. For example, phrases like the following can be difficult to translate:

Strip the leading character and remove the last quote character.
Unable to fork daemon.
Receives discarded.
Unable to close all users.

When you name a new feature, also avoid idioms, colloquialisms, or metaphors, which may be meaningless in other cultures.

Correct	Incorrect
Your design is finished in minutes.	Now how's that for instant design!
These simple steps complete the task.	That's all there is to it.

Do not assign a new or broader meaning to an existing term. Doing so may add extra effort during the translation process. Also, avoid joining words to create new words.

Phrasing that includes compound nouns also makes translation more complex. For example, the phrase "Last member query interval" can mean:

Last interval for the query "member"
Interval for the query "last member"
Interval for the last query "member"
Query interval for the "last member"

Use articles or personal pronouns with product or feature names only if they help clearly identify the product or feature. For example, in the phrase "Remove Remote Storage program files only," it is not clear whether "remove" is part of the program name or if the Remote Storage program files are to be removed. In this case, "Remove the Remote Storage program files" is much clearer.

Layout

Translation from English to other languages can affect the size of your application in a variety of ways:

- Localization to most other languages increases the length of text in the interface.

- It can affect the layout of controls.

- It can result in larger file sizes, potentially requiring changes to the layout of your installation disks and setup software.

Text Expansion

To handle expansion of your interface text, avoid sizing text to your content. You must allow for 30 percent or more space than you use in your English version, as shown in Figure 15.3.

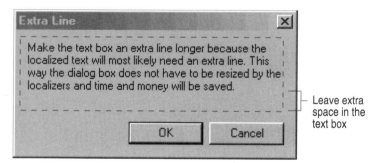

Figure 15.3 Text expansion space

Depending on the language and the wording, you might even need to provide twice as much space. For example, in German, the word "move" becomes "verschieben" and the word "prompt" becomes "Eingabeafforderung." Accordingly, if the amount of space available in the interface is strictly limited, as in a status bar, restrict the length of the English text to half of the available space.

When possible, avoid sizing text to the actual content. For message boxes or explanatory text, include an extra blank line, as shown in Figure 15.4.

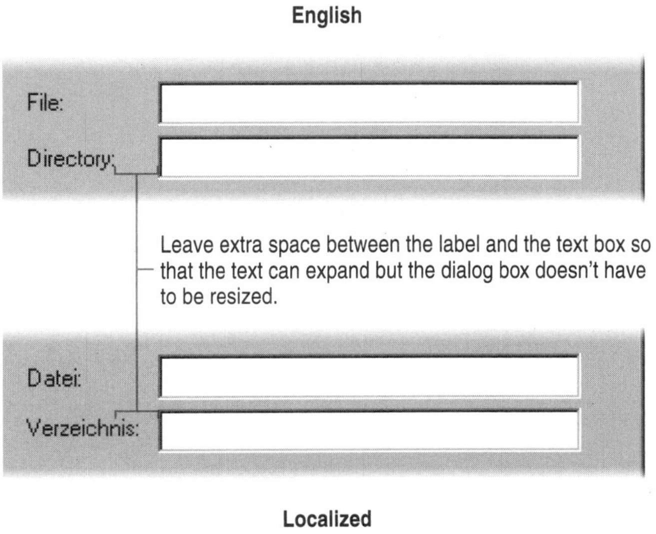

English

Localized

Figure 15.4 Allow for text expansion for explanatory text

For text labels for text boxes, leave extra space so that the label text can expand, as shown in Figure 15.5. This avoids the need to resize and adjust the layout for localization, saving time and money. It also reduces potential layout errors.

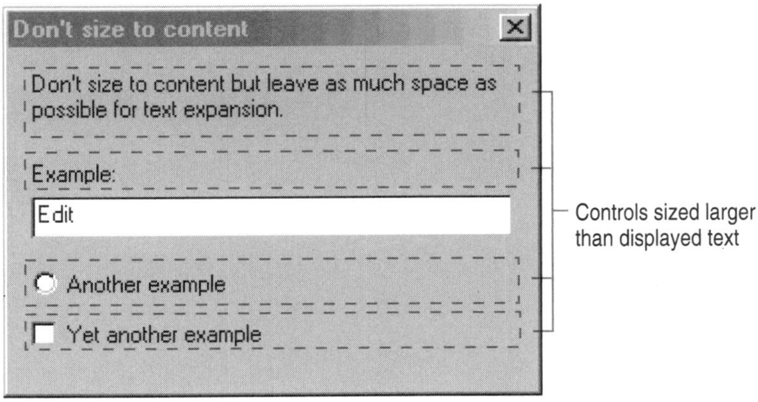

Figure 15.5 Allow for text expansion of text box labels

For some controls, such as option button labels, provide space not only for horizontal expansion, but also for an extra line, as shown in Figure 15.6.

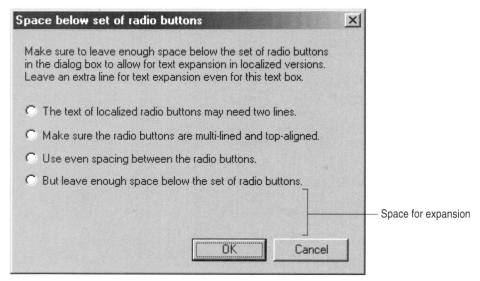

Figure 15.6 Example of vertical expansion spacing

For resizable controls that contain text within a frame, make sure you allow enough space for the control itself to be resized without requiring that the window be resized. For example, drop-down lists don't include a horizontal scroll bar, so important information may be hidden when the text is localized. Allow enough space to widen the list to avoid truncated text, as shown in Figure 15.7.

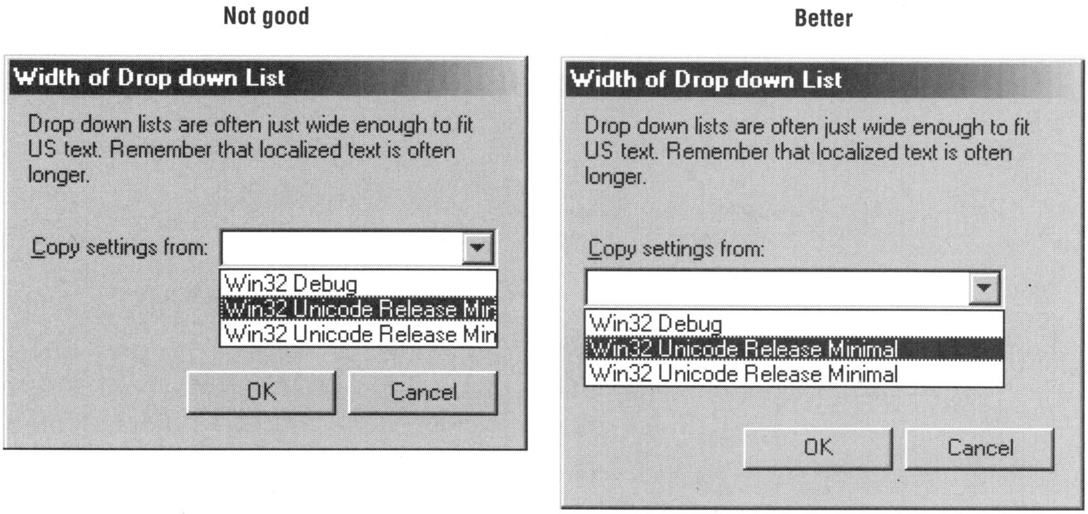

Not good   **Better**

Figure 15.7 Sizing to avoid truncation

When the label for a text box is already long, consider placing the label above the text box rather than in front of it, as shown in Figure 15.8. Then you won't have to reduce the width of the text box. Consider this also when you place a button adjacent to the text box.

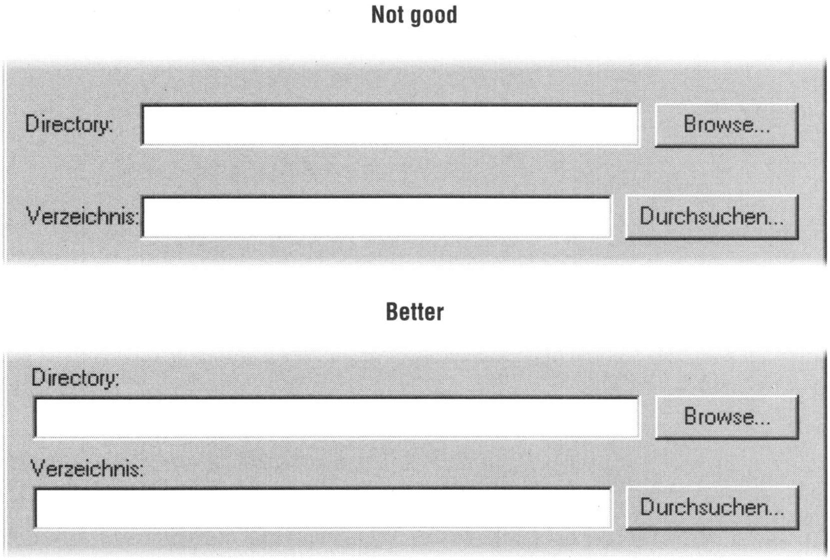

Not good

Better

Figure 15.8 Label above text box

Instead of using long phrases for text box labels, split the information into descriptive text, then use a word or short phrase for the label, as shown in Figure 15.9.

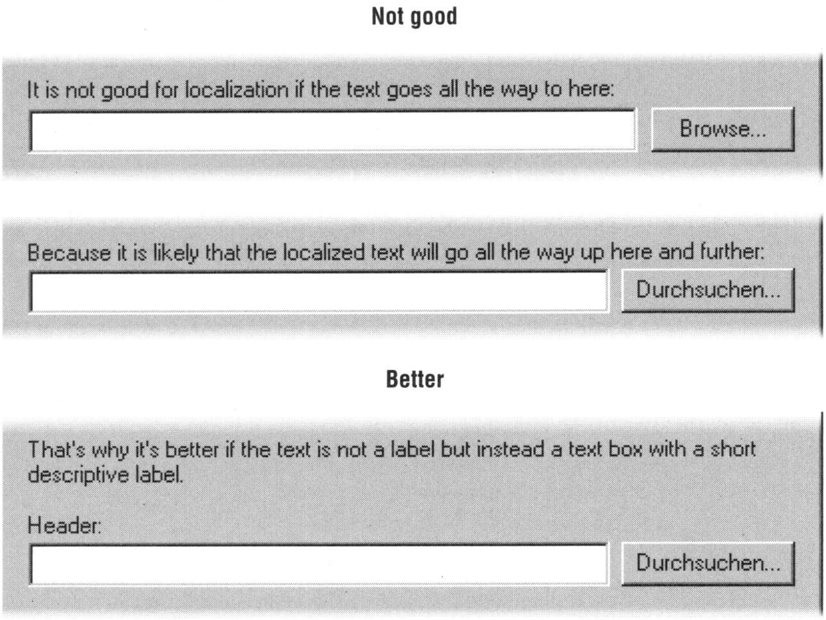

Not good

It is not good for localization if the text goes all the way to here:

[   ] [Browse...]

Because it is likely that the localized text will go all the way up here and further:

[   ] [Durchsuchen...]

Better

That's why it's better if the text is not a label but instead a text box with a short descriptive label.

Header:

[   ] [Durchsuchen...]

Figure 15.9 Splitting long labels into descriptive text and the label

Avoid using text that is dynamically linked from a string table, as shown in Figure 15.10. Many controls, such as buttons, are sized based on their labels. Control labels that use dynamically linked strings can make it difficult to lay out the controls properly when they are localized.

Not good

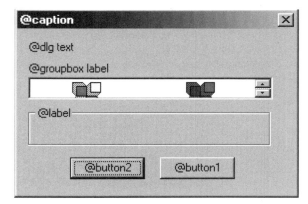

Figure 15.10 Avoid dynamically linked text labels

Similarly, avoid dynamic, or run-time, concatenation of different strings to form new strings — for example, composing messages by combining frequently used strings. An exception is the construction of file names and names of paths.

Placement

Avoid having your software rely on the position of text in a control or window, because translation may require movement of the text. Similarly, word forms, length, order, or number are likely to be different from language to language.

As a result, avoid placing controls within a sentence, as shown in Figure 15.11. This can require you to lay out the position of the controls differently for different languages. In the following example, you would have to relocate the combo box directly after the option button. Placing the control at the end of the text label for the option button provides a better alternative.

Not good

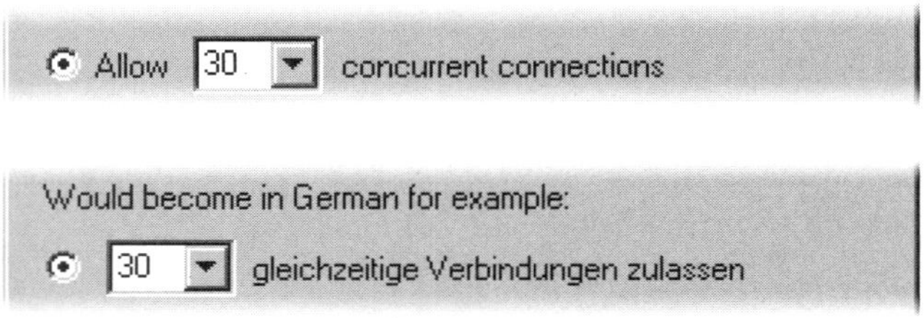

Better

Figure 15.11 Example of control placement

Also avoid placing text or other controls on top of other controls, as shown in Figure 15.12. Overlapped or hidden controls can result in access key or sizing problems.

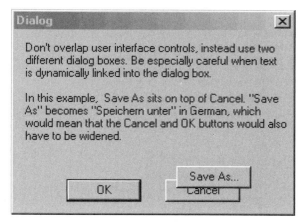

Figure 15.12 Avoid hidden or overlapping controls

In Hebrew and Arabic countries, information is written right to left. When you localize for these countries, your design needs to support reversing your U.S. presentation.

Some languages include diacritical marks that distinguish particular characters. Fonts associated with these characters can require additional spacing.

Graphics

It is best to review proposed graphics early in your design cycle to make sure they are applicable for international versions. Although graphics communicate more universally than text, graphical aspects of your software — especially for icons and toolbar button images — may need to be revised to address an international audience. Images, idioms, metaphors, or symbols with a strong meaning in one culture may not have any meaning in another. For example, many symbols for U.S. holidays and seasons are not shared around the world. Similarly, for example, the concept of a "wizard" may not include the concept of magic in many languages; therefore, a toolbar image of a magic wand that represents access to a wizard interface may not be an obvious reference. A "dog-eared" book won't work in some languages because they use a different animal or might not associate this idea with animals at all. Some symbols can even be offensive in some cultures. For example, the open palm commonly used at U.S. crosswalk signals is offensive in some countries.

Therefore, wherever possible, use neutral images and avoid including text. Localizing graphics can be time-consuming. Even if you can create custom designs for each language, having different images for different languages can confuse users who work with more than one language version.

Keyboards

International keyboards also differ from those used in the U.S. Avoid using punctuation character keys as shortcut keys, because they are not always found on international keyboards or easily produced by the user. Remember too, that what seems like an effective shortcut because of its mnemonic association (for example, CTRL+B for Bold) can warrant a change to fit a particular language. Similarly, macros or other utilities that invoke menus or commands based on access keys are not likely to work in an international version, because the command names on which the access keys are based differ.

Keys do not always occupy the same positions on all international keyboards. Even when they do, the interpretation of the unmodified keystroke can be different. For example, on U.S. keyboards, pressing SHIFT+8 results in an asterisk character. However, on French keyboards, it generates the number 8. Use the following guidelines when you work with key combinations:

- Avoid using CTRL+ALT combinations, because the system interprets this combination for some language versions as the ALTGR key, which generates some alphanumeric characters.

- Avoid using the ALT key as a modifier, because it is the primary keyboard interface for accessing menus and controls. In addition, the system uses many specialized versions for special input. For example, ALT+~ invokes special input editors in Far East versions of Windows. For text fields, pressing ALT+*number* enters characters in the upper range of a character set.

- Avoid using the following characters when you assign shortcut keys.

  @ £ $ { } [ ] \ ~ | ^ ` < >

Character Sets

Some international countries require support for different character sets (sometimes referred to as *code pages*). The system provides a standard interface for supporting multiple character sets and sort tables. Use these interfaces wherever possible for sorting and case conversion. In addition, consider the following guidelines:

The **SystemParametersInfo** function allows you to determine the current keyboard configuration. For more information about this function, see the Microsoft Platform SDK on the MSDN Online Web site at http://msdn.microsoft.com/ui/guide/sdk.asp.

- Do not assume that the character set is U.S. ANSI. Many ANSI character sets are available. For example, the Russian version of Windows 98 uses the Cyrillic ANSI character set, which is different than the U.S. ANSI set. Windows 2000 uses UNICODE character sets.

- Use the system functions for supporting font selection (such as the common font dialog box).

- Always save the character set with font names in documents. If you use the system's rich text control, it will automatically handle preserving the correct font and character set information.

Formats

Different countries often use substantially different formats for dates, time, money, measurements, and telephone numbers. This collection of language-related user preferences for a specific area is referred to as a *locale*. Designing your software to accommodate international audiences requires supporting these different formats.

Windows provides a standard way to find out what the default format is for a given locale. It also allows users to 'use different formats within a locale. Your software can also allow users to change formats, but you should change only those that affect your application or document type, not those that affect system defaults. The following table lists the most common format categories.

For more information about the functions that provide access to the current locale formats, see the Microsoft Platform SDK on the MSDN Online Web site at http://msdn.microsoft.com/ui/guide/sdk.asp.

Formats for International Software

Category	Format considerations
Date	Order, separator, long or short format, leading zero
Time	Separator and cycle (12-hour vs. 24-hour), leading zero
Physical quantity	Metric vs. U.S. measurement system
Currency	Symbol and format (for example, trailing vs. preceding symbol)
Separators	List, decimal, thousandths
Telephone numbers	Separator for area codes and exchanges
Calendar	Calendar used, starting day of the week
Addresses	Order, postal code format
Paper sizes	U.S. vs. European paper and envelope size

Access Key Definition

Access keys for control labels in double-byte languages (Japanese, Chinese, and Korean) follow conventions different from those of other languages. Instead of identifying an access key with an underline character, display the character in parentheses at the end of the text. Typically, you would use a Roman character, which is generally accessible even on foreign keyboards.

References to Unsupported Features

Avoid confusing international users by leaving in references to features that do not exist in their language version. Adapt the interface appropriately for features that do not apply. For example, some language versions may not include a grammar checker or support for bar codes on envelopes. Remove references to features such as menus, dialog boxes, and Help files from the installation program.

Other Issues

Take into account differences in international names and addresses. For example, middle names are not used in some countries. Many countries do not have an equivalent for states in the U.S.

Avoid hard-coding file names in a binary file. File names may need to be translated. Also, use the system interface to locate common system directories, such as Program Files.

Political unrest, disputes over national borders, and other geopolitical issues can also affect your application. For example, your product might be banned in a country that views its national borders differently than you present them. If your interface deals with maps, country names, international or political organizations and leaders, or any other politically sensitive subjects, consult an expert on geopolitical issues for advice.

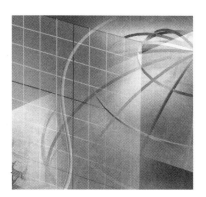

Appendixes and References

Mouse Interface Summary

The tables in this appendix summarize the basic mouse interface, including selection and direct manipulation, such as drag-and-drop operations.

If the user selects single-click activation, then use hover (pointer held for time-out) for click operations and click for double-click operations. Drag-and-drop operations remain unaffected.

Interaction Guidelines for Common Unmodified Mouse Actions

User Action	Target	Effect on current selection state	Effect on anchor point location	Resulting operation using primary mouse button	Resulting operation using secondary mouse button
Press	Object	Clears the active selection	Resets the anchor point to the object	Selects the object	Selects the object
	Selected object	None	None	None[1]	None
	White space (background)	Clears the active selection	Resets the anchor point to location of the pressed button	Initiates a region (marquee) selection	Initiates a region (marquee) selection
Click	Object	Clears the active selection	Resets the anchor point to the object	Selects the object	Selects the object and displays its shortcut menu
	Selected object	None[2]	None[2]	Selects the object[1]	Selects the object[1] and displays its shortcut menu
	White space (background)	Clears the active selection	None	None	Displays the shortcut menu for the white space[3]

Interaction Guidelines for Common Unmodified Mouse Actions *(continued)*

User Action	Target	Effect on current selection state	Effect on anchor point location	Resulting operation using primary mouse button	Resulting operation using secondary mouse button
Drag	Object	Clears the active selection	Resets the anchor point to the object	Selects object and performs the default transfer operation[4] at the location of the button release	Selects object and displays the non-default transfer shortcut menu[4] at the location of the button release
	Selected object	None	None	Performs the default transfer operation[4] on the selection at the location of the button release	Displays the non-default transfer shortcut menu[4] at the location of the button release
	White space (background)	Clears the active selection	None	Selects everthing logically included from anchor point to active end	Selects everthing logically included from anchor point to active end and displays shortcut menu for the selection
Double-click	Object	Clears the active selection	Resets the anchor point to the object	Selects the object and performs the default operation	Selects the object
	Selected object	None	None	Performs the selection's default operation	Selects the object
	White space (background)	Clears the active selection	None	Performs the default operation for the white space[3]	None

[1] Alternatively, you can support subselection for this action, which means to distinguish an object in a selection for some purpose. For example, in a selection of objects, subselecting an object may define it as the reference point for alignment commands.

[2] Alternatively, you can support clearing the active selection and resetting the anchor point to the object if this better fits the context of the user's task.

[3] The white space (or background) is an access point for commands of the view, the container, or both. For example, white space can include commands related to selection (**Select All**), magnification (**Zoom**), type of view (**Outline**), arrangement (**Arrange by Date**), display of specific view elements (**Show Grid**), general operation of the view (**Refresh**), and containment commands that insert objects (**Paste**).

[4] The default transfer operation is determined by the destination of the drag-and-drop operation. Similarly, the destination determines the transfer commands displayed in the resulting shortcut menu when the mouse button is released. If the object cannot be dragged, then you can optionally use this action to create a range selection.

Interaction Guidelines for Using the SHIFT Key to Modify Mouse Actions

User Action	Target	Effect on current selection state	Effect on anchor point location	Resulting operation using primary mouse button	Resulting operation using secondary mouse button
SHIFT+ Press	Object	Clears the active selection[1]	None	Extends the selection state from the anchor point to the object[2]	Extends the selection state from the anchor point to the object[3]
	Selected object	Clears the active selection[1]	None	Extends the selection state from the anchor point to the object[2]	Extends the selection state from the anchor point to the object[3]
	White space (background)	Clears the active selection[1]	None	Extends the selection state from the anchor point to the object logically included by the pressed button[2]	Extends the selection state from the anchor point to the object logically included by the pressed button[3]
SHIFT+ Click	Object	Clears the active selection[1]	None	Extends the selection state from the anchor point to the object[2]	Extends the selection state from the anchor point to the object[2] and displays the shortcut menu for the selection[3]
	Selected object	Clears the active selection[1]	None	Extends the selection state from the anchor point to the object[2]	Extends the selection state from the anchor point to the object[2] and displays the shortcut menu for the selection[3]
	White space (background)	Clears the active selection[1]	None	Extends the selection state from the anchor point to the object logically included by the pressed button[2]	Extends the selection state from the anchor point to the object[2] logically included by the pressed button point and displays the shortcut menu for the selection[3]

Interaction Guidelines for Using the SHIFT Key to Modify Mouse Actions *(continued)*

User Action	Target	Effect on current selection state	Effect on anchor point location	Resulting operation using primary mouse button	Resulting operation using secondary mouse button
SHIFT+ Drag	Object	Clears the active selection[1]	None	Extends the selection state from the anchor point to the object[2]	Extends the selection state from the anchor point to the object[2] and displays the shortcut menu for the selection[3]
	Selected object	Clears the active selection[1]	None	Extends the selection state from the anchor point to the object[2]	Extends the selection state from the anchor point to the object[2] and displays the shortcut menu for the selection[3]
	White space (background)	Clears the active selection[1]	None	Extends the selection state from the anchor point to the object logically included by the pressed button[2]	Extends the selection state from the anchor point to the object logically included by the pressed button[2] and displays the shortcut menu for the selection[3]

Interaction Guidelines for Using the SHIFT Key to Modify Mouse Actions *(continued)*

User Action	Target	Effect on current selection state	Effect on anchor point location	Resulting operation using primary mouse button	Resulting operation using secondary mouse button
SHIFT+ Double-click	Object	Clears the active selection[1]	Resets the anchor point to the object	Extends the selection state from the anchor point to the object[2] and performs the default command on the selection[3]	Extends the selection state from the anchor point to the object[2]
	Selected object	None	None	Extends the selection state from the anchor point to the object[2] and performs the default command on the selection[3]	Extends the selection state from the anchor point to the object[2]
	White space (background)	Clears the active selection[1]	None	Extends the selection state from the anchor point to the object logically included by the pressed button[2] and performs the default command on the selection[3]	Extends the selection state from the anchor point to the object logically included by the pressed button[2]

[1] Only the active selection is cleared. The active selection is the selection made from the current anchor point. Other selections made by disjoint selection techniques are not affected, unless the new selection includes those elements.

[2] The resulting selection state is based on the selection state of the object at the anchor point. If that object is selected, all the objects in the range are selected. If the object is not selected, all the objects included in the range are not selected.

[3] If by extending the selection, an object or a range of objects is removed from the selection, the operation applies only to the remaining selected objects.

Interaction Guidelines for Using the CTRL Key to Modify Mouse Actions

User Action	Target	Effect on current selection state	Effect on anchor point location	Resulting operation using primary mouse button	Resulting operation using secondary mouse button
CTRL+ Press	Object	None	Resets the anchor point to the object	Selects the object[1]	Selects the object[1]
	Selected object	None	Resets the anchor point to the object	None	None
	White space (background)	None	Resets the anchor point to the location of the pressed button	Initiates a disjoint region selection	Initiates a disjoint region selection
CTRL+ Click	Object	None	Resets the anchor point to the object	Selects the object[1]	Selects the object[1] and displays the shortcut menu for the entire selection
	Selected object	None	Resets the anchor point to the object	Cancels the object[1] selection	Cancels the object[1] selection and displays the shortcut menu for the remaining selection
	White space (background)	None	None	None	Displays the shortcut menu for the selection
CTRL+ Drag	Unselected object	None	Resets the anchor point to the object	Selects the object[1] and copies the entire selection[2]	Selects the object[1] and displays the transfer shortcut menu at the location of the button release
	Selected object	None	Resets the anchor point to the object	Copies the entire selection to the location of the button release[2]	Selects the object[1] and displays the transfer shortcut menu at the location of the button release
	White space (background)	None	None	Toggles the selection state of objects logically included by region selection[3]	Toggles the selection state of objects logically included by region selection[3] and displays the shortcut menu for the resulting selection[4]

Interaction Guidelines for Using the CTRL Key to Modify Mouse Actions *(continued)*

User Action	Target	Effect on current selection state	Effect on anchor point location	Resulting operation using primary mouse button	Resulting operation using secondary mouse button
CTRL+ Double-click	Object	None	Resets the anchor point to the object	Selects the object[1] and performs the default command on the entire selection	Selects the object[1]
	Selected object	None	Resets the anchor point to the object	Cancels the object selection and performs the default command on the entire selection[4]	Unselects the object
	White space (background)	None	None	Performs the default command on the selection[5]	None

[1] The CTRL key toggles the selection state of an object; this table entry shows the result.

[2] If the user releases the CTRL key before releasing the mouse button, the operation reverts to the default transfer operation as determined by the destination. If the destination does not support a copy operation, it may reinterpret the operation. If the object cannot be dragged, you can optionally use this operation to create a disjoint range selection.

[3] The range of objects is toggled to the same selection state, which is based on the first object included by the bounding region (marquee).

[4] If the effect of toggling cancels the selection of the object, the operation applies to the remaining selected objects.

[5] The white space (background) is an access point to the commands of the view, the container, or both.

Keyboard Interface Summary

This appendix summarizes the common keyboard operations, shortcut keys, and access key assignments.

The following table displays a summary of the keys used for navigation.

Common Navigation Keys

Key	Cursor movement	CTRL+cursor movement
LEFT ARROW	Left one unit	Left one proportionally larger unit
RIGHT ARROW	Right one unit	Right one proportionally larger unit
UP ARROW	Up one unit or line	Up one proportionally larger unit
DOWN ARROW	Down one unit or line	Down one proportionally larger unit
HOME	To the beginning of the line	To the beginning of the data (topmost position)
END	To the end of the line	To the end of the data (bottommost position)
PAGE UP	Up one screen (previous screen, same position)[1]	Left one screen (or previous unit, if left does not apply)
PAGE DOWN	Down one screen (next screen, same position)[1]	Right one screen (or next unit, if right does not apply)
TAB[2]	Next field	To next tab position (in property sheets, next page)

[1] "Screen" is defined as the height of the visible area being viewed. When scrolling, you should leave a nominal portion of the previous screen to provide context. For example in text, PAGE DOWN includes the last line of the previous screen as its first line.

[2] Use the SHIFT key with the TAB key to navigate in the reverse direction.

The following table lists the common shortcut keys. Avoid assigning these keys to functions other than those listed.

Common Shortcut Keys

Key	Meaning
CTRL+A	Select All
CTRL+C[1]	Copy
CTRL+F	Find
CTRL+N	New
CTRL+O	Open
CTRL+P	Print
CTRL+S	Save
CTRL+V[1]	Paste
CTRL+X[1]	Cut
CTRL+Z[1]	Undo
F1	Display contextual Help window
SHIFT+F1	Activate context-sensitive Help mode (What's This?)
SHIFT+F10	Display shortcut menu
SPACEBAR[2]	Select (same as primary mouse button click)
ESC	Cancel
ALT	Activate or inactivate menu bar mode
ALT+TAB[3]	Display next primary window (or application)
ALT+ESC[3]	Display next window
ALT+SPACEBAR	Display shortcut menu for the window
ALT+HYPHEN	Display shortcut menu for the active child window (MDI)
ALT+ENTER	Display property sheet for current selection
ALT+F4	Close active window
ALT+F6[3]	Switch to next window within application (between modeless secondary windows and their primary window)
ALT+PRINT SCREEN	Capture active window image to the Clipboard
PRINT SCREEN	Capture desktop image to the Clipboard

Common Shortcut Keys *(continued)*

Key	Meaning
CTRL+ESC	Access Start button on the taskbar
CTRL+F6	Display next child window (MDI)
CTRL+TAB	Display next tabbed page or child window (MDI)
CTRL+ALT+DEL	Reserved for system use

[1] The system supports shortcut assignments available in earlier versions of Microsoft Windows (ALT+BACKSPACE, SHIFT+INSERT, CTRL+INSERT, SHIFT+DELETE). You should consider supporting them (though not documenting them) to support the transition of users.

[2] If the context (for example, a text box) uses the SPACEBAR for entering a space character, you can use CTRL+SPACEBAR. If that is also defined by the context, define your own key.

[3] Using the SHIFT key with this key combination navigates in the reverse direction.

The following table lists shortcut key assignments for keyboards supporting the new Windows keys. The left Windows key and right Windows key are handled the same as in earlier versions of Windows. All Windows key combinations, whether currently assigned or not, are reserved for definition by the system only. Do not use these keys for your own application-defined functions.

Windows Keys

Key	Meaning
APPLICATION key	Display shortcut menu for the selected object
WINDOWS key	Display Start button menu
WINDOWS+F1	Display Help Topics browser dialog box for the main Windows Help file
WINDOWS+TAB	Activate next application window
WINDOWS+E	Explore My Computer
WINDOWS+F	Find a file
WINDOWS+CTRL+F	Find a computer
WINDOWS+M	Minimize All
SHIFT+WINDOWS+M	Undo Minimize All
WINDOWS+R	Display Run dialog box

Windows key and Application key

Windows Keys *(continued)*

Key	Meaning
WINDOWS+BREAK	Reserved for system function
WINDOWS+*number*	Reserved for computer manufacturer use

The following table lists the key combinations and sequences the system uses to support accessibility. Support for these options is set by users from the Accessibility Options in Control Panel.

Accessibility Keys

Key	Meaning
LEFT ALT+LEFT SHIFT+PRINT SCREEN	Toggle High Contrast mode
LEFT ALT+LEFT SHIFT+NUM LOCK	Toggle MouseKeys
SHIFT (pressed five consecutive times)	Toggle StickyKeys
RIGHT SHIFT (held eight or more seconds)	Toggle FilterKeys (SlowKeys, RepeatKeys, and BounceKeys)
NUM LOCK (held five or more seconds)	Toggle ToggleKeys

The following table lists the recommended access key assignments for common commands. Though the context of a command may impact specific assignments, use these access keys for the following commands in menus and for command buttons.

Access Key Assignments

About	Insert	Properties
Always on Top	Insert Object	Quick View
Apply	Link Here	Redo
Back	Maximize	Repeat
Browse	Minimize	Restore
Close	Move	Resume
Copy	Move Here	Retry
Copy Here	New	Run
Create Shortcut	Next	Save
Create Shortcut Here	No	Save As
Cut	Open	Select All
Delete	Open With	Send To
Edit	Options	Show
Exit	Paste	Size
Explore	Paste Link	Split
File	Paste Shortcut	Stop
Find	Page Setup	Tools
Font	Paste Special	Undo
Forward	Pause	View
Help	Play	What's This?
Help Topics	Print	Window
Hide	Print Here	Yes

Avoid assigning access keys to OK and Cancel when the ENTER key and ESC key, respectively, are assigned to them by default.

Glossary

A

accelerator key *See* shortcut key.

access bar *See* desktop toolbar.

access key The key that corresponds to an underlined letter on a menu or control (also referred to as a mnemonic or mnemonic access key).

accessibility The principle of designing software to be usable and accessible to the widest range of users, including users with disabilities.

activate To make an object's state available.

active The state of an object that is the focus of user input, with its operations available.

active end The ending point for a selected range of objects. It is usually established at the object logically nearest the hot spot of the pointer when a user releases the primary mouse button. *Compare* anchor point.

active window The window in which a user is currently working or directing input. An active window is typically at the top of the Z order and is distinguished by the color of its title bar. *Compare* inactive window.

adornment A control or status area that is attached to the edge of a pane or window, such as a toolbar or ruler.

anchor point The starting point for a selected range of objects. An anchor point is usually established at the object logically nearest the hot spot of the pointer when a user presses a mouse button. *Compare* active end.

anti-aliasing A graphic design technique that involves adding colored pixels to smooth the jagged edges of a graphic.

apply To commit a set of changes or pending transactions made in a secondary window, typically without closing that window.

auto-exit A text box in which the input focus automatically moves to the next control as soon as a user types the last character.

auto-joining The movement of text to fill a gap that remains after a user deletes other text.

automatic scrolling A technique whereby a display area automatically scrolls without direct interaction with a scroll bar.

auto-repeat An event or interaction that is automatically repeated. Auto-repeat events usually occur when a user holds down a keyboard key or clicks and holds a special control (for example, scroll bar buttons).

B

balloon tip   A ToolTip style design to provide message information about a control or object.

C

cancel   To halt an operation or process and return to the prior state. *Compare* stop.

caret   *See* insertion point.

cascading menu   A menu that is a submenu of a menu item (also referred to as a hierarchical menu, child menu, or submenu).

check box   A standard Windows control that displays a setting or a set of non-mutually exclusive settings, either selected (set) or cleared (not set). *Compare* option button.

child menu   *See* cascading menu.

child window   A document window used within an MDI window. *See also* multiple document interface.

chord   To press more than one mouse or keyboard button at the same time.

click   (v.) To position the pointer over an object and then press and release a mouse button. (n.) The act of clicking. *See also* press.

Clipboard   The area of storage for objects, data, or their references after a user carries out a Cut or Copy command.

close   To remove a window.

code page   A collection of characters that make up a character set.

collection   A set of objects that share some common aspect.

column heading   A standard Windows control that can be used to provide interactive column titles for a list.

combo box   A standard Windows control that combines a text box and interdependent list box. *Compare* drop-down combo box.

command button   A standard Windows control that initiates a command or sets an option (also referred to as a push button).

composite   An aggregated set or group of objects that is recognized as an object itself (for example, characters in a paragraph, a named range of cells in a spreadsheet, or a grouped set of drawing objects).

constraint   A relationship between a set of objects, where making a change to one object affects another object in the set.

container   An object that holds other objects.

context menu   *See* shortcut menu.

context-sensitive Help   Information about an object and its current condition that is requested by the user. It answers the questions "What is this" and "Why would I want to use it?" *Compare* procedural Help and reference Help.

contextual   Specific to the conditions in which something exists or occurs.

contiguous selection   A selection that consists of a set of objects that are logically sequential or adjacent to each other (also referred to as range selection). *Compare* disjoint selection.

control   An object that enables user interaction or input, often to initiate an action, display information, or set values.

Control menu   The menu, also referred to as the System menu, displayed on the left end of a title bar in Microsoft Windows version 3.1. The context menu of a window replaces the Control menu.

cursor   A generic term for the visible indication of where a user's interaction will occur. *See also* input focus, insertion point, and pointer.

D

data link   A link that propagates a value between two objects or locations.

data-centered design   A design in which users interact with their data directly without having to first start an appropriate editor or application.

default   An operation or value that the system or application provides, unless a user makes an explicit choice.

default button   The command button that is invoked when a user presses the ENTER key. A default button typically appears in a secondary window.

delete   To remove an object or value.

desktop   The visual work area that fills the screen. The desktop is also a container and can be used as a convenient location to place objects stored in the file system.

desktop toolbar   A toolbar that docks to the desktop, similar to the taskbar (also referred to as an *access bar*). *See also* taskbar.

dialog box   A secondary window that gathers additional information from a user. *Compare* message box, palette window, and property sheet.

dialog unit   A device-independent measure to use for layout. One horizontal unit is equal to one-fourth of the average character width for the current system font. One vertical unit is equal to one-eighth of an average character height for the current system font.

dimmed   *See* unavailable.

disabled   *See* unavailable.

disjoint selection   A selection that consists of a set of objects that are not logically sequential or physically adjacent to each other. *Compare* contiguous selection. *See also* extended selection.

dock   To manipulate an interface element, such as a toolbar, in order to align it with the edge of another interface element, typically a window or pane.

document   A common unit of data (typically a file) used in user tasks and exchanged between users.

document window   A window that provides a primary view of a document (typically its content).

double-click   (v.) To press and release a mouse button twice in rapid succession. (n.) The act of double-clicking to select an object or to perform an operation.

drag   To press and hold a mouse button while moving the mouse.

drag-and-drop operation   A technique for moving, copying, or linking an object by dragging. The destination determines the interpretation of the operation. *Compare* nondefault drag-and-drop operation.

drop-down combo box   A standard Windows control that combines the characteristics of a text box with a drop-down list box. *Compare* combo box.

drop-down list box A standard Windows control that displays a current setting, but can be opened to display a list of choices.

drop-down menu A menu that is displayed from a menu bar. *See also* menu and shortcut menu.

E

edit field *See* text box.

Edit menu A common drop-down menu that includes general purpose commands for editing objects displayed within a window, such as Cut, Copy, and Paste.

ellipsis The "..." suffix added to a menu item or button label to indicate that the command requires additional information from the user in order to be performed. When a user chooses the command, a dialog box is usually displayed for user input of this additional information.

embedded object A data object that retains the original editing and operating functionality of the application that created it, while physically residing in another document.

event An action or occurrence to which an application can respond. Examples of events are clicks, key presses, and mouse movements.

explicit selection A selection that a user intentionally makes with an input device. *Compare* implicit selection.

extended selection A selection technique that is optimized for the selection of a single object or single range using contiguous selection techniques (that is, canceling any existing selection when a new selection is made). However, it also supports modifying an existing selection using disjoint selection techniques. *See also* disjoint selection.

extended-selection list box A list box that supports multiple selection, but is optimized for a selection of a single object or single range. *See also* extended selection and list box. *Compare* multiple-selection list box.

F

File menu A common drop-down menu that includes commands for file operations, such as Open, Save, and Print.

flat appearance The recommended visual display of a control when it is nested inside another control or scrollable region.

folder A type of container for objects; typically for files.

font A set of attributes for text characters.

font size The size of a font, typically represented in points.

font style The stylistic attributes of a font — such as bold, italic, and underline.

G

glyph A generic term used to refer to any graphic or pictorial image that can be used on a button or in a message box. *Compare* icon.

grayed *See* unavailable.

group box A standard Windows control that groups a set of controls.

H

handle An interface element added to an object that provides a control point for moving, sizing, reshaping, or other operations pertaining to that object.

Help menu A common drop-down menu that includes commands that provide access to online Help or other forms of user assistance. *See also* context-sensitive Help, procedural Help, reference Help, and task-oriented Help.

heterogeneous selection A selection that includes objects of different types or with different properties. *Compare* homogeneous selection.

hierarchical menu *See* cascading menu.

hold To continue to press a keyboard key or mouse button.

homogeneous selection A selection that includes objects of the same type or with the same properties. *Compare* heterogeneous selection.

hot spot The specific portion of the pointer (or pointing device) that defines the exact location, or object, to which a user is pointing.

hot zone The interaction area of a particular object or location with which a pointer or pointing device's hot spot must come in contact.

hover selection A selection technique designed to optimize selection and activation of an object. Selection is initiated when the user moves the pointer over the object for a length of time that is longer than a time-out.

hyperlink A special form of link used to navigate to another location.

I

icon A pictorial representation of an object. *Compare* glyph.

implicit selection A selection that is the result of inference or the context of some other operation. *See also* explicit selection.

inactive The state of an object when it is not the focus of a user's input.

inactive window A window in which a user's input is not currently being directed. An inactive window is typically distinguished by the color of its title bar. *Compare* active window.

indeterminate *See* mixed-value appearance.

InfoTip A ToolTip used to provide a description for desktop, window, and Start menu items, in Web views, and in the Windows Explorer Comment column when Details view is used. Do not use the term to refer to ToolTips for toolbar buttons.

input focus The location where the user is currently directing input.

input focus appearance The visual display of a control or other object that indicates it has the input focus.

insertion point The location where text or graphics will be inserted (also referred to as the caret). Also used for text box controls to indicate input focus.

inside-out activation A technique that allows a user to directly interact with the content of an embedded object without executing an explicit activation command. *Compare* outside-in activation.

J

jump See hyperlink.

L

label The text (or graphic) that identifies a control (also referred to as a caption).

landscape An orientation where the long dimension of a rectangular area (for example, screen or paper) is horizontal.

link (v.) To form a connection between two objects. (n.) A reference to an object that is linked to another object. *See also* linked object.

link path The descriptive form, or explicit connecting points, of referring to the location of a link source (also referred to as a moniker).

linked object An object that represents or provides access to another object that resides in another location in the same container or in a different container. *See also* link.

list box A standard Windows control that displays a list of choices. *See also* extended selection list box.

list view A standard Windows list box control that displays a set of objects. The control also supports different views and drag-and-drop operations.

locale A collection of language-related user preferences for formatting information, such as time, currency, or dates.

localization The process of adapting software for different countries, languages, cultures, or markets.

M

marquee *See* region selection.

maximize To display a window at its largest size. *See also* minimize.

MDI *See* multiple document interface.

menu A list of textual or graphical choices from which a user can choose. *See also* drop-down menu and shortcut menu.

menu bar A horizontal bar at the top of a window, below the title bar, that contains menus. *See also* drop-down menu.

menu button A command button that displays a menu.

menu item A choice on a menu.

menu title A text or graphic label that describes a particular menu. For drop-down menus, the title is the entry in the menu bar; for cascading menus, the menu title is the name of its parent menu item.

message box A secondary window that is displayed to inform a user about a particular condition. *Compare* dialog box, palette window, and property sheet.

minimize To minimize the size or appearance of a window; in some cases this means to hide the window. *See also* maximize.

mixed-value appearance The visual display for a control which reflects a mixed set of values.

mnemonic *See* access key.

modal Restrictive or limited interaction due to operating in a mode. Modal often describes a secondary window that restricts a user's interaction with other windows. A secondary window can be modal with respect to its primary window or to the entire system. *Compare* modeless.

mode A particular state of interaction, often exclusive in some way to other forms of interaction.

modeless Non-restrictive or non-limited interaction. Modeless often describes a secondary window that does not restrict a user's interaction with other windows. *Compare* modal.

modifier key A keyboard key that, when pressed (and held), changes the actions of ordinary input.

moniker *See* link path.

mouse   A commonly used input device that has one or more buttons for the user to interact with a computer. Also used as a generic term to include other pointing devices that operate similarly (for example, trackballs and headpointers).

multiple-document interface (MDI)   A technique for managing a set of windows whereby documents are opened into windows (sometimes called child windows) that are constrained to a single primary (parent) window. *See also* child window and parent window.

multiple-selection list box   A list box that is optimized for making multiple, independent selections. *Compare* extended selection list box and single selection list box.

My Computer   A standard Windows icon that represents a user's private, usually local, storage.

N

Network Neighborhood   A standard Windows icon that represents access to objects that are stored on the network file system.

nondefault drag-and-drop operation   A drag (transfer) operation whose interpretation is determined by a user's choice of command. These commands are included in a shortcut menu displayed at the destination where the object is dropped. *Compare* drag-and-drop operation.

O

object   An entity or component identifiable by a user that can be distinguished by its properties, operations, and relationships.

object-action paradigm   The basic interaction model for the user interface in which the object to be acted upon is specified first, followed by the command to be executed.

OLE (Microsoft OLE)   Also known as Object Linking and Embedding, OLE describes the technology and interface for implementing support for object interaction.

open appearance   The visual display of an object when the user opens the object into its own window.

operation   A generic term that refers to the actions that can be done to or with an object.

option button   A standard Windows control that allows a user to select from a fixed set of mutually exclusive choices (also referred to as a radio button). *Compare* check box.

option-set appearance   The visual display for a control when its value is set.

outside-in activation   A technique that requires a user to perform an explicit activation command to interact with the content of an embedded object. *Compare* inside-out activation.

P

package   An encapsulation of a file so that it can be embedded into a container.

palette window   A modeless secondary window that displays a toolbar or other choices, such as colors or patterns. *Compare* dialog box and message box. *See also* property sheet.

pane   A separate area in a split window.

parent window   A primary window that provides window management for a set of child windows. *See also* child window and multiple document interface.

persistence   The principle that the state or properties of an object is automatically preserved.

point (v.) To position the pointer over a particular object and location. (n.) A unit of measurement for type (1 point equals approximately 1/72 inch).

pointer A graphical image displayed on the screen that indicates the location of a pointing device (also referred to as a cursor).

pop-up menu *See* shortcut menu.

pop-up window A secondary window with no title bar that is displayed next to an object; it provides contextual information about that object.

portrait An orientation where the long dimension of a rectangular area (for example, screen or paper) is vertical.

press To press and release a keyboard key. *See also* click.

pressed appearance The visual display for an object, such as a control, when it is being "pressed."

primary window The window in which the main interaction with an object takes place. *See also* secondary window and window.

procedural Help Information about the steps involved in carrying out a particular task. *Compare* context-sensitive Help, reference Help, and task-oriented Help.

progress indicator Any form of feedback that provides the user with information about the state of a process.

progress indicator control A standard Windows control that displays the percentage of completion of a particular process as a graphical bar.

progressive disclosure A technique for hiding the complexity of an interface by presenting the user with the primary or common options or choices at the topmost level, and then revealing more advanced or complex options through another means, such as explicit user action or navigation.

project A window or task management technique that consists of a container holding a set of objects, such that when the container is opened, the windows of the contained objects are restored to their former positions.

properties Attributes or characteristics of an object that define its state, appearance, or value.

property inspector A dynamic properties viewer that displays the properties of the current selection, usually of a particular type of object. *Compare* property sheet.

property page A grouping of properties on a tabbed page of a property sheet. *See also* property sheet.

property sheet A secondary window that displays the properties of an object when a user chooses its Properties command. *Compare* dialog box and property inspector. *See also* property page.

property sheet control A standard Windows control used to create property sheet interfaces.

push button *See* command button.

R

radio button *See* option button.

range selection *See* contiguous selection.

recognition The interpretation of strokes or gestures as characters or operations.

Recycle Bin   The standard Windows icon that represents the container for deleted files.

reference Help   A form of online Help that contains conceptual and explanatory information. *Compare* context-sensitive Help, procedural Help, and task-oriented Help.

region selection   A selection technique that involves dragging out a bounding outline (also referred to as a marquee) to define the selected objects.

relationship   The context or way an object relates to its environment.

rich-text box   A standard Windows control that is similar to a standard text box, except that it also supports individual character and paragraph properties.

roam   The ability for a user to move between different computers and have the same user experience on both computers.

S

scope   The definition of the extent to which a selection is logically independent from other selections. For example, selections made in separate windows are typically considered to be independent of each other.

scrap   An icon created when the user transfers a data selection from within a file to a shell container.

scroll   To move the viewable area of an object or information in order to make a different portion visible.

scroll arrow button   A component of a scroll bar that allows the information to be scrolled by defined increments when the user clicks it. The direction of the arrow indicates the direction in which the information scrolls.

scroll bar   A standard Windows control that supports scrolling.

scroll bar shaft   The component of a scroll bar that provides the visual context for the scroll box. Clicking in the scroll bar shaft scrolls the information by a screenful. *See also* scroll box.

scroll box   A component of a scroll bar that indicates the relative position (and optionally the proportion) of the visible information relative to the entire amount of information. The user can drag the scroll box to view areas of information not currently visible. *See also* scroll bar shaft.

secondary window   A window that provides information or supplemental interaction related to objects in a primary window. *See also* primary window and window.

select   To identify one or more objects upon which an operation can be performed.

selection   An object or set of objects that have been selected.

selection appearance   The visual display of an object when it has been selected.

selection handle   A graphical control point of an object that provides direct manipulation support for operations of that object, such as moving, sizing, or scaling.

separator   An entry in a menu used to both group and separate menu items.

shell   A generic term that refers to the interface that gives the user control over the system.

shortcut   A generic term that refers to an action or technique that invokes a particular command or performs an operation with less interaction than the usual method.

shortcut icon A link presented as an icon that provides a user with access to another object.

shortcut key A keyboard key or key combination that invokes a particular command (also referred to as an accelerator key).

shortcut menu A menu that is displayed for a selected object (also referred to as a context menu or pop-up menu). The menu contains commands that are contextually relevant to the selection.

single-selection list box A list box that supports only selection of a single item in the list.

size grip A special control that appears at the junction of a horizontal and vertical scroll bar or the right end of a status bar and provides an area that a user can drag to size the lower right corner of a window.

slider A standard Windows control that displays and sets a value from a continuous range of possible values, such as brightness or volume.

spin box A control composed of a text box and incremental and decremental buttons that allows a user to adjust a value from a limited range of possible values.

split bar A division between window panes in a split window; the split bar visually separates window panes.

split box A special control added to a window, typically adjacent to the scroll bar, that allows a user to split a window or adjust a window split.

status bar An area that displays state information for the content in the window, typically placed at the bottom of a window.

status bar control A standard Windows control that provides the functionality of a status bar.

stop To halt a process or action, typically without restoring the prior state. *Compare* cancel.

submenu *See* cascading menu.

System menu *See* Control menu.

T

tab control A standard Windows control that looks similar to a notebook or file divider and provides navigation between different pages or sections of information in a window.

task-oriented Help Information about the steps involved in carrying out a particular task. *Compare* context-sensitive Help, procedural Help, and reference Help.

taskbar A special toolbar that docks on an edge of the desktop supplied by the system. The taskbar includes the Start button, a button for each open primary window, and a status area.

template An object that automates the creation of new objects of a particular type.

text box A standard Windows control in which a user can enter and edit text (also referred to as the edit field).

thread A process that is part of a larger process or program.

title bar The horizontal area at the top of a window that identifies the window. The title bar also acts as a handle for dragging the window.

toggle key A keyboard key that alternates between turning a particular operation, function, or mode on or off.

toolbar A frame or special area that contains a set of other controls.

toolbar button A command button used in a toolbar (or status bar).

toolbar control A standard Windows control designed with the same characteristics as the toolbar.

ToolTip A standard Windows control that provides a small pop-up window with descriptive text, such as a label, for a control or graphic object.

transfer appearance The visual feedback displayed during a transfer operation.

transaction A unit of change to an object.

tree control A standard Windows control that allows a set of hierarchically-related objects to be displayed as an expandable outline.

type (v.) To enter a character from the keyboard. (n.) A classification of an object based on its characteristics, behavior, and attributes.

U

unavailable The state of a control in which normal functionality is not presently available to a user (also referred to as grayed, dimmed, and disabled).

unavailable appearance The visual display for a control when it is unavailable.

undo To reverse a transaction.

unfold button A command button used to expand a secondary window to a larger size to reveal additional controls or information.

V

visual editing The ability to edit an embedded object in place, without opening it in its own window.

W

white space The background area of a window. (The color need not literally be white.)

window A standard Windows object that displays information. A window is a separately controllable area of the screen that typically has a rectangular border. *See also* primary window and secondary window.

wizard A form of user assistance that automates a task through a dialog with the user. A wizard is typically composed of property sheets.

wordwrap The convention where, as a user enters text, existing text is automatically moved from the end of a line to the next line.

workbook A window or task management technique that consists of a set of views that are organized like a tabbed notebook.

workspace A window or task management technique that consists of a container holding a set of objects, where the windows of the contained objects are constrained to a parent window. Similar to the multiple document interface, except that the windows displayed within the parent window corresponding to objects that are also contained in the workspace.

Z

Z order The layered relationship of a set of objects, such as windows, on the display screen.

Bibliography

General Design

Baecker, Ronald M., Jonathan Grudin, William A.S. Buxton, and Saul Greenberg. *Readings in Human-Computer Interaction: Toward the Year 2000*. San Francisco, CA: Academic Press/Morgan Kaufmann, 1995.

Beyer, Hugh and Karen Holtzblatt. *Contextual Design: Defining Customer-Centered Systems*. San Francisco, CA: Academic Press/Morgan Kaufmann, 1997.

Blum, Bruce I. *Beyond Programming: To a New Era of Design (John Hopkins University/Applied Physics Laboratory Series in Science and Engineering)*. New York, NY: Oxford University Press, 1995.

Brooks Jr., Frederick P. *The Mythical Man-Month: Essays on Software Engineering*. Reading, MA: Addison-Wesley Pub. Co., 1995.

Helander, Martin G., Thomas K. Landauer, and Prasad Prabhu. *Handbook of Human-Computer Interaction*. Elsevier Science Pub. Co., 1997.

Hix, Deborah and H. Rex Hartson. *Developing User Interfaces: Ensuring Usability Through Product & Process*. New York, NY: John Wiley & Sons, 1993.

Lakoff, George and Mark Johnson. *Metaphors We Live By*. Chicago, IL: University of Chicago Press, 1983.

Landauer, Thomas K. *The Trouble with Computers: Usefulness, Usability and Productivity*. Cambridge, MA: MIT Press, 1996.

Laurel, Brenda, Ed. *The Art of Human-Computer Interface Design*. Reading, MA: Addison-Wesley Pub. Co., 1990.

Norman, Donald A. *The Design of Everyday Things*. New York, NY: Currency/Doubleday, 1990.

Norman, Donald A. and Stephen W. Draper, Eds. *User Centered System Design*: *New Perspectives on Human-Computer Interaction*. Hillsdale, NJ: Lawrence Erlbaum Associates, 1986.

Petroski, Henry. *The Evolution of Useful Things*. New York, NY: Knopf, 1992.

Preece, Jenny, Yvonne Rogers, Helen Sharp, and David Benyon. *Human-Computer Interaction*. Reading, MA: Addison-Wesley Pub. Co., 1994.

Shneiderman, Ben. *Designing the User Interface: Strategies for Effective Human-Computer Interaction*. Third ed., Reading, MA: Addison-Wesley Pub. Co., 1997.

Tognazzini, Bruce. *Tog on Interface*. Reading, MA: Addison-Wesley Pub. Co., 1992.

Graphic Design

Blair, Preston. *Cartoon Animation (How to Draw and Paint Series)*. Tustin, Calif.: Walter Foster Pub., 1995.

Dreyfuss, Henry. *Symbol Sourcebook: An Authoritative Guide to International Graphic Symbols*. New York, NY: John Wiley & Sons, 1997.

Horton, William. *The Icon Book: Visual Symbols for Computer Systems and Documentation*. New York, NY: John Wiley & Sons, 1994.

Mullet, Kevin and Darrell Sano. *Designing Visual Interfaces*: Communication Oriented Techniques. Englewood Cliffs, NJ: Prentice Hall, 1995.

Thomas, Frank and Ollie Johnston. *The Illusion of Life: Disney Animation*. Rev. ed., New York, NY: Hyperion, 1995.

Tufte, Edward R. *Envisioning Information*. Cheshire, CT: Graphics Press, 1990.

Tufte, Edward R. *The Visual Display of Quantitative Information*. Reprint ed., Cheshire, CT: Graphics Press, 1992.

Winograd, Terry, Ed., et al. *Bringing Design to Software*. Reading, MA: Addison-Wesley, 1996.

Usability

Dumas, Joseph S. and Janice C. Redish. *A Practical Guide to Usability Testing*. Norwood, NJ: Intellect, 1993.

Hackos, Joann T. and Janice C. Redish. *User and Task Analysis for Interface Design*. New York, NY: John Wiley & Sons, 1998.

Nielsen, Jakob. *Usability Engineering*. Boston, MA: Academic Press Professional, 1994.

Rubin, Jeffrey. *Handbook of Usability Testing: How to Plan, Design, and Conduct Effective Tests*. New York, NY: John Wiley & Sons, 1994.

Whiteside, John, John Bennett, and Karen Holtzblatt. "Usability Engineering: Our Experience and Evolution." *Handbook of Human-Computer Interaction*. Martin Helander, Ed., Amsterdam: Elsevier Science Pub. Co., 1989.

Wilson, John R. and E. Nigel Corlett. *Evaluation of Human Work: A Practical Ergonomics Methodology*. Second ed., London: Taylor & Francis, 1995.

Wixon, Dennis and Judith Ramey. *Field Methods Casebook for Software Design*. New York, NY: John Wiley & Sons, 1996.

Object-Oriented Design

Booch, Grady. *Object-Oriented Analysis and Design with Applications (Addison-Wesley Object Technology Series)*. Second ed., Reading, MA: Addison-Wesley Pub. Co., 1994.

Roberts, Berry D., D. Isensee, and J. Mullaly. *Designing for the User with OVID: Bridging the Gap Between Software Engineering and User Interface Design*. Indianapolis, IN: Macmillan, 1997.

Rumbaugh, James, et al. *Object-Oriented Modeling and Design*. Englewood Cliffs, NJ: Prentice Hall, 1991.

Wood, Larry E. *User Interface Design: Bridging the Gap from User Requirements to Design*. Boca Raton, FL: CRC Press, 1998.

Organizations

The following organizations publish journals and sponsor conferences on topics related to user interface design and usability assessment.

SIGCHI (Special Interest Group in Computer Human Interaction)
Association for Computing Machinery
1515 Broadway
New York, NY 10036-5701
(212) 869-7440
http://www.acm.org/sigchi

SIGGRAPH (Special Interest Group on Graphics)
Association for Computing Machinery
1515 Broadway
New York, NY 10036-5701
(212) 869-7440
http://www.siggraph.org/

Human Factors and Ergonomics Society
P.O. Box 1369
Santa Monica, CA 90406-1369
(310) 394-1811
http://www.hfes.org/

Usability Professionals' Association
4020 McEwen, Suite 105
Dallas, TX 75244-5019
(972) 233-9107
http://www.upassoc.org/

Accessibility

For a list of accessibility aids available for Microsoft Windows, accessibility software vendors, potential test sites, or facilities for producing accessible documentation, contact:

Microsoft Sales Information Center
One Microsoft Way
Redmond, WA 98052-6399
(800) 426-9400 (voice)
(800) 892-5234 (text telephone)
(206) 936-7329 (FAX)

An assistive technology program in your area can provide referrals to programs and services available to you. To locate an assistive technology program near you, contact:

National Information System
Center for Development Disabilities
University of South Carolina
Benson Building
Columbia, SC 29208
(803) 777-4435 (voice or text telephone)
(803) 777-6058 (FAX)

The Trace Research and Development Center publishes references and materials on accessibility, including:

Vanderheiden, Gregg C., and Katherine R. Vanderheiden. *Accessible Design of Consumer Products: Guidelines for the Design of Consumer Products to Increase Their Accessibility to People with Disabilities or Who Are Aging.* Madison, WI: Trace Research and Development Center, 1991.

Vanderheiden, Gregg C. *Application Software Design Guidelines: Increasing the Accessibility of Applications Software to People with Disabilities and Older Users (Version 1.1).* Madison, WI: Trace Research and Development Center, 1994.

Borden, Fatherly, Ford, and Vanderheiden, Eds. *Trace Resource Book: Assistive Technologies for Communication, Control and Computer Access.* Madison, WI: Trace Research and Development Center, 1993.

For information on these books and other resources available from the Trace Research and Development Center, contact:

Trace Research and Development Center
University of Wisconsin - Madison
S-151 Waisman Center
1500 Highland Avenue
Madison, WI 5705-2280
(608) 263-2309 (voice)
(608) 263-5408 (text telephone)
(608) 262-8848 (FAX)
http://www.trace.wisc.edu/

Index

Property sheets *(continued)*
   size 448
   title text 218, 447
   usability guidelines 18–19
   using instead of group boxes 454
Protected system files 11 *See also* Hidden files
Prototyping 32
Punctuation guidelines 439
Push buttons *See* Command buttons

Q

Quadruple-clicking 58
Question mark
   avoiding in message boxes 243
   interface text guidelines 439
   mouse pointer 56
Quick Launch bar 15, 49, 301
Quick View command 150
Quitting installation before completion 296
Quotation marks enclosing file names
   Open dialog box 230
   Save As dialog box 233–234

R

Radio buttons *See* Option buttons
Raised border styles 418
Range selection *See* Contiguous selection
Read-only program files, storing 9, 273
Read-only static text fields 185
Read-only text boxes 182
Readability of information 412
Readme information
   improving 6
   in application setup, avoiding 296
   in the Start menu, avoiding 294
Rebar control 202–203 *See also* Toolbar frame control
Rebooting the computer after running Setup 6, 296
Record processing 114
Recycle Bin integration 305
Redo command 94, 142
Redundancy, avoiding in interface text 441
Reference Help 382–383

Referencing other Help topics *See* Related Topics links
Refresh command 436
Refresh operation, defined 82
Region selection 77–78
Registry
   associating file types 283, 286
   enabling printing 285
   excluding applications from Open With dialog box 286
   purpose of 277
   registering application path information 289–290
   registering application state information 287–289
   registering commands 281–283
   registering file types
      file name extension key 278
      file type identifier key 279–280
      NoOpen value 283
      setting values for file types 286
      supporting the New command 283–284
   registering icons 281
   registering InfoTip descriptions 285
   registering NoOpenWith 286–287
   registering shared files 293
   registering sound events 312
   registering System folder location 292
   registering uninstall programs 299
   supporting the New command 283–284
   vs. Win.ini file 293
Related Topics links
   HTML Help 397
   procedural Help 382
Relationship of elements in visual design 412
Relationships between objects 42–43
Relative path to link source 112–114
Reminder balloon tips 196
Removing applications *See* Uninstall programs
Removing files to the Recycle Bin 305
Removing text 92
Rename command 149, 150
Repeat command 94
Replace command 143
Replace dialog box 235
Reset command 220

The *definitive* guide to the **Win32 API**

The industry bible
for
Visual C++
development

PROGRAMMING MICROSOFT® VISUAL C++,® Fifth Edition, is the newest edition of the book that has become the industry's most trusted text (previously published as *Inside Visual C++*). Newly expanded and updated for Microsoft Visual C++ 6.0, it offers even more of the detailed, comprehensive coverage that's consistently made this title the best overall explanation of the capabilities of this powerful and complex development tool. You'll find a full discussion of control development with ATL, the latest database programming enhancements, recent COM improvements, C++ programming for the Internet, and loads more.

U.S.A.   **$49.99**
U.K.   £46.99 [V.A.T. included]
Canada $71.99
ISBN 1-57231-857-0

Microsoft®
mspress.microsoft.com

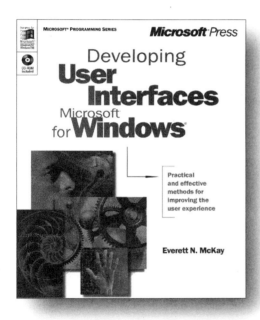